THE LOEB CLASSICAL LIBRARY

FOUNDED BY JAMES LOEB, LL.D.

EDITED BY

T. E. PAGE, LITT.D.

E. CAPPS, PH.D., LL.D.   W. H. D. ROUSE, LITT.D.

SILIUS ITALICUS
I

SILIUS ITALICUS
PUNICA

WITH AN ENGLISH TRANSLATION BY

J. D. DUFF

M.A., HON.D.LITT. DURHAM
FELLOW OF TRINITY COLLEGE, CAMBRIDGE

IN TWO VOLUMES

I

LONDON
WILLIAM HEINEMANN LTD
CAMBRIDGE, MASSACHUSETTS
HARVARD UNIVERSITY PRESS
MCMXXXIV

Printed in Great Britain

TO
A. E. H.
AND
W. T. V.

PREFACE

THE introduction deals first with the life of Silius Italicus, as it is described by Pliny and Martial, and then with his poem, the *Punica*, which deserves, in the translator's opinion, more respectful treatment than it has generally received in modern times. A short account is added of the manuscripts, editions, and translations.

The text follows, in the main, that of L. Bauer (Teubner, Leipzig, 1890); but many of the emendations proposed by Bentley, Bothe, Heinsius, and others, which Bauer includes in his *apparatus*, are here promoted to the text. The most important of these emendations are indicated in notes below the text.

In the translation I have tried to be true to the original and, at the same time, merciful to the English reader. The poem is so full of allusion that it seemed necessary to add a number of notes, elucidating points of biography, geography, history, and mythology. I have done my best to keep each note within compass. It should be understood that these notes refer to the translation only and not to the Latin text.

Silius is not, in general, an obscure writer. But

PREFACE

his poem, like all ancient poems, includes corrupt or difficult passages, on which I have often applied for aid to two powerful allies, Professor A. E. Housman and Mr. W. T. Vesey, Fellow of Gonville and Caius College ; it is a pleasure to record here my indebtedness to both these scholars.

J. D. DUFF.

July, 1933.

CONTENTS OF VOLUME I

INTRODUCTION

I. LIFE OF SILIUS ITALICUS

SILIUS ITALICUS lived to the age of seventy-five and died A.D. 101 ; he was therefore born A.D. 26. At the time of his birth Tiberius was emperor ; and he lived to see Trajan succeed Nerva. His death did not come in the course of nature : he was afflicted by a chronic ailment and put an end to his sufferings by abstaining from food—a manner of death which was not regarded by the Romans of that age as a crime but as a brave and virtuous action.

Our knowledge of this fact and of his life in general is derived from a letter of Pliny's (iii. 7). Pliny regarded his friend as a fortunate man and happy down to the last day of his life. Of his two sons Silius had lost one ; but the survivor was the more satisfactory son of the two and had even risen, in his father's life-time, to the dignity of the consulship.

Silius was not merely a poet. His poem was the work of his old age when he had retired from public affairs and was living in studious seclusion near Naples. He was consul himself A.D. 68—the year of Nero's downfall and death ; and he gained a high reputation when he governed the province of Asia as proconsul. Pliny hints that his political conduct during Nero's reign had been open to censure, but says that his later life atoned for any early indiscretions. We learn also from Martial [a] that he was famous in his younger days as a pleader in the law-courts.

Silius was a rich man and was able to gratify expensive tastes. He bought one fine country-house after another, and filled them with books, pictures, and statues. Upon his busts of Virgil he set special value. He bought the site of Virgil's tomb at Naples, which had fallen into neglect, and restored it. He made pilgrimages to the spot, and kept Virgil's birthday, October 15, with more ceremony than his own. Another of his acquisitions was a house that had belonged to Cicero,[b] whom Silius revered as the greatest of Roman orators.[c]

His life of retirement was not a solitary life : he received many visitors, with whom he liked to converse on literary topics, generally lying on his sofa ; and at times he entertained his guests by reading extracts from his poem, and asked for their criticism. (Pliny himself did not think highly of the poem : it was painstaking, he thought, but lacked genius.)

Thus Silius lived on, respected and courted, until he put an end to his life by his own act. The ailment from which he suffered is described by the word *clavus* ; the name that modern medical science would give to this affliction is uncertain, but it was incurable ; and, like a guest who had eaten his fill, he withdrew from the scene.

[a] vii. 63.
[b] Mart. xi. 48. 2.
[c] His reverence for both Virgil and Cicero is recorded in his poem : see viii. 593, 594, and viii. 408-413.

INTRODUCTION

II. The Poem of Silius Italicus

The *Punica* of Silius Italicus is the longest Latin poem : it contains upwards of 12,000 verses. Its subject is the Second Punic War, the most critical period in the history of the Republic. Hannibal is the true hero of the story, though Silius evidently intended to cast Scipio for that part. The narrative begins with Hannibal's oath and ends with the battle of Zama. There are two long digressions : the first (of 500 lines) fills most of the Sixth Book and contains the story of Regulus which properly belongs to the First Punic War ; and the second digression (in the Eighth Book) devotes 200 lines to the adventures of Anna, the sister of Dido, who has become the Nymph of an Italian river, so that her sympathies are, or ought to be, divided between the combatants. Otherwise, the narrative proceeds in orderly sequence from beginning to end.[a] It was certainly based upon Livy's Third Decad. But Silius owes much more to Virgil's *Aeneid* than to any other source. He had soaked his mind in Virgil.

There are undoubtedly long stretches in the poem which no modern reader can enjoy. Silius gives ample space, too ample, to the six great battles of the war —Ticinus, Trebia, Lake Trasimene, Cannae, the Metaurus, and Zama ; and the details of slaughter become in him, as they become in better poets, monotonous and repulsive. Then there are the

---

[a] There is serious disorder in Book XVII. about l. 290. But I agree with those editors who assume a lacuna here ; and it may well be a very large lacuna. For the lacuna in Book VIII. see p. xvii.

catalogues. The Catalogue was an indispensable part of an ancient Epic, and Silius has many of them —a catalogue of the Carthaginian forces, a catalogue of the Italian contingents who fought at Cannae, a catalogue of Sicilian towns and rivers, and others as well ; and these long lists of names and places, many of them quite obscure, are wearisome. Few poets have had the art to make catalogues interesting. Milton could do it ; and a very different poet from Milton wrote an excellent catalogue—the first part of Macaulay's *Horatius*. " From lordly Volaterrae " and so on is a catalogue of the Tuscan cities, which the reader, especially the youthful reader, finds delightful.

But the *Punica* does not consist entirely of carnage and catalogues. What of the poem as a whole ? Does it deserve its deplorable reputation ?

Of some writers it is the custom to say that they are more praised than read ; but no one ever said this of Silius. Of him it would be truer to say that he is more blamed than read. Even Madvig, who does not blame him, admits that he had only read the poem in parts and *celerrime*.[a] There is no doubt about the verdict pronounced by modern critics and historians of Roman literature. They say very little about Silius,[b] but they are all of one opinion—that he was a dull man who wrote a bad poem. And this is the view of the educated public. I believe myself that this judgement is much too summary, and that

[a] *Adversaria Critica*, ii. p. 161.

[b] This is not true of Professor J. Wight Duff, the latest critic of Silius. His discussion of the poem is full and careful (*Literary History of Rome in the Silver Age* (1927), pp. 452 foll.) ; but he seems to me somewhat blind to its merits.

scholars would think better of the poem if they would condescend to read it.

We know that it was the work of an old man, and the fire and vigour of youth are not to be found in it ; its merits are of another sort. The versification is in general pleasing, and much less monotonous than that of Lucan. Not that Silius had a really fine ear for the beautiful arrangement of vowels and consonants : he is capable of beginning a line with *certatis fatis*, and ending another with *genitore Pelore*.[a] Then too many of his verses end with a trochee ; and the Latin hexameter verse, unlike the Greek in this respect, is shorn of its true majesty if the trochaic ending is used too often.

The chief fault of style in the poem is tautology. Silius evidently thought that a plain statement of fact was improved, if he repeated it over again in different words. Examples may be found on almost every page.

Then there is another peculiarity of expression which is decidedly disconcerting to the reader. I believe that Silius did himself serious injury by what might seem a trifling matter—his system of nomenclature. The subject of his poem, the struggle between Carthage and Rome, is stated in the first two lines. But the Romans are not there called *Romani* : they are called *Aeneadae* ; and the " supremacy of Italy " is expressed by *Oenotria iura*, though Oenotria is not Italy but a name given by Greeks in early times to a district or kingdom in the southernmost part of Italy.

Silius evidently felt that *Romani* and *Itali* might

---

[a] ix. 543 : xvi. 426.

xiii

recur too often, and that aliases must be found. Variety is good ; but here it was carried to excess. The following list of variants for *Romani* may not be exhaustive, but is surely too long : *Aeneadae, Aurunci, Ausonidae* and *Ausonii, Dardanidae, Dardani* and *Dardanii, Dauni* and *Daunii, Evandrei, Hectorei, Hesperii, Idaei, Iliaci, Itali, Laomedontiadae, Latii* and *Latini, Laurentes, Martigenae, Oenotri, Phryges* and *Phrygii, Priamidae, Rhoetei, Saturnii, Sigei, Teucri, Troes, Troiugenae,* and *Tyrrheni.* The Carthaginians also are called by nearly a dozen different names. I have thought it best not always to follow Silius in this particular.

The great Roman poets, Lucretius and Virgil, Catullus and Horace, have their place apart ; and Silius has no claim to be ranked with these or near them. Yet, when defects are admitted and due qualifications made, the reader of the *Punica,* once he has surmounted the obstacles, will find much pleasant walking there. If anyone doubts whether Silius could write poetry, let him read the twenty-three lines in which the aspect and habits of the god Pan are described (xiii. 326-347). If Ovid had written these charming verses, every scholar would know them and critics would be eloquent in their praise. Silius is full of incidental narrative, and he tells a short story well, though it must be admitted that his main narrative is too apt to hang fire. And one quality he has which is a constant comfort and satisfaction to some at least of his readers. Though inferior to Statius in brilliance and far inferior to Lucan in intellectual force, he is almost entirely free from that misplaced ingenuity which pervades the whole of their works and makes the reader feel too often as if he were solving puzzles rather than reading poetry.

I shall end by referring to four passages (none of which seems to have been noticed by the contemptuous critics) as proofs of Silius's narrative power.

(i.) v. 344 foll. Silius describes how Mago, Hannibal's brother, was wounded ; how Hannibal flew to the spot, conveyed the wounded man to the camp, and summoned medical aid to dress the wound. For Hannibal had a famous physician, a descendant of Jupiter Ammon, in his train. (He had also a prophet, whose name was not, to our ears, a recommendation : he was called Bogus.)

(ii.) vii. 282 foll. This is a night scene and recalls the beginning of Matthew Arnold's " Sohrab and Rustum." [a] Hannibal has been caught in a trap by Quintus Fabius, the famous *Cunctator*. Unable to sleep for anxiety, he rises and wakens his brother, Mago ; they make a round of the camp together, and visit the chief captains, to suggest a plan of escape.

Both these extracts are vivid and swift pieces of narrative.

(iii.) The third passage (xvi. 229 foll.) has even higher merit. The scene is dramatic and picturesque ; it is even romantic. The place is the palace of Syphax, king of Numidia, whose alliance Scipio was anxious to secure against Carthage. Scipio had crossed over from Spain to Africa for this purpose.[b] We read how the Roman general, the conqueror of Spain, rose from his bed before sunrise and went to

---

[a] Both Silius and Arnold doubtless had in mind the beginning of the Tenth Book of the *Iliad*.

[b] This is a historical fact.

the palace, where he found the king playing with the lion-cubs that he kept as pets. Both were young men, and the younger of the two had a young man's generous hero-worship for his Roman visitor, and expresses it in the conversation that follows.

(iv.) ix. 401 foll. This is a scene from the battle of Cannae. It describes the friendship between Marius and Caper, two natives of Praeneste who fell side by side in the battle. There is no doubt that there were really no such persons, and that the entire incident, like many others, was invented by Silius. But the man who wrote these lines was certainly a poet; and I shall venture to say of them

$$\mu\omega\mu\eta\sigma\epsilon\tau\alpha\iota\ \tau\iota\varsigma\ \mu\hat{\alpha}\lambda\lambda\text{ov}\ \mathring{\eta}\ \mu\iota\mu\eta\sigma\epsilon\tau\alpha\iota.$$

III. Manuscripts, Editions, Translations

(a) In 1416 or 1417, during the Council of Constance, Poggio, the learned Florentine who unearthed so many Latin authors, found, probably at St. Gall, a manuscript of Silius; a copy of this was taken by Poggio or one of his companions; and from that copy all the existing MSS. are descended. Neither the original MS. nor the original copy of it is now extant. Editors use the letter S to denote this MS., and C to denote another MS. which was once in the Cathedral library at Cologne; this MS. also is lost, and its readings are known only from notes made by two scholars towards the end of the sixteenth century. Of the extant MSS. four, all written in the fifteenth century, are thought to be better than the rest. Their readings are cited in the critical editions mentioned below.

INTRODUCTION

(*b*) The two earliest editions were printed at Rome in 1471 ; many others followed, most of them printed in Italy and others in France and Germany. The Aldine edition of 1523 is important in the history of the text, because it offers 81 lines of the poem (viii. 145-225) which are found in no manuscript and in none of the previous editions, though some of the editors had pointed out that there must be a lacuna in the text. The source from which these verses are derived is a matter of dispute : some critics believe them to be the work of a forger ; others hold that they were written by Silius and that the loss of them was due to some mutilation of S, the original MS. at St. Gall. It is certain that the verses fit in perfectly with the context, and that they are such as Silius might have written.[a]

Of later editions the most important are those of G. A. Ruperti (Göttingen, 1795), F. H. Bothe (Stuttgart, 1855), L. Bauer (Leipzig, 1890), and W. C. Summers (London, 1905) in Postgate's *Corpus Poetarum Latinorum*.

Ruperti's edition (which was reprinted in a more convenient form by N. E. Lemaire, Paris, 1823) combines immense learning with a candour and simplicity that are most attractive. But he is not an ideal editor : too often he explains at great length what is perfectly clear already, and says nothing where explanation is needed. But his book is indispensable.

Bothe did not publish a text. He translated the

---

[a] For a full discussion of this lacuna see Mr. Heitland's article in the *Journal of Philology*, vol. xxiv. pp. 179-211 : he has no doubt that the verses are genuine : and his opinion carries weight.

whole poem into German hexameters, archaic both in vocabulary and style, and added below his version notes which deal both with text and interpretation. He is too ready to meddle with the text; but his brief business-like notes are most valuable. His translation is close and correct, and has fewer lines than the original, which is surely a remarkable feat of compression.

Bauer's text is the work of a competent and careful scholar. The revision by Professor W. C. Summers deserves the same praise and contains some important corrections, by himself and Postgate, of the text of Silius; and in punctuation it is much superior to any other text.

(c) Three translations of Silius are known to me. The earliest is by Thomas Ross, " Keeper of His Majesties' Libraries, and Groom of His most Honourable Privy-Chamber." The king was Charles II. The preface is dated at Bruges, November 18, 1657, and the work was published in London in 1672, twelve years after the Restoration. The translator added a supplement of his own in three books, carrying the story down to the death of Hannibal. The first book is dedicated to the King, the second to the Duke of York, afterwards James II., and the third to the memory of the Duke of Gloucester, the third son of Charles I. Ross was a fairly good scholar, but his versification is unpleasing. The rhyming heroic verse which he chose for his metre was still in its infancy : Dryden had not yet seriously taken it in hand. The second translation, by F. H. Bothe, is spoken of above. The third, printed below the Didot text, has little merit and many mistakes.

SILIUS ITALICUS

BOOKS I–VIII

PUNICORUM

LIBER PRIMUS

ARGUMENT

The subject of the poem is the Second Punic War (1-20). The cause of the war was Juno's hatred of Rome. She chooses Hannibal as her instrument (21-55). Hannibal's character, and the oath he swore in boyhood (56-139). Hasdrubal succeeds Hamilcar as commander in Spain : his character, conquests, and death (140-181). Hannibal is chosen to succeed Hasdrubal by all the army in Spain, both

Ordior arma, quibus caelo se gloria tollit
Aeneadum patiturque ferox Oenotria iura
Carthago.   da, Musa, decus memorare laborum
antiquae Hesperiae, quantosque ad bella crearit
et quot Roma viros, sacri cum perfida pacti   5
gens Cadmea super regno certamina movit,
quaesitumque diu, qua tandem poneret arce
terrarum Fortuna caput.   ter Marte sinistro
iuratumque Iovi foedus conventaque patrum
Sidonii fregere duces, atque impius ensis   10
ter placitam suasit temerando rumpere pacem.

---

a Oenotria, the Greek name of an ancient kingdom in
S. Italy, is one of the many synonyms for Italy which occur
in the poem : see p. xiii.

b Sidonians, Tyrians, Cadmeans, and other names are
used by Silius to denote the Carthaginians.

2

PUNICA

BOOK I

HERE I begin the war by which the fame of the Aeneadae was raised to heaven and proud Carthage submitted to the rule of Italy.[a] Grant me, O Muse, to record the splendid achievements of Italy in ancient days, and to tell of all those heroes whom Rome brought forth for the strife, when the people of Cadmus [b] broke their solemn bond and began the contest for sovereignty ; and for long it remained uncertain, on which of the two citadels Fortune would establish the capital of the world. Thrice over with unholy warfare did the Carthaginian leaders violate their compact with the Senate and the treaty they had sworn by Jupiter to observe ; and thrice over the lawless sword induced them wantonly to break the peace they had approved. But in the

3

sed medio finem bello excidiumque vicissim
molitae gentes, propiusque fuere periclo,
quis superare datum : reseravit Dardanus arces
ductor Agenoreas, obsessa Palatia vallo   15
Poenorum, ac muris defendit Roma salutem.
　Tantarum causas irarum odiumque perenni
servatum studio et mandata nepotibus arma
fas aperire mihi superasque recludere mentes.
iamque adeo magni repetam primordia motus.   20
　Pygmalioneis quondam per caerula terris
pollutum fugiens fraterno crimine regnum
fatali Dido Libyes appellitur orae.
tum pretio mercata locos nova moenia ponit,
cingere qua secto permissum litora tauro.   25
hic Iuno ante Argos (sic credidit alta vetustas)
ante Agamemnoniam, gratissima tecta, Mycenen
optavit profugis aeternam condere gentem.
verum ubi magnanimis Romam caput urbibus alte
exerere ac missas etiam trans aequora classes   30
totum signa videt victricia ferre per orbem,
iam propius metuens bellandi corda furore
Phoenicum extimulat.　sed enim conanime primae
contuso pugnae fractisque in gurgite coeptis
Sicanio Libycis, iterum instaurata capessens   35

---

　^a There were three Punic wars : the second of these is
the subject of the poem.
　^b Scipio Africanus, in 202 B.C.　Silius often uses *Dardanus*
as equivalent to *Romanus*, because the Romans were
descendants of Aeneas, an exile from Troy.
　^c Pygmalion, king of Tyre, treacherously murdered
Sychaeus, his brother-in-law and Dido's husband, for the
sake of his wealth ; but Dido managed to carry the treasure
off to Africa.

second war [a] each nation strove to destroy and exterminate her rival, and those to whom victory was granted came nearer to destruction : in it a Roman general [b] stormed the citadel of Carthage, the Palatine was surrounded and besieged by Hannibal, and Rome made good her safety by her walls alone.

The causes of such fierce anger, the hatred maintained with unabated fury, the war bequeathed by sire to son and by son to grandson—these things I am permitted to reveal, and to disclose the purposes of Heaven. And now I shall begin by tracing the origin of this great upheaval.

When Dido long ago fled across the sea from the land of Pygmalion,[c] leaving behind her the realm polluted by her brother's guilt, she landed on the destined shore of Libya. There she bought land for a price and founded a new city, where she was permitted to lay strips of a bull's hide round the strand. Here—so remote antiquity believed—Juno elected to found for the exiles a nation to last for ever, preferring it to Argos, and to Mycenae, the city of Agamemnon and her chosen dwelling-place. But when she saw Rome lifting her head high among aspiring cities, and even sending fleets across the sea to carry her victorious standards over all the earth, then the goddess felt the danger close and stirred up in the minds of the Phoenicians a frenzy for war. But the effort of their first campaign was crushed, and the enterprise of the Carthaginians was wrecked on the Sicilian sea [d] ; and then Juno took up the sword again

---

[d] The first Punic war ended in a great victory at sea for the Romans, near the Aegatian islands off the promontory of Lilybaeum (242 B.C.).

arma remolitur ; dux omnia sufficit unus
turbanti terra[1] pontumque movere paranti.

Iamque deae cunctas sibi belliger induit iras
Hannibal ; hunc audet solum componere fatis.
sanguineo tum laeta viro atque in regna Latini   40
turbine mox saevo venientum haud inscia cladum,
" intulerit Latio, spreta me, Troïus," inquit,
" exul Dardaniam et bis numina capta penates
sceptraque fundarit victor Lavinia Teucris,
dum Romana tuae, Ticine, cadavera ripae   45
non capiant, famulusque[2] mihi per Celtica rura
sanguine Pergameo Trebia et stipantibus armis
corporibusque virum retro fluat, ac sua largo
stagna reformidet Thrasymennus turbida tabo ;
dum Cannas, tumulum Hesperiae, campumque cruore
Ausonio mersum sublimis Iapyga cernam   51
teque vadi dubium coëuntibus, Aufide, ripis
per clipeos galeasque virum caesosque per artus
vix iter Hadriaci rumpentem ad litora ponti."
haec ait ac iuvenem facta ad Mavortia flammat.   55

Ingenio motus avidus fideique sinister
is fuit, exsuperans astu, sed devius aequi.
armato nullus divum pudor ; improba virtus
et pacis despectus honos ; penitusque medullis

---

[1] omnia . . . terra *Madvig*: agmina . . . terras *edd.*
[2] famulus *Postgate*: similis *edd.*

---

[a] The legendary king of Laurentum who welcomed
Aeneas on his arrival in Italy. The " realm of Latinus "
stands for either Rome or Italy.

[b] Aeneas.

[c] Troy: and so "Teucrians" below stands for " Romans."

[d] Troy was taken first by Hercules, when he had been
deceived by Laomedon, king of Troy ; and secondly by
the Greeks under Agamemnon.

[e] Juno enumerates the four main victories gained by

6

for a fresh conflict. When she upset all things on earth and was preparing to stir up the sea, she found a sufficient instrument in a single leader.

Now warlike Hannibal clothed himself with all the wrath of the goddess; his single arm she dared to match against destiny. Then, rejoicing in that man of blood, and aware of the fierce storm of disasters in store for the realm of Latinus,[a] she spoke thus : " In defiance of me, the exile from Troy[b] brought Dardania[c] to Latium, together with his household gods—deities that were twice taken prisoners[d] ; and he gained a victory and founded a kingdom for the Teucrians at Lavinium. That may pass—provided that the banks of the Ticinus[e] cannot contain the Roman dead, and that the Trebia, obedient to me, shall flow backwards through the fields of Gaul, blocked by the blood of Romans and their weapons and the corpses of men ; provided that Lake Trasimene shall be terrified by its own pools darkened with streams of gore, and that I shall see from heaven Cannae, the grave of Italy, and the Iapygian plain inundated with Roman blood, while the Aufidus, doubtful of its course as its banks close in, can hardly force a passage to the Adriatic shore through shields and helmets and severed limbs of men." With these words she fired the youthful warrior for deeds of battle.

By nature he was eager for action and faithless to his plighted word, a past master in cunning but a strayer from justice. Once armed, he had no respect for Heaven; he was brave for evil and despised the glory of peace ; and a thirst for human blood burned

Hannibal over the Romans in Italy : (1) on the Ticinus ; (2) on the Trebia ; (3) at Lake Trasimene ; (4) at Cannae, by the river Aufidus.

sanguinis humani flagrat sitis. his super, aevi   60
flore virens, avet Aegates abolere, parentum
dedecus, ac Siculo demergere foedera ponto.
dat mentem Iuno ac laudum spe corda fatigat.
iamque aut nocturno penetrat Capitolia visu
aut rapidis fertur per summas passibus Alpes.   65
saepe etiam famuli turbato ad limina somno
expavere trucem per vasta silentia vocem,
ac largo sudore virum invenere futuras
miscentem pugnas et inania bella gerentem.

   Hanc rabiem in fines Italum Saturniaque arva   70
addiderat laudem puero patrius furor orsus.[1]
Sarrana prisci Barcae de gente, vetustos
a Belo numerabat avos. namque orba marito
cum fugeret Dido famulam Tyron, impia diri
Belides iuvenis vitaverat arma tyranni   75
et se participem casus sociarat in omnes.
nobilis hoc ortu et dextra spectatus Hamilcar,
ut fari primamque datum distinguere lingua
Hannibali vocem, sollers nutrire furores,
Romanum sevit puerili in pectore bellum.   80

   Urbe fuit media sacrum genetricis Elissae
manibus et patria Tyriis formidine cultum,
quod taxi circum et piceae squalentibus umbris
abdiderant caelique arcebant lumine, templum.
hoc sese, ut perhibent, curis mortalibus olim   85

---

[1] *Thus emended by Housman* : tantam puero patris heu
furor altus *Bauer*.

---

  [a] See note to l. 35.
  [b] The legendary ruler of Latium, whose reign was the
Golden Age.
  [c] A king of Tyre, also called Sarra; perhaps a title borne by
all the kings of Tyre. The father of Dido was called Belus.
  [d] Barcas.

8

in his inmost heart. Besides all this, his youthful vigour longed to blot out the Aegates,[a] the shame of the last generation, and to drown the treaty of peace in the Sicilian sea. Juno inspired him and tormented his spirit with ambition. Already, in visions of the night, he either stormed the Capitol or marched at speed over the summits of the Alps. Often too the servants who slept at his door were roused and terrified by a fierce cry that broke the desolate silence, and found their master dripping with sweat, while he fought battles still to come and waged imaginary warfare.

When he was a mere child, his father's passion had kindled in Hannibal this frenzy against Italy and the realm of Saturn,[b] and started him on his glorious career. Hamilcar, sprung from the Tyrian house of ancient Barcas, reckoned his long descent from Belus.[c] For, when Dido lost her husband and fled from a Tyre reduced to slavery, the young scion of Belus[d] had escaped the unrighteous sword of the dread tyrant,[e] and had joined his fortunes with hers for weal or woe. Thus nobly born and a proved warrior, Hamilcar, as soon as Hannibal could speak and utter his first distinct words, sowed war with Rome in the boy's heart; and well he knew how to feed angry passions.

In the centre of Carthage stood a temple, sacred to the spirit of Elissa,[f] the foundress, and regarded with hereditary awe by the people. Round it stood yew-trees and pines with their melancholy shade, which hid it and kept away the light of heaven. Here, as it was reported, the queen had cast off long ago the ills

[e] Pygmalion.
[f] Another name for Dido.

9

exuerat regina loco.   stant marmore maesto
effigies, Belusque parens omnisque nepotum
a Belo series ; stat gloria gentis Agenor,
et qui longa dedit terris cognomina Phoenix.
ipsa sedet tandem aeternum coniuncta Sychaeo ;   90
ante pedes ensis Phrygius iacet ; ordine centum
stant arae caelique deis Erebique potenti.
hic, crine effuso, atque Hennaeae numina divae
atque Acheronta vocat Stygia cum veste sacerdos.
immugit tellus rumpitque horrenda per umbras   95
sibila ; inaccensi flagrant altaribus ignes.
tum magico volitant cantu per inania manes
exciti, vultusque in marmore sudat Elissae.
Hannibal haec patrio iussu ad penetralia fertur ;
ingressique habitus atque ora explorat Hamilcar. 100
non ille euhantis Massylae palluit iras,
non diros templi ritus aspersaque tabo
limina et audito surgentes carmine flammas.
olli permulcens genitor caput oscula libat
attollitque animos hortando et talibus implet :   105
" Gens recidiva Phrygum Cadmeae stirpis alumnos
foederibus non aequa premit ; si fata negarint
dedecus id patriae nostra depellere dextra,

---

^a Phoenicia. The Roman name for the Carthaginians was
Poeni.

^b The sword given her by Aeneas, with which she killed
herself.

^c Erebus is one of many names for Hades ; Acheron
(l. 94), properly a river in Hades, is another such name.

^d Proserpina : she was gathering flowers at Henna in
Sicily, when Pluto carried her down to Hades to be his
queen.

^e *i.e.* African. The Massyli were a powerful tribe who
occupied what is now called Algeria : see note to iii. 282.

that flesh is heir to. Statues of mournful marble
stood there—Belus, the founder of the race, and
all the line descended from Belus ; Agenor also, the
nation's boast, and Phoenix who gave a lasting name[a]
to his country. There Dido herself was seated, at
last united for ever to Sychaeus ; and at her feet
lay the Trojan sword.[b] A hundred altars stood here
in order, sacred to the gods of heaven and the lord of
Erebus.[c] Here the priestess with streaming hair and
Stygian garb calls up Acheron and the divinity of
Henna's goddess.[d] The earth rumbles in the gloom
and breaks forth into awesome hissings ; and fire
blazes unkindled upon the altars. The dead also are
called up by magic spells and flit through empty
space ; and the marble face of Elissa sweats. To
this shrine Hannibal was brought by his father's
command ; and, when he had entered, Hamilcar
examined the boy's face and bearing. No terrors
for him had the Massylian[e] priestess, raving in her
frenzy, or the horrid rites[f] of the temple, the
blood-bespattered doors, and the flames that mounted
at the sound of incantation. His father stroked the
boy's head and kissed him ; then he raised his
courage by exhortation and thus inspired him :

"The restored race of Phrygians[g] is oppressing with
unjust treaties the people of Cadmean stock. If
fate does not permit my right hand to avert this dis-
honour from our land, you, my son, must choose this

[f] This is probably an allusion to the human sacrifices,
especially of infants, which were common at Carthage :
see iv. 765 foll.
[g] The Romans are here called " Phrygians," " Lauren-
tines," and " Tuscans ": see p. xiii. The Carthaginians are
called " Cadmeans," because Cadmus, the founder of Thebes,
came from Phoenicia : see l. 6.

11

haec tua sit laus, nate, velis ; age, concipe bella
latura exitium Laurentibus ; horreat ortus   110
iam pubes Tyrrhena tuos, partusque recusent,
te surgente, puer, Latiae producere matres."
    His acuit stimulis, subicitque haud mollia dictu :
" Romanos terra atque undis, ubi competet aetas,
ferro ignique sequar Rhoeteaque fata revolvam.   115
non superi mihi, non Martem cohibentia pacta,
non celsae obstiterint Alpes Tarpeiaque saxa.
hanc mentem iuro nostri per numina Martis,
per manes, regina, tuos."   tum nigra triformi
hostia mactatur divae, raptimque recludit   120
spirantes artus poscens responsa sacerdos
ac fugientem animam properatis consulit extis.
    Ast ubi quaesitas artis de more vetustae
intravit mentes superum, sic deinde profatur :
" Aetolos late consterni milite campos   125
Idaeoque lacus flagrantes sanguine cerno.
quanta procul moles scopulis ad sidera tendit,
cuius in aërio pendent tua vertice castra !
iamque iugis agmen rapitur ; trepidantia fumant
moenia, et Hesperio tellus porrecta sub axe   130
Sidoniis lucet flammis.   fluit ecce cruentus
Eridanus.   iacet ore truci super arma virosque,
tertia qui tulerat sublimis opima Tonanti.

---

    [a] The treaty of peace between Rome and Carthage.
    [b] Hecate, who was worshipped also as Diana and Luna.
    [c] She foresees various episodes of the war : the battles
of Cannae and Lake Trasimene ; the crossing of the Alps ;
the battles of Ticinus and Trebia ; the death of Marcellus ;
the storm which drove Hannibal away from Rome (211 B.C.).
The " Aetolian fields " are Apulia, so called because Diomede,
the Aetolian king, settled there after the Trojan war.
    [d] Marcellus won " choice spoils " by killing in battle a
Gallic chief; he fell in an ambush in 208 B.C. : see xv. 334 foll.
12

as your field of fame. Be quick to swear a war that
shall bring destruction to the Laurentines ; let the
Tuscan people already dread your birth ; and when
you, my son, arise, let Latian mothers refuse to rear
their offspring.''

With these incentives he spurred on the boy and
then dictated a vow not easy to utter : " When I
come to age, I shall pursue the Romans with fire and
sword and enact again the doom of Troy. The gods
shall not stop my career, nor the treaty that bars
the sword,[a] neither the lofty Alps nor the Tarpeian
rock. I swear to this purpose by the divinity of our
native god of war, and by the shade of Elissa.'' Then
a black victim was sacrificed to the goddess of triple
shape [b] ; and the priestess, seeking an oracle, quickly
opened the still breathing body and questioned the
spirit, as it fled from the inward parts that she had
laid bare in haste.

But when, following the custom of her ancient art,
she had entered into the mind of the gods whom
she inquired of, thus she spoke aloud : " I see the
Aetolian fields [c] covered far and wide with soldiers'
corpses, and lakes red with Trojan blood. How huge
the rampart of cliffs that rises far towards heaven !
And on its airy summit your camp is perched. Now
the army rushes down from the mountains ; terrified
cities send up smoke, and the land that lies beneath
the western heavens blazes with Punic fires. See !
the river Po runs blood. Fierce is that face that lies
on a heap of arms and men—the face of him who was
the third to carry in triumph choice spoils [d] to the

These spoils, only thrice won in Roman history, were the
prize of a commander who killed with his own hand the
commander of the hostile army.

heu quaenam subitis horrescit turbida nimbis
tempestas, ruptoque polo micat igneus aether !   135
magna parant superi : tonat alti regia caeli,
bellantemque Iovem cerno." venientia fata
scire ultra vetuit Iuno, fibraeque repente
conticuere. latent casus longique labores.

    Sic clausum linquens arcano pectore bellum   140
atque hominum finem Gades Calpenque secutus,
dum fert Herculeis Garamantica signa columnis,
occubuit saevo Tyrius certamine ductor.

    Interea rerum Hasdrubali traduntur habenae,
occidui qui solis opes et vulgus Hiberum   145
Baeticolasque viros furiis agitabat iniquis.
tristia corda ducis, simul immedicabilis ira,
et fructus regni feritas erat ; asper amore
sanguinis, et metui demens credebat honorem ;
nec nota docilis poena satiare furores.   150
ore excellentem et spectatum fortibus ausis
antiqua de stirpe Tagum, superumque hominumque
immemor, erecto suffixum robore maestis
ostentabat ovans populis sine funere regem.
auriferi Tagus ascito cognomine fontis   155
perque antra et ripas nymphis ululatus Hiberis,
Maeonium non ille vadum, non Lydia mallet
stagna sibi, nec qui riguo perfunditur auro
campum atque illatis Hermi flavescit harenis.

---

   a Gibraltar and Cadiz. The Pillars of Hercules are now
the Straits of Gibraltar.
   b The son-in-law of Hamilcar.
   c The Guadalquivir.
   d The Pactolus. This and the Hermus were rivers of
Lydia (also called here Maeonia), both rich in gold. In
Europe the Tagus was famous for the gold contained in
its waters ; and this chief had taken his name from it.

Thunder-god. Ah ! what wild storm is this that
rages with sudden downpour, while the sky is
rent asunder and the fiery ether flashes ! The
gods are preparing mighty things, the throne of
high heaven thunders, and I see Jupiter in arms."
Then Juno forbade her to learn more of coming
events, and the victims suddenly became dumb.
The dangers and the endless hardships were con-
cealed.

So Hamilcar left his design of war concealed in
his secret heart, and made for Calpe and Gades,[a] the
limit of the world; but, while carrying the standards
of Africa to the Pillars of Hercules, he fell in a hard-
fought battle.

Meanwhile the direction of affairs was handed over
to Hasdrubal[b] ; and he harried with savage cruelty
the wealth of the western world, the people of Spain,
and the dwellers beside the Baetis.[c] Hard was
the general's heart, and nothing could mitigate his
ferocious temper ; power he valued because it gave
him the opportunity to be cruel. Thirst for blood
hardened his heart ; and he had the folly to believe
that to be feared is glory. Nor was he willing to sate
his rage with ordinary punishments. Tagus, a man
of ancient race, remarkable for beauty and of proved
valour, Hasdrubal, defying gods and men, fastened
high on a wooden cross, and displayed in triumph to
the sorrowing natives the unburied body of their king.
Tagus, who had taken his name from the gold-bearing
river, was mourned by the Nymphs of Spain through all
their caves and banks ; nor would he have preferred
the river of Maeonia[d] and the pools of Lydia, nor
the plain watered by flowing gold and turned yellow
by the sands of Hermus pouring over it. Ever first

15

primus inire manus, postremus ponere Martem ;   160
cum rapidum effusis ageret sublimis habenis
quadrupedem, non ense virum, non eminus hasta
sistere erat ; volitabat ovans aciesque per ambas
iam Tagus auratis agnoscebatur in armis.
quem postquam diro suspensum robore vidit   165
deformem leti famulus, clam corripit ensem
dilectum domino pernixque irrumpit in aulam
atque immite ferit geminato vulnere pectus.
at Poeni, succensa ira turbataque luctu
et saevis gens laeta, ruunt tormentaque portant. 170
non ignes candensque chalybs, non verbera passim
ictibus innumeris lacerum scindentia corpus,
carnificaeve manus penitusve infusa medullis
pestis et in medio lucentes vulnere flammae
cessavere ; ferum visu dictuque, per artem   175
saevitiae extenti, quantum tormenta iubebant,
creverunt artus, atque, omni sanguine rupto,
ossa liquefactis fumarunt fervida membris.
mens intacta manet ; superat ridetque dolores,
spectanti similis, fessosque labore ministros   180
increpitat dominique crucem clamore reposcit.

Haec inter spretae miseranda piacula poenae
erepto trepidus ductore exercitus una
Hannibalem voce atque alacri certamine poscit.
hinc studia accendit patriae virtutis imago,   185
hinc fama in populos iurati didita belli,

---

a Carthaginian and Spanish.
b i.e. Hasdrubal's.   c Hamilcar.

16

to enter the battle and last to lay down the sword,
when he sat high on his steed and urged it on with
loosened reins, no sword could stop him nor spear
hurled from far; on he flew in triumph, and the
golden armour of Tagus was well known throughout
both armies.[a] Then a servant, when he saw that
hideous death and the body of Tagus hanging on the
fatal tree, stole his master's favourite sword and
rushed into the palace, where he smote that savage
breast [b] once and again. Carthaginians are cruel; and
now, in their anger and grief, they made haste to
bring the tortures. Every device was used—fire and
white-hot steel, scourges that cut the body to ribbons
with a rain of blows past counting, the hands of the
torturers, the agony driven home into the marrow,
the flame burning in the heart of the wound. Dread-
ful to see and even to relate, the limbs were expanded
by the torturers' ingenuity and grew as much as
the torment required; and, when all the blood had
gushed forth, the bones still smoked and burned on,
after the limbs were consumed. But the man's spirit
remained unbroken; he was the master still and
despised the suffering; like a mere looker-on he
blamed the myrmidons of the torturer for flagging
in their task and loudly demanded to be crucified like
his master.

While this piteous punishment was inflicted on a
victim who made light of it, the soldiers, disturbed by
the loss of their general, with one voice and with
eager enthusiasm demanded Hannibal for their leader.
Their favour was due to many causes—the reflection
in him of his father's [c] valour; the report, broadcast
among the nations, that he was the sworn enemy of
Rome; his youth eager for action and the fiery spirit

SILIUS ITALICUS

hinc virides ausis anni fervorque decorus
atque armata dolis mens et vis insita fandi.
  Primi ductorem Libyes clamore salutant,
mox et Pyrenes populi et bellator Hiberus.   190
continuoque ferox oritur fiducia menti,
cessisse imperio tantum terraeque marisque.
Aeoliis candens austris et lampade Phoebi
aestifero Libye torretur subdita Cancro,
aut ingens Asiae latus, aut pars tertia terris.   195
terminus huic roseos amnis Lageus ad ortus
septeno impellens tumefactum gurgite pontum ;
at qua diversas clementior aspicit Arctos,
Herculeo dirimente freto, diducta propinquis
Europes videt arva iugis ; ultra obsidet aequor,   200
nec patitur nomen proferri longius Atlas,
Atlas subducto tracturus vertice caelum.
sidera nubiferum fulcit caput, aetheriasque
erigit aeternum compages ardua cervix.
canet barba gelu, frontemque immanibus umbris 205
pinea silva premit ; vastant cava tempora venti,
nimbosoque ruunt spumantia flumina rictu.
tum geminas laterum cautes maria alta fatigant,
atque ubi fessus equos Titan immersit anhelos,
flammiferum condunt fumanti gurgite currum.   210
sed qua se campis squalentibus Africa tendit,
serpentum largo coquitur fecunda veneno ;
felix qua pingues mitis plaga temperat agros,
nec Cerere Hennaea Phario nec victa colono.

---

  ^a African peoples subject to Carthage.
  ^b Aeolus was the ruler of all winds and kept them in prison.
  ^c The Nile, which flows into the sea by seven mouths.
Lagus, a Macedonian general, founded the dynasty of the
Ptolemies.
  ^d The Bears are the two northern constellations so named.
  ^e Atlas, the mountain range which bounds N.W. Africa,

18

that well became him ; his heart equipped with guile, and his native eloquence.

The Libyans [a] were first to hail him with applause as their leader, and the Pyrenean tribes and warlike Spaniards followed them.   At once his heart swelled with pride and satisfaction that so much of land and sea had come under his sway.   Libya lies under the burning sign of Cancer, and is parched by the south winds of Aeolus [b] and the sun's disk.   It is either a huge offshoot of Asia, or a third continent of the world. It is bounded on the rosy east by the river of Lagus,[c] which strikes the swollen sea with seven streams. But, where the land in milder mood faces the opposing Bears,[d] it is cut off by the straits of Hercules, and, though parted from them, looks on the lands of Europe from its adjacent heights ; the ocean blocks its further extension, and Atlas [e] forbids its name to be carried further—Atlas, who would bring down the sky, if he withdrew his shoulders.   His cloud-capt head supports the stars, and his soaring neck for ever holds aloft the firmament of heaven.   His beard is white with frost, and pine-forests crown his brow with their vast shade ; winds ravage his hollow temples, and foaming rivers rush down from his streaming open jaws.   Moreover, the deep seas assail the cliffs on both his flanks, and, when the weary Titan [f] has bathed his panting steeds, hide his flaming car in the steaming ocean.   But, where Africa spreads her un-tilled plains, the burnt-up land bears nothing but the poison of snakes in plenty ; though, where a temperate strip blesses the fields, her fertility is not surpassed by the crops of Henna[g] nor by the Egyptian

was personified by the Greeks as a giant who supports heaven on his shoulders.   [f] The sun.   [g] Sicily.

hic passim exultant Numidae, gens inscia freni,   215
quis inter geminas per ludum mobilis aures
quadrupedem flectit non cedens virga lupatis.
altrix bellorum bellatorumque virorum
tellus, nec fidens nudo sine fraudibus ensi.
 Altera complebant Hispanae castra cohortes,   220
auxilia Europae genitoris parta tropaeis.
Martius hinc campos sonipes hinnitibus implet,
hinc iuga cornipedes erecti bellica raptant ;
non Eleus eat campo ferventior axis.
prodiga gens animae et properare facillima mortem.
namque ubi transcendit florentes viribus annos,   226
impatiens aevi spernit novisse senectam,
et fati modus in dextra est.   his omne metallum :
electri gemino pallent de semine venae,
atque atros chalybis fetus humus horrida nutrit.   230
sed scelerum causas operit deus : Astur avarus
visceribus lacerae telluris mergitur imis
et redit infelix effosso concolor auro.
hinc certant, Pactole, tibi Duriusque Tagusque,
quique super Gravios lucentes volvit harenas,   235
infernae populis referens oblivia Lethes.
nec Cereri terra indocilis nec inhospita Baccho,
nullaque Palladia sese magis arbore tollit.

---

  [a] This fact is asserted by Virgil and Lucan, and repeatedly
by Silius : see ii. 64, iii. 293, xvi. 200.
  [b] They poison their weapons.
  [c] At the Olympic games.
  [d] He puts an end to his own life.
  [e] Electrum was a natural metal, called by the Greeks
" white gold " : it was partly gold and partly silver.
  [f] There was in Spain, in the land of the Gravii, a river
called *Oblivio* and therefore said to recall Lethe, the river

husbandman. Here the Numidians rove at large, a nation that knows not the bridle; for the light switch they ply between its ears turns the horse about in their sport, no less effectively than the bit.[a] This land breeds wars and warriors; nor do they trust to the naked sword but use guile[b] also.

A second camp was filled with Spanish troops, European allies whom the victories of Hamilcar had gained. Here the war-horse filled the plains with his neighings, and here high-mettled steeds drew along chariots of war; not even the drivers at Olympia[c] could dash over the course with more fiery haste. That people recks little of life, and they are most ready to anticipate death. For, when a man has passed the years of youthful strength, he cannot bear to live on and disdains acquaintance with old age; and his span of life depends on his own right arm.[d] All metals are found here: there are veins of electrum,[e] whose yellow hue shows their double origin, and the rugged soil feeds the black crop of iron. Heaven covered up the incentives to crime; but the covetous Asturian plunges deep into the bowels of the mangled earth, and the wretch returns with a face as yellow as the gold he has dug out. The Durius and the Tagus of this land challenge the Pactolus; and so does the river which rolls its glittering sands over the land of the Gravii and reproduces for the inhabitants the forgetfulness of Lethe in the nether world.[f] Spain is not unfit for corn-crops nor unfriendly to the vine; and there is no land in which the tree of Pallas[g] rises higher.

in Hades whose water takes away the memory of past events. The *Durius* (now Duero) is a river in Portugal.

[g] The olive.

SILIUS ITALICUS

Hae postquam Tyrio gentes cessere tyranno,
utque dati rerum freni, tunc arte paterna   240
conciliare viros ; armis consulta senatus
vertere, nunc donis.   primus sumpsisse laborem,
primus iter carpsisse pedes partemque subire,
si valli festinet opus.   nec cetera segnis,
quaecumque ad laudem stimulant ; somnumque
        negabat   245
naturae noctemque vigil ducebat in armis,
interdum proiectus humi turbaeque Libyssae
insignis sagulo duris certare maniplis ;
celsus et in magno praecedens agmine ductor
imperium praeferre suum ; tum vertice nudo   250
excipere insanos imbres caelique ruinam.
spectarunt Poeni tremuitque exterritus Astur,
torquentem cum tela Iovem permixtaque nimbis
fulmina et excussos ventorum flatibus ignes
turbato transiret equo ; nec pulvere fessum   255
agminis ardenti labefecit Sirius astro.
flammiferis tellus radiis cum exusta dehiscit,
candentique globo medius coquit aethera fervor,
femineum putat humenti iacuisse sub umbra
exercetque sitim et spectato fonte recedit.   260
idem correptis sternacem ad proelia frenis
frangere equum et famam letalis amare lacerti
ignotique amnis tranare sonantia saxa
atque e diversa socios accersere ripa.
idem expugnati primus stetit aggere muri,   265
et quotiens campo rapidus fera proelia miscet,

---

^a Spaniards. Asturia was a province of Spain, famous for
its breed of horses and its gold-mines : see l. 231.
^b The ancients supposed that lightning was caused by the
action of wind upon the clouds.

22

When these peoples had yielded to the Tyrian ruler and he had received the reins of government, then with his father's craft he gained men's friendship; by arms or by bribes he caused them to reverse the Senate's decrees. He was ever first to undertake hardship, first to march on foot, and first to bear a hand when the rampart was reared in haste. In all other things that spur a man on to glory he was untiring: denying sleep to nature, he would pass the whole night armed and awake, lying sometimes upon the ground; distinguished by the general's cloak, he vied with the hardy soldiers of the Libyan army; or mounted high he rode as leader of the long line; again he endured bare-headed the fury of the rains and the crashing of the sky. The Carthaginians looked on and the Asturians *a* trembled for fear, when he rode his startled horse through the bolts hurled by Jupiter, the lightnings flashing amid the rain, and the fires driven forth by the blasts of the winds *b*; he was never wearied by the dusty march nor weakened by the fiery star of Sirius. *c* When the earth was burnt and cracked by fiery rays, and when the heat of noon parched the sky with its blazing orb, he thought it womanish to lie down in the shade where the ground was moist; he practised thirst and looked on a spring only to leave it. He would grasp the reins also and break in for battle the steed that tried to throw him; he sought the glory of a death-dealing arm; he would swim through the rattling boulders of an unknown river and then summon his comrades from the opposite bank. He was first also to stand on the rampart of a city stormed; and, whenever he dashed over the plain where fierce battle was joined, a broad

c Sirius, the Dog-star, stands for the heat of summer.

qua sparsit ferrum, latus rubet aequore limes.
ergo instat fatis, et rumpere foedera certus,
quo datur, interea Romam comprendere bello
gaudet et extremis pulsat Capitolia terris.   270
   Prima Saguntinas turbarunt classica portas,
bellaque sumpta viro belli maioris amore.
haud procul Herculei tollunt se litore muri,
clementer crescente iugo, quis nobile nomen
conditus excelso sacravit colle Zacynthos.   275
hic comes Alcidae remeabat in agmine Thebas
Geryone extincto caeloque ea facta ferebat.
tres animas namque id monstrum, tres corpore dextras
armarat ternaque caput cervice gerebat.
haud alium vidit tellus, cui ponere finem   280
non posset mors una viro, duraeque sorores
tertia bis rupto torquerent stamina filo.
hinc spolia ostentabat ovans captivaque victor
armenta ad fontes medio fervore vocabat,
cum tumidas fauces accensis sole venenis   285
calcatus rupit letali vulnere serpens
Inachiumque virum terris prostravit Hiberis.
mox profugi ducente Noto advertere coloni,
insula quos genuit Graio circumflua ponto
atque auxit quondam Laërtia regna Zacynthos.   290
firmavit tenues ortus mox Daunia pubes,
sedis inops, misit largo quam dives alumno,

---

[a] To the ancients Spain was the western limit of the world.
[b] Saguntum in Spain, like Massilia in Gaul, claimed to
be a Greek city.   The name was identified with Zacynthus,
a companion of Hercules, whose tomb was shown there.
The seizure of Geryon's cattle was one of the Labours of
Hercules.   Further, settlers were said to have come there
from the Greek island of Zacynthus (now Zante).
[c] The three Fates or *Parcae*.

red lane was left on the field, wherever he hurled his spear. Therefore he pressed hard upon the heels of Fortune ; and, resolved as he was to break the treaty, he rejoiced meantime to involve Rome, as far as he could, in war ; and from the end of the world *a* he struck at the Capitol.

His war-trumpets sounded first before the gates of dismayed Saguntum,*b* and he chose this war in his eagerness for a greater war to come. The city, founded by Hercules, rises on a gentle slope not far from the coast, and owes its sacred and famous name to Zacynthus, who is buried there on the lofty hill. For he was on the march back to Thebes in company with Hercules, after the slaying of Geryon, and was praising the exploit up to the skies. That monster was furnished with three lives and three right arms in a single body, and carried a head on each of three necks. Never did earth see another man whom a single death could not destroy—for whom the stern Sisters *c* span a third lease of life when the thread had twice been snapped. Zacynthus displayed in triumph the prize taken from Geryon, and was calling the cattle to the water in the heat of noon, when a serpent that he trod on discharged from its swollen throat poison envenomed by the sun. The wound was fatal, and the Greek hero lay dead on Spanish soil. At a later time exiled colonists sailed hither before the wind—sons of Zacynthus, the island surrounded by the Ionian sea that once formed part of the kingdom of Laertes.*d* These small beginnings were afterwards strengthened by men of Daunia in search of a habitation ; they were sent forth by

d In Homer Zacynthus forms part of the dominions of Ulysses, son of Laërtes.

25

magnanimis regnata viris, clarum Ardea nomen.
libertas populis pacto servata decusque
maiorum, et Poenis urbi imperitare negatum.   295
   Admovet abrupto flagrantia foedere ductor
Sidonius castra et latos quatit agmine campos.
ipse caput quassans circumlustravit anhelo
muros saevus equo, mensusque paventia tecta,
pandere iamdudum portas et cedere vallo   300
imperat, et longe clausis sua foedera, longe
Ausoniam fore, nec veniae spem Marte subactis ;
scita patrum et leges et iura fidemque deosque
in dextra nunc esse sua.   verba ocius acer
intorto sancit iaculo figitque per arma   305
stantem pro muro et minitantem vana Caicum.
concidit exacti medius per viscera teli,
effusisque simul praerupto ex aggere membris,
victori moriens tepefactam rettulit hastam.
at multo ducis exemplum clamore secuti   310
involvunt atra telorum moenia nube.
clara nec in numero virtus latet ; obvia quisque
ora duci portans, ceu solus bella capessit.
hic crebram fundit Baliari verbere glandem
terque levi ducta circum caput altus habena   315
permissum ventis abscondit in aëre telum,
hic valido librat stridentia saxa lacerto,

---

   [a] Daunia, properly a part of Apulia, is used here and else-
where by Silius as another name for Italy.   Ardea was a
city in Latium, the capital of the Rutulians, and an important
place about the beginning of authentic history.   Hence the
Saguntines are often called " Rutulians " by Silius.
   [b] Here and often the " treaty " means the conditions of
peace dictated by Rome after the First Punic War.

Ardea [a] of famous name—a city ruled by heroic kings, and rich in the number of her sons. The freedom of the inhabitants and their ancestral glory were preserved by treaty ; and by it the Carthaginians were forbidden to rule the city.

The Carthaginian leader broke the treaty [b] and brought his camp-fires close and shook the wide plains with his marching host. He himself, shaking his head in fury, rode round the walls on his panting steed, taking the measure of the terrified buildings. He bade them open their gates at once and desert their rampart ; he told them that, now they were besieged, their treaties and Italy would be far away, and that they could not hope for quarter, if defeated : " Decrees of the Senate," he cried, " law and justice, honour and Providence, are all in my hand now." In eager haste he confirmed his taunts by hurling his javelin and struck Caicus through his armour, as he stood on the wall and uttered idle threats. Pierced right through the middle, down he fell ; his body at once slipped down from the steep rampart ; and in death he restored to his conqueror the spear warmed with his blood. Then with loud shouting the soldiers followed the example of their leader, and wrapped the walls round with a black cloud of missiles. Their prowess was seen and not hidden by their numbers ; turning his face to the general, each man fought as if he were the only combatant. One hurled volleys of bullets with Balearic sling [c] : standing erect, he brandished the light thong thrice round his head, and launched his missile in the air, for the winds to carry ; another poised whizzing stones with strong arm ; a

[c] The best slingers of that age came from the Balearic islands.

27

huic impulsa levi torquetur lancea nodo.
ante omnes ductor, patriis insignis in armis,
nunc picea iactat fumantem lampada flamma,   320
nunc sude, nunc iaculo, nunc saxis impiger instat
aut hydro imbutas, bis noxia tela, sagittas
contendit nervo atque insultat fraude pharetrae :
Dacus ut armiferis Geticae telluris in oris,
spicula qui patrio gaudens acuisse veneno   325
fundit apud ripas inopina binominis Histri.
    Cura subit, collem turrita cingere fronte
castelloque urbem circumvallare frequenti.
heu priscis numen populis, at nomine solo
in terris iam nota Fides ! stat dura iuventus   330
ereptamque fugam et claudi videt aggere muros,
sed dignam Ausonia mortem putat esse Sagunto,
servata cecidisse fide. iamque acrius omnes
intendunt vires ; adductis stridula nervis
Phocaïs effundit vastos balista molares ;   335
atque eadem, ingentis mutato pondere teli,
ferratam excutiens ornum media agmina rumpit.
alternus resonat clangor. certamine tanto
conseruere acies, veluti circumdata vallo
Roma foret ; clamatque super : " tot milia, gentes
inter tela satae, iam capto stamus in hoste ?   341
anne pudet coepti ? pudet ominis ? en bona virtus

---

    a A thong or strap was often attached to the middle of the
spear-shaft to increase its speed and force.
    b The Getae were Scythians : the Dacians lived in what
is now Hungary and Wallachia.
    c The Danube had two names in antiquity—Danubius and
Hister.

third threw a lance speeded by a light strap.[a] In front of them all their leader, conspicuous in his father's armour, now hurls a brand smoking with pitchy flame, now presses on unwearied with stake or javelin or stone, or shoots arrows from the string— missiles dipped in serpent's poison and doubly fatal— and exults in the guile of his quiver. So the Dacian, in the warlike region of the Getic[b] country, delighting to sharpen his arrows with the poison of his native land, pours them forth in sudden showers on the banks of the Hister, the river of two names.[c]

The next task was to surround the hill with a front of towers and blockade the city with a ring of forts. Alas for Loyalty, worshipped by former ages but now known on earth by name only! The hardy citizens stand there, seeing escape cut off and their walls enclosed by a mound; but they think it a death worthy of Italy, for Saguntum to fall with her loyalty preserved. Now they exert all their strength with increased ardour: the catapult of Marseilles[d] launches with a roar huge boulders from its tightened cords, and also, when the burden of the mighty engine is changed, discharges tree-trunks tipped with iron, and breaks a way through the ranks. Loud rose the noise on each side. They joined battle with as much fierceness as if Rome were besieged. Hannibal also shouted: "So many thousand men, people born in the midst of arms—why do we stand still before an enemy we have already conquered? Are we ashamed of our enterprise, or ashamed of our beginning? So much for splendid valour and the first

[d] The catapult was probably made at Marseilles: it is called Phocaean, because Marseilles was a colony from Phocaea in Asia Minor.

primitiaeque ducis ! taline implere paramus
Italiam fama ? tales praemittere pugnas ? "
   Accensae exultant mentes, haustusque medullis
Hannibal exagitat, stimulantque sequentia bella. 346
invadunt manibus vallum caesasque relinquunt
deiecti muris dextras. subit arduus agger
imponitque globos pugnantum desuper urbi.
armavit clausos ac portis arcuit hostem   350
librari multa consueta falarica dextra,
horrendum visu robur celsisque nivosae
Pyrenes trabs lecta iugis, cui plurima cuspis
vix muris toleranda lues ; sed cetera pingui
uncta pice atque atro circumlita sulphure fumant. 355
fulminis haec ritu summis e moenibus arcis
incita, sulcatum tremula secat aëra flamma,
qualis sanguineo praestringit lumina crine
ad terram caelo decurrens ignea lampas.
haec ictu rapido pugnantum saepe per auras,   360
attonito ductore, tulit fumantia membra ;
haec vastae lateri turris cum turbine fixa,
dum penitus pluteis Vulcanum exercet adesis,
arma virosque simul pressit flagrante ruina.
tandem condensis artae testudinis armis   365
subducti Poeni vallo caecaque latebra
pandunt prolapsam suffossis moenibus urbem.

---

^a The war in Italy.
  ^b The *falarica* was a missile of the largest dimensions,
hurled by machinery from towers called *falae.* It had an
iron head and wooden shaft ; and the iron just under the
head was enveloped in tow steeped in pitch, which was
ignited before the weapon was discharged.
  ^c This name was given to a formation often adopted by
soldiers when besieging a town. The shields were carried
above the men's heads and overlapped so as to form a pro-
tection like the shell of a tortoise.

exploit of your general! Is this the glorious news
with which we intend to fill Italy? Are these the
battles whose rumour we send before us?"

Fired by his words their courage rose high; the
spirit of Hannibal sank deep into their hearts and
inspired them; and the thought of wars to come [a]
spurred them on. They attack the rampart with
bare hands and, when thrust down from the walls,
leave there their severed limbs. A high mound was
erected and placed parties of combatants above the
city. But the besieged were protected and the enemy
kept away from the gates by the *falarica*,[b] which many
arms at once were wont to poise. This was a missile
of wood, terrible to behold, a beam chosen from
the high mountains of the snow-covered Pyrenees,
a weapon whose long iron point even walls could
scarce withstand. Then the shaft, smeared with
oily pitch and rubbed all round with black sulphur,
sent forth smoke. When hurled like a thunder-
bolt from the topmost walls of the citadel, it clove
the furrowed air with a flickering flame, even as
a fiery meteor, speeding from heaven to earth,
dazzles men's eyes with its blood-red tail. This
weapon often confounded Hannibal when it carried
aloft the smoking limbs of his men by its swift
stroke; and, when in its flight it struck the side of a
huge tower, it kindled a fire which burnt till all the
woodwork of the tower was utterly consumed, and
buried men and arms together under the blazing
ruins. But at last the Carthaginians retreated from
the rampart, sheltered by the close-packed shields of
the serried "tortoise,"[c] and sapped the wall unseen
till it collapsed, and made a breach into the town.

terribilem in sonitum procumbens aggere victo
Herculeus labor atque immania saxa resolvens
mugitum ingentem caeli dedit. Alpibus altis   370
aeriae rupes, scopulorum mole revulsa,
haud aliter scindunt resonanti fragmine montem.
surgebat †cumulo certantum†[1] prorutus agger,
obstabatque iacens vallum, ni protinus instent
hinc atque hinc acies media pugnare ruina.   375
   Emicat ante omnes primaevo flore iuventae
insignis Rutulo Murrus de sanguine ; at idem
matre Saguntina Graius geminoque parente
Dulichios Italis miscebat prole nepotes.
hic magno socios Aradum clamore vocantem,   380
qua corpus loricam inter galeamque patescit,
conantis motus speculatus, cuspide sistit ;
prostratumque premens telo, voce insuper urget:
" fallax Poene, iaces ; certe Capitolia primus
scandebas victor : quae tanta licentia voti ?   385
nunc Stygio fer bella Iovi ! " tum fervidus hastam
adversi torquens defigit in inguine Hiberi ;
oraque dum calcat iam singultantia leto,
" hac iter est," inquit, " vobis ad moenia Romae,
o metuenda manus: sic, quo properatis, eundum." 390
mox instaurantis pugnam circumsilit arma
et rapto nudum clipeo latus haurit Hiberi.

---

[1] *The words obelized seem to be corrupt.*

[a] Ulysses ruled over the islands of Ithaca, Dulichium, and
Zacynthos : hence Silius perversely uses " Dulichian " for
" Saguntine," because men of Zacynthos had taken part in
founding Saguntum.
   [b] Aradus, who hoped to attack Jupiter on the Capitol
at Rome, is told to fight Pluto instead, the Jupiter of
Hades. The Styx is one of the infernal rivers : see note to
ii. 610.

The rampart gave way, the walls built by Hercules
sank down with a fearful crash, and the huge stones
fell apart, and a mighty rumbling of the sky
followed their fall. So the towering peaks of the
high Alps, when a mass of rock is torn away from
them, furrow the mountain-side with the roar of an
avalanche. With haste the ruined rampart was raised
again ; and nought but the prostrate wall prevented
both armies from fighting on in the wreckage that
divided them.

First of all Murrus sprang forward, conspicuous for
his youthful beauty. He was of Rutulian blood, born
of a Saguntine mother ; but he had Greek blood too,
and by his two parents he combined the seed of Italy
with that of Dulichium.[a] When Aradus summoned
his comrades with a mighty shout, Murrus watched
his forward movement and stopped him ; and the
spear-point pierced the gap that came between the
breastplate and the helmet. Then pinning him to
the ground with his spear he taunted him as well :
" False Carthaginian, you lie low ; you were to be
foremost, forsooth, in mounting the Capitol as a
conqueror ; was ever ambition so presumptuous ?
Go now, and fight the deity of the Styx instead ! "[b]
Next, brandishing his fiery spear, he buried it in
the groin of Hiberus who stood before him ; and,
treading on the features already convulsed in death,
he cried : " Terrible as is your host, by this path
must ye march to the walls of Rome ; thus must ye go
to the place whither ye are hastening." Then, when
Hiberus[c] tried to renew the combat, Murrus evaded
the weapon and snatched the shield of his foe, and

[c] There is some error here : Hiberus was a dying man in
l. 388 ; in l. 387 *Hiberi* has ousted some other name.

dives agri, dives pecoris famaeque negatus
bella feris[1] arcu iaculoque agitabat Hiberus,
felix heu nemorum et vitae laudandus opacae,   395
si sua per patrios tenuisset spicula saltus.
hunc miseratus adest infesto vulnere Ladmus.
cui saevum arridens : " narrabis Hamilcaris umbris
hanc," inquit, " dextram, quae iam post funera vulgi
Hannibalem vobis dederit comitem "—et ferit alte
insurgens gladio cristatae cassidis aera   401
perque ipsum tegimen crepitantia dissipat ossa.
tum frontem Chremes intonsam umbrante capillo
saeptus et horrentes effingens crine galeros ;
tum Masulis crudaque virens ad bella senecta   405
Kartalo, non pavidus fetas mulcere leaenas,
flumineaque urna caelatus Bagrada parmam
et vastae Nasamon Syrtis populator Hiempsal,
audax in fluctu laceras captare carinas—
una omnes dextraque cadunt iraque perempti ;   410
nec non serpentem diro exarmare veneno
doctus Athyr tactuque graves sopire chelydros
ac dubiam admoto subolem explorare ceraste.
tu quoque fatidicis Garamanticus accola lucis,
insignis flexo galeam per tempora cornu,   415
heu frustra reditum sortes tibi saepe locutas
mentitumque Iovem increpitans, occumbis, Hiarba.

---

[1] feris *Summers* : ferens *Bauer*.

---

[a] She was supposed to be especially fierce then.

[b] Bagrada is a river in N. Africa, after which this man was
named. The " urn " of the river is its source. The Syrtes,
as formidable to Roman mariners as the Goodwin Sands
once were to us, are two rocky gulfs on the N. coast of
Africa, between Cyrene and Carthage.

[c] If he was a true-born child, the snake would not frighten
him.

[d] The horn showed his connexion with the oracle of

pierced his unprotected side. Rich in land and rich
in flocks but unknown to fame, Hiberus used to wage
war against wild beasts with bow and javelin, happy,
alas, in his forests and worthy of praise in his life of
retirement, if he had never carried his arrows outside
his ancestral woodlands. In pity for him Ladmus
came up, intent to strike. But Murrus cried with a
savage laugh : "Tell Hamilcar's ghost of my right
arm, which, when the rabble are slain, shall send
Hannibal to keep company with you all." Then,
rising erect, he smote with his sword the crested
brazen helmet and scattered the rattling bones of the
skull right through their covering. Next, Chremes,
whose unshorn brow was surrounded and shaded by
his hair, and who made a shaggy cap of his locks ;
then Masulis, and Kartalo, vigorous for war in green
old age, who feared not to stroke the lioness with
cubs [a] ; and Bagrada, whose shield was blazoned with
the river's urn [b] ; and Hiempsal, one of the Nasa-
monians who plunder the devouring Syrtis and make
bold to pillage shipwrecks ; —all these were slain
alike by that wrathful right hand ; and so was Athyr,
skilled to disarm serpents of their fell poison, to send
fierce water-snakes to sleep by his touch, and to test
a child of doubtful birth by placing a horned snake
beside it.[c] Slain too was Hiarbas, who dwelt near
the prophetic groves of the Garamantes, and whose
helmet was conspicuous for the horn that curved
over his temples [d] ; in vain, alas, he blamed the oracle
that had so often promised a safe return, and Jupiter [e]
for his breach of faith. By this time the rampart had

Ammon, the supreme deity of Libya, who was commonly
represented as wearing a ram's head.
   [e] Ammon was often called Jupiter Ammon.

et iam corporibus cumulatus creverat agger,
perfusaeque atra fumabant caede ruinae.
tum ductorem avido clamore in proelia poscit.　　420

　　At parte ex alia, qua se insperata iuventus　　426
extulerat portis, ceu spicula nulla manusque
vim ferre exitiumve queant, permixtus utrisque
Hannibal agminibus passim furit et quatit ensem,
cantato nuper senior quem fecerat igni　　430
litore ab Hesperidum Temisus, qui carmine pollens
fidebat magica ferrum crudescere lingua,
quantus Bistoniis late Gradivus in oris
belligero rapitur curru telumque coruscans,
Titanum quo pulsa cohors, flagrantia bella　　435
cornipedum afflatu domat et stridoribus axis.
iamque Hostum Rutulumque Pholum ingentemque
　　　　Metiscum,
iam Lygdum Duriumque simul flavumque Galaesum
et geminos, Chromin atque Gyan, demiserat umbris.
Daunum etiam, grata quo non spectatior alter　　440
voce movere fora atque orando fingere mentes
nec legum custos sollertior, aspera telis
dicta admiscentem : " quaenam te, Poene, paternae
huc adigunt Furiae ? non haec Sidonia tecta
feminea fabricata manu pretiove parata,　　445
exulibusve datum dimensis litus harenis.
fundamenta deum Romanaque foedera cernis."
ast illum, toto iactantem talia campo,
ingenti raptum nisu medioque virorum

---

　　^a A Thracian people.
　　^b The Giants, sons of Earth who fought against the gods
at Phlegra and were imprisoned under volcanoes when
defeated.

grown higher with heaps of corpses, and the ruins smoked with horrid slaughter. Then with eager shout Murrus challenged Hannibal to combat.

But Hannibal was far away, where a band of defenders had issued unexpected from the gates. As if no missiles or swords could bring him injury or death, he mingled with both armies and raged far and wide, brandishing the sword which old Temisus from the shore of the Hesperides had lately forged with magic spells—Temisus the powerful enchanter who believed that iron was hardened by incantations. Mighty was Hannibal as Mars when he careers far and wide in his war-chariot through the land of the Bistones,[a] brandishing the weapon that defeated the band of Titans,[b] and ruling the flame of battle by the snorting of his steeds and the noise of his chariot. Already Hannibal had sent down to Hades Hostus and Pholus the Rutulian and huge Metiscus, and, with them, Lygdus and Durius and fair-haired Galaesus, and a pair of twins, Chromis and Gyas. Next came Daunus, than whom no man was more skilled to move assemblies by the charm of eloquence and to mould men's minds by speech ; nor was any man a more sagacious guardian of the laws. He mingled taunts with his blows : " What madness, inherited from your father, brings you hither, man of Carthage ? This is no Tyrian city built by a woman's hands or bought for money ; this is not a shore with a measured space of sand conceded to exiles[c] : you see here walls raised by gods, and allies of Rome." But even as he shouted such boasts over all the plain, Hannibal seized him with a mighty effort, and bore

[c] This is an allusion to the circumstances in which Dido built Carthage : see i. 24, 25.

avulsum inter tela globo et post terga revinctum   450
Hannibal ad poenam lentae mandaverat irae ;
increpitansque suos inferri signa iubebat
perque ipsos caedis cumulos stragemque iacentum
monstrabat furibundus iter cunctosque ciebat   454
nomine et in praedas stantem dabat improbus urbem.
  Sed postquam a trepidis allatum fervere partem
diversam Marte infausto, Murroque secundos
hunc superos tribuisse diem, ruit ocius amens
lymphato cursu atque ingentes deserit actus.
letiferum nutant fulgentes vertice cristae,   460
crine ut flammifero terret fera regna cometes,
sanguineum spargens ignem : vomit atra rubentes
fax caelo radios, ac saeva luce coruscum
scintillat sidus terrisque extrema minatur.
praecipiti dant tela viam, dant signa virique,   465
atque ambae trepidant acies ; iacit igneus hastae
dirum lumen apex, ac late fulgurat umbo.
talis ubi Aegaeo surgente ad sidera ponto
per longum vasto Cauri cum murmure fluctus
suspensum in terras portat mare, frigida nautis   470
corda tremunt ; sonat ille procul flatuque tumescens
curvatis pavidas tramittit Cycladas undis.
non cuncta e muris unum incessentia tela
fumantesque ante ora faces, non saxa per artem
tormentis excussa tenent. ut tegmina primum   475
fulgentis galeae conspexit et arma cruento
inter solem auro rutilantia, turbidus infit :

---

  [a] Comets were supposed to portend a change of dynasty
and to menace kings more than private men.

him from the centre of the fighting men, and bound his hands behind him, and reserved him to suffer the punishment of wrath deferred. Then, reproaching his men, he ordered the standards to be advanced, and right through the piled corpses and heaps of dead he pointed out the way in his frenzy, calling to each man by name, and boldly promising them as booty the still untaken city.

But when frightened messengers brought news that in a different quarter the fighting was fierce and they were losing the day, and that propitious gods had granted this day to Murrus, then Hannibal, abandoning his mighty exploits, flew off with frantic haste and the speed of a madman. The plume that nodded on his head showed a deadly brightness, even as a comet terrifies fierce kings [a] with its flaming tail and showers blood-red fire : the boding meteor spouts forth ruddy rays from heaven, and the star flashes with a dreadful menacing light, threatening earth with destruction. Weapons, standards, and men gave way before his headlong career, and both armies were terrified ; the fiery point of his spear shed a dreadful light, and his shield flashed far and wide. So, when the Aegean sea rises to the stars, and all along the coast, with a mighty roaring of the North-west wind, the waves carry ashore the piled-up sea, the hearts of seamen turn cold and tremble ; the wind roars far away, and with swelling blast and arching waves crosses the frightened Cyclades. Neither missiles from the walls, all aimed at him alone, nor smoking brands before his face, nor boulders hurled cunningly from engines, can arrest his course. As soon as he saw the glittering helmet on the head of Murrus, and his arms shining in the sunlight with blood-bedabbled gold, he began

" en, qui res Libycas inceptaque tanta retardet,
Romani Murrus belli mora ! foedera, faxo
iam noscas, quid vana queant et vester Hiberus. 480
fer tecum castamque fidem servataque iura,
deceptos mihi linque deos." cui talia Murrus :
" exoptatus ades : mens olim proelia poscit
speque tui flagrat capitis ; fer debita fraudum
praemia et Italiam tellure inquire sub ima. 485
longum in Dardanios fines iter atque nivalem
Pyrenen Alpesque tibi mea dextera donat."

Haec inter cernens subeuntem comminus hostem
praeruptumque loci fidum sibi, corripit ingens
aggere convulso saxum et nitentis in ora 490
devolvit, pronoque silex ruit incitus ictu.
subsedit duro concussus fragmine muri.
tum pudor accendit mentem, nec conscia fallit
virtus pressa loco ; frendens luctatur et aegro
scandit in adversum per saxa vetantia nisu. 495
sed postquam propior vicino lumine fulsit
et tota se mole tulit, velut incita clausum
agmina Poenorum cingant et cuncta paventem
castra premant, lato Murrus caligat in hoste.
mille simul dextrae densusque micare videtur 500
ensis, et innumerae nutare in casside cristae.
conclamant utrimque acies, ceu tota Saguntos
igne micet ; trahit instanti languentia leto

---

^a In the treaty between Rome and Carthage, the river
Ebro (*Hebrus*) was the limit beyond which Carthage was
forbidden to advance; and the freedom of Saguntum was
guaranteed : see ll. 294, 295.
^b The ground was littered with the stones that had formed
the wall. Hannibal stood on an eminence formed by these,
and Murrus had to climb over them.

in his rage : " Behold Murrus ! Murrus is the man to impede the prowess of Libya and our mighty enterprise, the man to hinder the war against Rome ! Soon will I make you learn the power of your useless treaty and your river Ebro.ᵃ Take with you loyalty unstained and observance of law; leave to me the gods whom I have deceived ! " And Murrus addressed him thus : " I have longed for your coming ; my heart has long been eager for battle and aflame with hope to take your life ; take the deserved reward of your guile, and seek for Italy in the bowels of the earth. My right hand spares you the long march to Roman territory and the ascent of the snowy Pyrenees and the Alps."

Meanwhile, seeing his foe come close, and that he could trust the overhanging ground where he stood, Hannibal rent the rampart and seized a huge rock and hurled it down upon the head of the climber ; and the stone fell swiftly with downward force. Smitten by the tough fragment of the wall, Murrus crouched down. But soon shame fired his heart ; and conscious courage, though taken at a disadvantage, did not fail him. Grinding his teeth, he struggled on, and with difficult effort climbed up over the stones ᵇ that barred his way. But when Hannibal shone closer with nearer light, and moved on in all his bulk, then the eyes of Murrus grew dark before his mighty foe ; it seemed as if the whole Carthaginian army were moving to close round him, and as if all the host were attacking him. He seemed to see a thousand arms and countless flashing swords, and a forest of plumes waving on his foe's helmet. Both armies shouted, as if all Saguntum were on fire ; Murrus in fear dragged along his limbs faint with the

41

membra pavens Murrus supremaque vota capessit :
" conditor Alcide, cuius vestigia sacra   505
incolimus terra, minitantem averte procellam,
si tua non segni defenso moenia dextra."

   Dumque orat caeloque attollit lumina supplex,
" cerne," ait, " an nostris longe Tirynthius ausis
iustius affuerit.   ni displicet aemula virtus,   510
haud me dissimilem, Alcide, primoribus annis
agnosces, invicte, tuis ; fer numen amicum
et, Troiae quondam primis memorate ruinis,
dexter ades Phrygiae delenti stirpis alumnos."
sic Poenus pressumque ira simul exigit ensem,   515
qua capuli statuere morae, teloque relato
horrida labentis perfunditur arma cruore.
ilicet ingenti casu turbata iuventus
procurrit ; nota arma viri corpusque superbo
victori spoliare negant : coit aucta vicissim   520
hortando manus, et glomerata mole feruntur.
hinc saxis galea, hinc clipeus sonat aereus hastis ;
incessunt sudibus librataque pondera plumbi
certatim iaciunt.   decisae vertice cristae
direptumque decus nutantum in caede iubarum.   525
iamque agitur largus per membra fluentia sudor,
et stant loricae squamis horrentia tela.
nec requies tegimenve datur mutare sub ictu.
genua labant, fessique humeri gestamina laxant.
tum creber penitusque trahens suspiria sicco   530

---

   ^a Another name for Hercules.
   ^b Hercules : he lived for many years at Tiryns, an ancient
city near Argos.
   ^c See note to l. 43.

approach of death, and uttered his latest prayer :
" Alcides,[a] our founder, whose footprints we inhabit
on hallowed ground, turn aside the storm that
threatens us, if I defend thy walls with no sluggish
arm."

And, while he prayed and raised his eyes to heaven
in supplication, the other spoke thus : " Consider
whether the hero of Tiryns [b] will not far more
justly assist us in our enterprise. If thou frownest
not on rival valour, invincible Alcides, thou wilt recog-
nize that I come not short of thy young years ; bring
thy power to help me; and, as thou art renowned
for the destruction of Troy long ago,[c] so support me
when I destroy the scions of the Phrygian race."
Thus Hannibal spoke ; and at the same time, clutch-
ing his sword in fury, he drove it home till the hilt
stopped it ; then he drew back the weapon, and his
dread armour was drenched with the blood of the
dying man. At once the fighters rush forward,
troubled by the great man's fall, and defy the proud
conqueror to take the famous armour and body of
Murrus. Their numbers grow by mutual encourage-
ment ; they unite and charge in a serried mass.
Now stones rattle on Hannibal's helmet, and now
spears on his brazen shield ; they attack with stakes,
and vie with one another in swinging and hurling
weights of lead. The plume was shorn from his
head, and the glorious horsehair crest that nodded
over the slain was torn in pieces. And now streams
of sweat started out and bathed his limbs, and pointed
missiles stuck fast in the scales of his breastplate.
No respite was possible and no change of armour,
beneath the rain of blows. His knees shake, and
his weary arms lose hold of his shield. Now too a

43

fumat ab ore vapor, nisuque elisus anhelo
auditur gemitus fractumque in casside murmur. 532
fulmineus ceu Spartanis latratibus actus,   421
cum silvam occursu venantum perdidit, hirto
horrescit saetis dorso et postrema capessit
proelia, canentem mandens aper ore crurorem,
iamque gemens geminat contra venabula dentem. 425
mente adversa domat gaudetque nitescere duris 533
virtutem et decoris pretio discrimina pensat.

   Hic subitus scisso densa inter nubila caelo   535
erupit quatiens terram fragor, et super ipsas
bis pater intonuit geminato fulmine pugnas.
inde inter nubes ventorum turbine caeco
ultrix iniusti vibravit lancea belli
ac femine adverso librata cuspide sedit.   540
Tarpeiae rupes superisque habitabile saxum
et vos, virginea lucentes semper in ara
Laomedonteae, Troiana altaria, flammae,
heu quantum vobis fallacis imagine teli
promisere dei ! propius si pressa furenti   545
hasta foret, clausae starent mortalibus Alpes,
nec, Thrasymenne, tuis nunc Allia cederet undis.

   Sed Iuno, aspectans Pyrenes vertice celsae
nava rudimenta et primos in Marte calores,
ut videt impressum coniecta cuspide vulnus,   550

---

   [a] It is a historical fact that Hannibal was wounded before
Saguntum. Silius seems to imply that Jupiter hurled the
weapon.
   [b] The ever-burning fire in the temple of Vesta is meant.
The fire was brought from Troy, where Laomedon once was
king, by Aeneas, and was kept alight at Rome.
   [c] The Allia is a tributary of the Tiber where the Romans
were defeated with great slaughter by the Gauls (390 B.C.).

44

constant steam comes smoking from his parched lips,
with deep-drawn breaths, and men heard a groaning
forced out with panting effort, and an inarticulate
cry that broke against the helmet. So the furious
wild boar, when pursued by baying hounds of Sparta,
and when debarred from the forest by the hunters
in his way, erects the bristles on his shaggy back
and fights his last battle, champing his own foaming
blood ; and now with a yell he dashes his twin tusks
against the spears. By courage Hannibal overcomes
disaster ; he is glad that valour is made brighter by
hardship ; and he finds an equivalent for danger in
the reward of glory.

Now the sky was cloven, and a sudden earth-shak-
ing crash burst forth among the thick clouds, and
right above the battle the Father of heaven thundered
twice with repeated bolt. Then, mid the blind hurri-
cane of the winds, there sped between the clouds a
spear to punish unrighteous warfare, and the well-
aimed point lodged in the front of Hannibal's thigh.[a]
Ye Tarpeian rocks, where the gods have their dwell-
ing, and ye fires of Laomedon, altars of Troy,[b] that
burn for ever with a flame tended by Vestals, how
much, alas, Heaven promised to you by the appear-
ance of that deceptive weapon ! If the spear had
pierced deeper into the fierce warrior, the Alps had
been for ever closed to mortal men, and Allia [c] would
not now rank after the waters of Lake Trasimene.[d]

But Juno, surveying from the summit of the lofty
Pyrenees his youthful prowess and martial ardour,
when she saw the wound inflicted by the point of

But, says Silius, the slaughter at Lake Trasimene was even
greater.

[d] The third of the great battles won by Hannibal in Italy.

45

advolat, obscura circumdata nube, per auras
et validam duris evellit ab ossibus hastam.
ille tegit clipeo fusum per membra cruorem,
tardaque paulatim et dubio vestigia nisu
alternata trahens, aversus ab aggere cedit.   555
    Nox tandem optatis terras pontumque tenebris
condidit et pugnas erepta luce diremit.
at durae invigilant mentes, molemque reponunt,
noctis opus.   clausos acuunt extrema pericli
et fractis rebus violentior ultima virtus.   560
hinc puer invalidique senes, hinc femina ferre
certat opem in dubiis miserando nava labori,
saxaque mananti subvectat vulnere miles.
iam patribus clarisque senum sua munia curae.
concurrunt lectosque viros hortantur et orant,   565
defessis subeant rebus revocentque salutem
et Latia extremis implorent casibus arma.
" ite citi, remis velisque impellite puppim,
saucia dum castris clausa est fera ; tempore Martis
utendum est rupto et grassandum ad clara periclis. 570
ite citi, deflete fidem murosque ruentes
antiquaque domo meliora accersite fata.
mandati summa est : dum stat, remeate, Saguntos."
ast illi celerant, qua proxima litora, gressum
et fugiunt tumido per spumea caerula velo.   575
    Pellebat somnos Tithoni roscida coniux,
ac rutilus primis sonipes hinnitibus altos
afflarat montes roseasque movebat habenas.
iam celsa e muris exstructa mole iuventus

---

    a i.e. Hannibal.   *b* Ardea, which is near Rome.
          c Aurora, Dawn.

the flying spear, hastened thither through the sky, veiled by a dark cloud, and plucked forth the stout spear from the tough bone. He covered with his shield the blood that poured over his limbs, and went back from the rampart, dragging his feet one after the other slowly and gradually with uncertain effort.

Night at last buried land and sea in welcome darkness, and separated the combatants by robbing them of light. But resolute hearts kept watch, and they rebuilt the wall—their task for the night. The besieged were spurred on by the extremity of their danger, and their last stand was more furious in their desperate plight. Here boys and feeble old men, and there women, strove valiantly to carry on the piteous task in the hour of peril, and soldiers with streaming wounds carried stones to the wall. And now the senators and noble elders were heedful of their special duty. Meeting in haste, they chose envoys, and urged them with entreaties to be active in this grievous plight and bring safety back, and to entreat the aid of Roman armies in their extremity. " Go with speed ; urge on your ship with oar and sail, while the wounded wild beast [a] is shut up in his camp ; we must take advantage of the interruption of war, and rise to fame by danger. Go with speed ; lament our loyalty and our crumbling walls, and bring us better fortune from our ancient home.[b] This is our final charge—return before Saguntum falls." Then the men hasten to the nearest coast, and fly with swollen sail over the foaming sea.

The dewy spouse [c] of Tithonus was banishing sleep, and her ruddy steeds had breathed on the mountain-tops with their first neighings, and tugged at their roseate reins. Now high on the walls the inhabitants,

47

clausam nocturnis ostentat turribus urbem.   580
rerum omnes pendent actus, et milite maesto
laxata obsidio, ac pugnandi substitit ardor,
inque ducem versae tanto discrimine curae.

    Interea Rutulis longinqua per aequora vectis
Herculei ponto coepere exsistere colles,   585
et nebulosa iugis attollere saxa Monoeci.
Thracius hos Boreas scopulos immitia regna
solus habet semperque rigens nunc litora pulsat,
nunc ipsas alis plangit stridentibus Alpes ;
atque ubi se terris glaciali fundit ab Arcto,   590
haud ulli contra fiducia surgere vento.
verticibus torquet rapidis mare, fractaque anhelant
aequora, et iniecto conduntur gurgite montes ;
iamque volans Rhenum Rhodanumque in nubila tollit.
hunc postquam Boreae dirum evasere furorem,   595
alternos maesti casus bellique marisque
et dubium rerum eventum sermone volutant.
" o patria, o Fidei domus inclita, quo tua nunc sunt
fata loco ? sacraene manent in collibus arces ?
an cinis, heu superi ! tanto de nomine restat ?   600
ferte leves auras flatusque ciete secundos,
si nondum insultat templorum Poenicus ignis
culminibus, Latiaeque valent succurrere classes."

    Talibus illacrimant noctemque diemque querellis,

---

a Saguntines : see note to l. 377.
b Now Monaco, named after Hercules Monoecus as a
protector of seamen : he had a temple on the promontory.

aloft on their finished work, point from the walls
to their city, fenced in by towers that grew in
the night. All activity was suspended; for the
sorrowing Carthaginians relaxed the vigour of the
blockade, and their martial ardour paused; it was
to their leader in his great danger that their thoughts
were turned.

Meantime the Rutulians[a] had travelled far over
the waters, and the hills of Hercules began to emerge
from the sea, and to lift up from the range the cloud-
capt cliffs of Monoecus.[b] Thracian Boreas is the sole
lord of these rocks, a savage domain; ever freezing,
he now lashes the shore, and now beats the Alps
themselves with his hissing wings; and, when he
spreads over the land from the frozen Bear,[c] no wind
dares to rise against him. He churns the sea in
rushing eddies, while the broken billows roar and the
mountains are buried beneath water piled above
them; and now in his career he raises the Rhine and
the Rhone up to the clouds. Having escaped this
awful fury of Boreas, the envoys spoke sadly one to
another of the hazards of war succeeded by the
hazards of the sea, and about the doubtful issue of
events. "Alas for our country, the famous home of
Loyalty! how do thy fortunes now stand? is thy
sacred citadel still erect upon the hills? Or—alas,
ye gods!—are ashes all that remain of so mighty a
name? Grant us light airs, and send forth favouring
breezes, if the Carthaginian fire is not yet triumphant
over the tops of our temples, and if the Roman fleets
have power to help us."

Thus night and day they mourned and wept, until

---

[c] The Bear denotes the North.

donec Laurentes puppis defertur ad oras,   605
qua pater, acceptis Anienis ditior undis,
in pontum flavo descendit gurgite Thybris.
hinc consanguineae subeunt iam moenia Romae.

  Concilium vocat augustum castaque beatos
paupertate patres ac nomina parta triumphis   610
consul et aequantem superos virtute senatum.
facta animosa viros et recti sacra cupido
attollunt ; hirtaeque togae neglectaque mensa
dexteraque a curvis capulo non segnis aratris ;
exiguo faciles et opum non indiga corda,   615
ad parvos curru remeabant saepe penates.

  In foribus sacris primoque in limine templi
captivi currus, belli decus, armaque rapta
pugnantum ducibus saevaeque in Marte secures,
perfossi clipei et servantia tela cruorem   620
claustraque portarum pendent ; hic Punica bella,
Aegates cernas fusaque per aequora classe
exactam ponto Libyen testantia rostra ;
hic galeae Senonum pensatique improbus auri
arbiter ensis inest, Gallisque ex arce fugatis   625
arma revertentis pompa gestata Camilli ;
hic spolia Aeacidae, hic Epirotica signa

---

  a Laurentum was a town and district of Latium, about
sixteen miles from Rome. In the legendary history it is the
capital of Latium, and was the residence of King Latinus
at the time when Aeneas landed in Italy. *Laurentes* is in
Silius an equivalent of *Romani*.

  b An anachronism : Scipio was the first Roman general to
take a name from a conquered country ; see note to xvii. 626.

  c This is a reference to Cincinnatus, who was summoned
from his plough to be consul in 438 B.C.

  d The Senate-house. The Senate often met in one of the
temples at Rome.

  e See note to l. 35.

their ship put in at the shore of Laurentum,*a* where
father Tiber, richer by the tribute of the Anio's
waters, runs down with yellow stream into the sea.
From here they soon reached the city of their Roman
kinsmen.

The consul summoned the worshipful assembly—
the Fathers rich in unstained poverty, with names
acquired by conquests *b*—a senate rivalling the gods in
virtue.   Brave deeds and a sacred passion for justice
exalted these men ; their dress was rough and their
meals simple, and the hands they brought from the
crooked plough were ready with the sword-hilt *c* ;
content with little, uncovetous of riches, they often
went back to humble homes from the triumphal car.

At the sacred doors and on the threshold of the
temple *d* captured chariots were hung, glorious spoils
of war, and armour taken from hostile generals, and
axes ruthless in battle, and perforated shields, and
weapons to which the blood still clung, and the bolts
of city-gates.   Here one might see the wars with
Carthage, the Aegatian *e* islands, and the ships' prows
which testified that Carthage had been driven from
the sea when her fleet was defeated on the water.
Here were the helmets of the Senones and the in-
solent sword that decreed the weight of gold paid
down,*f* and the armour that was borne in the proces-
sion of Camillus on his return, when the Gauls had
been repulsed from the citadel ; here were the spoils
of the scion of Aeacus, and here the standards of the

---

f In 390 B.C. the Senones, a Gallic tribe, took Rome and
burnt it.   The Romans paid gold for a ransom ; and when
the gold was being weighed, Brennus, the leader of the Gauls,
threw his sword into the scale, as a gesture of contempt.
Brennus was afterwards defeated by Camillus.

et Ligurum horrentes coni parmaeque relatae
Hispana de gente rudes Alpinaque gaesa.

    Sed postquam clades patefecit et horrida bella   630
orantum squalor, praesens astare Sagunti
ante oculos visa est extrema precantis imago.
tum senior maesto Sicoris sic incipit ore :
" sacrata gens clara fide, quam rite fatentur
Marte satam populi ferro parere subacti,   635
ne crede emensos levia ob discrimina pontum.
vidimus obsessam patriam murosque trementes ;
et, quem insana freta aut coetus genuere ferarum,
vidimus Hannibalem.   procul his a moenibus, oro,
arcete, o superi, nostroque in Marte tenete   640
fatiferae iuvenem dextrae !   qua mole sonantes
exigit ille trabes ! et quantus crescit in armis !
trans iuga Pyrenes, medium indignatus Hiberum,
excivit Calpen et mersos Syrtis harenis
molitur populos maioraque moenia quaerit.   645
spumeus hic, medio qui surgit ab aequore, fluctus,
si prohibere piget, vestras se effringet in urbes.
an tanti pretium motus ruptique per enses
foederis hoc iuveni iurata in bella ruenti
creditis, ut statuat superatae iura Sagunto ?   650
ocius ite, viri, et nascentem extinguite flammam,
ne serae redeant post aucta pericula curae.
quamquam o, si nullus terror, non obruta iam nunc
semina fumarent belli, vestraene Sagunto

---

    [a] Pyrrhus, king of Epirus, who made war against Rome
282–275 B.C. He claimed descent from Achilles, the grandson
of Aeacus.
    [b] See note to l. 141.   [c] See note to l. 408.

Epirote,[a] the bristling plumed helmets of the Ligures, the rude targets brought back from Spanish natives, and Alpine javelins.

But when the mourning garb of the suppliants made plain their calamities and sufferings in war, the Senate seemed to see before them the figure of Saguntum appealing for help in her last hour. Then aged Sicoris thus began his sorrowful tale : " O people famous for keeping of your oaths, people whom the nations defeated by your arms admit with reason to be the seed of Mars, think not that we have crossed the sea because of trifling dangers. We have seen our native city besieged and its walls rocking ; we have looked on Hannibal, a man to whom raging seas or some union of wild beasts gave birth. I pray that Heaven may keep the deadly arm of that stripling far from these walls, and confine him to war against us. With what might he hurls the crashing beam ! How his stature increases in battle ! Scorning the limit of the Ebro, and crossing the range of the Pyrenees, he has roused up Calpe[b] and stirs up the peoples hidden in the sands of the Syrtis,[c] and has greater cities in his eye. This foaming billow, rising in mid-ocean, will dash itself against the cities of Italy, if you refuse to stop it. Do you believe that Hannibal, frantic for the war he has sworn to wage, will be content with this reward of his great enterprise and his breach of treaty by force of arms—the conquest and submission of Saguntum ? Hasten, ye men of Rome, to put out the flame in its beginning, or the trouble may recur too late when the danger has grown greater. And yet—ah me !—if no danger threatened you, if the hidden sparks of war were not at this moment smoking, would it be beneath you to

spernendum consanguineam protendere dextram ?
omnis Hiber, omnis rapidis fera Gallia turmis,   656
omnis ab aestifero sitiens Libys imminet axe.
per vos culta diu Rutulae primordia gentis
Laurentemque larem et genetricis pignora Troiae,
conservate pios, qui permutare coacti   660
Acrisioneis Tirynthia culmina muris.
vos etiam Zanclen Siculi contra arma tyranni
iuvisse egregium ; vos et Campana tueri
moenia, depulso Samnitum robore, dignum
Sigeis duxistis avis.   vetus incola Daunus,   665
testor vos, fontes et stagna arcana Numici,
cum felix nimium dimitteret Ardea pubem,
sacra domumque ferens et avi penetralia Turni,
ultra Pyrenen Laurentia nomina duxi.
cur ut decisa atque avulsa a corpore membra   670
despiciar, nosterque luat cur foedera sanguis ? "
    Tandem, ut finitae voces, (miserabile visu)
summissi palmas, lacerato tegmine vestis,
affigunt proni squalentia corpora terrae.
inde agitant consulta patres curasque fatigant.   675
Lentulus, ut cernens accensae tecta Sagunti,
poscendum poenae iuvenem celerique negantis
exuri bello Carthaginis arva iubebat.

---

   [a] A reference to the Palladium, a statue of Pallas, which was brought from Troy to Rome and assured the safety of the city which contained it.

   [b] That is, to migrate from Ardea to Saguntum : Danae, daughter of Acrisius, was said to have founded Ardea.

   [c] Zancle, afterwards called Messana, when occupied by the Mamertines, was defended by Rome against Hiero, king of Syracuse.

   [d] In 343 B.C. the Romans rescued Capua, the capital of Campania, from the Samnites.

   [e] A name for Italy.

hold out to your city of Saguntum a kindred hand?
All Spain threatens us, all Gaul with her swift horse-
men, and all thirsty Libya from the torrid zone. By
the long-cherished origins of the Rutulian race, by the
household gods of Laurentum, and by the pledges [a]
of our mother Troy, preserve those righteous men
who were forced to leave the walls of Acrisius for
the towers of Hercules. [b] It was your glory to help
Zancle against the armies of the Sicilian despot [c];
you deemed it worthy of your Trojan ancestors to
defend the walls of Capua and drive away the strength
of the Samnites. [d] I was once a dweller in Daunia [e]—
bear witness, ye springs and secret pools of the river
Numicius [f]!—and when Ardea sent forth the sons in
which she was too rich, I bore forth [g] the sacred things
and the inner shrine from the house of Turnus, my
ancestor, and carried the name of Laurentum beyond
the Pyrenees. Why should I be scorned, like a limb
cut off and torn from the body? and why should our
blood expiate the breach of the treaty?"

At last, when they ceased to speak, it was pitiful
to see them dash their unkempt bodies down upon
the floor, with their open hands held up and their
garments torn. Next the Fathers held counsel and
carried on anxious debate. Lentulus, as if he actually
saw the houses of Saguntum burning, moved that
they should demand the surrender of Hannibal for
punishment, and that, if Carthage refused to give
him up, her territory should be ravaged with instant

[f] A small river of Latium running into the sea between
Ardea and Laurentum: it was believed that Aeneas was
buried beside the river.

[g] The speaker identifies himself with the original settlers
at Saguntum.

55

at Fabius, cauta speculator mente futuri
nec laetus dubiis parcusque lacessere Martem   680
et melior clauso bellum producere ferro :
prima super tantis rebus pensanda, ducisne
ceperit arma furor, patres an signa moveri
censuerint ; mittique viros, qui exacta reportent.
providus haec, ritu vatis, fundebat ab alto   685
pectore praemeditans Fabius surgentia bella.
ut saepe e celsa grandaevus puppe magister,
prospiciens signis venturum in carbasa Caurum,
summo iam dudum substringit lintea malo.
sed lacrimae atque ira mixtus dolor impulit omnes
praecipitare latens fatum ; lectique senatu,   691
qui ductorem adeant ; si perstet surdus in armis
pactorum, vertant inde ad Carthaginis arces
nec divum oblitis indicere bella morentur.

---

a See note to ii. 6.
b The Carthaginians were unmindful of the gods, when
they violated a treaty which they had sworn by the gods to
observe.

war. But Fabius,[a] peering warily into the future, no lover of doubtful courses, slow to provoke war, and skilful to prolong a campaign without unsheathing the sword, was next to speak. He said that in so grave a matter they must first find out whether the madness of Hannibal began the war, or the senate of Carthage ordered the army to advance ; they must send envoys to examine and report. Mindful of the future and musing on the war to come, Fabius, prophet-like, uttered this advice from his lofty soul. Thus many a veteran pilot, when from his high poop he sees by tokens that the gale will soon fall upon his canvas, reefs his sails in haste upon the top-mast. But tears, and grief mixed with resentment, made them all eager to hasten the unknown future. Senators were chosen to approach Hannibal ; if he turned a deaf ear to his engagements and fought on, they must then turn their steps to the city of Carthage and declare war without delay against men unmindful of the gods.[b]

LIBER SECUNDUS

ARGUMENT

The Roman envoys, dismissed by Hannibal, proceed to Carthage (1-24). Hannibal addresses his men and goes on with the siege (25-269). The Roman envoys are received in the Carthaginian senate: speeches of Hanno and Gestar: Fabius declares war (270-390). Hannibal deals with some rebellious tribes and returns to the siege: he receives a gift of armour from the Spanish peoples (391-456). The

Caeruleis provecta vadis iam Dardana puppis
tristia magnanimi portabat iussa senatus
primoresque patrum. Fabius, Tirynthia proles,
ter centum memorabat avos, quos turbine Martis
abstulit una dies, cum Fors non aequa labori   5
patricio Cremerae maculavit sanguine ripas.
huic comes aequato sociavit munere curas
Publicola, ingentis Volesi Spartana propago.
is, cultam referens insigni nomine plebem,
Ausonios atavo ducebat consule fastos.   10
    Hos ut depositis portum contingere velis

---

a Q. Fabius Maximus, the famous Dictator often mentioned later in the poem, was one of the envoys. The Fabii claimed Hercules as their ancestor. In 480 B.C., three hundred Fabii with 4000 clients went out to fight against the people of Veii, and all but one of them fell by the river Cremera in Etruria.

BOOK II

ARGUMENT (*continued*)

sufferings of Saguntum (457-474). The goddess Loyalty is sent to the city by Hercules, its founder, and encourages them to resist (475-525). But Juno sends a Fury from Hell who drives the people mad (526-649). They build a great pyre and light it. Hannibal takes the city (650-695). Epilogue by the poet (696-707).

AND now the Roman vessel, sailing forth over the blue water, carried leading senators with the stern behests of the high-souled Senate. Fabius, descended from Hercules, could tell of ancestors three hundred in number, who were swept away in a single day by the hurricane of war, when Fortune frowned on the enterprise of the patricians and stained the banks of the Cremera with their blood.[a] With Fabius went Publicola, the Spartan descendant of mighty Volesus, and shared the duty in common with his colleague. Publicola showed by his name his friendship for the people, and the name stood first on the roll of Roman consuls, when his ancestor held office.[b]

When word was brought to Hannibal that the

[b] Volesus, the founder of the famous Valerian family, was a Sabine, who settled at Rome. The Sabines claimed a Spartan origin. One of his descendants gained the name of Publicola (Friend of the People), and was elected consul in the first year of the Republic, 509 B.C.

allatum Hannibali consultaque ferre senatus
iam medio seram bello poscentia pacem
ductorisque simul conceptas foedere poenas,
ocius armatas passim per litora turmas   15
ostentare iubet minitantia signa recensque
perfusos clipeos et tela rubentia caede.
haud dictis nunc esse locum ; strepere omnia clamat
Tyrrhenae clangore tubae gemituque cadentum.
dum detur, relegant pontum neu se addere clausis   20
festinent ; notum, quid caede calentibus armis,
quantum irae liceat, motusve quid audeat ensis.
sic ducis affatu per inhospita litora pulsi,
converso Tyrios petierunt remige patres.

  Hic alto Poenus fundentem vela carinam   25
incessens dextra : " Nostrum, pro Iupiter ! " inquit,
" nostrum ferre caput parat illa per aequora puppis.
heu caecae mentes tumefactaque corda secundis !
armatum Hannibalem poenae petit impia tellus !
ne deposce, adero ; dabitur tibi copia nostri   30
ante expectatum, portisque focisque timebis,
quae nunc externos defendis, Roma, penates.
Tarpeios iterum scopulos praeruptaque saxa
scandatis licet et celsam migretis in arcem,
nullo iam capti vitam pensabitis auro."   35
  Incensi dictis animi, et furor additus armis.
conditur extemplo telorum nubibus aether,

---

  ^a The war-trumpet was an Etruscan invention.
^b Italy.
^c The first time was during the Gallic invasion in 390 B.C.
  ^d See note to i. 624.

envoys had lowered sail and were gaining the harbour, and that they brought a decree of the Senate demanding peace—a belated peace when war was already raging—and also the punishment of the general as laid down in the treaty, he quickly ordered squadrons in arms to display all along the shore menacing standards, shields newly dyed with blood, and weapons red with slaughter. " This is no time for words," he cried ; " all the land is loud with the blare of the Tyrrhene *a* trumpet and the groans of the dying. Let them, while they may, put to sea again, and not make haste to join the besieged Saguntines ; we know the licence of passion and of weapons reeking with slaughter, and the boldness of the sword, when once unsheathed." Thus accosted by Hannibal, the envoys, driven away along the unfriendly shore, turned their course about and made for the Carthaginian senate.

Then Hannibal shook his fist at the vessel as she spread her sails : " Ye gods," he cried, " it is my head, even mine, which yonder ship seeks to carry across the sea ! Woe be to minds that cannot see, and to hearts puffed up with prosperity ! The unrighteous land *b* demands Hannibal, sword in hand, for punishment. Without your asking, I shall come ; you shall see enough of me before you expect me ; and Rome, which is now protecting foreign households, shall tremble for her own gates and her own hearths. Though ye clamber a second time *c* up the steep cliffs of the Tarpeian rock and take refuge in your lofty citadel, ye shall not again, when made prisoners, ransom your lives for any weight of gold." *d*

These words fired the courage of his troops, and they fought with fresh fury. Instantly the sky was hidden with clouds of missiles, and the towers of

et densa resonant saxorum grandine turres.
ardor agit, provecta queat dum cernere muros,
inque oculis profugae Martem exercere carinae.   40
ipse autem incensas promissa piacula turmas
flagitat, insignis nudato vulnere, ductor
ac repetens questus furibundo personat ore :
" poscimur, o socii, Fabiusque e puppe catenas
ostentat, dominique vocat nos ira senatus.   45
si taedet coepti, culpandave movimus arma,
Ausoniam ponto propere revocate carinam.
nil moror, evincta lacerandum tradite dextra.
nam cur, Eoi deductus origine Beli,
tot Libyae populis, tot circumfusus Hiberis,   50
servitium perferre negem ?   Rhoeteius immo
aeternum imperet et populis saeclisque propaget
regna ferox ; nos iussa virum nutusque tremamus."
effundunt gemitus atque omina tristia vertunt
in stirpem Aeneadum ac stimulant clamoribus iras.   55
    Discinctos inter Libyas populosque bilingues
Marmaricis audax in bella Oenotria signis
venerat Asbyte, proles Garamantis Hiarbae.
Hammone hic genitus, Phorcynidos antra Medusae
Cinyphiumque Macen et iniquo a sole calentes   60
Battiadas late imperio sceptrisque regebat ;
cui patrius Nasamon aeternumque arida Barce,

---

    [a] Hannibal himself.   [b] See note to i. 73.
    [c] Silius here uses " Rhoetean " as an equivalent of
" Roman."   Rhoeteum was a promontory in the Trojan
country.   This is more surprising than the names of Trojans,
Phrygians, Dardanids, Priamids, Teucri, etc., which he con-
stantly applies to the Romans : see p. xiii.
    [d] *i.e.* the doom foreseen by Hannibal for Carthage.
    [e] Speaking Libyan and Egyptian.
    [f] Asbyte is clearly modelled upon Camilla in the *Aeneid* (vii.
803 foll.).   The chief nations of Libya are enumerated below.

Saguntum rattled under a thick hail of stones. Men were spurred on by their eagerness to wage war under the eyes of the retreating vessel, while she could still see the walls in her course. But their leader, conspicuous with his wound exposed to view, himself demanded of his excited soldiers the promised scapegoat,[a] and shouted his repeated complaint with frenzied utterance : " Comrades, the Romans demand my surrender ; and Fabius on the deck displays the fetters for me, and the wrath of the imperious Senate summons me. If you are weary of our enterprise, if the war we have begun is blame-worthy, then make haste to recall the Roman ship from the sea. I am ready : hand me over to the torturers with fettered wrists. For why should I, though I trace my pedigree to Belus [b] of the East, and am girt about by so many nations of Africa and Spain—why should I refuse to endure slavery ? Nay, let the Roman [c] rule for ever, and proudly spread his tyranny over the world for all generations : let us tremble at their nod and obey their bidding." His men groan aloud, and turn the evil omen [d] upon the race of the Aeneadae, and increase their ardour by shouting.

Among the loosely-girt Libyans and the peoples of two tongues,[e] Asbyte [f] had come boldly to fight against Rome with troops from Marmarica. She was the child of Hiarbas the Garamantian ; and he was the son of Ammon and ruled with extended sway the caves of Medusa, daughter of Phorcys, and the Macae who dwell by the river Cinyps, and the Cyrenians whom the cruel sun scorches ; he was obeyed by the Nasamones, hereditary subjects, by ever-parched Barce, by the forests of the Autololes,

cui nemora Autololum atque infidae litora Syrtis
parebant nullaque levis Gaetulus habena.
atque is fundarat thalamos Tritonide nympha,   65
unde genus proavumque Iovem regina ferebat
et sua fatidico repetebat nomina luco.
haec, ignara viri vacuoque assueta cubili,
venatu et silvis primos dependerat annos ;
non calathis mollita manus operatave fuso,   70
Dictynnam et saltus et anhelum impellere planta
cornipedem ac stravisse feras immitis amabat.
quales Threïciae Rhodopen Pangaeaque lustrant
saxosis nemora alta iugis cursuque fatigant
Hebrum innupta manus : spreti Ciconesque Getaeque
et Rhesi domus et lunatis Bistones armis.   76

    Ergo habitu insignis patrio, religata fluentem
Hesperidum crinem dono dextrumque feroci
nuda latus Marti ac fulgentem tegmine laevam
Thermodontiaca munita in proelia pelta,   80
fumantem rapidis quatiebat cursibus axem.
pars comitum biiugo curru, pars cetera dorso
fertur equi ; nec non Veneris iam foedera passae
reginam cingunt, sed virgine densior ala est.
ipsa autem gregibus per longa mapalia lectos   85
ante aciem ostentabat equos ; tumuloque propinqua
dum sequitur gyris campum, vibrata per auras
spicula contorquens summa ponebat in arce.

---

    [a] The oracular shrine of Jupiter Ammon : see note to i. 415.
    [b] A name of Diana, the Huntress.
    [c] A warlike race of women, who play a great part in
Greek mythology and art. They were supposed to live
among the Thracian mountains, Rhodope and Pangaeus,
and by the river Hebrus.
    [d] A golden clasp is meant : the Hesperides were nymphs
who guarded the golden apples near Mount Atlas.

by the shore of treacherous Syrtis, and by the Gae-
tulians who ride without reins. And he had built
a marriage-bed for the nymph Tritonis, from whom
the princess was born; she claimed Jupiter as her
forefather and derived her name from the prophetic
grove.[a] She was a maiden and ever lay alone, and had
spent her early years in the forest-chase; never did the
wool-basket soften her hands nor the spindle give her
occupation; but she loved Dictynna[b] and the wood-
lands, and to urge on with her heel the panting steed
and lay low wild beasts without mercy. Even so
the band of Amazons[c] in Thrace traverse Rhodope
and the high forests on the stony ridges of Mount
Pangaeus, and tire out the Hebrus by their speed;
they spurn all suitors—the Cicones and Getae, the
royal house of Rhesus, and the Bistones with their
crescent-shaped shields.

And thus conspicuous in her native dress—with
her long hair bound by a gift from the Hesperides,[d]
with her right breast bared for battle, while the
shield glittered on her left arm and the target of
the Amazons protected her in battle—she urged on
her smoking chariot with furious speed. Some of her
companions drove two-horse chariots, while others
rode on horseback; and some of the princess's escort
had already submitted to the bond of wedlock, but
the maidens of the troop outnumbered these. She
herself proudly displayed before the line the steeds
which she had chosen from the droves among distant
native huts; keeping near the mound, she drove
round the plain in circles; and, hurling her whizzing
missiles through the air, she planted them in the
summit of the citadel.

Hanc hasta totiens intrantem moenia Mopsus
non tulit et celsis senior Gortynia muris   90
tela sonante fugat nervo liquidasque per auras
dirigit aligero letalia vulnera ferro.
Cres erat, aerisonis Curetum advectus ab antris,
Dictaeos agitare puer levioribus annis
pennata saltus assuetus harundine Mopsus.   95
ille vagam caelo demisit saepe volucrem ;
ille procul campo linquentem retia cervum
vulnere sistebat ; rueretque inopina sub ictu
ante fera incauto, quam sibila poneret arcus.
nec se tum pharetra iactavit iustius ulla,   100
Eois quamquam certet Gortyna sagittis.
verum ut, opum levior, venatu extendere vitam
abnuit, atque artae res exegere per aequor,
coniuge cum Meroë natisque inglorius hospes
intrarat miseram, fato ducente, Saguntum.   105
coryti fratrum ex humeris calamique paterni
pendebant volucerque chalybs, Minoia tela.
hic, medius iuvenum, Massylae gentis in agmen
crebra Cydoneo fundebat spicula cornu.
iam Garamum audacemque Thyrum pariterque
    ruentes   110
Gisgonem saevumque Bagam indignumque sagittae,
impubem malas, tam certae occurrere Lixum
fuderat et plena tractabat bella pharetra.
tum, vultum intendens telumque in virginis ora,
desertum non grata Iovem per vota vocabat.   115

---

a Arrows in Latin poetry are generally " Dictaean " or
" Gortynian " or " Cretan." Crete was famous for its
archers ; and Dicte and Gortyn are Cretan cities.
b The Curetes were the guardians of the infant Zeus
(Jupiter) in Crete and drowned his cries by clashing their
shields and cymbals. *c* The Parthian archers are meant.

Again and again she hurled her weapons within the
walls ; but old Mopsus resented it, and sped from the
high walls Cretan [a] arrows from his twanging bow,
and launched through the clear sky deadly wounds
with the winged steel. He was a Cretan, who had
voyaged from the caverns of the Curetes [b] that ring
with brass. When young and nimble, he was wont
to beat the coverts of Dicte with feathered shafts :
oft did he bring down from the sky the wandering
bird ; from a distance he would strike and stay the
stag that was escaping from the nets along the plain ;
and the beast would collapse, surprised by a blow
unforeseen, before the bow had ceased to twang.
Gortyna, though she rivals the arrows of the East, [c]
had more reason then to boast of Mopsus than of any
other archer. But when, grown poor, he was un-
willing to pass his whole life in hunting, and when his
poverty drove him across the sea, he had come, a
humble guest, with his wife Meroë and his sons ; and
destiny had led him to ill-fated Saguntum. From
the young men's shoulders there hung quivers and
their father's arrows and the winged steel that is
Crete's weapon. Mopsus, between his sons, was
raining arrows from his Cydonian [d] bow of horn upon
the Massylian warriors. Already he had laid low
Garamus and bold Thyrus, and Gisgo rushing on
together with fierce Bagas, and Lixus, yet beardless,
who did not deserve to meet an arrow so unerring ;
and he fought on with his quiver filled. Now he
turned his eyes and his weapon against the face of
Asbyte, and prayed to Jupiter ; but his prayer found
no favour with the god whom he had deserted. [e] For

[d] Cydon is another city of Crete.
[e] By leaving Crete, the birthplace of Jupiter.

namque ut fatiferos converti prospicit arcus,
opposito procul insidiis Nasamonias Harpe
corpore praeripuit letum calamumque volantem,
dum clamat, patulo excipiens tramisit hiatu,
et primae ferrum a tergo videre sorores.　　　120
at comitis frendens casu labentia virgo
membra levat parvaque oculos iam luce natantes
irrorat lacrimis totisque annisa doloris
viribus intorquet letalem in moenia cornum.
illa volans humerum rapido transverberat ictu　125
conantis Dorylae, iunctis iam cornibus arcus,
educti spatium nervi complente sagitta,
excutere in ventos resoluto pollice ferrum.
tum subitum in vulnus praeceps devolvitur altis
aggeribus muri, iuxtaque cadentia membra　　130
effusi versa calami fluxere pharetra.
exclamat paribus frater vicinus in armis
Icarus ulciscique parat lacrimabile fatum.
atque illum raptim promentem in proelia telum
Hannibal excussi praevertit turbine saxi.　　　135
labuntur gelido torpentia frigore membra,
deficiensque manus pharetrae sua tela remisit.
　　At pater in gemino natorum funere Mopsus
correptos arcus ter maesta movit ab ira,
ter cecidit dextra, et notas dolor abstulit artes.　140
paenitet heu sero dulces liquisse penates,
arreptoque avide, quo concidis, Icare, saxo,
postquam aevum senior percussaque pectora frustra
sentit et, ut tantos compescat morte dolores,
nil opis in dextra, vastae se culmine turris　　　145

---

　　a The Nasamones were an African tribe who lived near
the Syrtes and had an evil reputation as wreckers : see i. 409.
　　b This phrase is found elsewhere in Latin poetry : we
should say " fell forward."

Harpe, a Nasamonian [a] maid, when she saw the fatal bow turned about, placed herself in the way of the distant danger, and anticipated the mortal blow; and even as she shouted, the flying arrow struck her open mouth and passed through; and her sisters first saw the point standing out behind her. But Asbyte, furious at the fall of her comrade, raised the prostrate body and wetted with her tears the swimming eyes with their failing light; and then, putting forth all the strength of sorrow, she hurled her deadly spear against the city walls. On it flew and pierced with sudden blow the shoulder of Dorylas, as he strove to launch the steel into the air with loosened thumb— the ends of the bow already met, and the arrow filled the space left by the expanded string. Then he fell down headlong towards his sudden wound [b] from the high bastions of the wall, and beside his falling body the arrows poured forth from his upset quiver. His brother, Icarus, armed alike and standing near him, cried aloud and sought to avenge that pitiable death. But, as he put forth his weapon in haste for battle, Hannibal hurled a great stone and stopped him with its whirling mass. His limbs collapsed, stiff with icy cold, and his failing hand returned to the quiver the arrow that belonged to it.

But Mopsus, when both his sons were slain, caught up his bow in his grief and rage, and bent it thrice; but thrice his hand fell, and sorrow robbed him of his accustomed skill. Too late, alas! he regrets to have left the land he loved. Eagerly he clutched the stone that had felled Icarus; but, when the old man felt that his feeble blows on his own breast were vain, and knew that his arm could not help him to end his sore grief by death, he threw him-

praecipitem iacit et delapsus pondere prono
membra super nati moribundos explicat artus.
  Dum cadit externo Gortynius advena bello,
iam nova molitus stimulato milite Theron,
Alcidae templi custos araeque sacerdos,   150
non expectatum Tyriis effuderat agmen
et fera miscebat reserata proelia porta.
atque illi non hasta manu, non vertice cassis,
sed, fisus latis humeris et mole iuventae,
agmina vastabat clava, nihil indigus ensis.   155
exuviae capiti impositae tegimenque leonis
terribilem attollunt excelso vertice rictum.
centum angues idem Lernaeaque monstra gerebat
in clipeo et sectis geminam serpentibus hydram.
ille Iubam Thapsumque patrem clarumque Micipsam
nomine avi Maurumque Sacen, a moenibus actos   161
palantesque fuga, praeceps ad litora cursu
egerat, atque una spumabant aequora dextra.
nec contentus Idi leto letoque Cothonis
Marmaridae nec caede Rothi nec caede Iugurthae, 165
Asbytes currum et radiantis tegmina laenae
poscebat votis gemmataque lumina peltae
atque in belligera versabat virgine mentem.
quem ruere ut telo vidit regina cruento,
obliquos detorquet equos laevumque per orbem   170
fallaci gyro campum secat ac velut ales
averso rapitur sinuata per aequora curru.

---

  [a] For each head of the Hydra (a water-snake) that Her-
cules cut off, two new heads grew. The priest of Hercules
displays on his shield one of the Labours of Hercules.
  [b] The allusion has not been explained. In 148 B.C. a
Micipsa became king of Numidia and adopted Jugurtha.
Perhaps the text is corrupt. Silius appears to be giving to

self headlong from the top of the huge tower ; and, falling heavily down, laid at full length his dying limbs on his son's body.

While the Cretan stranger fell thus in foreign war, Theron, who guarded Hercules' temple and was priest at his altar, urged on the fighters and attempted a fresh effort. Unbarring a gate, he sent out a force to surprise the Carthaginians, and the fighting was fierce. He bore no spear in his hand nor helmet on his head ; but, trusting in his broad shoulders and youthful strength, he laid the enemy low with a club, and craved no sword. The skin stripped from a lion was laid on his head, and raised the terrible open mouth aloft on his tall figure. He bore likewise on his shield a hundred snakes and the monster of Lerna —the hydra [a] that multiplied when the serpents were cut in two. Juba and his father Thapsus ; Micipsa, famous for the glory of his ancestor,[b] and Saces the Moor—all these he had driven from the walls and pursued headlong to the shore as they fled in disorder ; and his unaided arm made the sea foam with blood. Not satisfied with the death of Idus and the death of Cotho of Marmarica, nor with the slaughter of Rothus and the slaughter of Jugurtha, he raised his ambition to Asbyte's chariot, the glittering mantle that covered her, and her bright jewelled target ; and all his mind was fixed on the warrior maiden. When the princess saw him rushing on with bloodstained weapon, she made her horses swerve aside ; and thus, evading him by wheeling to the left, she cleaves the plain and flies like a bird over the curving field, showing him the back of her chariot. And,

fictitious persons names that were famous later in Roman history. He does the same thing elsewhere.

71

dumque ea se ex oculis aufert, atque ocior Euro
incita pulveream campo trahit ungula nubem,
adversum late stridens rota proterit agmen,   175
ingerit et crebras virgo trepidantibus hastas.
hic cecidere Lycus Thamyrisque et nobile nomen
Eurydamas, clari deductum stirpe parentis ;
qui thalamos ausus quondam sperare superbos,
heu demens ! Ithacique torum ; sed enim arte pudica
fallacis totiens revoluto stamine telae   181
deceptus, mersum pelago iactarat Ulixen ;
ast Ithacus vero ficta pro morte loquacem
affecit leto, taedaeque ad funera versae.
gens extrema viri campis deletur Hiberis   185
Eurydamas Nomados dextra ; superinstrepit ater
et servat cursum perfractis ossibus axis.
   Iamque aderat remeans virgo, inter proelia post-
      quam
distringi Therona videt, saevamque bipennem
perlibrans mediae fronti, spolium inde superbum 190
Herculeasque tibi exuvias, Dictynna, vovebat.
nec segnis Theron tantae spe laudis in ipsos
adversus consurgit equos villosaque fulvi
ingerit obiectans trepidantibus ora leonis.
attoniti terrore novo rictuque minaci   195
quadrupedes iactant resupino pondere currum.
tum saltu Asbyten conantem linquere pugnas
occupat, incussa gemina inter tempora clava,
ferventesque rotas turbataque frena pavore
disiecto spargit collisa per ossa cerebro ;   200
ac rapta properans caedem ostentare bipenni,

---

[a] Silius seems to have made a mistake. In Homer the
suitor whom Penelope put off by her device of unravelling
her web every night is called Eurymachus.
  [b] Ulysses.   [c] See note to l. 71.

while she vanished from his sight, and the hoofs of
her horses, galloping swifter than the wind, raised a
cloud of dust on the field, her crashing wheels crushed
the opposing ranks far and wide ; and the maiden
launched spear after spear upon them in their con-
fusion. Here Lycas fell, and Thamyris, and Eury-
damas [a] of famous name, the scion of a noble stock.
His ancestor, poor fool ! had dared long ago to covet
a splendid marriage with the wife of the Ithacan [b] ;
but he was taken in by the trick of the chaste wife,
who unravelled every night the threads of her web.
He had declared that Ulysses was drowned at sea ;
but the Ithacan inflicted death upon the prater—real
death and no fiction ; and funeral took the place of
marriage. Now his latest descendant, Eurydamas,
was slain by the hand of the Numidian queen : the
fatal chariot thundered over his broken bones and
kept its course.

And now Asbyte came back to the place, when she
saw Theron busy with battle ; and, aiming her fierce
battle-axe at the centre of his brow, she vowed to
Dictynna [c] a glorious spoil from it, even the lion-skin
of Hercules. Nor did Theron hang back : eager for
so great a prize, he rose up right in front of the horses
and held before them the shaggy head of the tawny
lion and thrust it in their frightened faces. Frantic
with fear unfelt before—fear of the menacing open
jaws—the coursers upset the heavy car and turned it
over. Then, as Asbyte tried to flee from the fight,
he sprang to stop her, and smote her between the
twin temples with his club ; he spattered the glowing
wheels and the reins, disordered by the terrified
horses, with the brains that gushed from the broken
skull. . Then he seized her axe and, eager to display

amputat e curru revolutae virginis ora.
necdum irae positae ; celsa nam figitur hasta
spectandum caput ; id gestent ante agmina Poenum,
imperat, et propere currus ad moenia vertant.   205
haec caecus fati divumque abeunte favore
vicino Theron edebat proelia leto.
namque aderat toto ore ferens iramque minasque
Hannibal et caesam Asbyten fixique tropaeum
infandum capitis furiata mente dolebat.   210
ac simul aerati radiavit luminis umbo,
et concussa procul membris velocibus arma
letiferum intonuere, fugam perculsa repente
ad muros trepido convertunt agmina cursu.
sicut agit levibus per sera crepuscula pennis   215
e pastu volucres ad nota cubilia vesper ;
aut, ubi Cecropius formidine nubis aquosae
sparsa super flores examina tollit Hymettos,
ad dulces ceras et odori corticis antra
mellis apes gravidae properant densoque volatu   220
raucum connexae glomerant ad limina murmur.
praecipitat metus attonitos, caecique feruntur.
heu blandum caeli lumen ! tantone cavetur
mors reditura metu nascentique addita fata ?
consilium damnant portisque atque aggere tuto   225
erupisse gemunt ; retinet vix agmina Theron
interdumque manu, interdum clamore minisque :
" state, viri ; meus ille hostis ; mihi gloria magnae,

---

a Cecropian = Athenian. Cecrops was an ancient king of
Athens : Hymettus, famous for its honey, is a hill at Athens.
b Cp. xvi. 73.

his slaughter of her, cut off the head of the maiden when she rolled out of her chariot. Not yet was his rage sated; for he fixed her head on a lofty pike, for all to see, and bade men bear it in front of the Punic army, and drive the chariot with speed to the town. Blind to his doom and deserted by divine favour, Theron fought on; but death was near him. For Hannibal came up, with wrath and menace expressed in every feature; with frenzied heart he raged at the slaughter of Asbyte, and at the horrid trophy of her head borne aloft. And, as soon as his shield of glittering brass shone out, and the armour on his swift limbs, rattling afar, thundered forth doom, the enemy were suddenly stricken with fear and fled in haste towards the town. So, in the late twilight, evening sends the birds on their light wings back from their feeding-ground to their familiar roosts; or so, when Cecropian Hymettus [a] scares with menace of a rain-cloud the swarms scattered over the flowers, the bees, heavy with honey, hasten back to their luscious combs and hives of fragrant cork; they fly in a close pack, and unite in a deep humming noise outside the hives. Thus panic drove the frightened soldiers headlong, and they rushed on blindly. Ah! how sweet is the light of heaven! [b] Why do men shun with such terror the death that must some day come, and the sentence pronounced against them at birth? They curse their design, and lament their sally from the protection of the gates and the wall. Theron can hardly stop their flight, using force sometimes and sometimes loud threats: " Stand fast, my men; yon enemy belongs to me; stand fast—victory in a mighty combat is coming to me. My right hand shall

state, venit pugnae : muro tectisque Sagunti
hac abigam Poenos dextra ; spectacula tantum   230
ferte, viri ; vel, si cunctos metus acer in urbem,
heu deforme ! rapit, soli mihi claudite portas."
  At Poenus rapido praeceps ad moenia cursu,
dum pavitant trepidi rerum fessique salutis,
tendebat ; stat primam urbem murosque patentes
postposita caede et dilata invadere pugna.   236
id postquam Herculeae custos videt impiger arae,
emicat et velox formidine praevenit hostem.
gliscit Elissaeo violentior ira tyranno :
"tu solve interea nobis, bone ianitor urbis,   240
supplicium, ut pandas," inquit, " tua moenia leto."
nec plura effari sinit ira, rotatque coruscum
mucronem ; sed contortum prior impete vasto
Daunius huic robur iuvenis iacit ; arma fragore
icta gravi raucum gemuere, alteque resultant   245
aere illisa cavo nodosae pondera clavae.
at viduus teli et frustrato proditus ictu,
pernici velox cursu rapit incita membra
et celeri fugiens perlustrat moenia planta.
instat atrox terga increpitans fugientia victor.   250
conclamant matres, celsoque e culmine muri
lamentis vox mixta sonat ; nunc nomine noto
appellant, seras fesso nunc pandere portas
posse volunt ; quatit hortantum praecordia terror,
ne simul accipiant ingentem moenibus hostem.   255
incutit umbonem fesso assultatque ruenti

---

[a] Daunian = Italian = Saguntine.

drive away the Carthaginians from the wall and houses of Saguntum : do your part as mere spectators ; or, if urgent fear drives you all into the city—a sorry sight—then shut your gates against me alone."

But Hannibal was hastening with headlong speed towards the walls, while the besieged were in fear, trembling for their safety and despairing of life ; his purpose was to attack the city first through its open gates, deferring the slaughter of his foe. When the bold guardian of the temple of Hercules saw this, he sprang forward and, urged to speed by his fears, outstripped the foeman. The wrath of the Tyrian leader waxed yet fiercer : " You, worthy keeper of the city's gates, shall first suffer death at my hands, and by your death throw open the walls." Rage prevented further speech, and he whirled round his flashing sword ; but the Daunian *a* warrior was before him and swinging his club with mighty force threw it at Hannibal. Beneath that heavy blow his armour rang with a hollow sound ; and the weighty knotted club, crashing upon the hollow metal, rebounded high. Then, unarmed and betrayed by his unsuccessful stroke, Theron urged his limbs to hasty flight and ran round the walls, seeking to escape by his speed. The conqueror pursued fiercely and taunted the back of the fugitive. The matrons cried out together, and their voices, together with wailings, rose up from the lofty summit of the wall ; now they address Theron by his familiar name, and now, too late, they wish for power to open the gate to him in his extremity ; but, even as they encourage him, their hearts are shaken by the fear that, together with him, they may admit within the walls their mighty foe. Hannibal struck the weary runner with

77

Poenus et ostentans spectantem e moenibus urbem :
" i, miseram Asbyten leto solare propinquo."
haec dicens, iugulo optantis dimittere vitam
infestum condit mucronem ac regia laetus   260
quadrupedes spolia abreptos a moenibus ipsis,
quis aditum portae trepidantum saepserat agmen,
victor agit curruque volat per ovantia castra.

At Nomadum furibunda cohors miserabile humandi
deproperat munus tumulique adiungit honorem   265
et rapto cineres ter circum corpore lustrat.
hinc letale viri robur tegimenque tremendum
in flammas iaciunt ; ambustoque ore genisque
deforme alitibus liquere cadaver Hiberis.

Poenorum interea quis rerum summa potestas,   270
consultant bello super, et quae dicta ferantur
Ausoniae populis, oratorumque minaci
adventu trepidant.   movet hinc foedusque fidesque
et testes superi iurataque pacta parentum,
hinc popularis amor coeptantis magna iuventae, 275
et sperare iuvat belli meliora.   sed, olim
ductorem infestans odiis gentilibus, Hannon
sic adeo increpitat studia incautumque favorem :
" cuncta   quidem, patres, (neque   enim   cohibere
          minantum
irae se valuere) premunt formidine vocem.   280
haud tamen abstiterim, mortem licet arma propin-
          quent.

---

^a Hanno, surnamed The Great, was a Carthaginian general
and statesman, who possessed great influence in the Cartha-
ginian senate, and always used it to oppose Hamilcar, and
Hamilcar's sons, Hannibal and Hasdrubal.

his shield and sprang upon him as he fell ; then, pointing to the citizens watching from the walls, " Go ! " he cried, " and comfort hapless Asbyte by your speedy death ! " and at the same time buried his fatal sword in the throat of a victim who was fain to lose his life. Then the conqueror drove off with joy the horses taken from Asbyte, carrying them off from before the very walls, where the body of fugitives had used them to block the entrance of the gate ; and off he sped in the chariot through the triumphant lines.

But the band of Numidians, frantic with grief, made haste with the sad office of burial, and gave Asbyte the tribute of a pyre, and seized the dead man's body and carried it thrice round her ashes. Next they cast into the flames his murderous club and his dreadful head-dress ; and, when the face and beard were burnt, they left the unsightly corpse to the Spanish vultures.

Meanwhile the rulers of Carthage took counsel concerning the war and the answer they must send to the Italian people ; and the formidable approach of the envoys made them uneasy. On the one hand they were swayed by loyalty to the treaty, by the gods who witnessed it, and by the compact to which their fathers swore ; and on the other by the popularity of the ambitious young leader ; and they nursed a hope of victory. But Hanno,[a] hereditary foe and constant assailant of Hannibal, with these words rebuked their zeal and heedless partiality : " Senators, all things indeed intimidate me from speaking ; for the angry threats of my opponents have proved unable to restrain themselves. Yet I shall not flinch, not even though I must soon die by violence. I shall

testabor superos et caelo nota relinquam,
quae postrema salus rerum patriaeque reposcit.
nec nunc obsessa demum et fumante Sagunto
haec serus vates Hannon canit ; anxia rupi   285
pectora, ne castris innutriretur et armis
exitiale caput, monui et, dum vita, monebo,
ingenitum noscens virus flatusque paternos ;
ut, qui stelligero speculatur sidera caelo,
venturam pelagi rabiem Caurique futura   290
praedicit miseris haud vanus flamina nautis.
consedit solio rerumque invasit habenas :
ergo armis foedus fasque omne abrumpitur armis,
oppida quassantur, longeque in moenia nostra
Aeneadum arrectae mentes, disiectaque pax est.   295
exagitant manes iuvenem furiaeque paternae
ac funesta sacra et conversi foedere rupto
in caput infidum superi Massylaque vates.
an nunc ille novi caecus caligine regni
externas arces quatit ? haud Tirynthia tecta   300
(sic propria luat hoc poena nec misceat urbis
fata suis), nunc hoc, hoc inquam, tempore muros
oppugnat, Carthago, tuos teque obsidet armis.
lavimus Hennaeas animoso sanguine valles
et vix conducto produximus arma Lacone.   305
nos ratibus laceris Scyllaea replevimus antra
classibus et refluo spectavimus aequore raptis
contorta e fundo revomentem transtra Charybdin.

---

^a This refers to the oath which Hamilcar made his son
swear in Dido's temple, in the presence of the Massylian
priestess : *cf.* i. 81-139.

^b " Henna "=" Sicily."   Hanno is referring to the First
Punic War, when Sparta sent troops under Xanthippus, and
Regulus, the Roman general, was defeated (258 B.C.).

^c When defeated at sea near the Aegatian islands : see
note to i. 35.

appeal to the gods, and I shall tell Heaven, ere I die,
the measures demanded by the safety of the state
and of our country in its extremity. Not now only,
when it is too late, when Saguntum is besieged and
burning, do I prophesy these evils : I made a clean
breast of my fears : I warned you before and, while
I live, shall go on warning you, not to suffer that
instrument of destruction to be bred up in camps and
in war ; for I marked the poison of his nature and his
hereditary ambition, even as the watcher of the starry
heavens foretells, not in vain, to hapless seamen the
coming fury of the sea and the approaching blasts
of the North-west wind. Hannibal has taken his
seat on a throne and seized the reins of government ;
and therefore the treaty is broken by the sword, and
by the sword every obligation is broken ; cities are
shaken, and the distant Aeneadae are alert to attack
Carthage, and peace has been thrown to the winds.
The young man is driven mad by the ghost and evil
spirit of his father, by that fatal ceremony,[a] by the
gods who have turned against the breaker of faith
and treaties, and by the Massylian priestess. Blinded
and dazzled by new-gained power, he is overthrowing
cities ; but are they foreign cities ? It is not Sagun-
tum that he is attacking—so may he atone for this
crime in his own person and not involve his country
in his punishment—now, even now, I declare, he is
attacking the walls of Carthage and besieging us with
his army. We drenched the valleys of Henna with
the blood of the brave, and could hardly carry on
the war by hiring the Spartan.[b] We filled Scylla's
caverns with shipwrecks [c] ; and, when our fleets were
borne away by the tide, we saw Charybdis whirling
the rowers' benches round and spouting them forth

respice, pro demens ! pro pectus inane deorum !
Aegates Libyaeque procul fluitantia membra.   310
quo ruis ? et patriae exitio tibi nomina quaeris ?
scilicet immensae, visis iuvenilibus armis,
subsident Alpes, subsidet mole nivali
Alpibus aequatum attollens caput Apenninus.
sed campos fac, vane, dari. num gentibus istis   315
mortales animi ? aut ferro flammave fatiscunt ?
haud tibi Neritia cernes cum prole laborem.
pubescit castris miles, galeaque teruntur
nondum signatae flava lanugine malae.
nec requies aevi nota, exsanguesque merendo   320
stant prima inter signa senes letumque lacessunt.
ipse ego Romanas perfosso corpore turmas
tela intorquentes correpta e vulnere vidi ;
vidi animos mortesque virum decorisque furorem.
si bello obsistis nec te victoribus offers,   325
quantum heu, Carthago, donat tibi sanguinis Hannon ! ''
     Gestar ad haec (namque impatiens asperque co-
          quebat
iamdudum immites iras mediamque loquentis
bis conatus erat turbando abrumpere vocem) :
'' concilione,'' inquit, '' Libyae Tyrioque senatu,   330
pro superi ! Ausonius miles sedet ? armaque tantum
haud dum sumpta viro ? nam cetera non latet hostis.
nunc geminas Alpes Apenninumque minatur,
nunc freta Sicaniae et Scyllaei litoris undas ;

---

     [a] By '' limbs '' it seems that separate parts of the Cartha-
ginian empire, such as Sicily and Sardinia, are meant.
     [b] The false statement must be attributed to rhetorical
licence.
     [c] The Saguntines are meant : they came originally from
Zacynthus, an Ionian island ; and Neritus is a mountain in
Ithaca, another Ionian island.

from her depths. Madman, with no fear of God in
your heart, look at the Aegatian islands and the
limbs *a* of Libya drifting far away ! Whither are you
rushing ? Do you seek fame for yourself by the
ruin of your country ? The huge Alps will sink down,
forsooth, at sight of the stripling warrior ; and the
snowy mass of the Apennines, that raise their summit
as high as the Alps,*b* will sink down also. But sup-
pose, vain pretender, that you reach the plains ; that
nation has a spirit that never dies ; sword and flame
can never wear them out. You will not find yourself
fighting there against the stock that came from
Neritus.*c* Their soldiers grow to manhood in the
camp, and their faces rub against the helmet before
they are marked by the golden down. Nor is rest
known to them in age ; even old men, who have shed
their blood in long service, stand in the front rank and
challenge death. My own eyes have seen Roman
soldiers, when run through the body, snatch the
weapon from their wound and hurl it at the foe ; I
have seen their courage and the way they die and
their passion for glory. From how much bloodshed
does Hanno save Carthage, if she sets her face against
war and does not wantonly confront the conquerors!"

To this speech Gestar replied. Harsh and im-
patient, he had long been nursing bitter wrath, and
twice had he tried to raise a disturbance and silence
Hanno in the middle of his speech. " Ye gods ! " he
cried : " is this a Roman soldier, seated in the
council of Libya and the Carthaginian senate ? Arms
he has not yet taken up ; but in all else the foeman
stands declared before us. Now he threatens us
with the twin ranges of Alps and Apennines, now
with the Sicilian sea and the waves on Scylla's

nec procul est, quin iam manes umbrasque pavescat
Dardanias ; tanta accumulat praeconia leto   336
vulneribusque virum ac tollit sub sidera gentem.
mortalem, mihi crede, licet formidine turpi
frigida corda tremant, mortalem sumimus hostem.
vidi ego, cum, geminas artis post terga catenis   340
evinctus palmas, vulgo traheretur ovante
carceris in tenebras spes et fiducia gentis
Regulus Hectoreae ; vidi, cum robore pendens
Hesperiam cruce sublimis spectaret ab alta.
nec vero terrent puerilia protinus ora   345
sub galea et pressae properata casside malae.
indole non adeo segni sumus. aspice, turmae
quot Libycae certant annos anteire labore
et nudis bellantur equis. ipse, aspice, ductor,
cum primam tenero vocem proferret ab ore,   350
iam bella et lituos ac flammis urere gentem
iurabat Phrygiam atque animo patria arma movebat.
proinde polo crescant Alpes, astrisque coruscos
Apenninus agat scopulos : per saxa nivesque
(dicam etenim, ut stimulent atram vel inania
       mentem)   355
per caelum est qui pandat iter. pudet Hercule tritas
desperare vias laudemque timere secundam.
sed Libyae clades et primi incendia belli
aggerat atque iterum pro libertate labores
Hannon ferre vetat. ponat formidinis aestus   360
parietibusque domus imbellis femina servet
singultantem animam ; nos, nos contra ibimus hostem,

---

    a The Trojans, identified by Silius with the Romans.
    b Regulus was tortured to death : see vi. 539 foll. ; and
his dead body seems to have been crucified : see l. 435.

shore ; he is not far from fearing the very shades
and ghosts of the Romans : such praise does he
heap upon their wounds and deaths, and exalts
the nation to the sky. But, though his cold heart
trembles with base fear, take my word for it, that
the foe whom we are engaging is mortal. I was
looking on, when Regulus, the hope and pride of
Hector's race,[a] was dragged along amid the shouts of
the populace to his dark dungeon, with both hands
bound fast behind his back ; I was looking on, when
he hung high upon the tree and saw Italy from his
lofty cross.[b] Nor again do I dread the brows that
wear the helmet in early boyhood, nor the heads that
carry the steel cap before their time. The temper of
our people is not so sluggish. Look at the Libyan
squadrons : how many of them vie in exertions beyond
their years, and go to war on bare-backed horses !
Look at Hannibal himself. When he was first able to
utter speech from his childish lips, he pledged himself
to war and the clarion's sound, and swore to consume
the Phrygian people with fire, and fought in fancy
the campaigns of his father, Hamilcar. Therefore,
let the Alps soar to heaven, and the Apennines lift
their glittering peaks to the stars : through rocks and
snows—I will say it, that even an idle boast may sting
a traitor's heart—through the sky itself our pioneer
will find a way. Shameful is it to shun a path that
Hercules trod and to shrink back from repeating his
exploit. Hanno exaggerates the defeats of Libya and
the conflagration of our first war with Rome, and for-
bids us to bear hardship again in defence of freedom.
Let Hanno still his agitation and fears, and keep his
sobbing breath, like an unwarlike woman, behind the
walls of his house. But we shall march against the

quis procul a Tyria dominos depellere Byrsa,
vel Iove non aequo, fixum est.   sin fata repugnant,
et iam damnata cessit Carthagine Mavors,   365
occumbam potius nec te, patria inclita, dedam
aeternum famulam liberque Acheronta videbo.
nam quae, pro superi ! Fabius iubet ? ocius arma
exuite et capta descendite ab arce Sagunti.
tum delecta manus scutorum incendat acervos,   370
uranturque rates, ac toto absistite ponto.
di, procul o, merita est numquam si talia plecti
Carthago, prohibete nefas nostrique solutas
ductoris servate manus ! "   ut deinde resedit
factaque censendi patrum de more potestas,   375
hic Hannon reddi propere certamine rapta
instat et auctorem violati foederis addit.
tum vero attoniti, ceu templo irrumperet hostis,
exsiluere patres, Latioque id verteret omen,
oravere deum.   at postquam discordia sensit   380
pectora et infidas ad Martem vergere mentes,
non ultra patiens Fabius rexisse dolorem,
consilium propere exposcit, patribusque vocatis,
bellum se gestare sinu pacemque profatus,
quid sedeat, legere ambiguis neu fallere dictis   385
imperat ac, saevo neutrum renuente senatu,
ceu clausas acies gremioque effunderet arma :
" accipite infaustum Libyae eventuque priori

---

a The citadel of Carthage, built by Dido. The name is
Semitic (Bozra = " a citadel "), but was corrupted by Greeks
into Byrsa, " a bull's hide " ; and hence arose the legend
that the settlers bought as much land as they could cover
with a hide ; but they were ingenious people and cut up the
hide into strips and surrounded with them as much space as
they could.

foe—we who are determined, even if Jupiter is not
on our side, to drive foreign rulers far from Tyrian
Byrsa.[a] But, if Fate fights against us and Mars has
already condemned Carthage and departed from her,
I shall choose rather to fall ; I shall not hand over my
glorious fatherland to eternal slavery, and I shall go
down free to Acheron.[b] For, ye gods ! what are the
demands of Fabius ? ' Lay down your arms at once
and depart from the captured citadel of Saguntum.
Next, your picked troops must pile their shields and
burn them ; your ships must be burnt, and you must
withdraw altogether from the sea.' Ye gods, if
Carthage never deserved such punishment, prevent
the abomination, and keep the hands of our general
unfettered." Then he sat down, and the senators
were permitted to vote according to custom. But
Hanno insisted that the spoils of war should be at
once given up, and also the first breaker[c] of the treaty.
Then indeed the senate, as excited as if the enemy
were bursting into the temple, sprang up and prayed
the gods to turn the evil omen against Latium. But
when Fabius perceived the division of opinion, and
that their disloyal minds were inclining to war, he
could master his resentment no longer ; and he de-
manded a swift decision. When the senate was sum-
moned, he began thus : " I carry war and peace here
in my lap ; choose which ye will have, and cheat me
not by an ambiguous answer." The angry senators
said they would accept neither. Then, as if he were
pouring out battle and war enclosed in his arms,
" Take war," he cried, " a fatal war for Libya, and

[b] Acheron, one of the rivers in Hades, is often used for
Hades itself.
[c] Hannibal.

par," inquit, " bellum "—et laxos effundit amictus.
tum patrias repetit pugnandi nuntius arces.   390

  Atque ea dum profugae regnis agitantur Elissae,
accisis velox populis, quis aegra lababat
ambiguo sub Marte fides, praedaque gravatus
ad muros Poenus revocaverat arma Sagunti.

  Ecce autem clipeum saevo fulgore micantem   395
Oceani gentes ductori dona ferebant,
Callaicae telluris opus, galeamque coruscis
subnexam cristis, vibrant cui vertice coni
albentis niveae tremulo nutamine pennae ;
ensem, unam ac multis fatalem milibus hastam ;   400
praeterea textam nodis auroque trilicem
loricam, nulli tegimen penetrabile telo.
haec, aere et duri chalybis perfecta metallo
atque opibus perfusa Tagi, per singula laetis
lustrat ovans oculis et gaudet origine regni.   405

  Condebat primae Dido Carthaginis arces,
instabatque operi subducta classe iuventus.
molibus hi claudunt portus, his tecta domosque
partiris, iustae Bitia venerande senectae.
ostentant caput effossa tellure repertum   410
bellatoris equi atque omen clamore salutant.
has inter species orbatum classe suisque
Aenean pulsum pelago dextraque precantem
cernere erat. fronte hunc avide regina serena
infelix ac iam vultu spectabat amico.   415

---

  a Dido.

  b Gallicia is the northern part of Portugal, beyond the
river Douro. The district was rich in metals, especially gold.

  c In what follows Silius has in mind the shield of Achilles
described by Homer (*Il.* xviii. 478 foll.) and the shield of
Aeneas described by Virgil (*Aen.* viii. 626 foll.).

  d The horse's head, supposed to be an omen of victory,
appears on coins of Carthage.

like in its issue to the last "—and therewith he shook
loose the folds of his gown. Then he returned to
his native city, a harbinger of war.

While this debate went on in the kingdom of the
exile, Elissa,[a] Hannibal swiftly despoiled those tribes
whose loyalty was waxing faint as the war dragged
on ; then, loaded with plunder, he took his army back
to the walls of Saguntum.

But behold ! the peoples who dwell by the Atlantic
brought gifts to the general. They gave him a
shield that glittered with cruel sheen, the work of
Gallician[b] craftsmen; a helmet wreathed with flashing
plumes, on the height of whose white crest snowy
feathers nodded and waved ; a sword and a spear
that, though it was but one, was to slay its thousands.
There was also a cuirass wrought with triple bosses of
gold, a defence that no weapon could pierce. This
armour was wrought throughout of bronze and tough
steel, and covered richly with the gold of the Tagus ;
and Hannibal surveyed each part of it with joy and
triumph in his eyes, and he delighted to see there
depicted the beginnings of Carthage.[c]

Dido was shown building the city of infant Carthage;
her men had beached their ships and were busily en-
gaged. Some were enclosing a harbour with piers ; to
others dwellings were assigned by Bitias, a righteous
and venerable old man. Men pointed to the head of
a warhorse which they had found in the soil when
digging, and hailed the omen with a shout.[d] Amid
these scenes Aeneas was shown, robbed of his ships
and men and cast up by the sea ; with his right hand
he made supplication. The hapless queen looked
eagerly upon him with unclouded brow and with
looks already friendly. Next, the art of Gallicia had

89

hinc et speluncam furtivaque foedera amantum
Callaicae fecere manus ; it clamor ad auras
latratusque canum, subitoque exterrita nimbo
occultant alae venantum corpora silvis.
nec procul Aeneadum vacuo iam litore classis   420
aequora nequicquam revocante petebat Elissa.
ipsa, pyram super ingentem stans, saucia Dido
mandabat Tyriis ultricia bella futuris ;
ardentemque rogum media spectabat ab unda
Dardanus et magnis pandebat carbasa fatis.   425
parte alia supplex infernis Hannibal aris
arcanum Stygia libat cum vate cruorem
et primo bella Aeneadum iurabat ab aevo.
at senior Siculis exultat Hamilcar in arvis—
spirantem credas certamina anhela movere,   430
ardor inest oculis, torvumque minatur imago.
   Necnon et laevum clipei latus aspera signis
implebat Spartana cohors ; hanc ducit ovantem
Ledaeis veniens victor Xanthippus Amyclis.
iuxta triste decus pendet sub imagine poenae   435
Regulus et fidei dat magna exempla Sagunto.
laetior at circa facies, agitata ferarum
agmina venatu et caelata mapalia fulgent.
nec procul usta cutem nigri soror horrida Mauri
assuetas mulcet patrio sermone leaenas.   440
it liber campi pastor, cui fine sine ullo
invetitum saltus penetrat pecus ; omnia Poenum
armenti vigilem patrio de more secuntur ;

---

    [a] Dido and Aeneas.   [b] Aeneas.
    [c] See note to l. 305.   Amyclae is a city of Laconia, on
the river Eurotas.
    [d] See note to l. 344.
    [e] This seems to refer to the tortures that preceded his
crucifixion: see vi. 539 foll.

fashioned the cave and the secret tryst of the lovers[a];
high rose the shouting and the baying of hounds;
and the mounted huntsmen, alarmed by a sudden
rainfall, took shelter in the forest. Not far away, the
fleet of the Aeneadae had left the shore and was
making for the open sea, while Elissa was calling
them back in vain. Then Dido by herself was stand-
ing wounded on a huge pyre, and charging a later
generation of Tyrians to avenge her by war; and
the Dardan,[b] out at sea, was watching the blazing
pile and spreading his sails for his high destiny. On
another part of the shield Hannibal prayed at the
altars of the nether gods, and, with the Stygian
priestess, made a secret libation of blood, and swore
to fight against the Aeneadae from his youth up.
And old Hamilcar was there, riding proudly over the
Sicilian fields; one might think that he was alive and
rousing breathless conflict—fire shines in his eyes, and
his image is grim with menace.

The left side also of the shield was filled with
Spartan warriors, carved in high relief; they were
led in triumph by victorious Xanthippus,[c] who came
from Amyclae, the city of Leda. Near them hung
Regulus,[d] glorious in suffering, beneath a picture of
his punishment,[e] setting to Saguntum a noble example
of loyalty. Hard by was a happier scene—herds of
wild beasts chased by hunters, and African huts,
carved in shining metal. Not far away the savage
sunburnt sister of a blackamoor soothed lionesses,
her companions, with her native speech. The shep-
herd roamed free over the plains, and his flock, un-
forbidden, made their way into pastures without
limit; the Punic guardian of the herd took all his
possessions with him, according to the custom of his

gaesaque latratorque Cydon tectumque focique
in silicis venis et fistula nota iuvencis.   445
eminet excelso consurgens colle Saguntos,
quam circa immensi populi condensaque cingunt
agmina certantum pulsantque trementibus hastis.
extrema clipei stagnabat Hiberus in ora,
curvatis claudens ingentem flexibus orbem.   450
Hannibal, abrupto transgressus foedere ripas,
Poenorum populos Romana in bella vocabat.
tali sublimis dono, nova tegmina latis
aptat concutiens humeris celsusque profatur :
" heu quantum Ausonio sudabitis, arma, cruore ! 455
quas, belli iudex, poenas mihi, Curia, pendes ! "
    Iamque senescebat vallatus moenibus hostis,
carpebatque dies urbem, dum signa manusque
expectant fessi socias.   tandem aequore vano
avertunt oculos frustrataque litora ponunt   460
et propius suprema vident.   sedet acta medullis
iamdudum atque inopes penitus coquit intima pestis.
est furtim lento misere durantia tabo
viscera et exurit siccatas sanguine venas
per longum celata fames ; iam lumina retro   465
exesis fugere genis, iam lurida sola
tecta cute et venis male iuncta trementibus ossa
extant, consumptis visu deformia membris.
humentes rores noctis terramque madentem
solamen fecere mali, cassoque labore   470
e sicco frustra presserunt robore sucos.

---

[a] This appears to mean that the Roman Senate claim a
right to forbid Carthage making war on Saguntum.

country—his javelins, his barking Cretan hound, his
tent, his fire hidden in the veins of flint, and the reed-
pipe which his steers know well. Conspicuous on the
shield was Saguntum, rising on its lofty eminence ;
and round it swarmed countless hosts and serried
ranks of fighters, who assailed it with their quivering
spears. On the outer rim of the shield flowed the
Ebro, enclosing the vast circuit with its curves and
windings. And there was Hannibal ; having broken
the treaty by crossing the river, he was summoning
the Punic nations to battle against Rome. Proud
of such a gift, the leader fitted the new armour to
his broad shoulders with a clang. Then, with head
held high, he spoke thus : " Ah ! what torrents of
Roman blood will drench this armour ! How great a
penalty shall the Senate, the disposer of war,[a] pay
to me ! "

By now the beleaguered enemy was growing
feebler, and time sapped the strength of the citizens,
while they looked in their extremity for the eagles
and troops of their ally. At last they turned their
gaze away from the delusive sea, and gave up the
shore as hopeless, and saw their doom at hand. In-
ward pangs, piercing to the marrow, had long been
fixed there, utterly consuming the starving people.
Famine, long concealed, devoured their much-enduring
flesh with slow and secret poison, and burnt up their
bloodless veins ; by now their eyes sank back from
the emaciated cheeks ; the bones, a hideous sight
when the flesh was gone, stuck out, covered only by
the yellow skin and ill-joined by the shaking arteries.
They tried to ease their suffering by the moist dews
and damp soil of night, and with useless toil squeezed
in vain the sap from dry wood. They shrank from

nil temerare piget ; rabidi ieiunia ventris
insolitis adigunt vesci ; resolutaque, nudos
linquentes clipeos, armorum tegmina mandunt.
    Desuper haec caelo spectans Tirynthius alto   475
illacrimat fractae nequicquam casibus urbis.
namque metus magnique tenent praecepta parentis,
ne saevae tendat contra decreta novercae.
sic igitur, coepta occultans, ad limina sanctae
contendit Fidei secretaque pectora tentat.   480
arcanis dea laeta polo tum forte remoto
caelicolum magnas volvebat conscia curas ;
quam tali alloquitur Nemeae pacator honore :
" ante Iovem generata, decus divumque hominumque,
qua sine non tellus pacem, non aequora norunt,   485
iustitiae consors tacitumque in pectore numen,
exitiumne tuae dirum spectare Sagunti
et tot pendentem pro te, dea, cernere poenas
urbem lenta potes ? moritur tibi vulgus, et unam
te matres, vincente fame, te maesta virorum   490
ora vocant, primaque sonant te voce minores.
fer caelo auxilium et fessis da surgere rebus."
    Haec satus Alcmena ; contra cui talia virgo :
" cerno equidem, nec pro nihilo est mihi foedera
        rumpi ;
statque dies, ausis olim tam tristibus ultor.   495
sed me, pollutas properantem linquere terras,
sedibus his tectisque novis succedere adegit
fecundum in fraudes hominum genus ; impia liqui

---

    ^a Juno.
    ^b By killing the lion of Nemea, whose skin he wore ever
after.
    ^c This is said more often of Astraea, the goddess of Justice—
that she was forced to leave the earth because of the wicked-
ness of men.

no pollution ; their fierce hunger forced them to eat strange food ; they stripped their shields bare and gnawed the loosened coverings of their bucklers.

Hercules looked down from high heaven and beheld these things and wept over the calamities of the stricken town ; but he was helpless, and respect for the bidding of his mighty sire hindered him from opposing the decrees of his cruel stepmother.[a] Therefore, hiding his intent, he took his way to the abode of sacred Loyalty, seeking to discover her hidden purpose. It chanced that the goddess, who loves solitude, was then in a distant region of heaven, pondering in her heart the high concerns of the gods. Then he who gave peace to Nemea[b] accosted her thus with reverence : " Goddess more ancient than Jupiter, glory of gods and men, without whom neither sea nor land finds peace, sister of Justice, silent divinity in the heart of man, canst thou look on unmoved at the awful doom of thine own Saguntum, and watch the city while it suffers so many penalties in thy defence ? For thy sake the people die ; the matrons, conquered by famine, call on thee alone ; the pitiful cries of the men invoke thee ; thy name is heard in the first utterance of their little ones. Bring help from heaven, and grant that the fallen may rise."

Thus spoke Alcmena's son, and the goddess made answer : " I see it indeed, and the breaking of treaties is not disregarded by me : the day is fixed that shall hereafter punish such evil deeds. But, when I hastened to leave the sin-stained earth, I was forced to settle here and change my habitation, because the human race was so fertile in wickedness[c] ; I fled from

et, quantum terrent, tantum metuentia regna
ac furias auri nec vilia praemia fraudum   500
et super haec ritu horrificos ac more ferarum
viventes rapto populos luxuque solutum
omne decus multaque oppressum nocte pudorem.
vis colitur, iurisque locum sibi vindicat ensis,
et probris cessit virtus.   en, aspice gentes !   505
nemo insons ; pacem servant commercia culpae.
sed, si cura tua fundata ut moenia dextra
dignum te servent memorando fine vigorem,
dedita nec fessi tramittant corpora Poeno,
quod solum nunc fata sinunt seriesque futuri,   510
extendam leti decus atque in saecula mittam
ipsaque laudatas ad manes prosequar umbras.''

   Inde severa levi decurrens aethere virgo
luctantem fatis petit inflammata Saguntum.
invadit mentes et pectora nota pererrat   515
immittitque animis numen ; tum, fusa medullis,
implicat atque sui flagrantem inspirat amorem.
arma volunt tentantque aegros ad proelia nisus.
insperatus adest vigor, interiusque recursat
dulcis honor divae et sacrum pro virgine letum.   520
it tacitus fessis per ovantia pectora sensus,
vel leto graviora pati saevasque ferarum
attentare dapes et mensis addere crimen.

wicked kings, who themselves fear as much as they
are feared, and the frenzy for gold, and the rich
rewards of wickedness. I fled also from nations hate-
ful in their customs and living by violence like wild
beasts, where all honour is undermined by luxury,
and where shame is buried in deep darkness. Force
is worshipped, and the sword usurps the place of
justice, and virtue has given place to crime. Behold
the nations ! no man is innocent ; fellowship in guilt
alone preserves peace. But, if thou desirest the
walls built by thy hand to keep a manhood worthy
of thee by a noble ending, and not, worn out
as they are, surrender themselves as prisoners
to the Carthaginian, I will grant the only boon
now allowed by fate and by the chain of coming
events : I will prolong the renown of their death
and send it down to posterity ; and I myself
will follow their glorious spirits to the nether
world."

Then the austere goddess sped down the light ether
and, burning with anger, made for Saguntum and
found it struggling with doom. Taking possession
of their minds and pervading their breasts, her
familiar habitation, she instilled her divine power into
their hearts. Then, piercing even to their marrow,
she filled them with a burning passion for herself.
They call for arms and put forth their feeble efforts in
battle. Strength beyond their hopes is forthcoming ;
to honour their loved goddess, and to die nobly in
her defence—this purpose comes still closer to their
hearts. An unspoken resolve fills the triumphant
hearts of the sufferers—to endure things even worse
than death, to imitate the diet of wild beasts, and
make their meals an abomination. But stainless

sed prohibet culpa pollutam extendere lucem
casta Fides paribusque famem compescere membris.

Quam simul invisae gentis conspexit in arce, 526
forte ferens sese Libycis Saturnia castris,
virgineum increpitat miscentem bella furorem
atque, ira turbata gradum, ciet ocius atram
Tisiphonen, imos agitantem verbere manes, 530
et palmas tendens : " hos," inquit, " Noctis alumna,
hos muros impelle manu populumque ferocem
dextris sterne suis ; Iuno iubet, ipsa propinqua
effectus studiumque tuum de nube videbo.
illa deos summumque Iovem turbantia tela, 535
quis Acheronta moves, flammam immanesque chely-
    dros
stridoremque tuum, quo territa comprimit ora
Cerberus, ac, mixto quae spumant felle, venena
et quicquid scelerum, poenarum quicquid et irae
pectore fecundo coquitur tibi, congere praeceps 540
in Rutulos totamque Erebo demitte Saguntum.
hac mercede Fides constet delapsa per auras."

Sic voce instimulans dextra dea concita saevam
Eumenida incussit muris ; tremuitque repente
mons circum, et gravior sonuit per litora fluctus. 545
sibilat insurgens capiti et turgentia circa
multus colla micat squalenti tergore serpens.
Mors graditur, vasto cava pandens guttura rictu,
casuroque inhiat populo : tunc Luctus et atri

---

  [a] They were willing to prolong their lives by cannibalism ;
but Loyalty forbade this.   [b] Juno.

  [c] The Furies, called Eumenides by the Greeks, were three
in number. Their names were Alecto, Megaera, and Tisi-
phone. They lived in Hades, where they tormented the
wicked spirits ; and they could also appear on earth, where
they invariably spread terror and madness.

  [d] The hound of Hades had three mouths.

Loyalty forbids them to prolong a life defiled by crime, and to stay their hunger with the flesh of fellow-creatures.[a]

It chanced that Saturn's daughter [b] was repairing to the Carthaginian camp ; and, soon as she saw the maiden, Loyalty, in the citadel of the hated people, she rebuked her eagerness to stir up war, and, stumbling in her rage, summoned at once dark Tisiphone [c] who drives with her scourge the spirits in the depths of hell. Stretching out her hands she said : " Daughter of Night, use your power to overthrow yonder walls, and lay the proud people low by their own hands. This is Juno's bidding; I myself shall keep near and watch from a cloud your handiwork and your zeal. Take up the weapons that confound the gods and even supreme Jupiter, and that make Acheron tremble—flame and hideous serpents and that hissing which belongs to you alone and makes Cerberus shut his mouths [d] for fear ; take frothing venom mixed with gall ; take all the crime and punishment and wrath that are nursed in your teeming breast, and heap them headlong upon the Rutulians,[e] and send all Saguntum down to Erebus. Let this be the price they pay for Loyalty's descent from heaven."

With these words the angry goddess spurred on the ruthless Fury, and hurled her with her own hand against the walls ; and suddenly the mountain shook all round, and the waves along the shore made a deeper sound. Upon the Fury's head and round her swollen neck a brood of scaly-backed serpents glittered and hissed. Opening wide his hollow jaws, Death stalked abroad and gaped for the doomed citizens ; and round him stood Mourning and Wailing

[e] Saguntines.

99

SILIUS ITALICUS

pectora circumstant Planctus Maerorque Dolorque,
atque omnes adsunt Poenae, formaque trifauci   551
personat insomnis lacrimosae Ianitor aulae.
protinus assimulat faciem mutabile monstrum
Tiburnae gressumque simul sonitumque loquentis.
haec bello vacuos et saevi turbine Martis   555
lugebat thalamos, Murro spoliata marito ;
clara genus Daunique trahens a sanguine nomen.
cui vultus induta pares disiectaque crinem
Eumenis in medios irrumpit turbida coetus
et maestas lacerata genas, " quis terminus ? " in-
    quit,   560
" sat Fidei proavisque datum ! vidi ipsa cruentum,
ipsa meum vidi lacerato vulnere nostras
terrentem Murrum noctes et dira sonantem :
eripe te, coniux, miserandae casibus urbis
et fuge, si terras adimit victoria Poeni,   565
ad manes, Tiburna, meos ; cecidere penates,
occidimus Rutuli, tenet omnia Punicus ensis.
mens horret, nec adhuc oculis absistit imago.
nullane iam posthac tua tecta, Sagunte, videbo ?
felix, Murre, necis patriaque superstite felix.   570
at nos, Sidoniis famulatum matribus actas,
post belli casus vastique pericula ponti
Carthago aspiciet victrix ; tandemque suprema
nocte obita, Libyae gremio captiva iacebo.
sed vos, o iuvenes, vetuit quos conscia virtus   575
posse capi, quis telum ingens contra aspera mors est,
vestris servitio manibus subducite matres.

---

   a These are often identified with the Furies.
   b Cerberus.
   c See i. 376 foll.
   d Her name, Tiburna, suggests that her ancestors came
from Tibur, the city in Latium.

100

with blackened breast and Grief and Pain ; and all the
Avengers [a] were there ; and the sleepless guardian [b]
of the dismal dwelling bayed from his triple throat.
At once the Fiend changed her shape and took the
likeness of Tiburna and her gait withal and the
sound of her voice. Tiburna, robbed of her husband,
Murrus,[c] was mourning for her marriage-bed made
empty by war and the fierce blast of battle ; she was
of noble birth and derived her name from the blood
of Daunus.[d] The Fury assumed her likeness and
then, with hair dishevelled and cheeks torn in sign of
mourning, rushed wildly into the midst of the crowd.
" How long ? " she cried. " We have done enough
for the sake of Loyalty and our forefathers ; my own
eyes have seen the bleeding form of my loved Murrus,
have seen him startling my nights with his mangled
body, and speaking fearful words : ' Save yourself,
dear wife, from the calamities of this hapless city ;
and, if the victory of the Carthaginian leaves no land
for refuge, seek safety, Tiburna, with my ghost. Our
gods are overthrown, we Rutulians are undone, the
Punic sword is master of all.' My heart quakes with
fear, and his ghost is still before my eyes. Shall I
then see the dwellings of Saguntum vanish utterly ?
Fortunate Murrus, to die and leave his country still
alive ! But as for us—we shall be carried off to wait
on the women of Carthage ; and, after the calamities
of war and the dangers of the great deep, victorious
Carthage will behold us ; and at last, when the final
darkness of death comes, I shall be laid a captive in
the lap of Libya. But you, young men, whose con-
scious valour has denied that you can ever be taken
captive, you who have in death a mighty weapon
against misfortune, rescue your mothers from slavery

ardua virtutem profert via.   pergite primi
nec facilem populis nec notam invadere laudem."
   His ubi turbatas hortatibus impulit aures,   580
inde petit tumulum, summo quem vertice montis
Amphitryoniades spectandum ex aequore nautis
struxerat et grato cineres decorarat honore.
excitus sede, horrendum ! prorumpit ab ima
caeruleus maculis auro squalentibus anguis ;   585
ignea sanguinea radiabant lumina flamma,
oraque vibranti stridebant sibila lingua ;
isque inter trepidos coetus mediamque per urbem
volvitur et muris propere delabitur altis
ac similis profugo vicina ad litora tendit   590
spumantisque freti praeceps immergitur undis.
   Tum vero excussae mentes, ceu prodita tecta
expulsi fugiant manes, umbraeque recusent
captivo iacuisse solo.   sperare saluti
pertaesum, damnantque cibos, agit abdita Erinnys.
haud gravior duris divum inclementia rebus,   596
quam leti proferre moras ; abrumpere vitam
ocius attoniti quaerunt lucemque gravantur.
certatim structus surrectae molis ad astra
in media stetit urbe rogus ; portantque trahuntque
longae pacis opes quaesitaque praemia dextris,   601
Callaico vestes distinctas matribus auro
armaque Dulichia proavis portata Zacyntho
et prisca advectos Rutulorum ex urbe penates ;

---

   [a] Hercules.
   [b] Zacynthus : see i. 276 foll.
   [c] So the spirit of Anchises appeared to Aeneas in the form
of a serpent (*Aen.* v. 84 foll.).
   [d] This snake might be supposed to be the soul of Zacynthus
who was buried on the top of the hill.
   [e] See note to i. 379.

with your swords. Steep is the path that makes virtue seen. Hasten to be the first to snatch a glory that few can attain to, a glory unknown till now ! ''

When she had stirred up her hearers' troubled minds with this appeal, next she sought the mound which Amphitryon's son[a] had built on the topmost peak of the mountain, as a sea-mark for sailors and a welcome tribute of honour to the dead.[b] Then— dreadful to behold—a snake burst forth at her summons from its abode in the depths of the mound ; its body was dark-green and rough with spots of gold ; its fiery eyes glittered with blood-red flame ; and the mouth with its flickering tongue made a loud hissing. Between the terrified groups its coils moved on through the centre of the city, and swiftly it glided down from the high walls ; then, as if escaping, it made its way to the shore near the town, and plunged headlong into the waves of the foaming sea.[c]

Then indeed men's reason tottered : it seemed that the dead were fleeing forth from abodes no longer safe, and that their ghosts refused to lie in conquered soil.[d] They were sick with disappointed hope of deliverance ; they refused food ; the disguised Fury possessed them. To postpone the date of death is as grievous as Heaven's refusal to pity their suffering ; in their frenzy they find existence a burden and long to snap the thread of life instantly. Built by many hands, a pyre whose height rose to heaven was erected in the centre of the city. Hither they dragged or carried the wealth of a long peace, the prizes won by valour, robes embroidered with Gallician gold by their matrons, weapons brought by their ancestors from Dulichian[e] Zacynthus, and the household gods that came across the sea from the

huc, quicquid superest captis, clipeosque simulque 605
infaustos iaciunt enses et condita bello
effodiunt penitus terrae gaudentque superbi
victoris praedam flammis donare supremis.

Quae postquam congesta videt feralis Erinnys,
lampada flammiferis tinctam Phlegethontis in undis
quassat et inferna superos caligine condit.   611
inde opus aggressi, toto quod nobile mundo
aeternum invictis infelix gloria servat.
princeps Tisiphone, lentum indignata parentem,
pressit ovans capulum cunctantemque impulit ensem
et dirum insonuit Stygio bis terque flagello.   616
invitas maculant cognato sanguine dextras
miranturque nefas aversa mente peractum
et facto sceleri illacrimant.   hic, turbidus ira
et rabie cladum perpessaeque ultima vitae,   620
obliquos versat materna per ubera visus ;
hic, raptam librans dilectae in colla securim
coniugis, increpitat sese mediumque furorem
proiecta damnat stupefactus membra bipenni.
nec tamen evasisse datur ; nam verbera Erinnys 625
incutit atque atros insibilat ore tumores.
sic thalami fugit omnis amor, dulcesque marito
effluxere tori, et subiere oblivia taedae.
ille iacit, totis connisus viribus, aegrum
in flammas corpus, densum qua turbine nigro   630
exundat fumum piceus caligine vertex.

---

^a Ardea.
^b One of the rivers in Hades, a river not of water but of
fire.   The other three rivers, often mentioned in Silius, are
Acheron, Cocytus, and Styx.
^c The father is trying to kill his own child.
^d He intends to kill his mother but finds it impossible to
look straight at her.

ancient city of the Rutulians.[a] They throw on the
pile all that the conquered still possess, and their
shields too and swords that could not save ; and they
dig up from the bowels of the earth hoards buried
in time of war, and with joy and pride consign the
conqueror's booty to the all-devouring flames.

When the fatal Fury saw this pile, she brandished
the torch that was dipped in the fiery waves of Phlege-
thon [b] ; and she hid the gods above with the darkness
of Hell. Then the people, ever unconquered, began
a work, which glory in defeat keeps famous for ever
throughout the world. First Tisiphone, resenting a
father's [c] half-hearted stroke, pushed the hilt forward
in triumph and drove in the reluctant sword, and
cracked her hellish scourge again and again with
hideous noise. Against their will men stain their
hands with kindred blood ; they marvel at the crime
they have committed with loathing, and weep over
the wickedness they have wrought. One man, dis-
traught with rage and the madness of disaster and
extreme suffering, turns a sidelong glance [d] at the
breast of his mother. Another, snatching an axe and
aiming it at the neck of his loved wife, reproaches
himself and curses his unfinished crime, and, as if
paralysed, throws his weapon down. Yet he is not
suffered to escape ; for the Fury repeats her blows,
and breathes black passion into him with her hissing
mouth. Thus there is an end of all wedded love :
the husband has forgotten the joys of his marriage-
bed, and remembers his bride no more. Another,
exerting all his strength, throws a suffering body
into the flames where the crest of the dark-
rolling fire sends up thick smoke and pitchy black-
ness.

At medios inter coetus pietate sinistra,
infelix Tymbrene, furis, Poenoque parentis
dum properas auferre necem, reddentia formam
ora tuam laceras temerasque simillima membra. 635
vos etiam primo gemini cecidistis in aevo,
Eurymedon fratrem et fratrem mentite Lycorma,
cuncta pares ; dulcisque labor sua nomina natis
reddere et in vultu genetrici stare suorum.
iam fixus iugulo culpa te solverat ensis, 640
Eurymedon, inter miserae lamenta senectae,
dumque malis turbata parens deceptaque visis
" quo ruis ? huc ferrum," clamat, " converte,
 Lycorma,"
ecce simul iugulum perfoderat ense Lycormas.
sed magno, " quinam, Eurymedon, furor iste ? "
 sonabat 645
cum planctu, geminaeque nota decepta figurae,
funera mutato revocabat nomine mater,
donec, transacto tremebunda per ubera ferro,
tunc etiam ambiguos cecidit super inscia natos.

Quis diros urbis casus laudandaque monstra 650
et Fidei poenas ac tristia fata piorum
imperet evolvens lacrimis ? vix Punica fletu
cessassent castra ac miserescere nescius hostis.
urbs, habitata diu Fidei caeloque parentem
murorum repetens, ruit inter perfida gentis 655
Sidoniae tela atque immania facta suorum,
iniustis neglecta deis ; furit ensis et ignis,

Again, in the midst of the crowd, ill-starred Tym-
brenus, distraught with love assuming strange dis-
guise, and eager to rob the Carthaginian of his father's
death, mutilates the features that resemble his own,
and desecrates a body that is the image of himself.
Twin brethren also, alike in every point, Eurymedon
and Lycormas, each an exact likeness of the other,
were slain there in their prime. To their mother it
had been a sweet perplexity to name her sons aright,
and to be uncertain of her own children's features.
The sword that pierced the throat of Eurymedon,
while the poor old mother lamented, had already
cleared him of guilt [a]; and while she, distraught with
sorrow and mistaking whom she saw, cried out,
"What mean you, madman? Turn your sword
against me, Lycormas," lo! Lycormas had already
stabbed himself in the throat. But she cried aloud:
"Eurymedon, what madness is this?"—and the
mother, misled by the likeness of the twins, called
back her dead sons by wrong names; at last, driving
the steel through her own quivering breast, she sank
down over the sons whom even then she could not
distinguish.

Who could command his tears when recounting
the dreadful fate of the city, the crimes that deserve
praise, the penalty paid by Loyalty, and the piteous
doom of pious souls? Even the Punic army, enemies
incapable of pity, could scarce have refrained from
weeping. A city, that was long the abode of Loyalty
and that claimed a god as the founder of her walls,
is falling now, disregarded by the injustice of Heaven,
amid the treacherous warfare of Carthaginians and
horrors committed by her own citizens; fire and
sword run riot, and any spot that is not burning is

quique caret flamma, scelerum est locus.   erigit atro
nigrantem fumo rogus alta ad sidera nubem.
ardet in excelso proceri vertice montis   660
arx, intacta prius bellis (hinc Punica castra
litoraque et totam soliti spectare Saguntum)
ardent tecta deum ; resplendet imagine flammae
aequor, et in tremulo vibrant incendia ponto.

Ecce inter medios caedum Tiburna furores,   665
fulgenti dextram mucrone armata mariti
et laeva infelix ardentem lampada quassans
squalentemque erecta comam ac liventia planctu
pectora nudatis ostendens saeva lacertis,
ad tumulum Murri super ipsa cadavera fertur.   670
qualis, ubi inferni dirum tonat aula parentis,
iraque turbatos exercet regia manes,
Alecto solium ante dei sedemque tremendam
Tartareo est operata Iovi poenasque ministrat.
arma viri, multo nuper defensa cruore,   675
imponit tumulo illacrimans ; manesque precata,
acciperent sese, flagrantem lampada subdit.
tunc rapiens letum : " tibi ego haec," ait, " optime
     coniux,
ad manes, en, ipsa fero."   sic ense recepto
arma super ruit et flammas invadit hiatu.   680
Semiambusta iacet nullo discrimine passim
infelix obitus, permixto funere, turba.
ceu, stimulante fame, cum victor ovilia tandem
faucibus invasit siccis leo, mandit hianti
ore fremens imbelle pecus, patuloque redundat   685

---

a These are names for Pluto, or Dis, the Ruler of Hades.
For Alecto, see note to l. 530.

a scene of crime. The pyre sends up aloft a sable
cloud of black smoke. On the high top of the lofty
mountain the citadel that former wars had spared
is blazing—from this point the citizens were wont to
see the Punic camp and the shore and the whole of
Saguntum,—the temples of the gods are blazing.
The sea is lit up by the reflection of the fire, and the
conflagration quivers on the restless water.

Lo! in the midst of madness and murder, unhappy
Tiburna was seen. Her right hand was armed with
her husband's bright sword, and in her left she brand-
ished a burning torch; her disordered hair stood
on end, her shoulders were bare, and she displayed
a breast discoloured by cruel blows. She hurried
right over the corpses to the tomb of Murrus. Such
seems Alecto, when the palace of the Infernal
Father *a* thunders doom, and the monarch's wrath
troubles and vexes the dead; then the Fury, standing
before the throne and terrible seat of the god, does
service to the Jupiter of Tartarus *a* and deals out
punishments. Her husband's armour, lately rescued
with much bloodshed, she placed on the mound with
tears; then she prayed to the dead to welcome her,
and applied her burning torch to the pile. Then,
rushing upon death, "Best of husbands," she cried,
"see, I myself carry this weapon to you in the shades."
And so she stabbed herself and fell down over the
armour, meeting the fire with open mouth.

Unhappy in their death, half-consumed by the fire,
without distinction or order, the bodies of the people
lay pell-mell, one upon another. Even so, when a
lion, driven by hunger, has at last prevailed and
stormed the sheepfold with parched gorge, he roars
with gaping jaws and devours the helpless sheep, and

gutture ructatus large cruor ; incubat atris
semesae stragis cumulis, aut, murmure anhelo
infrendens, laceros inter spatiatur acervos.
late fusa iacent pecudes custosque Molossus
pastorumque cohors stabulique gregisque magister,
totaque vastatis disiecta mapalia tectis.   691
irrumpunt vacuam Poeni tot cladibus arcem.
tum demum ad manes, perfecto munere, Erinnys
Iunoni laudata redit magnamque superba
exultat rapiens secum sub Tartara turbam.   695
   At vos, sidereae, quas nulla aequaverit aetas,
ite, decus terrarum, animae, venerabile vulgus,
Elysium et castas sedes decorate piorum.
cui vero non aequa dedit victoria nomen
(audite, o gentes, neu rumpite foedera pacis   700
nec regnis postferte fidem) vagus exul in orbe
errabit toto, patriis proiectus ab oris,
tergaque vertentem trepidans Carthago videbit.
saepe Saguntinis somnos exterritus umbris
optabit cecidisse manu ; ferroque negato,   705
invictus quondam Stygias bellator ad undas
deformata feret liventi membra veneno.

---

    a At the battle of Zama (202 B.C.) Hannibal was utterly
defeated by Scipio.
    b Hannibal, fearing to be given up to the Romans, escaped
from Africa in 193 B.C. and went from place to place—
Tyre, Ephesus, Crete, Bithynia. It was in Bithynia that he
swallowed poison which he carried in a ring. The year of
his death is uncertain ; but it was probably 182 B.C.

streams of blood are vomited forth from his vast
gape; he couches down on dark heaps of victims half-
devoured, or, gnashing his teeth with panting and
roaring, stalks between the piles of mangled carcasses.
Around him in confusion lie the sheep with the
Molossian dog that guarded them, and the band of
shepherds with the owner of the flock and fold ; and
their huts are utterly destroyed and their dwellings
demolished. The Carthaginians rushed into the
citadel which so many disasters had left undefended.
And then at last the Fiend, her duty done, returned,
with thanks from Juno, to the nether world, proud
and triumphant that she carried with her to Tartarus
a multitude of victims.

But you, ye star-like souls, whom no succeeding age
shall ever match—go, glory of the earth, a worship-
ful company, and adorn Elysium and the pure abodes
of the righteous. Whereas he, who gained glory
by an unjust victory—hear it, ye nations, and break
not treaties of peace nor set power above loyalty !—
banished from his native land he shall wander, an
exile, over the whole earth ; and terrified Carthage
shall see him in full retreat.[a] Often, startled in his
sleep by the ghosts of Saguntum, he shall wish that he
had fallen by his own hand ; but the steel will be
denied him, and the warrior once invincible in earlier
years shall carry down to the waters of Styx a body
disfigured and blackened by poison.[b]

LIBER TERTIUS

ARGUMENT

*After the taking of Saguntum, Bostar is sent to Africa to
consult Jupiter Ammon (1-13). Hannibal goes to Gades,
where he is shown the famous temple of Hercules and marvels
at the tides of the Atlantic (14-60). He sends his wife,
Himilce, and his infant son to Carthage (61-157). He
dreams of the coming campaign (158-213). He sets off:
a catalogue of his forces (214-405). He crosses the Pyrenees*

Postquam rupta fides Tyriis, et moenia castae,
non aequo superum genitore, eversa Sagunti,
extemplo positos finiti cardine mundi
victor adit populos cognataque limina Gades.
nec vatum mentes agitare et praescia corda   5
cessatum super imperio.   citus aequore Bostar
vela dare et rerum praenoscere fata iubetur.
prisca fides adytis longo servatur ab aevo,
qua sublime sedens, Cirrhaeis aemulus antris,
inter anhelantes Garamantas corniger Hammon   10
fatidico pandit venientia saecula luco.
hinc omen coeptis et casus scire futuros
ante diem bellique vices novisse petebat.
   Exin clavigeri veneratus numinis aras

---

   [a] A common description of Spain.
   [b] Gades (now Cadiz) was a colony from Tyre and the
chief Phoenician settlement outside the Mediterranean.
   [c] For Jupiter Ammon see note to i. 415.

112

BOOK III

AFTER the Carthaginians had broken faith, and the walls of faithful Saguntum, frowned on by the Father of Heaven, had been overthrown, the conqueror at once visited the peoples who dwell at the limit where the world ends,[a] and Gades,[b] the home of a race akin to Carthage. Nor did he omit to consult the wisdom and foresight of prophets concerning the struggle for power. Bostar was ordered to set sail at once and to inquire into the future before it came. From early times men have always trusted the shrine where horned Ammon[c] sits on high, a rival of the Delphian[d] caves, and reveals future ages in his prophetic grove among the thirsty Garamantes. From there Hannibal sought a good omen for his enterprise; he sought to know coming events before their date and to learn the changing fortunes of the war.

Thereafter he worshipped at the altars of the god

[d] See note to l. 98.

captivis onerat donis, quae nuper ab arce   15
victor fumantis rapuit semusta Sagunti.
vulgatum, nec cassa fides, ab origine fani
impositas durare trabes solasque per aevum
condentum novisse manus. hinc credere gaudent
consedisse deum seniumque repellere templis.   20
tum, quis fas et honos adyti penetralia nosse,
femineos prohibent gressus ac limine curant
saetigeros arcere sues ; nec discolor ulli
ante aras cultus ; velantur corpora lino,
et Pelusiaco praefulget stamine vertex.   25
discinctis mos tura dare atque e lege parentum
sacrificam lato vestem distinguere clavo.
pes nudus tonsaeque comae castumque cubile ;
irrestincta focis servant altaria flammae.
sed nulla effigies simulacrave nota deorum   30
maiestate locum et sacro implevere timore.
    In foribus labor Alcidae : Lernaea recisis
anguibus hydra iacet, nexuque elisa leonis
ora Cleonaei patulo caelantur hiatu.
at Stygius, saevis terrens latratibus umbras,   35
ianitor, aeterno tum primum tractus ab antro,
vincla indignatur, metuitque Megaera catenas.
iuxta Thraces equi pestisque Erymanthia et altos

---

^a The temple of Hercules at or near Gades was very
ancient, greatly venerated, and immensely wealthy. The
timber that never decayed is mentioned by other writers.
Silius gives more details about the ritual than any other
extant author.

^b The priests are meant.

^c Pelusium is a district near one mouth of the Nile.

^d Cleonae was a little town near Nemea.

^e Cerberus, whom Hercules chained and brought up from
Hades.

114

who bears the club,[a] and loaded them with offerings lately snatched by the conqueror from the fire and smoke of the citadel of Saguntum. Men said— and it was no idle tale—that the timber, of which the temple was built at first, never decayed, and for ages never felt the handiwork of any others than the first builders. Hence men take pleasure in the belief that the god has taken up his abode there and defends his temple from decay. Further, those who are per- mitted and privileged to have access to the inner shrine[b] forbid the approach of women, and are careful to keep bristly swine away from the threshold. The dress worn before the altars is the same for all : linen covers their limbs, and their foreheads are adorned with a head-band of Pelusian[c] flax. It is their custom to offer incense with robes ungirt ; and, following their fathers' rule, they adorn the garment of sacrifice with a broad stripe. Their feet are bare and their heads shaven, and their bed admits no partner ; the fires on the hearth-stones keep the altars alight perpetually. But no statues or familiar images of the gods filled the place with solemnity and sacred awe.

The doors displayed the Labours of Hercules. The Hydra of Lerna lay there with her snakes lopped off, and the strangled head of the Nemean[d] lion was carved there with jaws agape. There too the door- keeper of the Styx,[e] who terrifies the dead by his savage barking, raged at his bonds, when dragged for the first time from his everlasting cavern ; and Megaera stood by, fearing to be fettered too. Near by were the Thracian horses,[f] and the bane of Ery-

[f] The horses which Diomede, king of Thrace, fed on human flesh.

115

aeripedis ramos superantia cornua cervi.
nec levior vinci Libycae telluris alumnus   40
matre super stratique genus deforme bimembres
Centauri frontemque minor nunc amnis Acarnan.
inter quae fulget sacratis ignibus Oete,
ingentemque animam rapiunt ad sidera flammae.

Postquam oculos varia implevit virtutis imago,   45
mira dehinc cernit : surgentis mole profundi
iniectum terris subitum mare nullaque circa
litora et infuso stagnantes aequore campos.
nam qua caeruleis Nereus evolvitur antris
atque imo freta contorquet Neptunia fundo,   50
proruptum exundat pelagus, caecosque relaxans
Oceanus fontes torrentibus ingruit undis.
tum vada, ceu saevo penitus permota tridenti,
luctantur terris tumefactum imponere pontum.
mox remeat gurges tractoque relabitur aestu,   55
ac ratis erepto campis deserta profundo,
et fusi transtris expectant aequora nautae.
Cymothoës ea regna vagae pelagique labores
Luna movet, Luna, immissis per caerula bigis,
fertque refertque fretum, sequiturque reciproca
    Tethys.   60
Haec propere spectata duci ; nam multa fatigant.
curarum prima exercet, subducere bello

---

^a A wild boar that laid waste Erymanthus in Arcadia.
^b A stag (or hind) sacred to Diana, which Hercules hunted
for a whole year in Arcadia.
^c Antaeus, who gained fresh strength every time that he
touched his mother, Earth.
^d The Achelous, which lost a horn in contest with Hercules.
When ancient rivers are personified, they generally have a
bull's head and horns.
^e The mountain in Thrace on which Hercules was
cremated.

manthus,[a] and the antlers of the brazen-footed stag [b] that rose above tall trees. And the child of the Libyan land, no easy conquest when he stood upon his mother,[c] lay low, and low lay the ungainly race of Centaurs, half men and half horses, and the river of Acarnania,[d] now robbed of one horn. Amid these figures Oeta [e] shines with sacred fires, and the flames carry the hero's soul up to Heaven.

When Hannibal's eyes were sated with the picture of all that valour, he saw next a marvellous sight [f]— the sea suddenly flung upon the land with the mass of the rising deep, and no encircling shores, and the fields inundated by the invading waters. For, where Nereus rolls forth from his blue caverns and churns up the waters of Neptune from the bottom, the sea rushes forward in flood, and Ocean, opening his hidden springs, rushes on with furious waves. Then the water, as if stirred to the depths by the fierce trident,[g] strives to cover the land with the swollen sea. But soon the water turns and glides back with ebbing tide; and then the ships, robbed of the sea, are stranded, and the sailors, lying on their benches, await the waters' return. It is the Moon that stirs this realm of wandering Cymothoe [h] and troubles the deep; the Moon, driving her chariot through the sky, draws the sea this way and that, and Tethys [i] follows with ebb and flow.

Hannibal viewed these things in haste; for he had much to trouble him. His first anxiety was to remove

[f] To the Greeks and ancient Romans, accustomed only to the Mediterranean, the tides of the Atlantic Ocean, visible at Gades, were a marvellous sight.

[g] The trident is the sceptre with which Neptune rules the sea.   [h] One of the Nereids, or sea-nymphs.

[i] The wife of Oceanus and mother of the sea-nymphs.

consortem thalami parvumque sub ubere natum.
virgineis iuvenem taedis primoque Hymenaeo
imbuerat coniux memorique tenebat amore.   65
at puer, obsessae generatus in ore Sagunti,
bissenos lunae nondum compleverat orbes.
quos ut seponi stetit et secernere ab armis,
affatur ductor : " spes o Carthaginis altae,
nate, nec Aeneadum levior metus, amplior, oro,   70
sis patrio decore et factis tibi nomina condas,
quis superes bellator avum ; iamque aegra timoris
Roma tuos numerat lacrimandos matribus annos.
ni praesaga meos ludunt praecordia sensus,
ingens hic terris crescit labor ; ora parentis   75
agnosco torvaque oculos sub fronte minaces
vagitumque gravem atque irarum elementa mearum.
si quis forte deum tantos inciderit actus
et nostro abrumpat leto primordia rerum,
hoc pignus belli, coniux, servare labora.   80
cumque datum fari, duc per cunabula nostra ;
tangat Elissaeas palmis puerilibus aras
et cineri iuret patrio Laurentia bella.
inde ubi flore novo pubescet firmior aetas,
emicet in Martem et, calcato foedere, victor   85
in Capitolina tumulum mihi vindicet arce.
tu vero, tanti felix quam gloria partus
expectat, veneranda fide, discede periclis
incerti Martis durosque relinque labores.

---

[a] This tomb must have been a cenotaph.

from war the sharer of his bed and their little son, an
infant at his mother's breast. She was a maiden and
he a youth, when they first were wedded ; and she
clung to him with a love full of memories. But the
child, born in front of besieged Saguntum, had not
yet completed twelve circuits of the moon. When
he had resolved to send off mother and child and
remove them from the army, Hannibal addressed
them thus : " O my son, hope of high Carthage, and
dread, no less, of the Aeneadae, may you, I pray, be
more glorious than your father and make a name for
yourself by works of war which shall surpass your
grandsire's. Rome, sick with fear, already reckons
up your years—years that shall make mothers weep.
If my prophetic soul does not deceive my feeling,
vast suffering for the world is growing up in you ; I
recognize my father's countenance, and the defiant
eyes beneath a frowning brow ; I note the depth of
your infant cries and the beginnings of a fierceness
like my own. If haply some god shall check my
great career and nip my glory in the bud by death,
then be it your task, my wife, to keep safe this pledge
of war. And, when he is able to speak, lead him
through the scenes of my childhood : let him lay his
baby hands on the altar of Elissa, and vow to his
father's ashes that he will fight against Rome. Then,
when his riper age shall put on the down of youth, let
him rush forth to war, treading the treaty under
foot; and let him, when victorious, demand a tomb [a]
for me upon the Capitoline hill. But you, whose love
deserves my worship, you who can look forward to
the glory and happiness of so mighty a son, depart
from the dangers and uncertainty of war, and turn
away from hardship. We men must face heights

nos clausae nivibus rupes suppostaque caelo   90
saxa manent ; nos Alcidae, mirante noverca,
sudatus labor et, bellis labor acrior, Alpes.
quod si promissum vertat Fortuna favorem
laevaque sit coeptis, te longa stare senecta
aevumque extendisse velim ; tua iustior aetas,   95
ultra me improperae ducant cui fila sorores."
    Sic ille.   at contra Cirrhaei sanguis Imilce
Castalii, cui materno de nomine dicta
Castulo Phoebei servat cognomina vatis,
atque ex sacrata repetebat stirpe parentes ;   100
tempore quo Bacchus populos domitabat Hiberos,
concutiens thyrso atque armata Maenade Calpen,
lascivo genitus Satyro nymphaque Myrice,
Milichus indigenis late regnabat in oris,
cornigeram attollens genitoris imagine frontem.   105
hinc patriam clarumque genus referebat Imilce,
barbarica paulum vitiato nomine lingua.
quae tunc sic lacrimis sensim manantibus infit :
" mene, oblite tua nostram pendere salutem,
abnuis inceptis comitem ?   sic foedera nota   110
primitiaeque tori, gelidos ut scandere tecum
deficiam montes coniux tua ?   crede vigori
femineo ; castum haud superat labor ullus amorem.
sin solo aspicimur sexu, fixumque relinqui,
cedo equidem nec fata moror ; deus annuat, oro : 115

---

[a] Juno.
[b] Hannibal's wife, Imilce, was a native of Castulo, a Spanish town on the Guadalquivir. Silius derives the name of the city from a man, Castalius, a native of Delphi. Castalia is the name of the spring near Delphi. Cirrha, the port of Delphi, is often identified with Delphi itself.

barred by snow, and crags that reach the sky ; we must face the labour that brought the sweat to the brow of Alcides and made his stepmother [a] marvel ; we must face the Alps, a sharper ordeal than war. But, if Fortune withhold her promised favour and frown on my enterprise, I should wish you long life and peaceful old age ; your youth deserves that the unhasting Fates should prolong your threads beyond my span."

Thus he spoke, and Imilce answered him. She was descended from Castalius,[b] a man of Cirrha, who named his city, Castulo, after his mother, and it still keeps the name of Apollo's priest. Thus Imilce traced her pedigree to a sacred stock. When Bacchus was conquering the Spanish peoples and attacking Calpe with the staves and spears of his Maenads, Milichus was born of a lustful Satyr and the nymph Myrice, and had held wide dominion in his native land ; and horns, like those of his father, grew upon his forehead.[c] From him Imilce drew her nationality and noble blood ; but the name of Milichus had suffered a slight corruption in the native speech. Thus she then began with slowly dropping tears : " Do you forget that my life depends on yours ? Do you reject me as a partner of your enterprise ? Does our union, do our first nuptial joys, make you believe that I, your wife, would fall back when climbing with you the frozen mountains ? Doubt not a woman's hardihood ; no danger is too great for wedded love to face. But if you judge me by sex alone, and are determined to leave me, I yield indeed and will not stay the course of destiny. I pray God to bless you.

[c] Satyrs were generally represented with horns and goats' feet : they escorted Bacchus on his journeys of conquest.

i felix, i numinibus votisque secundis
atque acies inter flagrantiaque arma relictae
coniugis et nati curam servare memento.
quippe nec Ausonios tantum nec tela nec ignes,
quantum te, metuo ; ruis ipsos acer in enses   120
obiectasque caput telis ; nec te ulla secundo
eventu satiat virtus, tibi gloria soli
fine caret, credisque viris ignobile letum
belligeris in pace mori. tremor implicat artus,
nec quemquam horresco, qui se tibi conferat unus.
sed tu, bellorum genitor, miserere nefasque   126
averte et serva caput inviolabile Teucris."

    Iamque adeo egressi steterant in litore primo,
et promota ratis, pendentibus arbore nautis,
aptabat sensim pulsanti carbasa vento,   130
cum, lenire metus properans aegramque levare
attonitis mentem curis, sic Hannibal orsus :
" ominibus parce et lacrimis, fidissima coniux.
et pace et bello cunctis stat terminus aevi,
extremumque diem primus tulit ; ire per ora   135
nomen in aeternum paucis mens ignea donat,
quos pater aetheriis caelestum destinat oris.
an Romana iuga et famulas Carthaginis arces
perpetiar ? stimulant manes noctisque per umbras
increpitans genitor ; stant arae atque horrida sacra
ante oculos, brevitasque vetat mutabilis horae   141
prolatare diem. sedeamne, ut noverit una
me tantum Carthago et, qui sim, nesciat omnis

---

^a Mars.
^b Here again the Romans are called *Teucri, i.e.* Trojans.
^c See i. 99 foll.

122

Go and prosper! Go with favouring gods and prayers!
And amid the battles and the blaze of arms, remember
to keep in mind the wife and child whom you leave
behind. For I fear the Romans, with their weapons
and their firebrands, less than I fear you: you rush
fiercely right upon the swords, and expose your life
to the missiles, nor does any successful feat of arms
content you; your ambition, unlike that of other
men, knows no bounds; and you think a peaceful
death an inglorious end for a soldier. Trembling
takes hold of my limbs; and yet I dread no man
who shall meet you in single combat. But thou, O
Father of battles,[a] have pity, and turn away evil
from us, and preserve that life from all assaults of
the Trojans [b]!"

And now they had gone forth and stood upon the
shore-line. The ship, rowed forward, was slowly
trimming her sails to the wind, and the sailors dangled
from the mast, when Hannibal, eager to allay her
fears and relieve her mind, sick with frantic anxieties,
thus began: " Have done with forebodings and with
tears, my faithful wife. In war, as in peace, the end
of each man's life is fixed, and the first day leads but
to the last; few there are whom a soul of fire permits
to be for ever famous on the lips of men; and such
the Divine Father marks out to dwell in heaven.
Shall I endure the yoke of Rome, and not resent the
slavery of Carthage? I am driven on by the spirit
of my father that rebukes me in the darkness of
night; that altar and that dreadful sacrifice [c] stand
clear before my sight; and my brief and changeful
span forbids me to defer the date. Am I to sit still,
in order that Carthage alone may know my name?
And is all the world to be ignorant of my quality?

gens hominum? letique metu decora alta relinquam?
quantum etenim distant a morte silentia vitae !   145
nec tamen incautos laudum exhorresce furores ;
et nobis est lucis honos, gaudetque senecta
gloria, cum longo titulis celebratur in aevo.
te quoque magna manent suscepti praemia belli ;
dent modo se superi, Thybris tibi serviet omnis   150
Iliacaeque nurus et dives Dardanus auri.''
dumque ea permixtis inter se fletibus orant,
confisus pelago celsa de puppe magister
cunctantem ciet. abripitur divulsa marito.
haerent intenti vultus et litora servant,   155
donec, iter liquidum voluci rapiente carina,
consumpsit visus pontus, tellusque recessit.
    At Poenus belli curis avertere amorem
apparat et repetit properato moenia gressu.
quae dum perlustrat crebroque obit omnia visu,   160
tandem sollicito cessit vis dura labori,
belligeramque datur somno componere mentem.
    Tum pater omnipotens, gentem exercere periclis
Dardaniam et fama saevorum tollere ad astra
bellorum meditans priscosque referre labores,   165
praecipitat consulta viri segnemque quietem
terret et immissa rumpit formidine somnos.
iamque per humentem noctis Cyllenius umbram
aligero lapsu portabat iussa parentis.
nec mora : mulcentem securo membra sopore   170
aggreditur iuvenem ac monitis incessit amaris :
'' turpe duci totam somno consumere noctem,
o rector Libyae : vigili stant bella magistro.

ᵃ See note to i. 14.
ᵇ The siege of Troy.
ᶜ Mercury, the messenger of the gods, was born on Cyllene,
a mountain of Arcadia.

Am I, from fear of death, to abandon the heights of glory ? How little does an obscure life differ from death ! Yet fear not rashness in my ardour for renown : I too value life, and the hero finds pleasure in old age, when he is famed for great deeds in the autumn of life. You too may look for great rewards from the war now begun : if only Heaven favours us, all Tiber and the Roman women and the Dardans,[a] rich in gold, shall be at your feet." While they conversed together thus and mingled their tears, the steersman, feeling that he could trust the sea, hailed the unwilling wife from his high seat on the stern. Torn from her husband's arms she is carried away. Her eager eyes still cling to him and watch the shore, until the sea made sight impossible and the land fell back, as the swift ship sped on its watery way.

But Hannibal sought to drown his love in the business of war : he went back quickly to the walls of Gades ; and, while he went round them and surveyed every part again and again, the ceaseless toil proved too much at last for that strong heart, and he was able to rest his warlike mind in sleep.

Then the Almighty Father, purposing to test the Roman people by peril, to raise their fame to heaven by victory in fierce warfare, and to repeat their ancient ordeal,[b] urged on Hannibal's design by breaking his peaceful rest and sending terrors to disturb his sleep. Quickly the god of Cyllene,[c] flying through the dewy darkness of the night, carried the message of his sire. At once he accosted Hannibal, where he lay at ease in untroubled sleep, and upbraided him with sharp reproof : " Ruler of Libya, it becomes not a leader to pass the whole night in slumber : war prospers when the commander wakes. You will see

iam maria effusas cernes turbare carinas
et Latiam toto pubem volitare profundo,   175
dum lentus coepti terra cunctaris Hibera.
scilicet, id satis est decoris memorandaque virtus,
quod tanto cecidit molimine Graia Saguntos ?
en age, si quid inest animo par fortibus ausis,
fer gressus agiles mecum et comitare vocantem ; 180
respexisse veto (monet hoc pater ille deorum) ;
victorem ante altae statuam te moenia Romae.''

Iamque videbatur dextram iniectare graduque
laetantem trahere in Saturnia regna citato,
cum subitus circa fragor et vibrata per auras   185
exterrent saevis a tergo sibila linguis ;
ingentique metu divum praecepta paventi
effluxere viro, et turbatus lumina flectit.
ecce iugis rapiens silvas ac robora vasto
contorta amplexu tractasque per invia rupes,   190
ater letifero stridebat turbine serpens.
quantus non aequas perlustrat flexibus Arctos,
et geminum lapsu sidus circumligat Anguis,
immani tantus fauces diducit hiatu
attollensque caput nimbosis montibus aequat.   195
congeminat sonitus rupti violentia caeli
imbriferamque hiemem permixta grandine torquet.
hoc trepidus monstro (neque enim sopor ille nec altae
vis aderat noctis, virgaque fugante tenebras
miscuerat lucem somno deus) ardua quae sit,   200
scitatur pestis terrasque urgentia membra
quo ferat et quosnam populos deposcat hiatu.

---

^a The epithet implies that Greeks are not really formidable
opponents—a view generally held by the Romans.

^b Italy : see note to i. 70.

^c Mercury carried a magic wand, the *caduceus*, with which
he could send mortals to sleep or wake them from sleep.

ships swarm forth ere long to plough the sea, and
Roman warriors speeding all over the deep, while you,
slow to begin, stand idle in the land of Spain. Is it
glory enough for you, and a memorable feat of arms,
to have overthrown Greek [a] Saguntum with so great
an effort? Arise! and if aught in your heart is
capable of bold action, then go quickly along with
me and accompany my summons (I forbid you to
look back: such is the command of Jupiter) and I
will set you victorious before the lofty walls of
Rome."

And now he dreamed that Mercury laid a hand upon
him and drew him in joy and haste to the land of
Saturn,[b] when he was startled by a sudden noise about
him and a hissing of fierce tongues behind him that
hurtled through the sky. Stricken with intense fear,
he forgot the divine command, and looked behind
him in his dismay. Behold! a black serpent, sweep-
ing along in its huge embrace woods, and forest-trees
torn from the hills, and rocks dragged along a path-
less track, was hissing with deadly blast. Huge as
the Serpent which moves with its coils round the
Great and Little Bear and encompasses both con-
stellations in its course, so huge it parts its jaws with
cavernous yawn, and raises its crest to the height of
rain-swept mountains. And the fury of the bursting
heavens redoubled the noise and discharged a storm
of rain mixed with hail. Terrified by this portent
(for his sleep was not real sleep, and the power of
night was waning, because the god whose rod dispels
darkness [c] had mingled night with day) Hannibal
asked what this terrible monster was, and whither it
was bearing that body which weighed down the
earth, and what nations were demanded by its open

cui gelidis almae Cyllenes editus antris :
" bella vides optata tibi. te maxima bella,
te strages nemorum, te moto turbida caelo   205
tempestas caedesque virum magnaeque ruinae
Idaei generis lacrimosaque fata secuntur.
quantus per campos populatis montibus actas
contorquet silvas squalenti tergore serpens
et late humectat terras spumante veneno,   210
tantus, perdomitis decurrens Alpibus, atro
involves bello Italiam tantoque fragore
eruta convulsis prosternes oppida muris."
    His aegrum stimulis liquere deusque soporque.
it membris gelidus sudor, laetoque pavore   215
promissa evolvit somni noctemque retractat.
iamque deum regi Martique sub omine fausto
instauratus honos ; niveoque ante omnia tauro
placatus meritis monitor Cyllenius aris.
extemplo edicit convellere signa, repensque   220
castra quatit clamor permixtis dissona linguis.
    Prodite, Calliope, famae, quos horrida coepta
excierint populos tulerintque in regna Latini,
et quas indomitis urbes armarit Hiberis
quasque Paraetonio glomerarit litore turmas   225
ausa sibi Libye rerum deposcere frenos
et terris mutare iugum. non ulla nec umquam
saevior it trucibus tempestas acta procellis ;

---

    [a] The mountain gets this epithet because it was the scene
of his birth and might be called his nurse.
    [i] The Romans : Ida is a mountain near Troy.
    [c] Sacrifices are meant.
    [d] The shafts of ancient standards ended in a metal point
which was driven into the ground when the army halted.
    [e] Paraetonian, more properly Egyptian, is used loosely for
African : cp. v. 356.

jaws. The god who was born in the cold caverns of fostering *a* Cyllene made reply : " You see the war you have prayed for : mighty wars follow in your train, and falling forests, and fierce storms in an angry sky, and slaughter of men, with mighty destruction and doleful doom to the people of Ida.*b* All this is your doing. As that huge serpent with scaly hide laid waste the mountains and hurled the uprooted forests over the plains and wetted the whole earth with its foaming slaver, so you, as huge, will rush down from the conquered Alps and wrap Italy in a black cloud of war ; and with a noise like the serpent's you will shatter the walls of towns and root out cities and dash them to the ground."

The god and slumber then left him, disturbed by these incitements. A cold sweat broke out on his body, while he turned over the promises of the dream with a fearful joy and reviewed the night once more. Soon was honour *c* paid to the King of Heaven and Mars, because of the favourable omen ; and first of all the god of Cyllene, in reward for his counsel, was propitiated with the sacrifice of a snow-white bull. At once Hannibal ordered that the standards should be plucked up,*d* and a sudden shout shook the camp filled with a babel of discordant tongues.

Hand down to fame, Calliope, the peoples summoned forth by this fell enterprise and borne against the realm of Latinus ! Name the cities of warlike Spaniards whom Carthage armed, and the squadrons that she mustered on the shore of Africa,*e* when she dared to claim for herself the reins of government, and to give a new ruler to mankind. Never at any time did a fiercer tempest rage, driven on by furious

nec bellum raptis tam dirum mille carinis
acrius infremuit trepidumque exterruit orbem.   230
  Princeps signa tulit Tyria Carthagine pubes,
membra levis celsique decus fraudata superbum
corporis, at docilis fallendi et nectere tectos
numquam tarda dolos. rudis his tum parma, brevique
bellabant ense ; at vestigia nuda, sinusque   235
cingere inassuetum, et rubrae velamine vestis
ars erat in pugna fusum occuluisse cruorem.
his rector fulgens ostro super altior omnes
germanus nitet Hannibalis gratoque tumultu
Mago quatit currus et fratrem spirat in armis.   240
  Proxima Sidoniis Utica est effusa maniplis,
prisca situ veterisque ante arces condita Byrsae.
tunc, quae Sicanio praecinxit litora muro,
in clipei speciem curvatis turribus, Aspis.
sed dux in sese converterat ora Sychaeus,   245
Hasdrubalis proles, cui vano corda tumore
maternum implebat genus, et resonare superbo
Hannibal haud umquam cessabat avunculus ore.
  Affuit undosa cretus Berenicide miles,
nec, tereti dextras in pugnam armata dolone,   250
destituit Barce sitientibus arida venis.
nec non Cyrene Pelopei stirpe nepotis
Battiadas pravos fidei stimulavit in arma.

---

  [a] The war in which Agamemnon launched a thousand
ships against Troy.
  [b] Utica, a colony of Tyre, was said to have been founded
287 years earlier than Carthage.
  [c] See note to ii. 363.
  [d] Aspis, called Clypea by the Romans (both names mean
"Shield"), was fortified by Agathocles, tyrant of Syracuse,
in 310 B.C., when he was making war against Carthage.
The city was shaped like a shield.
  [e] The mother of Sychaeus was Hannibal's sister.

winds; not even that dreadful war[a] that swept along a thousand ships raged with more violence or appalled more utterly a terror-stricken world.

Foremost in the ranks were the soldiers from Tyrian Carthage. Light of limb were they, and the glory of lofty stature was denied them; but they were readily taught to deceive, and never slow to lay secret traps for the enemy. They carried then a primitive shield, and fought with a short sword; their feet were bare, nor was it their custom to wear a belt; their dress was red, and they had skill to hide under its covering the blood shed in battle. Their leader was Mago, Hannibal's brother, and his purple-clad figure over-topped them all while he drove his chariot along, rejoicing in its clattering noise and bold as his brother in the fray.

Next to the men of Carthage, Utica poured forth her people—Utica hoary with age,[b] that was founded before the citadel of ancient Byrsa.[c] Next came Aspis,[d] which borders the sea with a wall built by the Sicilian, and whose ramparts form a crescent in the shape of a shield. But all eyes were turned upon their leader, Sychaeus, a son of Hasdrubal, who was filled with vainglory on the score of his mother's blood[e]; and the name of his uncle, Hannibal, came ever proudly from his lips.

The warlike sons of Berenicis by the sea were present; nor was Barce backward, a dry land of thirsty springs, whose men are armed for battle with long smooth pikes; and Cyrene too roused to arms the sons of Battus,[f] treacherous men, descendants from a

---

[f] Cyrene, a Greek settlement in Africa, was founded in 631 B.C. by Battus and a body of Dorian colonists. Why this people is called treacherous is not known.

quos trahit, antiquo laudatus Hamilcare quondam,
consilio viridis sed belli serus Ilertes.   255
  Sabratha tum Tyrium vulgus Sarranaque Leptis
Oeaque Trinacrios Afris permixta colonos
et Tingim rapido mittebat ab aequore Lixus.
tum Vaga et antiquis dilectus regibus Hippo,
quaeque procul cavit non aequos Ruspina fluctus,   260
et Zama et uberior Rutulo nunc sanguine Thapsus.
ducit tot populos, ingens et corpore et armis,
Herculeam factis servans ac nomine famam,
Antaeus celsumque caput super agmina tollit.
  Venere Aethiopes, gens haud incognita Nilo,   265
qui magneta secant ; solis honor ille, metalli
intactum chalybem vicino ducere saxo.
his simul, immitem testantes corpore solem,
exusti venere Nubae.   non aerea cassis
nec lorica riget ferro, non tenditur arcus ;   270
tempora multiplici mos est defendere lino
et lino munire latus scelerataque sucis
spicula dirigere et ferrum infamare veneno.
tum primum castris Phoenicum tendere ritu
Cinyphii didicere Macae ; squalentia barba   275
ora viris, humerosque tegunt velamine capri
saetigero ; panda manus est armata cateia.
versicolor contra caetra et falcatus ab arte
ensis Adyrmachidis ac laevo tegmina crure.
sed mensis asper populus victuque maligno ;   280

---

  [a] Sarra is an ancient name of Tyre. The reader would do
well to consult an Ancient Atlas for these places.
  [b] Thapsus was the scene of Caesar's defeat of the Pom-
peians (46 B.C.).
  [c] It is implied that Antaeus was descended from the giant
of that name conquered by Hercules : see l. 40.

Peloponnesian stock. They were led by Ilertes, whom old Hamilcar praised long ago, active still in council but slow in war.

Then Sabratha and Phoenician[a] Leptis sent their Tyrian folk, and Oea sent Sicilian colonists mixed with Africans, and the river Lixus sent the men of Tingis from the stormy shore. Next came Vaga, and Hippo dear to kings of old, and Ruspina, which guards herself by distance against sea-floods; and, with Zama, Thapsus, now made more fertile by Roman blood.[b] All these peoples were led by Antaeus, a giant in giant armour; by his deeds as by his name he kept alive the fame of Hercules,[c] and towered above the heads of his soldiers.

The Ethiopians came, a race whom the Nile knows well, who dig the loadstone from the earth; they alone have the power to attract the iron of the mine without the use of tools by placing the stone beside it. Together with them came the burnt-up Nubae, whose bodies show the fierce heat of their sun; they wear no helmet of brass nor tough cuirass of steel; nor do they bend the bow. It is their custom to protect their heads with many folds of linen, and with linen to cover their bodies, and to throw javelins steeped in noxious juices, thus disgracing the steel with poison. Then first the Macae, from the river Cinyps, learned how to pitch tents in their camp in Phoenician fashion—shaggy bearded men, whose backs are covered with the bristling hide of a wild goat, and the weapon they carry is a curved javelin. But the Adyrmachidae bear a target of many colours, and a sword fashioned by the smith in the shape of a sickle, and wear greaves on the left leg. Rough was this people's fare, and scanty their diet; for their

nam calida tristes epulae torrentur harena.
quin et Massyli fulgentia signa tulere,
Hesperidum veniens lucis domus ultima terrae.
praefuit, intortos demissus vertice crines,
Bocchus atrox, qui sacratas in litore silvas   285
atque inter frondes revirescere viderat aurum.

   Vos quoque desertis in castra mapalibus itis,
misceri gregibus Gaetulia sueta ferarum
indomitisque loqui et sedare leonibus iras.
nulla domus ; plaustris habitant ; migrare per arva
mos atque errantes circumvectare penates.   291
hinc mille alipedes turmae (velocior Euris
et doctus virgae sonipes) in castra ruebant.
ceu pernix cum densa vagis latratibus implet
venator dumeta Lacon, aut exigit Umber   295
nare sagax e calle feras, perterrita late
agmina praecipitant volucres formidine cervi.
hos agit haud laeto vultu nec fronte serena,
Asbytes nuper caesae germanus, Acherras.

   Marmaridae, medicum vulgus, strepuere catervis ;
ad quorum cantus serpens oblita veneni,   301
ad quorum tactum mites iacuere cerastae.
tum, chalybis pauper, Baniurae cruda iuventus,
contenti parca durasse hastilia flamma,
miscebant avidi trucibus fera murmura linguis.   305

---

  [a] The Massyli were the most powerful of the tribes which
occupied Numidia (now Algeria).   Bocchus, their leader, had
seen the Golden Apples in the garden of the Hesperides, which
legend placed in the far North-west of Africa.

sorry meals are roasted on the burning sand. The Massyli [a] also brought thither their glittering standards, the most remote inhabitants of earth, coming from the groves of the Hesperides. Fierce Bocchus was their leader; from his head the hair fell down in close curls; and he had seen the sacred trees beside the sea, and the glittering gold among the green leaves.

The Gaetulians also, who are wont to live among packs of wild beasts, and by their speech to allay the fierceness of untamed lions, left their settlements for the camp of Hannibal. Houseless men, they dwell in wagons; their custom is to stray from place to place and to carry with them their moving household gods. Of these a thousand wing-footed squadrons came speeding to the camp; their horses are swifter than the wind and taught to obey the switch.[b] So, when the speedy Spartan dog fills the thickets with his roving bark, or the Umbrian hound by his keen scent drives wild beasts forth from a mountain path, the flying deer in their terror rush headlong in their herds far and wide. Acherras led the Gaetulians; but his face was not joyful, nor his brow serene; for he was the brother of Asbyte [c] so lately slain.

Then came the Marmaridae with a sound of clashing arms, a people of magical powers, at whose spells the snake forgot its poison, and at whose touch horned serpents lay still and harmless. Next came the hardy warriors of Baniura; having little iron they are content to harden their spear-points over a scanty flame; eager for battle they uttered wild cries

[b] Their horses had no bridles: cp. i. 215 foll.
[c] See ii. 56 foll.

necnon Autololes, levibus gens ignea plantis ;
cui sonipes cursu, cui cesserit incitus amnis,
tanta fuga est ; certant pennae, campumque volatu
cum rapuere, pedum frustra vestigia quaeras.
spectati castris, quos suco nobilis arbor   310
et dulci pascit lotos nimis hospita baca.
quique atro rabidas effervescente veneno
dipsadas immensis horrent Garamantes harenis.
fama docet, caesae rapuit cum Gorgonis ora
Perseus, in Libyam dirum fluxisse cruorem ;   315
inde Medusaeis terram exundasse chelydris.
milibus his ductor spectatus Marte Choaspes,
Neritia Meninge satus, cui tragula semper
fulmineam armabat, celebratum missile, dextram.
huc coit aequoreus Nasamon, invadere fluctu   320
audax naufragia et praedas avellere ponto ;
huc, qui stagna colunt Tritonidos alta paludis,
qua virgo, ut fama est, bellatrix edita lympha
invento primam Libyen perfudit olivo.

  Necnon totus adest vesper populique reposti.   325
Cantaber ante omnes, hiemisque aestusque famisque
invictus palmamque ex omni ferre labore.
mirus amor populo, cum pigra incanuit aetas,
imbelles iam dudum annos praevertere fato

---

  [a] The companions of Ulysses, after eating the fruit of the
lotus, lost all desire to return home to Ithaca.
  [b] The Gorgon, Medusa, had snakes for hair.
  [c] For the adj. " Neritian " see note to ii. 317.
  [d] Pallas Athene : when she sprang from the head of her
father, Jupiter, she alighted first in Africa, near Lake
Tritonis.   The olive was her tree, and she introduced it first
into Africa.

together with fierce speech. The Autololes also came, a fiery race of nimble runners : no horse nor flooded river could match their pace, so great their speed. They vie with the birds ; and, when they have scoured the plain in their flight, you would look in vain for their footprints. There were seen also in the army the people who feed on the tree famous for its juices—on the sweet berries of the lotus, too friendly to the stranger.[a] The Garamantes were there, who dread the furious serpents that pour out black venom in their boundless deserts. Legend tells that, when Perseus slew the Gorgon and carried off her head, the horrid gore dripped over Libya, and from that time the land has abounded with the snakes of Medusa.[b] These thousands were led by Choaspes, a proved warrior, native of Meninx, an Ithacan[c] island ; his right arm, swift as the lightning, ever bore a javelin, his renowned weapon. Hither came the Nasamones from the sea, men who fear not to attack wrecked ships upon the water, and to snatch their booty from the deep ; and hither came the dwellers by the deep pools of Lake Tritonis, where the Maiden Warrior sprang, as legend tells, from the water and anointed Libya, before other lands, with the olive-oil which she herself had discovered.[d]

Moreover, all the West[e] with its remote nations was present too. First of all were the Cantabrians, proof against cold and heat and hunger, and victorious over every hardship. This people, when disabled by white old age, find a strange pleasure in cutting short the years of weakness by an instant death, and they

[e] The West stands for Spain : Spanish soldiers formed the backbone of Hannibal's armies.

nec vitam sine Marte pati : quippe omnis in armis 330
lucis causa sita, et damnatum vivere paci.
    Venit et, Aurorae lacrimis perfusus, in orbem
diversum, patrias fugit cum devius oras,
armiger Eoi non felix Memnonis Astyr.
his parvus sonipes nec Marti notus ; at idem 335
aut inconcusso glomerat vestigia dorso,
aut molli pacata celer rapit esseda collo.
Cydnus agit, iuga Pyrenes venatibus acer
metiri iaculove extendere proelia Mauro.
    Venere et Celtae sociati nomen Hiberis. 340
his pugna cecidisse decus, corpusque cremari
tale nefas : caelo credunt superisque referri,
impastus carpat si membra iacentia vultur.
    Fibrarum et pennae divinarumque sagacem
flammarum misit dives Callaecia pubem, 345
barbara nunc patriis ululantem carmina linguis,
nunc, pedis alterno percussa verbere terra,
ad numerum resonas gaudentem plaudere caetras.
haec requies ludusque viris, ea sacra voluptas.
cetera femineus peragit labor ; addere sulco 350
semina et impresso tellurem vertere aratro,
segne viris.   quicquid duro sine Marte gerundum,
Callaici coniux obit irrequieta mariti.
hos Viriathus agit Lusitanumque remotis
extractum lustris, primo Viriathus in aevo, 355
nomen Romanis factum mox nobile damnis.

---

   [a] The Astures inhabited Asturia in Spain.   Silius derives
their name from Astyr, the charioteer of Memnon.   When
Achilles slew Memnon before Troy, his mother, Aurora, shed
tears.
   [b] They were called *Celtiberi.*   [c] Portuguese.
   [d] The allusion is to a later Viriathus, who for fourteen
years fought a guerilla warfare against Rome for the
freedom of his country, and fell by treachery in 142 B.C.

refuse life except in arms. For war is their only reason for living, and they scorn a peaceful existence.

Then Astyr,[a] the ill-starred squire of Eastern Memnon, came; wetted by Aurora's tears, he had fled far from his native land to the opposite quarter of the world. The horses of the Astyrians are small and not notable in battle; yet they amble without shaking their rider, or with docile neck can draw a carriage with speed in time of peace. They were led by Cydnus, eager to scour the heights of the Pyrenees in the chase, or to fight from a distance with Moorish javelin.

The Celts who have added to their name that of the Hiberi [b] came also. To these men death in battle is glorious; and they consider it a crime to burn the body of such a warrior; for they believe that the soul goes up to the gods in heaven, if the body is devoured on the field by the hungry vulture.

Rich Gallicia sent her people, men who have knowledge concerning the entrails of beasts, the flight of birds, and the lightnings of heaven; they delight, at one time, to chant the rude songs of their native tongue, at another to stamp the ground in the dance and clash their noisy shields in time to the music. Such is the relaxation and sport of the men, and such their solemn rejoicings. All other labour is done by the women: the men think it unmanly to throw seed into the furrow and turn the soil by pressure of the plough; but the wife of the Gallician is never still and performs every task but that of stern war. These men, and the Lusitanians [c] drawn forth from their distant forests, were led by the young Viriathus —Viriathus, whose name was to win fame from Roman disasters at a later day.[d]

Nec Cerretani, quondam Tirynthia castra,
aut Vasco, insuetus galeae, ferre arma morati.
non, quae Dardanios post vidit, Ilerda, furores,
nec qui, Massageten monstrans feritate parentem, 360
cornipedis fusa satiaris, Concane, vena.
iamque Ebusus Phoenissa movet, movet Arbacus
    arma,
aclyde vel tenui pugnax instare veruto ;
iam cui Tlepolemus sator et cui Lindus origo,
funda bella ferens Baliaris et alite plumbo ;   365
et quos nunc Gravios violato nomine Graium
Oeneae misere domus Aetolaque Tyde.
dat Carthago viros, Teucro fundata vetusto,
Phocaïcae dant Emporiae, dat Tarraco pubem
vitifera et Latio tantum cessura Lyaeo.   370
hos inter clara thoracis luce nitebat
Sedetana cohors, quam Sucro rigentibus undis
atque altrix celsa mittebat Saetabis arce—
Saetabis et telas Arabum sprevisse superba
et Pelusiaco filum componere lino.   375
Mandonius populis domitorque insignis equorum
imperitat Caeso, et socio stant castra labore.
    At Vettonum alas Balarus probat aequore aperto.
hic adeo, cum ver placidum flatusque tepescit,
concubitus servans tacitos, grex perstat equarum   380

---

   a Ilerda in Spain was the scene of fighting between
Pompey's army and Caesar in 49 B.C.
   b The Massagetae were a Scythian tribe : other writers
attribute to them this practice, of bleeding their horses to get
a meal for themselves.
   c An island to the south of Spain.
   d Lindus is one of the three cities founded in Rhodes by
Tlepolemus, a son of Hercules and king of Argos.

140

The Cerretani, who once fought for Hercules, were
not slow now to bear arms ; nor the Vascones, un-
used to wear helmets ; nor Ilerda, that witnessed later
the madness of Romans [a] ; nor the Concanian, who
proves by his savagery his descent from the Massa-
getae, when he opens a vein of his horse to fill his own
belly.[b] Now Phoenician Ebusus [c] rises in arms ; and
the Arbacians, fierce fighters with the dart or slender
javelin ; and the Balearic islanders, whose sire was
Tlepolemus and Lindus [d] their native land, waging
war with the sling and flying bullet ; and the men
sent forth by the town of Oene and Aetolian Tyde,[e]
called Gravii by corruption of Graii, their former
name. Carthago,[f] founded by Teucer of old, supplied
men ; and also Emporiae, colony of Massilia, and
Tarraco, the land of vines, which allows precedence to
no vintage but that of Latium. Conspicuous among
these by the sheen of their cuirasses were the Sede-
tanian soldiers, who came from the icy waters of
the Sucro and the lofty citadel of their mother city,
Saetabis—Saetabis which dares to despise the
looms of the Arabs and to match her webs against
the linen of Egypt. These peoples were com-
manded by Mandonius and by Caeso, famous tamer
of horses ; and their joint exertions kept the host
together.

The squadrons of the Vettones were reviewed on
the open plain by Balarus. In that country, when
spring is mild and airs are warm, the drove of mares
stand still, mating in secret, and conceive a mysterious

[e] Diomedes, king of Aetolia, after leaving Troy, visited
Spain and there founded Tyde, in honour of his father,
Tydeus.
[f] Usually called New Carthage.

et Venerem occultam genitali concipit aura.
sed non multa dies generi, properatque senectus,
septimaque his stabulis longissima ducitur aestas.

   At non Sarmaticos attollens Uxama muros
tam levibus persultat equis ; hinc venit in arma   385
haud aevi fragilis sonipes crudoque vigore
asper frena pati aut iussis parere magistris.
Rhyndacus his ductor, telum sparus ; ore ferarum
et rictu horrificant galeas ; venatibus aevum
transigitur, vel more patrum vis raptaque pascunt. 390

   Fulget praecipuis Parnasia Castulo signis
et celebre Oceano atque alternis aestibus Hispal
ac Nebrissa dei Nysaeis conscia thyrsis,
quam Satyri coluere leves redimitaque sacra
nebride et arcano Maenas nocturna Lyaeo.   395
Arganthoniacos armat Carteia nepotes.
rex proavis fuit humani ditissimus aevi,
ter denos decies emensus belliger annos.
armat Tartessos, stabulanti conscia Phoebo,
et Munda, Emathios Italis paritura labores.   400
nec decus auriferae cessavit Corduba terrae.
hos duxere viros flaventi vertice Phorcys
spiciferisque gravis bellator Arauricus oris,

---

   [a] This fable of mares made pregnant by the wind is found
in Virgil (*Georg.* iii. 271): it was a way of accounting for
the speed of their progeny : see xvi. 364.
   [b] The connexion between Sarmatia (Poland) and the
Spanish town of Uxama is not elsewhere mentioned.
   [c] See note to l. 98.
   [d] Now Seville, near the mouth of the Guadalquivir : the
estuary rises and falls with the tide.

progeny begotten by the wind.[a] But their stock is short-lived: old age comes quick upon them, and the life of these horses lasts but seven years at the longest.

Less nimble on their feet are the horses from Uxama, a city whose walls are Sarmatian [b]; but her steeds that came to war were tenacious of life; their lusty youth found it hard to endure the bit or obey the commands of the rider. These men were led by Rhyndacus and armed with spears; they add terror to their helmets by decking them with the open jaws of wild beasts; they pass their lives in hunting, or support themselves, as their fathers did, by violence and rapine.

Bright beyond the rest shone the ensigns of Delphian Castulo [c]; and of Hispalis,[d] famous for commerce and for the ebb and flow of its tides; and of Nebrissa which knows the thyrsi of the Nysaean god [e] —Nebrissa haunted by nimble Satyrs and nightly Maenads, who wear the sacred fawn-skin and the mystic vine-leaf. Carteia sent to war the children of Arganthonius; king over their ancestors, he surpassed all mankind in length of days and waged war for the space of three hundred years. Tartessus, that sees the sun to rest, sprang to arms; and likewise Munda,[f] doomed to produce for Italy the suffering of Pharsalia; nor did Corduba hang back, the pride of a land rich in gold. These men were led by fair-haired Phorcys and by Arauricus whose arms were terrible to the corn-bearing lands; the two were of

---

[e] Bacchus, said to have been born at Nysa: Silius connects the name of the town with *nebris*, " a fawn-skin."

[f] At Munda Caesar defeated Pompey's sons (45 B.C.). The site of the battle of Pharsalia is often called Emathia.

aequales aevi ; genuit quos ubere ripa
Palladio Baetis umbratus cornua ramo.   405
   Talia Sidonius per campos agmina ductor
pulvere nigrantes raptat lustransque sub armis,
qua visu comprendere erat, fulgentia signa
ibat ovans longaque umbram tellure trahebat.
non aliter, quotiens perlabitur aequora curru   410
extremamque petit, Phoebea cubilia, Tethyn
frenatis Neptunus equis, fluit omnis ab antris
Nereidum chorus et sueto certamine nandi
candida perspicuo convertunt brachia ponto.
   At Pyrenaei frondosa cacumina montis   415
turbata Poenus terrarum pace petebat.
Pyrene celsa nimbosi verticis arce
divisos Celtis late prospectat Hiberos
atque aeterna tenet magnis divortia terris.
nomen Bebrycia duxere a virgine colles,   420
hospitis Alcidae crimen, qui, sorte laborum
Geryonae peteret cum longa tricorporis arva,
possessus Baccho saeva Bebrycis in aula
lugendam formae sine virginitate reliquit
Pyrenen, letique deus, si credere fas est,   425
causa fuit leti miserae deus.   edidit alvo
namque ut serpentem patriasque exhorruit iras,
confestim dulces liquit turbata penates.
tum noctem Alcidae solis plangebat in antris
et promissa viri silvis narrabat opacis,   430
donec maerentem ingratos raptoris amores

---

   [a] The olive-trees for which Corduba was famous.
   [b] Hannibal.   [c] Caused by the dust.
   [d] See note to i. 271.
   [e] King of the Bebryces, an Iberian people living on both sides of the Pyrenees.   Another people of the same name lived near the Black Sea.

equal age, and were born on the fertile banks where
the Baetis shelters his horns under the branches of
the tree of Pallas.[a]

Such was the host which the Carthaginian captain[b]
led on at speed over the dust-darkened plains; he
reviewed their glittering ensigns in the field, as far
as the eye could see, and rode on in triumph, leaving
a shadow[c] on all the land he traversed. Even so,
when Neptune glides over the deep in his chariot and
drives his bitted coursers to the outermost Ocean
where the sun sinks to rest, all the train of Nereids
issue from their caves and, as is their wont, swim in
rivalry, tossing their white arms in the transparent
water.

But now Hannibal, throwing a peaceful world into
confusion, made for the leafy summits of the Pyrenees.
From the eminence of their rain-swept peaks
they command a wide prospect and divide Spain
from Gaul, making an eternal barrier between two
great countries. These mountains took their name
from Pyrene, daughter of Bebryx and victim of Her-
cules. For Hercules, in the course of his appointed
Labours, was travelling to the distant land of three-
bodied Geryon,[d] when he was mastered by wine in
the savage court of Bebryx,[e] and left Pyrene robbed
of her maidenhood; her beauty was a cause for
mourning. The god (if it is not sinful to believe it),
the god was the cause of the poor maiden's death.
For when she gave birth to a serpent she fled at once
from the home she loved, in horror and dread of her
father's wrath. Then in lonely caves she mourned
for the night when she lay with Alcides, and told
his promises to the dark forests; till at last, as
she mourned the ingratitude of her ravisher, and

tendentemque manus atque hospitis arma vocantem
diripuere ferae.   laceros Tirynthius artus,
dum remeat victor, lacrimis perfudit et amens
palluit invento dilectae virginis ore.   435
at voce Herculea percussa cacumina montis
intremuere iugis ; maesto clamore ciebat
Pyrenen, scopulique omnes ac lustra ferarum
Pyrenen resonant.   tumulo tum membra reponit,
supremum illacrimans; nec honos intercidet aevo, 440
defletumque tenent montes per saecula nomen.

Iamque per et colles et densos abiete lucos
Bebryciae Poenus fines transcenderat aulae.
inde ferox quaesitum armis per inhospita rura
Volcarum populatur iter tumidique minaces   445
accedit Rhodani festino milite ripas.
aggeribus caput Alpinis et rupe nivali
proserit in Celtas ingentemque extrahit amnem
spumanti Rhodanus proscindens gurgite campos
ac propere in pontum lato ruit incitus alveo.   450
auget opes stanti similis tacitoque liquore
mixtus Arar, quem gurgitibus complexus anhelis
cunctantem immergit pelago raptumque per arva
ferre vetat patrium vicina ad litora nomen.
invadunt alacres inimicum pontibus amnem ;   455
nunc celso capite et cervicibus arma tuentur,
nunc validis gurges certatim frangitur ulnis.
fluminea sonipes religatus ducitur alno,

---

stretched forth her hands, imploring the aid of her
guest, she was torn in pieces by wild beasts. When
Hercules came back victorious,[a] he wetted the mangled
limbs with his tears ; and when he found the head
of the maid he had loved, he turned pale, distraught
with grief. Then the high mountain-tops, smitten
by his cries, were shaken ; with loud lament he
called Pyrene by name ; and all the cliffs and haunts
of wild beasts echoed the name of Pyrene. Then,
with a last tribute of tears, he laid her body in the
grave. And time shall never eclipse her fame ; for
the mountains retain for ever the name that caused
such grief.

And now, marching through hills and dense pine-
woods, Hannibal had crossed the territory of the
Bebrycian king. Thence he boldly forced his way
through the land of the inhospitable Volcae, and
ravaged it, till he came with rapid march to the for-
midable banks of the swollen Rhone. That river,
taking its rise in the Alpine heights and snow-
covered rocks, flows into Gaul, expanding into a
mighty stream, cleaving the plains with its foaming
waters, and rushing with utmost speed into the sea
in a broad estuary. The Arar, whose noiseless stream
seems to stand still, joins the Rhone and swells it ;
and the Rhone, embracing the reluctant Arar with its
restless waters, plunges it into the sea, and forbids
it, as it is hurried through the land, to carry its own
name to the neighbouring shore.[b] The river will
bear no bridges, and the soldiers eagerly plunged
in ; some protect their weapons by holding their head
and shoulders high, while others in keen rivalry stem
the flood with stout arms. The horses were haltered
and taken across in barges ; nor did the terror of the

belua nec retinet tardante Libyssa timore ;
nam trabibus vada et iniecta tellure repertum   460
connexas operire trabes ac ducere in altum
paulatim ripae resolutis aggere vinclis.
at gregis illapsu fremebundo territus atras
expavit moles Rhodanus stagnisque refusis
torsit harenoso minitantia murmura fundo.   465
   Iamque Tricastinis incedit finibus agmen,
iam faciles campos, iam rura Vocontia carpit.
turbidus hic truncis saxisque Druentia laetum
ductoris vastavit iter.   namque Alpibus ortus,
avulsas ornos et adesi fragmina montis   470
cum sonitu volvens, fertur latrantibus undis
ac vada translato mutat fallacia cursu,
non pediti fidus, patulis non puppibus aequus ;
et tunc, imbre recens fuso, correpta sub armis
corpora multa virum spumanti vertice torquens   475
immersit fundo laceris deformia membris.
   Sed iam praeteritos ultra meminisse labores
conspectae propius dempsere paventibus Alpes.
cuncta gelu canaque aeternum grandine tecta
atque aevi glaciem cohibent ; riget ardua montis   480
aetherii facies, surgentique obvia Phoebo
duratas nescit flammis mollire pruinas.
quantum Tartareus regni pallentis hiatus
ad manes imos atque atrae stagna paludis
a supera tellure patet, tam longa per auras   485
erigitur tellus et caelum intercipit umbra.

---

   [a] Elephants.
   [b] The cables served to secure the rafts : when the elephant
had reached midstream, the cable was slackened.
   [c] Now the Durance.
   [d] In Hades.

Libyan beasts *a* delay or hinder the crossing; for they contrived to throw rafts over the stream and to conceal the line of rafts beneath a covering of soil ; then they led the elephants out on to the deep, loosing little by little the cables *b* on the high bank. Scared by this invasion of trumpeting elephants, and fearing the dusky monsters, the Rhone turned back his stream and sent up ominous rumblings from his sandy depths.

Now Hannibal moved on through the territory of the Tricastini, and made an easy march through the land of the Vocontii. But here the Druentia,*c* rough with rocks and trunks of trees, turned his pleasant march to rack and ruin ; for, rising in the Alps, it carries along with a roar uprooted ash-trees and boulders washed away from the mountains, and rushes on with raging waters, often shifting its channel, and changing its deceitful fords. The foot-passenger cannot trust it ; no broad ship is safe upon it. Now, swollen by recent rains, it seized many of the armed men, and whirled them round in its foaming eddies, and buried in its depths their mutilated bodies and mangled limbs.

But now all memory of past hardships was dispelled by terror, when they saw the Alps close at hand. All that region is covered with rime and hail that never thaws, and imprisons the ice of ages ; the steep face of the lofty mountain rises stiffly up, and, though it faces the rising sun, can never melt its hardened crust in his rays. Deep as the chasm that divides the upper world from the pale kingdom of Tartarus, and descends to the dead below and the pools of the black marsh,*d* so high does the earth here rise towards heaven and shut out the sky by its shadow. There is

149

nullum ver usquam nullique aestatis honores.
sola iugis habitat diris sedesque tuetur
perpetuas deformis hiems ; illa undique nubes
huc atras agit et mixtos cum grandine nimbos.   490
iam cuncti flatus ventique furentia regna
Alpina posuere domo.   caligat in altis
obtutus saxis, abeuntque in nubila montes.
mixtus Athos Tauro Rhodopeque adiuncta Mimanti
Ossaque cum Pelio cumque Haemo cesserit Othrys.
primus inexpertas adiit Tirynthius arces.   496
scindentem nubes frangentemque ardua montis
spectarunt superi longisque ab origine saeclis
intemerata gradu magna vi saxa domantem.

At miles dubio tardat vestigia gressu,   500
impia ceu sacros in fines arma per orbem,
natura prohibente, ferant divisque repugnent.
contra quae ductor (non Alpibus ille nec ullo
turbatus terrore loci, sed languida maestis   504
corda virum fovet hortando revocatque vigorem) :
" non pudet obsequio superum fessosque secundis,
post belli decus atque acies, dare terga nivosis
montibus et segnes summittere rupibus arma ?
nunc, o nunc, socii, dominantis moenia Romae
credite vos summumque Iovis conscendere culmen.510
hic labor Ausoniam et dabit hic in vincula Thybrim."
nec mora, commotum promissis ditibus agmen
erigit in collem et vestigia linquere nota
Herculis edicit magni crudisque locorum

---

[a] The Capitoline Hill at Rome, where stood the temple of
Jupiter Optimus Maximus, the thunder-god.

no spring anywhere and no beauty of summer; un
sightly winter alone inhabits the gruesome heights
and dwells for ever there; from every quarter winter
drives hither black clouds and rain mixed with hail.
All winds and storms, moreover, have set up their
furious dominion in the Alps. The gaze turns giddy
on the high cliffs, and the mountains are lost in the
clouds. Athos added to Mount Taurus, Rhodope
united to Mimas, Pelion piled on Ossa and Othrys
on Mount Haemus—all these must bow before the
Alps. Hercules was the first to set foot on these
virgin fortresses; he was a sight for the gods as he
cleft the clouds, mastered the steep ascent, and with
main force tamed the rocks that no foot had ever
trodden during the long ages that followed their
birth.

The soldiers moved slow with lagging steps, think-
ing that they were marching over the world into a
forbidden land, in defiance of Nature and in opposition
to Heaven. But their general would have none of it
—*he* was not terrified by the Alps or all the horror of
the place; and his words raised the courage of his
men and revived their energy when they were faint
with fear. "Shame on you," he cried, "to grow
weary of success and Heaven's favour, and, after
glorious victories in the field, to retreat now before
snow-clad mountains, cowed and beaten by cliffs!
Now, comrades, now—believe that you are even now
scaling the walls of imperial Rome and the lofty hill
of Jupiter.ᵃ Our present toil shall make Italy and
the Tiber our prisoners." Straightway he led the
army uphill, persuading them by his rich promises.
He ordered the troops to abandon the track beaten
by great Hercules, to march over fresh ground, and

ferre pedem ac proprio turmas evadere calle.   515
rumpit inaccessos aditus atque ardua primus
exsuperat summaque vocat de rupe cohortes.
tum, qua durati concreto frigore collis
lubrica frustratur canenti semita clivo,
luctantem ferro glaciem premit.   haurit hiatu   520
nix resoluta viros, altoque e culmine praeceps
humenti turmas operit delapsa ruina.
interdum adverso glomeratas turbine Caurus
in media ora nives fuscis agit horridus alis ;
aut rursum immani stridens avulsa procella   525
nudatis rapit arma viris volvensque per orbem
contorto rotat in nubes sublimia flatu.
quoque magis subiere iugo atque, evadere nisi,
erexere gradum, crescit labor.   ardua supra
sese aperit fessis et nascitur altera moles,   530
unde nec edomitos exsudatosque labores
respexisse libet ;   tanta formidine plana
exterrent repetita oculis ;   atque una pruinae
canentis, quacumque datur promittere visus,
ingeritur facies.   medio sic navita ponto,   535
cum dulces liquit terras, et inania nullos
inveniunt ventos securo carbasa malo,
immensas prospectat aquas ac, victa profundis
aequoribus, fessus renovat sua lumina caelo.
    Iamque super clades atque importuna locorum 540
illuvie rigidaeque comae squalore perenni
horrida semiferi promunt e rupibus ora,

---

a Or " the steel " may refer to iron spikes on the soldiers'
boots.
b The landscape is " even " (not " level "), because all
irregularities of surface are obliterated by the snow.

climb up by a path of their own. He forced a passage where no man had passed; he was the first to master heights and from the crag's top called on his men to follow. Where the ascent was stiff with frozen ice and the slippery path over the snow-slopes baffled them, he cut steps with the steel [a] in the resisting ice. When the snow thawed, it swallowed down the men in its opened jaws, and, as it rushed down from a height, buried whole companies beneath an avalanche. At times the North-west wind, menacing with dark wings, drove the snow, packed tight by the opposing gale, full in their faces; or again, the fury of the raging storm stripped the men of their shields, and, rolling them round and round, whirled them aloft into the clouds with its circling blast. The higher they climbed in their struggle to reach the top, the harder grew their toil. When one height had been mastered, a second opens and springs up before their aching sight; and from it they cared not even to look back at the difficulties they had already mastered by their sweat; with such dread did the monotonous even landscape [b] strike their sight; and, as far as their eyes could reach, the same scene of frozen snow forced itself upon them. So the sailor in mid-ocean, when he has left behind the land he loves, and the flapping sails on his idle mast can find no wind, looks forth upon a boundless waste of water, and turns wearily to the sky, to refresh his eyes that cannot endure the sight of the deep any longer.

And now, on the top of the disasters and difficulties of the ascent, half-savage men peeped out from the rocks, showing faces hideous with filth and with the matted dirt of bristling locks. Pouring forth from

atque effusa cavis exesi pumicis antris
Alpina invadit manus assuetoque vigore
per dumos notasque nives atque invia pernix   545
clausum montivagis infestat cursibus hostem.
mutatur iam forma locis : hic sanguine multo
infectae rubuere nives, hic, nescia vinci,
paulatim glacies cedit tepefacta cruore ;
dumque premit sonipes duro vestigia cornu,   550
ungula perfossis haesit comprensa pruinis.
nec pestis lapsus simplex ; abscisa relinquunt
membra gelu, fractosque asper rigor amputat artus.
bis senos soles, totidem per vulnera saevas
emensi noctes, optato vertice sidunt   555
castraque praeruptis suspendunt ardua saxis.

   At Venus, ancipiti mentem labefacta timore,
affatur genitorem et rumpit maesta querellas :
" quis poenae modus aut pereundi terminus, oro,
Aeneadis erit ? et quando terrasque fretumque   560
emensis sedisse dabis ? cur pellere nostros
a te concessa Poenus parat urbe nepotes ?
Alpibus imposuit Libyam finemque minatur
imperio.   casus metuit iam Roma Sagunti.
quo Troiae extremos cineres sacramque ruinam   565
Assaracique larem et Vestae secreta feramus,
da sedem, genitor, tutisque iacere.   parumne est,
exilia errantes totum quaesisse per orbem ?
anne iterum capta repetentur Pergama Roma ? "

---

   [a] Assaracus, son of Tros, was a king of Troy.
   [b] The fire sacred to Vesta which Aeneas carried with him
from Troy to Italy. *Pergama* was the citadel of Troy.

caves in the hollow rock, the natives of the Alps
attacked them; with the ease of habit they sped
through thorn-brakes and their familiar snow-drifts
and pathless places; and soon the army was hemmed
in and assailed by the nimble mountaineers. And
now the place bore a different aspect. For here the
snow turned red, deeply dyed with blood; and here
the ice, unwilling to give way, yielded by degrees,
when the hot blood thawed it; and where the horse
stamps his horny feet, the hoof sticks fast in the ice he
has bored through. Nor is a fall the only danger; for
men leave arms and legs behind, severed by the frost,
and the cruel cold cuts off the limbs already broken.
Twelve days and as many dreadful nights they spent in
such suffering, before they rested on the longed-for
summit, and hung their camp aloft on precipitous cliffs.

But now Venus, her heart shaken with doubt and
fear, addressed her sire and broke into sorrowful
complaint. "What limit of their punishment will
the Aeneadae ever reach, I ask, or what end to their
destruction? When wilt thou grant them a fixed
abode, after all their wanderings over land and sea?
Why does the Carthaginian essay to drive my de-
scendants from the city which thou didst grant them?
He has planted Libya upon the Alps and threatens
an end to Roman power. Rome now dreads the
fate of Saguntum. Grant us a resting-place, O
Father, whither we may bear at last the ashes and
sacred relics of fallen Troy, with the house of
Assaracus [a] and the mysteries of Vesta. [b] Grant us
safety in our overthrow. Is it not enough that we
have wandered over the whole earth, seeking a place
of exile? Or shall Rome be taken and the doom
of Troy be repeated once more?"

His Venus ; et contra genitor sic deinde profatur :
" pelle metus, neu te Tyriae conamina gentis   571
turbarint, Cytherea ; tenet longumque tenebit
Tarpeias arces sanguis tuus.   hac ego Martis
mole viros spectare paro atque expendere bello.
gens ferri patiens ac laeta domare labores   575
paulatim antiquo patrum dissuescit honori ;
atque ille, haud umquam parcus pro laude cruoris
et semper famae sitiens, obscura sedendo
tempora agit, mutum volvens inglorius aevum,
sanguine de nostro populus, blandoque veneno   580
desidiae virtus paulatim evicta senescit.
magnae molis opus multoque labore parandum,
tot populos inter soli sibi poscere regna.
iamque tibi veniet tempus, quo maxima rerum
nobilior sit Roma malis.   hinc nomina nostro   585
non indigna polo referet labor ; hinc tibi Paulus,
hinc Fabius gratusque mihi Marcellus opimis.
hi tantum parient Latio per vulnera regnum,
quod luxu et multum mutata mente nepotes
non tamen evertisse queant.   iamque ipse creatus,
qui Poenum revocet patriae Latioque repulsum   591
ante suae muros Carthaginis exuat armis.
hinc, Cytherea, tuis longo regnabitur aevo.
exin se Curibus virtus caelestis ad astra

---

[a] A name of Venus, derived from the town of Cythera in
Crete.
[b] L. Aemilius Paulus was killed in the battle of Cannae
(216 B.C.).   His son, of the same name, defeated Perseus,
king of Macedonia.   Fabius is the famous dictator nick-
named " Slow-coach."   M. Claudius Marcellus in 222 B.C.
killed Viridomarus, king of the Insubrians, with his own
hand and so gained what were called *spolia opima*.   He
defeated Hannibal at Nola in 215 B.C.

Thus Venus spoke, and then her sire made answer thus : " Fear not, Cytherea,[a] nor be disturbed by the ambition of the Tyrian people. Your descendants hold the Tarpeian rock and long shall hold it. But I mean to test their manhood by this great conflict and to try them in war. A people, once steadfast in battle and triumphant over hardships, are forgetting by degrees the ancient glory of their sires. Then they never spared their blood in honour's cause, and ever thirsted for fame ; but now they pass their time in obscurity and inaction, and spend their lives amid inglorious silence, though my blood is in their veins ; and their manliness is slowly sapped and weakened by the seductive poison of indolence. But it is a mighty enterprise that must cost intense effort, to claim power for themselves alone among so many nations. Thou shalt see a time come, when Rome, mistress of the world, shall be more glorious for her calamities. Thus suffering shall produce famous men, worthy to dwell with us in heaven ; thou shalt see a Paulus, a Fabius, and a Marcellus who has pleased me by honourable spoils.[b] These men, by their defeats, will gain for Latium an empire so great, that their descendants will be unable to overthrow it, for all their luxury and degenerate hearts. Already the man [c] is born who shall drive Hannibal back from Latium to his own land, and strip him of his arms before the walls of his native Carthage. Thereafter thy descendants, Cytherea, shall reign for ages. Later still, godlike excellence shall come from Cures [d]

---

[c] P. Cornelius Scipio Africanus.

[d] Cures was an ancient city in the Sabine country, where Vespasian was born. An elaborate panegyric follows upon Vespasian and his sons and successors—Titus and Domitian.

efferet, et sacris augebit nomen Iulis   595
bellatrix gens bacifero nutrita Sabino.
hinc pater ignotam donabit vincere Thylen
inque Caledonios primus trahet agmina lucos ;
compescet ripis Rhenum, reget impiger Afros
palmiferamque senex bello domitabit Idumen.   600
nec Stygis ille lacus viduataque lumine regna
sed superum sedem nostrosque tenebit honores.
tum iuvenis, magno praecellens robore mentis,
excipiet patriam molem celsusque feretur,
aequatum imperio tollens caput : hic fera gentis 605
bella Palaestinae primo delebit in aevo.
at tu transcendes, Germanice, facta tuorum,
iam puer auricomo praeformidate Batavo.
nec te terruerint Tarpei culminis ignes,
sacrilegas inter flammas servabere terris ;   610
nam te longa manent nostri consortia mundi.
huic laxos arcus olim Gangetica pubes
summittet, vacuasque ostendent Bactra pharetras.
hic et ab Arctoo currus aget axe per urbem,
ducet et Eoos, Baccho cedente, triumphos.   615
idem, indignantem tramittere Dardana signa,
Sarmaticis victor compescet sedibus Histrum.
quin et Romuleos superabit voce nepotes,
quis erit eloquio partum decus.   huic sua Musae

---

  [a] The olive-berry.

  [b] The emperors of the Julio-Claudian line.

  [c] " Thule " stands for the far North—possibly the Shetlands, or Iceland.

  [d] Vespasian fought against Judaea before becoming emperor ; his elder son, Titus, took Jerusalem A.D. 70 and ended the war.   Idume (Edom) stands for Judaea.

  [e] One of the undeserved titles conferred by Domitian on himself.

  [f] The temple on the Capitol was burnt down in A.D. 69, and Domitian was nearly burnt inside it.

and soar to heaven; and a warrior family, reared
on the berry [a] that grows in the Sabine land, shall
increase the fame of the deified Julii. [b] The father of
that family shall give Rome victory over Thule, [c]
unknown till then, and shall be the first to lead an
army against the Caledonian forests; he shall set
banks to restrain the Rhine, he shall rule Africa with
vigour, and, in his old age, he shall subdue in war the
palm-groves of Idume. [d] Nor shall he descend to the
pools of the Styx and the realm deprived of light;
but he shall attain to the habitation of the gods and
the honours we enjoy. Then his son, unrivalled in
mighty strength of mind, shall take up his father's
task and move on in majesty, raising his head as high
as his power. While yet a youth, he shall put an
end to war with the fierce people of Palestine. But
thou, Conqueror of Germany, [e] shalt outdo the exploits
of thy father and brother; even in boyhood thou
wert dreaded by the yellow-haired Batavians. The
burning of the Tarpeian temple cannot alarm thee;
but in the midst of the impious flames thou shalt be
saved, for the sake of mankind; [f] for in the distant
future thou shalt share with me the kingdom of the
sky. The people of the Ganges shall one day lower
their unbent bows before him, and Bactra [g] display
its empty quivers. He shall drive the triumphal
car through Rome after conquering the North; he
shall triumph over the East, and Bacchus give place
to him. When the Danube refuses a passage to the
Roman legions, he shall be victorious and retain the
river in the land of the Sarmatians. Moreover, his
oratory shall surpass all the sons of Romulus who have
gained glory by their eloquence; the Muses shall

[g] The Parthians are meant here.

sacra ferent, meliorque lyra, cui substitit Hebrus   620
et venit Rhodope, Phoebo miranda loquetur.
ille etiam, qua prisca, vides, stat regia nobis,
aurea Tarpeia ponet Capitolia rupe
et iunget nostro templorum culmina caelo.
tunc, o nate deum divosque dature, beatas   625
imperio terras patrio rege.   tarda senectam
hospitia excipient caeli, solioque Quirinus
concedet, mediumque parens fraterque locabunt :
siderei iuxta radiabunt tempora nati."

   Dum pandit seriem venturi Iupiter aevi,   630
ductor Agenoreus, tumulis delatus iniquis,
lapsantem dubio devexa per invia nisu
firmabat gressum atque humentia saxa premebat.
non acies hostisve tenet, sed prona minaci
praerupto turbant et cautibus obvia rupes.   635
stant clausi maerentque moras et dura viarum.
nec refovere datur torpentia membra quiete ;
noctem operi iungunt et robora ferre coactis
approperant humeris ac raptas collibus ornos.
iamque ubi nudarunt silva densissima montis,   640
aggessere trabes ; rapidisque accensus in orbem
excoquitur flammis scopulus.   mox proruta ferro
dat gemitum putris resoluto pondere moles
atque aperit fessis antiqui regna Latini.

---

   [a] Domitian wrote an epic poem, "The War on the
Capitol," which described the fighting in Rome when
Vitellius fell ; but no line of it is preserved.
   [b] Orpheus.
   [c] Domitian rebuilt the temple of Jupiter with great magnificence : it was completed A.D. 82.
   [d] Domitian had one son who died in childhood.

bring him offerings, and Phoebus shall marvel at his song [a]—a sweeter strain than his [b] whose music made the Hebrus stand still and Mount Rhodope move on. He shall also erect a golden Capitol on the Tarpeian [c] rock, where, as thou seest, my ancient palace now stands, and raise the summit of the temple to reach our abode in the sky. Then, O son of gods and father of gods to be, [d] rule the happy earth with paternal sway. Heaven shall welcome thee at last, in thy old age, and Quirinus [e] give up his throne to thee ; thy father and brother shall place thee between them ; and hard by the head of thy deified son shall send forth rays."

While Jupiter thus revealed the sequence of future events, the Carthaginian leader, descending the dangerous heights, tried with uncertain effort to get a firm foothold, as he slid down pathless slopes and trod on dripping rocks. No hostile army detained him ; but he was troubled by the dreadful steepness of the descent and by rocks confronting cliffs. The men stand still, as if shut in, and lament the obstacles and difficulties of the way. Nor can they sleep and so revive their frozen bodies ; but they work on all night in haste, forced to carry wood on their shoulders and to tear up ash-trees from the hills. Then after stripping the mountain where the trees grew thickest, they piled the timber in a heap ; and the rock, set on fire all round, was melted by the devouring flames. Then demolished by the axe, the heavy mass crumbled and parted asunder with a rumbling sound and opened up to the weary soldiers the land of old Latinus. [f] At last, after all these

---

[e] The name given to Romulus when deified.
[f] Italy.

his tandem ignotas transgressus casibus Alpes, 645
Taurinis ductor statuit tentoria campis.
   Interea, voces Iovis atque oracula portans,
emensis aderat Garamantum laetus harenis
Bostar et ut viso stimulabat corda Tonante :
" maxime Belide, patriis qui moenibus arces 650
servitium dextra, Libycas penetravimus aras.
nos tulit ad superos perfundens sidera Syrtis,
nos paene aequoribus tellus violentior hausit.
ad finem caeli medio tenduntur ab orbe
squalentes campi. tumulum natura negavit 655
immensis spatiis, nisi quem cava nubila torquens
construxit turbo, impacta glomeratus harena,
vel si, perfracto populatus carcere terras,
Africus et, pontum spargens super aëra, Caurus
invasere truces capientem proelia campum 660
inque vicem ingesto cumularunt pulvere montes.
has observatis valles enavimus astris ;
namque dies confundit iter, peditemque profundo
errantem campo et semper media arva videntem
Sidoniis Cynosura regit fidissima nautis. 665
verum ubi defessi lucos nemorosaque regna
cornigeri Iovis et fulgentia templa subimus,
exceptos hospes tectis inducit Arisbas.
stat fano vicina, novum et memorabile, lympha,
quae nascente die, quae deficiente tepescit 670

---

^a The name of this Gallic tribe survives in the city of
Turin.
  ^b See ll. 6 foll.
  ^c See note to i. 408.
  ^d See note to i. 193.
  ^e The Phoenicians used the Little Bear (Cynosura) to
steer by ; the Greeks used the Great Bear (Helice) : see xiv.
457.
  ^f Jupiter Ammon : see note to i. 415.

sufferings, Hannibal crossed the untrodden Alps and pitched his camp on the plains of the Taurini.[a]

Meanwhile Bostar[b] arrived, bearing the oracular response of Jupiter. He came with joy, after traversing the deserts of the Garamantes, and encouraged Hannibal, as if he had seen the Thunder-god with his own eyes: " Mighty son of Belus, whose right arm defends your native walls from slavery, we made our way to the shrine of Libya. The Syrtis,[c] which spatters the stars with its foam, bore us on towards the gods ; and the land, more furious than the sea, almost swallowed us up. From the centre of earth to the limit of the sky the barren plains stretch out. Nowhere in that boundless tract does Nature suffer the level to rise, save where a whirlwind, thick with accumulated sand, and driving the hollow clouds along, has raised up a mound. Or sometimes the South-west wind breaks its prison[d] and devastates the earth ; and then a blast from the North-west, scattering the sea over the sky, falls fiercely on the plain that is large enough for their battle ; and the two winds, blowing against each other, raise mountains of heaped-up sand. We steered our course across these hollows by observation of the stars ; for daylight confuses the tracks, and the Little Bear, which never deceives the Phoenician mariner,[e] guides the traveller, as he strays over the sandy depths and ever sees the waste all round him. But when we came, weary travellers, to the groves and tree-clad abode and shining temple of Jupiter who has horns on his forehead,[f] Arisbas welcomed us as guests and took us to his house. Beside the temple is a wondrous marvel—a spring, whose water is lukewarm at morning and at evening, but

quaeque riget, medius cum sol accendit Olympum,
atque eadem rursum nocturnis fervet in umbris.
tum loca plena deo, dites sine vomere glebas
ostentat senior laetaque ita mente profatur :
' has umbras nemorum et connexa cacumina caelo 675
calcatosque Iovi lucos prece, Bostar, adora.
nam cui dona Iovis non divulgata per orbem,
in gremio Thebes geminas sedisse columbas ?
quarum, Chaonias pennis quae contigit oras,
implet fatidico Dodonida murmure quercum.   680
at quae, Carpathium super aequor vecta, per auras
in Libyen piceis¹ tranavit concolor alis,
hanc sedem templo Cythereïa condidit ales ;
hic, ubi nunc aram lucosque videtis opacos,
ductore electo gregis, admirabile dictu,   685
lanigeri capitis media inter cornua perstans,
Marmaricis ales populis responsa canebat.
mox subitum nemus atque annoso robore lucus
exiluit ; qualesque premunt nunc sidera quercus,
a prima venere die ; prisco inde pavore   690
arbor numen habet coliturque tepentibus aris.'
dumque ea miramur, subito stridore tremendum
impulsae patuere fores, maiorque repente
lux oculos ferit.   ante aras stat veste sacerdos
effulgens nivea, et populi concurrere certant.   695
inde ubi mandatas effudi pectore voces,
ecce intrat subitus vatem deus.   alta sonoro,
collisis trabibus, volvuntur murmura luco,

¹ piceis: niveis *edd.*

---

a Silius seems to mean Thebes in Greece ; but Herodotus
and others refer the legend to Thebes in Egypt.
  b A district of Epirus including the forest of Dodona.
  c Aegean.
  d A district of N. Africa : the inhabitants are called Mar-
maridae.

cold when the midday sun kindles the sky; and the
same water boils again in the darkness of night.
Then that old man showed us the places which the
god fills with his presence, and the fields that bear
crops without the plough; and thus he addressed us
with cheerful heart: 'Bostar, bow down in prayer
before these shady woods, this roof that soars to
heaven, and these groves where Jupiter has trodden.
For who upon earth has not heard of the gift of
Jupiter—the two doves that perched on the lap of
Thebe[a]? One of these flew to the land of Chaonia[b]
and there fills the oak of Dodona with prophetic
utterance; but the other bird of Venus sailed through
the sky over the Carpathian[c] sea, and flew on dusky
wings to the dusky people of Libya, and founded
here the site for a temple. Here, where now you see
the altar and the shady groves, the dove—marvellous
to tell—chose out a leader of the flock, and stood
between the horns of his fleecy head, and prophesied
to the people of Marmarica.[d] Later, trees sprang
suddenly from the earth, and a grove of ancient oaks;
and, as the branches now reach the skies, so they grew
on their first day. Hence the grove is sacred and
awful from ancient times, and is worshipped with
steaming altars.' While we marvelled at his words,
the doors suddenly flew open with a terrible crash,
and a brighter light suddenly struck upon our eyes.
Before the altar stood the priest, conspicuous in his
snow-white robe, and the people thronged eagerly to
the doors. Then when I had uttered the message
with which I was charged, behold! the god suddenly
entered the breast of the prophet. The trees clashed
against one another, and a deep humming noise
passed through the resounding grove; and then a

ac maior nota iam vox prorumpit in auras :
' tenditis in Latium belloque agitare paratis   700
Assaraci prolem, Libyes.   coepta aspera cerno
Gradivumque trucem currus iam scandere et atram
in latus Hesperium flammam expirare furentes
cornipedes multoque fluentia sanguine lora.
tu, qui pugnarum eventus extremaque fati   705
deposcis claroque ferox das vela labori,
invade Aetoli ductoris Iapyga campum ;
Sidonios augebis avos nullique relinques
altius Ausoniae penetrare in viscera gentis,
donec victa tibi trepidabunt Dardana regna.   710
nec ponet pubes umquam Saturnia curam,
dum carpet superas in terris Hannibal auras.' "
   Talia portabat laetis oracula Bostar
impleratque viros pugnae propioris amore.

---

   a The Romans : see note to l. 566.
   b This epithet, often applied to fire by Silius, may mean
"terrible," "awful" rather than "black."
   c Italy.
   d Diomede, the Homeric hero and King of Aetolia, after
returning from Troy, settled in Apulia and there founded
Argyripa, later called Arpi. The " Iapygian plain " is the

voice, louder than any we know, burst forth into the air : ' Men of Libya, ye move against Latium, and prepare to make war against the seed of Assaracus.[a] I see a perilous enterprise ; I see fierce Mars even now mounting his chariot ; I see his furious steeds breathing forth black[b] flame against the Western land,[c] and the blood that streams down from his reins. And thou, who seekest to know the issue of battle and the fated end, and boldly spreadest thy sail for the glorious adventure, advance against the Iapygian plain of the Aetolian leader[d] : thou shalt glorify thy Phoenician ancestors, and no man after thee shall be able to pierce deeper into the vitals of the Ausonian race, so long as the Dardan[e] realm shall tremble beneath thy conquests. Nor shall the race of Saturn[f] ever be free from fear, so long as Hannibal draws breath in the upper world.' "

Such was the welcome oracle that Bostar brought back ; and he filled the army with desire for instant battle.

site of the battle of Cannae : Iapygia is part of Apulia in S. Italy.
  [e] Dardan = Trojan = Roman.   [f] The Romans.

LIBER QUARTUS

ARGUMENT

Rome is greatly alarmed by the news that Hannibal has reached Italy : but the Senate does not lose heart (1-38). Hannibal courts the Gauls of N. Italy. Scipio hurries back from Marseilles (39-55). Both generals address their soldiers and prepare for battle (56-100). An omen precedes the battle (101-134). The battle of the Ticinus (135-479). Scipio withdraws to the Trebia, and is joined by an army under Ti. Sempronius Longus (480-497). Hannibal forces

Fama per Ausoniae turbatas spargitur urbes
nubiferos montes et saxa minantia caelo
accepisse iugum, Poenosque per invia vectos,
aemulaque Herculei iactantem facta laboris
descendisse ducem. diros canit improba motus   5
et gliscit gressu volucrique citatior Euro
terrificis quatit attonitas rumoribus arces.
astruit auditis, docilis per inania rerum
pascere rumorem vulgi, pavor. itur in acres
bellorum raptim curas, subitusque per omnem   10
Ausoniam Mavors strepit et ciet arma virosque.
pila novant, ac detersa rubigine saevus
induitur ferro splendor, niveumque repostae
instaurant galeae coni decus ; hasta iuvatur
ammento, revocantque novas fornace bipennes.   15

---

a For this contrivance see note to i. 318.

BOOK IV

RUMOUR, spreading through the dismayed cities
of Ausonia, told that cloud-capped mountains and
heaven-threatening peaks had been conquered, that
the Carthaginians had passed over trackless wilds, and
that Hannibal had descended from the Alps, boasting
an exploit that rivalled the labour of Hercules. Mis-
chievous Rumour prophesied dread commotions, and,
growing as she went, and moving swifter than the
wings of the wind, shook the panic-stricken cities with
alarming reports. Then fear, quick to feed the talk
of the populace with falsehood, exaggerated what it
heard. Men turned quickly to the fierce business of
war, and Mars suddenly raised a clamour throughout
Italy, summoning arms and men. They refashion
their javelins ; the steel is cleansed of rust and puts
on its cruel glitter ; and helmets, long laid by, renew
the beauty of their snowy plumes ; the spear is
strengthened by a thong,[a] and axes are brought back

169

conseritur tegimen laterum impenetrabile, multas
passurus dextras atque irrita vulnera, thorax.
pars arcu invigilant, domitat pars verbere anhelum
cornipedem in gyros saxoque exasperat ensem.
nec vero muris, quibus est luctata vetustas,   20
ferre morantur opem ; subvectant saxa cavasque
retractant turres, edit quas longior aetas.
hinc tela accipiunt arces, ac robora portis
et fidos certant obices accersere silva ;
circumdant fossas. haud segnis cuncta magister   25
praecipitat timor, ac vastis trepidatur in agris.
deseruere larem ; portant cervicibus aegras
attoniti matres ducentesque ultima fila
grandaevos rapuere senes ; tum crine soluto
ante agitur coniux, dextra laevaque trahuntur   30
parvi, non aequo comitantes ordine, nati.
sic vulgus ; traduntque metus, nec poscitur auctor.
at patres, quamquam exterrent immania coepta
inque sinu bellum, atque Alpes et pervia saxa
decepere, tamen crudam contra aspera mentem   35
et magnos tollunt animos : iuvat ire periclis
ad decus et dextra memorandum condere nomen,
quale dedit numquam rebus Fortuna secundis.
    Sed Libyae ductor tuto fovet agmina vallo,
fessa gradum multoque gelu torpentia nervos ;   40
solandique genus—laetis ostentat ad urbem

reforged from the furnace. The cuirass that must parry many a thrust and unsuccessful blow is fitted together, to form a protection for the body that nothing can pierce. Some sit late, to mend the bow; some tame the panting steed with the whip and make him wheel about; and others whet the sword upon the stone. Nor are men slow to repair the walls that time has attacked; they bring up stone in wagons and refashion the hollow towers eaten away by age. The citadels too are stored with missiles; men hasten to bring from the forest oak-timber for their gates and trusty bars, and dig moats around. Fear, an active taskmaster, speeds all the work; and terror is rife in the deserted fields. Men leave their homes; panic-stricken, they carry ailing mothers upon their shoulders and drag along old men whose span of life is almost ended; they drive their wives with dishevelled hair in front of them; behind them come the little children with shorter steps, clinging to their father's right hand and left. Thus the people flee, handing on their fear to one another; and no man asks the origin of the reports. But the Senate, though alarmed by the enemy at their doors and by his enormous enterprise, and disappointed by his passage over the Alps, nevertheless opposed the danger with unbroken spirit and high courage. They rejoice to march through peril to glory, and to build by strength of arm such a monument of fame as Fortune has never granted to prosperity.

But Hannibal nursed his army behind the protection of a camp, while the men were weary of marching and their muscles were stiff with continued frost; and, by way of consolation, he pointed out that the

per campos superesse viam, Romamque sub ictu.
at non et rerum curas consultaque belli
stare probat, solusque nequit perferre quietem.
armiferae quondam prisca inter tempora gentes   45
Ausonium invasere latus sedesque beatas
et metui peperere manu : mox impia bella
Tarpeius pater et capti sensere Quirites.
hos dum sollicitat donis et inania corda
ac fluxam morum gentem fovet armaque iungit,   50
iam consul, volucri pervectus litora classe,
Scipio Phocaicis sese referebat ab oris ;
ingentesque duces, pelagi terraeque laborem
diversum emensos, propiora pericula vallo
iungebant, magnaeque aderant primordia cladis.   55
namque ut, collatis admoto consule castris,
sustulerat Fortuna moras, signumque furoris
accensae viso poscebant hoste cohortes :
" debellata procul, quaecumque vocantur Hiberis,"
ingenti Tyrius numerosa per agmina ductor   60
voce sonat ; non Pyrenen Rhodanumve ferocem
iussa aspernatos, Rutulam fumasse Saguntum,
raptum per Celtas iter, et, qua ponere gressum
Amphitryoniadae fuerit labor, isse sub armis
Poenorum turmas, equitemque per ardua vectum   65
insultasse iugo, et fremuisse hinnitibus Alpes.
   Contra pulchra suos vocat ad discrimina consul :

---

   [a] Gauls made their appearance in Italy in the fifth century
B.C. and gradually spread southwards ; in 390 B.C. they took
and burnt Rome. Hannibal therefore hoped to lead the
Gauls of N. Italy against Rome a second time.
   [b] Massilia (Marseilles), founded by colonists from Phocaea
in Asia Minor. P. Cornelius Scipio, consul in 218 B.C., sailed

rest of the march to Rome was over level ground, and
that the city was at their mercy. But he did not
approve of any pause in his own survey of affairs and
plan of campaign ; and he alone could not endure
inaction. Once before, in ancient days, armed tribes
had invaded the happy land of Italy and caused terror
by their might ; and soon the Tarpeian Father and
the conquered Quirites felt the shock of sacrilegious
warfare.[a] But, while he was tempting the Gauls
with bribes, working on the folly and fickleness of
that people, and making an alliance with them, the
consul Scipio was returning from the land of the
Phocaeans,[b] sailing with speed along the coast. Each
mighty chief had completed his hard task, one on
land and the other by sea ; and now a more instant
danger brought their camps together ; and the be-
ginnings of a great disaster were present. For when
the consul arrived and the armies faced each other,
and Fortune put an end to delays, the soldiers, roused
by the sight of the enemy, demanded the signal for
the furious assault. Then Hannibal's voice rose in a
great shout over his mighty host : " We have subdued
all that distant land that bears the name of Spain ;
the Pyrenees and the proud Rhone have obeyed our
bidding ; Rutulian Saguntum has gone up in smoke ;
we forced a passage through Gaul ; and, where Her-
cules found it hard to tread, the soldiers of Carthage
have marched in arms ; our horsemen have ridden
up the heights and trampled on the peaks, and the
Alps have echoed with the snorting of our steeds."

On the other side the consul summoned his men
to danger and to glory : " Soldiers, your foes are

back in haste from Marseilles on hearing that Hannibal
had crossed the Alps : see xvi. 333 foll.

" hostem, miles, habes fractum ambustumque nivosis
cautibus atque aegre torpentia membra trahentem.
en age, qui sacros montes rupesque profundas   70
transiluit, discat, quanto stat celsius arce
Herculea vallum, et maius sit, scandere colles,
an vestros rupisse globos.   det inania famae,
dum magna fuso pugna retroque ruenti,
qua ventum est, obstent Alpes.   super ardua ductum
huc egere dei, Latios ut sanguine fines   76
imbueret, tellusque hostilis conderet ossa.
scire libet, nova nunc nobis atque altera bellum
Carthago, anne eadem mittat, quae, mersa sub aequor,
Aegates inter vasto iacet obruta ponto."   80
    Haec ait atque agmen Ticini flectit ad undas.
caeruleas Ticinus aquas et stagna vadoso
perspicuus servat turbari nescia fundo
ac nitidum viridi lente trahit amne liquorem.
vix credas labi ; ripis tam mitis opacis,   85
argutos inter volucrum certamine cantus,
somniferam ducit lucenti gurgite lympham.
    Iamque sub extremum noctis fugientibus umbris
lux aderat, Somnusque suas confecerat horas—
explorare locos consul collisque propinqui   90
ingenium, et campis quae sit natura, parabat.
par studium Poeno similesque in pectore curae.
ergo aderant, rapidis equitum comitantibus alis.
    Verum ubi commoto docuerunt pulvere nubes

---

    [a] He asserts that his camp is more impregnable than the
city had been.
    [b] See note to i. 35.
    [c] The river beside which Hannibal won the first of his
four great victories in Italy : a tributary of the Po.

enfeebled and frost-bitten by the Alpine snows, and drag their benumbed limbs with difficulty. They have crossed inviolate mountains and rocky chasms : well, let them learn how high our rampart [a] rises above the citadel of Saguntum, and which is the harder task—to climb hills or to break your ranks. Let them boast of their useless exploit—I care not, if only the Alps oppose them, when they have been routed in a great battle and are rushing back the way they came. Heaven brought them hither and led them over the heights, that they might dye the land of Latium with their blood and lay their bones in a hostile soil. I would fain know whether this war is launched by a new and different Carthage or by the same power which sank beneath the waves and now lies buried in the boundless deep near the Aegatian islands." [b]

Thus he spoke, and turned his march aside to the river Ticinus.[c] That crystal river keeps its pools of blue water free from all stain above its shallow bed, and slowly draws along its fair stream of greenish hue. One would scarce believe it was moving ; so softly along its shady banks, while the birds sing sweet in rivalry, it leads along in a shining flood its waters that tempt to sleep.

And now night was ending and the darkness departing ; dawn was near and Sleep had completed his allotted hours, when the consul made ready to examine the ground and ascertain the character of the neighbouring hill and plains. Hannibal had the same intention, and the same anxiety filled his heart. So the two came near, escorted by speedy squadrons of horsemen.

But when the rising cloud of dust showed that the

hostem ferre gradum, et propius propiusque sonoro 95
quadrupedum cornu tellus gemit, ac simul acer
vincentum lituos hinnitus saevit equorum :
" arma, viri, rapite arma, viri," dux instat uterque.
ambobus velox virtus geminusque cupido
laudis et ad pugnas Martemque insania concors. 100

Haud mora, iam tantum campi dirimebat ab ictu,
quantum impulsa valet comprendere lancea nodo,
cum subitum liquida, non ullis nubibus, aethra
augurium mentes oculosque ad sidera vertit.
accipiter, medio tendens a limite solis, 105
dilectas Veneri notasque ab honore Diones
turbabat violentus aves atque unguibus idem,
idem nunc rostro, duris nunc ictibus alae,
ter quinas dederat saeva inter vulnera leto ;
nec finis satiesve, novi sed sanguinis ardor 110
gliscere, et urgebat trepidam iam caede priorum
incertamque fugae, pluma labente, columbam,
donec Phoebeo veniens Iovis ales ab ortu
in tenues tandem nubes dare terga coegit.
tum victrix laetos signa ad Romana volatus 115
convertit, prolesque ducis qua parte decora
Scipio quassabat puerilibus arma lacertis,
clangorem bis terque dedit, rostroque coruscae
perstringens conum galeae, se reddidit astris.

Exclamat Liger (huic superos sentire monentes 120
ars fuit ac penna monstrare futura magistra) :
" Poene, bis octonos Italis in finibus annos,

---

    [a] See note to i. 318.
    [b] That is, from the South, the direction in which Carthage
lay.
    [c] A name of Venus : the dove was her favourite bird.
    [d] P. Cornelius Scipio Africanus, afterwards conqueror of
Hannibal.

enemy were on the march, and the earth rang with
the sound of hoofs coming ever nearer, and at the
same time the trumpet was drowned by the eager
neighing of the horses, then both leaders called
upon their troops : " To arms, my men ! to arms
with speed ! " Each had the same restless valour,
and the same thirst for glory, and they were kindred
spirits in their passion for war and battle.

There was no delay. Soon the combatants were
separated only by as much ground as a lance sped
by a thong *a* can cover, when suddenly all eyes and
thoughts were turned to the sky by a portent appear-
ing in the clear and cloudless heavens. A hawk,
flying from the sun in his meridian,*b* was fiercely
assailing a flock of the birds that are dear to Venus
and owe their fame to the favour of Dione *c* ;
now with talons, now with beak, and now with fierce
buffeting of his wings, he had cruelly wounded and
slain fifteen victims. Nor did he stop, satisfied : his
eagerness for a fresh victim grew, and he pressed
hard on the last dove, while she wavered in her flight
with flagging wing, terrified by the slaughter of the
rest. But now an eagle, coming up from the East,
forced the hawk at last to fly for refuge to the
unsubstantial clouds. Then the undefeated dove
turned and flew gladly towards the Roman standards
and the place where the general's son, Scipio,*d*
was brandishing shining weapons with his childish
strength ; then, when she had uttered her note thrice
and pecked at the plume of the boy's glittering
helmet, she went back to the sky.

A cry came from Liger—he was skilled to perceive
the warnings of heaven and to foretell the future by
watching the birds :—" Hannibal, you, like that bold

audaci similis volucri, sectabere pubem
Ausoniam multamque feres cum sanguine praedam.
sed compesce minas ; renuit tibi Daunia regna   125
armiger ecce Iovis.   nosco te, summe deorum.
adsis o firmesque tuae, pater, alitis omen.
nam tibi servantur (ni vano cassa volatu
mentitur superos praepes) postrema subactae
fata, puer, Libyae et maius Carthagine nomen."   130
    Contra laeta Bogus Tyrio canit omina regi,
et faustum accipitrem caesasque in nube volucres
Aeneadis cladem et Veneris portendere genti.
tum dictis comitem contorquet primus in hostes,
ceu suadente deo et fatorum conscius, hastam.   135
illa volans patuli longe per inania campi
ictum perdiderat spatio, ni, fusus habenas,
dum primae decus affectat decerpere pugnae,
obvia quadrupedis praeceps Catus ora tulisset.
sic elanguescens ac iam casura, petitum   140
invenit vulnus caedemque accepit ab hoste
cornus et oblatae stetit inter tempora frontis.
    Incurrunt acies, magnoque fragore per aequor
suspendunt cuncti frenis sublime reductos
cornipedes ultroque ferunt : erectus in auras   145
it sonipes, rapidaque volans per aperta procella,
tenuia vix summo vestigia pulvere signat.
Boiorum ante alias Crixo duce mobilis ala

---

^a The number of years corresponds to the number of
pigeons.   The young Scipio is the eagle.
    ^b A common title of the eagle which was supposed to carry
Jupiter's thunderbolts.
    ^c Africanus.
    ^d Not, to our ears, a felicitous name for a prophet.
    ^e A Celtic tribe.

bird, for twice eight years[a] shall pursue the men of
Rome in the land of Italy, and shall carry off much
booty and shed much blood. But restrain your
threats; for, lo! the armour-bearer of Jupiter[b] with-
holds from you the realm of Daunus. I recognize
thy hand, O mightiest of the gods. Be present, O
Father, and confirm the omen of thy bird! For,
unless the eagle is false to the gods and his flight
means nothing, it is reserved for this boy to seal the
fate of conquered Libya, and to gain a name[c] greater
than that of Carthage."

Bogus,[d] on the other hand, prophesied good fortune
to Hannibal: the hawk was a favourable sign, and the
slaughter of birds in the sky foretold disaster to the
Aeneadae, the descendants of Venus. Then, to suit
his words, he hurled the first spear against the foe, as
if prompted by heaven and aware of coming events.
The weapon flew far over the empty space of the
spreading plain, and distance would have robbed it of
its effect, but for the desire of Catus to reap glory in
the first battle. He galloped forward with loosened
rein and drove his horse's head to meet it; and so
the spear, when flagging in its course and ready to
fall, found the mark it sought and received from the
enemy power to kill; it lodged between the temples
of the brow that courted death.

The armies advance at speed, and a mighty noise
spreads over the field when all the riders raise their
horses' heads high with the bridle and then urge
them forward; rearing aloft, the chargers then rush
on and in their stormy flight over the plain leave
hardly a trace of their hoof-prints on the dusty
surface. A swift squadron of Boii,[e] commanded by
Crixus, takes the lead, dashing against the front rank

arietat in primos obicitque immania membra.
ipse, tumens atavis, Brenni se stirpe ferebat   150
Crixus et in titulos Capitolia capta trahebat.
Tarpeioque iugo demens et vertice sacro
pensantes aurum Celtas umbone gerebat.
colla viri fulvo radiabant lactea torque,
auro virgatae vestes, manicaeque rigebant   155
ex auro, et simili vibrabat crista metallo.

   Sternitur impulsu vasto perculsa Camertum
prima phalanx, spissaeque ruunt conferta per arma
undae Boiorum ; sociata examina densent
infandi Senones ; collisaque quadrupedantum   160
pectoribus toto volvuntur corpora campo.
arva natant, altusque virum cruor, altus equorum
lubrica belligerae sorbet vestigia turmae.
seminecum letum peragit gravis ungula pulsu
et circumvolitans taetros e sanguine rores   165
spargit humo miserisque suo lavit arma cruore.
spicula prima, puer, tumidi, Tyrrhene, Pelori
purpureo moriens victricia sanguine tinguis.
nam tibi, dum stimulas cornu atque in proelia mentes
accendis renovasque viros ad vulnera cantu,   170
haesit barbaricum sub anhelo gutture telum
et clausit raucum letali vulnere murmur.
at sonus, extremo morientis fusus ab ore,
flexa pererravit mutis iam cornua labris.

---

  [a] For this Gallic chief see note to i. 624-625.
  [b] A town in Umbria, whose inhabitants were called Camertes.
  [c] So called because the capture of Rome in 390 B.C. was effected by that tribe.
  [d] The names of the common soldiers were no doubt invented by Silius. He gives the name of Tyrrhenus to a trumpeter, because this epithet is often applied to the trumpet

of Romans, and blocking the way with their giant
bodies. Crixus himself, proud of his ancestry,
claimed descent from Brennus,[a] and the taking of the
Capitol was one of his titles to fame. Poor fool ! he
displayed on his shield the Gauls weighing the gold
on the sacred eminence of the Tarpeian hill. A golden
collar glittered on his snow-white neck ; his garments
were striped with gold, with gold his gauntlets were
stiff, and his helmet-crest sparkled with the same
metal.

Their fearful charge struck and overthrew the men
of Camerium[b] in the front rank, and the Boii rushed
over the close-packed spears like crowding waves ;
and the accursed[c] Senones joined them and swelled
their ranks ; and men's bodies, shattered by the
chests of the horses, tumble over all the plain. The
ground is drenched ; pools of blood, from men and
horses, swallow up the slippery footprints of the fight-
ing squadron. The heavy hoof kills outright those
who are half-dead already ; and the horses, as they
ride round, scatter on the ground a hideous dew of
blood, and the armour of the poor wretches is drenched
with their own gore. The first victorious javelin
was thrown by proud Pelorus, and stained by the red
life-blood of young Tyrrhenus.[d] For, while he blew
his horn, to stir the soldiers' hearts and kindle their
courage for battle, and to make them face fresh
wounds by his music, the barbarian's weapon stuck
fast in his windpipe and stopped with a deadly
wound the hoarse murmur of the horn. Yet the last
music that came from his dying lips trickled through
the curved instrument, after the lips themselves were

which was invented by the *Tyrrheni* (the Greek name for the
Etruscans or Tuscans).

181

Crixus Picentem Laurumque, nec eminus ambo, 175
sed gladio Laurum ; Picenti rasilis hasta,
ripis lecta Padi, letum tulit.   avia namque
dum petit ac laevo meditatur fallere gyro,
hasta viri femur et pariter per nuda volantis
ilia sedit equi et geminam dedit horrida mortem. 180
idem, sanguinea Venuli cervice revellens,
sternit praecipitem tepido te, Farfare, telo
et te sub gelido nutritum, Tulle, Velino,
egregium Ausoniae decus ac memorabile nomen,
si dent fata moras, aut servent foedera Poeni ;   185
tum Remulum atque, olim celeberrima nomina bello,
Tiburtes Magios Hispellatemque Metaurum
et Clanium, dubia meditatus cuspide vulnus.

 Nec locus est Tyriis belli pugnaeve, sed omnem
Celticus implevit campum furor ; irrita nulli   190
spicula torquentur, statque omne in corpore ferrum.
hic inter trepidos immane Quirinius audens,
cui fugere ignotum atque invicta mente placebat
rebus in adversis exceptum pectore letum,
cuspide flammat equum ac dispergit gaesa lacerto, 195
si reserare viam atque ad regem rumpere ferro
detur iter ; certusque necis petit omnibus ausis,
quod nequeat sentire, decus.   cadit inguine fosso
Teutalus, et vasto quatitur sub pondere tellus.
occumbit Sarmens, flavam qui ponere victor   200
caesariem crinemque tibi, Gradive, vovebat

---

 a The name of a river and lake in the Sabine country.
   b In which case there would have been no war.

182

dumb. Crixus slew Picens and Laurus, but not both
from a distance ; for Laurus fell by the sword, but
Picens was slain by a polished spear, once cut on
the banks of the Po. For, when Picens tried to turn
aside and sought to elude his foe by wheeling to the
left, the terrible spear pierced at the same time the
rider's thigh and the unprotected belly of the flying
steed, inflicting a double death. Crixus also plucked
his weapon from the gory neck of Venulus and, while
it was still warm, laid low Farfarus with it, and Tullus
who was reared near cold Velinus *ᵃ*—a proud boast
of Italy he would have been and a famous name, if
the Fates had granted him longer life or the Cartha-
ginians had adhered to the treaty.*ᵇ* Next Crixus slew
Remulus, and warriors whose names were once
famous in arms—the Magii of Tibur, Metaurus of
Hispellum, and Clanius,—and aimed his blow with a
spear which doubted whom to strike.

The Carthaginians had no room for fighting, because
the furious Gauls filled all the field ; not one of them
hurled his weapon in vain ; every missile was planted
in the body of a foe. And now Quirinius, to whom
flight was a thing unknown, and whose dauntless
heart chose death with wounds in front, when the
battle went against them, showed mighty daring,
while those around him trembled. He spurred his
horse with his spear-point and hurled javelins with
his strong arm, hoping to clear a passage and burst
his way by the steel to Crixus. Assured of death, he
sought with might and main the glory he could never
hope to enjoy. Teutalus, pierced in the groin, fell
before him, and the earth shook under his huge
weight ; and Sarmens next, who vowed, if victorious,
to offer to Mars his yellow locks—the hair that rivalled

auro certantem et rutilum sub vertice nodum.
sed Parcae intonsa non exaudita voventem
ad manes traxere coma ; per candida membra
it fumans cruor, et tellus perfusa rubescit.　　205
at, non tardatus iaculo occurrente, Ligaunus
irruit adversumque viro rotat obvius ensem
et ferit insurgens, humero qua brachia lenti
annectunt nervi, decisaque vulnere laeva[1]
laxatis paulum moribunda pependit habenis ;　　210
dumque micans tremulo conatu lora retemptat,
flectentem assuetos imitatur nescia frenos.
demetit aversi Vosegus tum colla, iubaque
suspensam portans galeam atque inclusa perempti
ora viri, patrio divos clamore salutat.　　215
　　Dumque ea Gallorum populi dant funera campo,
accitas propere castris in proelia consul
raptabat turmas primusque ruebat in hostem,
candenti sublimis equo.　trahit undique lectum
divitis Ausoniae iuvenem, Marsosque Coramque　　220
Laurentumque decus iaculatoremque Sabellum
et Gradivicolam celso de colle Tudertem
indutosque simul gentilia lina Faliscos,
quosque sub Herculeis taciturno flumine muris
pomifera arva creant Anienicolae Catilli,　　225
quosque in praegelidis duratos Hernica rivis
mittebant saxa et nebulosi rura Casini.
ibant in Martem terrae dominantis alumni,

[1] laeva *Ruperti*: dextra *edd.*

---

[a] The knot in which the Gauls tied up their long hair is
often mentioned by Latin writers.

[b] The men of Tibur (now Tivoli) are meant.　Hercules had
a famous temple there.　The city was said to have been
founded by Catillus and Tiburtus, sons of Amphiaraus.　The
district was famous for its fruit.

gold—and the ruddy topknot [a] on the crown of his head. But his vow was unheard, and the Fates drew him down to the shades below with his locks unshorn; the steaming blood drenched his white limbs, and the soaked earth turned red. But now Ligaunus, undeterred by the javelin that met him, rushed on and whirled his sword full in face of Quirinius, rising to his full height as he struck; and the left arm, where the tough muscles attach the limb to the shoulder, was cut off by the blow; for a space it hung dying over the slackened reins, and the quivering hand, while it felt again with feeble effort for the bridle, imitated unwittingly the familiar gesture of the horseman. Then Vosegus cut off his head from behind, and carried off the helmet hanging by its plume with the dead man's head inside it, and hailed his gods with the war-cry of his nation.

While the Gallic tribes dealt death thus over the field, the consul summoned his troops in hot haste from their camp, and charged foremost against the foe, borne aloft on his white steed. Behind him came the soldiers, chosen from every part of fertile Italy— Marsians and men of Cora, the pride of Laurentum and the Sabine throwers of javelins, the hill-dwellers of Tuder who worship Mars, and with them the men of Falerii who wear the flaxen stuff of their country; the men who were bred by the orchards of Catillus, dwellers by the Anio, where the stream runs silent under the walls of Hercules [b]; and the men sent forth by the misty fields of Casinum and by the Hernician rocks, where the people are made hardy by their icy streams. Thus the children of the ruling land [c] went forth to battle; but heaven had condemned them,

[c] Italy.

damnati superis nec iam reditura iuventus.
Scipio, qua medius pugnae vorat agmina vertex, 230
infert cornipedem atque, instinctus strage suorum,
inferias caesis mactat Labarumque Padumque
et Caunum et multo vix fusum vulnere Breucum
Gorgoneoque Larum torquentem lumina vultu.
occidis et tristi, pugnax Lepontice, fato ; 235
nam dum frena ferox obiecto corpore prensat
atque aequat celsus residentis consulis ora
ipse pedes, frontem in mediam gravis incidit ensis,
et divisum humeris iacuit caput.   at Batus, amens
qui luctatur equo parmaque incursibus obstat, 240
ictu quadrupedis fulva porrectus harena
elisa incussis amisit calcibus ora.
perfurit Ausonius turbata per aequora ductor,
ceu Geticus Boreas, totum cum sustulit imo
Icarium fundo victor mare ; navita vasto 245
iactatur sparsus, lacerata classe, profundo,
cunctaque canenti perfunditur aequore Cyclas.

Crixus, ut in tenui spes exiguumque salutis,
armat contemptu mentem necis ; horrida barba
sanguinea rutilat spuma, rictusque furentis 250
albet, et affuso squalent a pulvere crines.
invadit Tarium, vicino consule pugnas
miscentem, saevisque virum circumtonat armis.
volvitur ille solo ; nam pronum effundit in armos
fata extrema ferens abies, rapiturque pavore 255
tractus equi, vinctis connexa ad cingula membris.

---

^a That part of the Aegean Sea into which Icarus fell was
named after him.

and the army was doomed never to return. Scipio
urged his steed to where the central whirlpool of
battle was swallowing up the fighters; then, in-
furiated by the carnage of his men, he slaughtered,
as offerings to the dead, Labarus and Padus and
Caunus and Brucus, scarcely laid low with many a
wound, and Larus, as he rolled his eyes with the stare
of a Gorgon. Cruel too was the doom by which brave
Leponticus fell. For when he boldly threw himself
in the consul's way, catching hold of the reins, and,
though on foot, reaching up to the level of the
rider's face, down came the heavy sword on the centre
of his forehead, and the head, split in two, fell upon
the shoulders. Then Batus, while he fought madly
against Scipio's horse and warded off attacks with
his shield, was stretched on the yellow sand by a
blow from the steed, and his face was crushed out
of recognition by the stamping hoofs. Thus the
Roman general raged over the troubled plain, like the
Thracian North-wind, when in his might he has stirred
up from the bottom the whole Icarian *a* sea; ships
are wrecked, and seamen scattered and tossed on the
mighty deep; and all the Cyclades are drenched with
the foaming flood.

With slender hopes and little chance of safety,
Crixus steeled his heart with contempt of death : his
bristling beard was red with a bloody foam, foam
flew from his open mouth in his fury, and his hair was
rough with a coating of dust. He attacked Tarius,
who was fighting beside Scipio, and thundered round
him with furious assault. Tarius rolled upon the
ground; for the death-dealing spear drove him for-
ward upon his horse's neck, and he was dragged along
by the frightened beast, with his feet caught in the

187

longa cruor sparso linquit vestigia campo,
et tremulos cuspis ductus in pulvere signat.
laudabat leti iuvenem egregiosque parabat
ulcisci consul manes, cum dira per aures   260
vox venit, et Crixum ferri clamoribus audit,
haud notum vultu.   surgit violentior ira
comminus atque oculos optato in corpore figit.
tum, stimulans grato plausae cervicis honore,
cornipedem alloquitur : " vulgum Martemque mino-
          rem   265
mox, Gargane ; vocant superi ad maiora.   videsne,
quantus eat Crixus ? iam nunc tibi praemia pono
illum Sidonio fulgentem ardore tapeta,
barbaricum decus, et fulvis donabere frenis."
sic fatus, magno Crixum clamore ciebat   270
in pugnam ac vacuo poscebat proelia campo.
nec detractantem par ira accenderat hostem.
ut iussae cessere retro spatiumque dederunt
hinc atque hinc alae, medio stetit aequore pugna.
quantus Phlegraeis Telluris alumnus in arvis   275
movit signa Mimas caelumque exterruit armis,
tantus semifero Crixus sub pectore murmur
torquet et horrisonis ululatibus erigit iras :
" nemone incensae captaeque superfuit urbi,
ut tibi, quas Brenni populus ferremus in arma,   280
narraret, dextras ? disce en nunc," inquit et una
contorquet nodis et obusto robore diram
vel portas quassare trabem.   sonat illa tremendum
ac, nimio iactu servasse improvida campi
distantis spatium, propiorem transvolat hostem. 285

---

^a Phlegra, afterwards called Pallene, in Macedonia was
the place where Mimas and the other Titans fought against
the gods.
^b See note to i. 624.

188

encircling girth. His blood sprinkled the plain and left long traces there ; and the spear printed uneven marks on the sand. Scipio praised the young man's death, and was preparing to avenge his noble spirit, when a dreadful sound struck his ear, and he knew by the shouting that Crixus, whose face he did not know, was coming. His wrath grew fiercer as they got closer, and he fastened his gaze upon the coveted victim. Then encouraging his steed, and patting his neck to please and honour him, Scipio spoke thus : " Garganus, leave till later the common herd of lesser foes ; the gods summon us to greater things. Do you see the mighty Crixus coming ? Even now I promise to reward you with yonder saddle-cloth, glittering with Tyrian purple—an adornment fit for the barbarian ; and I shall give you the reins of gold." Thus Scipio spoke, and summoned Crixus to battle with a great shout, and demanded an open space for the duel. His enemy, fired with equal ardour, proved no laggard. When the squadrons on both sides fell back as they were bidden and left a clear space, the combatants took stand in the centre of the field. Like the Giant Mimas, the son of Earth, when he fought on the fields of Phlegra [a] and terrified Heaven, so the gigantic Crixus sent forth a cry from his brutish breast and roused his fury with hideous yells. "When Rome was taken and burnt,[b] was no survivor left, to tell you the strength of arm that the tribe of Brennus showed in battle ? Well, learn it now ! " As he spoke, he threw his spear, whose knotted strength and fire-hardened point were fit to batter down even a city gate. With a dreadful sound it flew ; but it went too far, misjudging the distance to be crossed, and the foe was too close ; so it passed over the consul's

189

cui consul : " ferre haec umbris proavoque memento,
quam procul occumbas Tarpeia sede, tibique
haud licitum sacri Capitolia cernere montis."
tum nodo cursuque levi simul adiuvat hastam,
dignum mole viri nisus.   fugit illa per oras   290
multiplicis lini subtextaque tegmina nervis
atque altum tota metitur cuspide pectus.
procumbit lata porrectus in arva ruina,
et percussa gemit tellus ingentibus armis.
haud aliter, structo Tyrrhena ad litora saxo,   295
pugnatura fretis subter caecisque procellis,
pila, immane sonans, impingitur ardua ponto :
immugit Nereus, divisaque caerula pulsu
illisum accipiunt irata sub aequora montem.
ductore amisso pedibus se credere Celtae ;   300
una spes anima tantusque pependerat ardor.
ac veluti summo venator densa Picano
cum lustra exagitat spississque cubilibus atram
immittit passim dumosa per invia pestem—
dum tacitas vires et flammam colligit ignis,   305
nigranti piceus sensim caligine vertex
volvitur et pingui contorquet nubila fumo ;
mox subita in toto lucent incendia monte—
fit sonitus, fugere ferae, fugere volucres,
atque ima longe trepidant in valle iuvencae.   310
    At Mago, ut vertisse globos primumque laborem,
qui solus genti est, cassum videt, arma suorum

---

    [a] For breastplates made of linen see iii. 272.
    [b] Silius refers to the houses built by rich Romans on the
Campanian coast : these often projected over the sea.
    [c] A mountain in Apulia.
    [d] Hannibal's brother.

head. But to him said Scipio: "Remember to tell the shades below and Brennus, your ancestor, how far from the Tarpeian temple you fell, and that *you* were not permitted to behold the sacred hill of the Capitol." Then he added force to his spear by the thong and by the trotting of his horse, and threw it with an effort worthy of his huge antagonist. Through the many folds of linen *a* it sped and through the shield fashioned of hide, and pierced with the length of its point his inmost breast. Down he sank, stretching far over the field in his overthrow, and the earth groaned, smitten by his gigantic armour. Even so, when masons build on the Tuscan shore,*b* they hurl a mass of stone from a height upon the water with a mighty noise, to battle with the sea and the invisible currents below: the sea roars; and the deep, parted by the blow, receives the huge mass as it crashes beneath the angry water. Deprived of their leader, the Gauls had recourse to flight; all their confidence and all their valour depended upon a single life. So the hunter on the top of Mount Picanus *c* harries the haunts of wild beasts, and all through the untrodden thickets spreads fell destruction in their crowded lairs; while the fire is silently gathering strength and flame, the tops of the pine-trees are gradually wrapt in black darkness, and the thick smoke goes eddying to the sky; but soon flames blaze out suddenly over the whole mountain: a crackling is heard, the wild beasts flee, the birds flee, and the heifers are startled in the lowland valleys far away.

When Mago *d* saw that the ranks of Gaul had turned back and that their first effort had failed (and that people is incapable of a second), he summoned

ac patrium in pugnas equitem vocat : undique nudi
assiliunt frenis infrenatique manipli.
nunc Itali in tergum versis referuntur habenis,   315
nunc rursus Tyrias retro pavor avehit alas ;
aut illi dextros lunatis flexibus orbes,
aut illi laevos sinuant in cornua gyros ;
texunt alterno glomerata volumina cursu
atque eadem refuga cedentes arte resolvunt.   320
hac pontum vice, ubi exercet discordia ventos,
fert Boreas Eurusque refert molemque profundi
nunc huc alterno, nunc illuc, flamine gestant.
    Advolat aurato praefulgens murice ductor
Sidonius, circaque Metus Terrorque Furorque.   325
isque ubi Callaici radiantem tegminis orbem
extulit et magno percussit lumine campos,
spes virtusque cadunt, trepidaque a mente recedit
vertere terga pudor ; nec leti cura decori
sed fugere infixum est, terraeque optantur hiatus. 330
sic, ubi Caucaseis tigris se protulit antris,
linquuntur campi, et tutas petit omne latebras
turbatum insano vultu pecus ; illa pererrat
desertas victrix valles, iamque ora reducto
paulatim nudat rictu, ut praesentia mandens   335
corpora, et immani stragem meditatur hiatu.
non illum Metabus, non illum celsior Ufens
evasere tamen, quamvis hic alite planta,
hic ope cornipedis totis ferretur habenis.
nam Metabum ad manes demisit cuspide fulgens 340

---

    [a] See note to i. 215 foll.
    [b] Silius seems here to describe not a real battle of cavalry,
but the *Troia*, a sham fight between boys armed and
mounted : there is a full account of it in Virgil (*Aen.* v. 545
foll.): and Silius has imitated Virgil.
    [c] For Hannibal's shield see ii. 395 foll.

to battle his own men and the cavalry of his country.
From all sides they rode up, men who used bridles
and men who used none.[a] At one time the Romans
turn their reins and retreat; at another, panic carries
back the squadrons of Carthage; either one force
wheels to the right in crescent-shaped curves, or the
other turns with a left wheel to outflank the foe;
riding forwards and then back, they weave their
massed moving ranks and then unweave them in the
skill of their retreat.[b] With such alternation, when
the winds are at variance, the North-wind drives the
sea one way and the East-wind another, and the two
with alternate blasts carry the mighty deep in different
directions.

Now the Carthaginian leader flew to the spot,
gleaming in purple and gold, and with him were Fear
and Terror and Madness. When he raised up the
beamy circle of his Gallician shield[c] and threw a great
light over the plains, then hope and courage fled, and
the shame of retreat was forgotten by fearful hearts;
none cared for a noble death, but all were resolved
to fly and prayed to the earth to swallow them. So,
when a tigress comes forth from her den in the
Caucasus, the plains are deserted, and every beast,
terrified by her furious mien, seeks a safe hiding-
place; she wanders victorious through the deserted
valleys, and presently draws back her lips and slowly
bares her teeth, as if tearing actual bodies, and devises
carnage with wide-gaping jaws. Metabus could not
escape Hannibal, nor could Ufens for all his greater
stature, though the last ran with winged feet, and
the other, with his horse to help him, galloped at
full speed. For the spear with shining point sent
Metabus to the lower world; and the sword slew

fraxinus, Ufentem collapsum poplite caeso
ensis obit laudemque pedum cum sanguine ademit.
iamque dedit leto Sthenium Laurumque domoque
Collinum gelida, viridi quem Fucinus antro
nutrierat dederatque lacum tramittere nando.   345
fit socius leti coniecta Massicus hasta,
vitiferi sacro generatus vertice montis
et Liris nutritus aquis, qui fronte quieta
dissimulat cursum ac, nullo mutabilis imbri,
perstringit tacitas gemmanti gurgite ripas.   350
exoritur rabies caedum, ac vix tela furori
sufficiunt ; teritur iunctis umbonibus umbo,
pesque pedem premit, et nutantes casside cristae
hostilem tremulo pulsant conamine frontem.

Tergemini primam ante aciem sacra proelia fratres
miscebant, quos Ledaeo Sidonia Barce   356
Xanthippo felix uteri inter bella crearat.
res Graiae ductorque parens ac nobile Amyclae
nomen et iniectus Spartanis colla catenis
Regulus inflabant veteri praecordia fama.   360
Marte probare genus factisque Lacona parentem
ardebant gelidosque dehinc invisere montes
Taygeta et tandem bellis innare subactis
Eurotan patrium ritusque videre Lycurgi.
sed Spartam penetrare deus fratresque negarunt   365
Ausonii, totidem numero, quos miserat altis

---

[a] Among the Apennine Hills, in the country of the Marsi.
[b] Mount Massicus in Campania, famous for its vines.
[c] See note to ii. 304. The " wars " are the First Punic
War, in which Regulus was taken prisoner. Leda was a
legendary queen of Sparta : hence Ledaean = Spartan.

194

Ufens when he fell hamstrung and so lost his life and
his repute for speed together. Next Hannibal slew
Sthenius and Laurus and Collinus, the son of a cool
country, whom Lake Fucinus [a] had reared in its
moss-covered grotto and had suffered to swim across
its waters. From these Massicus was not divided in
death, when the spear struck him—Massicus who
was born on the sacred top of the vine-clad hill,[b] and
drank the water of the Liris, a placid stream that
conceals its flow, and, never affected by rain, brushes
its silent banks with sparkling wave. And now began
a furious slaughter, and the madness of the combat-
ants could scarce find weapons ; shield met and
clashed against shield ; foot pressed on foot, and the
nodding helmet-plume waved as it struck the enemy's
brow.

Three brothers, all of an age, fought fiercely in the
first rank. They were the sons of Barce, a Cartha-
ginian, whom their fertile mother bore, during the
wars, to Xanthippus,[c] the Spartan. Their hearts
swelled with pride for the past—the victory of Greece
when their father led the host, the famous name of
Amyclae,[d] and the fetters that the Spartans fastened
upon the neck of Regulus. They burned to prove
by deeds of valour their descent from a Laconian
sire ; and then they were fain to visit the cold
heights of Taygetus, and at last, when war was over,
to swim in their native Eurotas,[e] and see the laws
of Lycurgus. But they never went to Sparta ; for
Heaven and three Italian brothers prevented them.
The three were of the same age and the same spirit ;

[d] An equivalent for Sparta.
[e] Taygetus is a mountain and Eurotas a river, both near
Sparta.

Egeriae genitos immitis Aricia lucis,
aetatis mentisque pares ; at non dabat ultra
Clotho dura lacus aramque videre Dianae.
namque ut in adversos, impacti turbine pugnae,   370
Eumachus et Critias et laetus nomine patris
Xanthippus iunxere gradus, ceu bella leones
inter se furibunda movent et murmure anhelo
squalentes campos ac longa mapalia complent—
omnis in occultas rupes atque avia pernix   375
Maurus saxa fugit, coniuxque Libyssa profuso,
vagitum cohibens, suspendit ab ubere natos ;
illi dira fremunt, perfractaque in ore cruento
ossa sonant, pugnantque feris sub dentibus artus—
haud secus Egeriae pubes, hinc Virbius acer,   380
hinc Capys, assiliunt paribusque Albanus in armis.
subsidens paulum perfossa proruit alvo
Albanum Critias (ast illi cuncta repente
implerunt clipeum miserando viscera lapsu),
Eumachus inde Capyn ; sed tota mole tenebat   385
ceu fixum membris tegimen ; tamen improbus ensis
annexam parmae decidit vulnere laevam,
inque suo pressa est non reddens tegmina nisu
infelix manus atque haesit labentibus armis.
ultima restabat fusis iam palma duobus   390
Virbius.   huic trepidos simulanti ducere gressus
Xanthippus gladio, rigida cadit Eumachus hasta,
et tandem aequatae geminato funere pugnae.
inde alterna viris transegit pectora mucro,
inque vicem erepta posuerunt proelia vita.   395

---

a The spring of the nymph Egeria was near Aricia ; and
here were the grove and temple of Diana, where the priest
obtained his office by killing his predecessor : hence the
epithet " ruthless."

they were bred in the tall groves of Egeria, and ruthless Aricia *a* sent them forth ; but stern Fate suffered them not to look again on Diana's lake *b* and temple. For Eumachus and Critias, with Xanthippus, proud to bear his father's name, were swept on by the tide of battle, and confronted the Romans. Even so, when lions fight one another with fury and fill the desert plains and distant huts with their hoarse roaring, every Moor hastens to remote rocks and untrodden crags, and the African mother raises her babes to her streaming breast, to still their cries ; the beasts roar terribly, the broken bones crack in their blood-stained jaws, and the limbs *c* still fight on, in the grip of the cruel teeth. Even so Egeria's sons, brave Virbius and Capys and their comrade Albanus, sprang forward. Critias, crouching down a moment, stabbed Albanus in the belly and overthrew him ; and at once his bowels all gushed out and filled his shield —a piteous sight. Next Eumachus attacked Capys ; and though he clutched his shield with all his strength as though it were fastened to his body, yet a cruel sword-cut lopped off the left arm as it clung to the shield ; and the luckless hand, refusing to surrender the buckler, still kept its grip and clung to the armour as it fell. Two were now slain, and Virbius alone was left to conquer. He, while shamming flight, slew Xanthippus with his sword and Eumachus with his unbending spear. So at last, when these two were slain, the combat was on equal terms. Then each ran his sword through the other's breast, and they ended the combat by mutual slaughter. Fortunate

b The Lake of Nemi.
c These must be the limbs of the lion, still fighting while being eaten ; but the phrase is strange.

197

felices leti, pietas quos addidit umbris !
optabunt similes venientia saecula fratres,
aeternumque decus memori celebrabitur aevo, ·
si modo ferre diem serosque videre nepotes
carmina nostra valent, nec famam invidit Apollo. 400
   At consul toto palantes aequore turmas
voce tenet, dum voce viget : " quo signa refertis ?
quis vos heu vobis pavor abstulit ?   horrida primi
si sors visa loci pugnaeque lacessere frontem,
post me state, viri, et pulsa formidine tantum   405
aspicite !   has dextras capti genuere parentes.
quo fugitis ?   quae spes victis ?   Alpesne petemus ?
ipsam turrigero portantem vertice muros
credite summissas Romam nunc tendere palmas.
natorum passim raptus caedemque parentum   410
Vestalesque focos extingui sanguine cerno.
hoc arcete nefas ! "   postquam inter talia crebro
clamore obtusae crassoque a pulvere fauces,
hinc laeva frenos, hinc dextra corripit arma
et latum obiectat pectus strictumque minatur   415
nunc sibi, nunc trepidis, ni restent, comminus ensem.
   Quas acies alto genitor dum spectat Olympo,
consulis egregii movere pericula mentem.
Gradivum vocat et patrio sic ore profatur :
" magnanimi, me nate, viri, ni bella capessis,   420
haud dubie extremus terret labor ; eripe pugnae
ardentem oblitumque sui dulcedine caedum.

---

    [a] He means that the Carthaginians had been conquered in the First Punic War, a generation ago.
    [b] Personifications of cities often wear this kind of crown.
    [c] He threatened to commit suicide if they disgraced him.

in death were they, whom love of kin and country
sent down to join the dead! Coming ages will pray
for brethren like them, and their undying fame shall
be for ever remembered, if only my verse has power
to endure and see a distant posterity, and if Apollo
has not begrudged me fame.

When the ranks were straggling over all the plain,
Scipio's voice (while his voice lasted) stopped them :
" Whither do you carry back your standards ? What
panic has robbed you of yourselves ? If it seemed a
dreadful thing to stand in the front rank and challenge
the van of the foe, then take your stand behind me,
soldiers, dismiss your fears, and merely look on !
Yonder warriors are the sons of our prisoners.[a]
Whither do you fly ? What hope have you, if defeated ?
Shall we make for the Alps ? Believe that Rome in
person, with her walls and her head crowned with
towers,[b] is now stretching out her hands in supplica-
tion. I see all our children carried captive, our
parents slain, and the fires of Vesta quenched with
blood. Keep this sacrilege far away ! " Thus he
shouted again and again, till the effort and the thick
dust choked his voice ; then he seized his reins with
the left hand and his sword with the right, and ex-
posed his broad breast to the foe, threatening to use
his bare blade at once, now against himself[c] and now
against the fugitives, if they refused to stand.

When the Father of Heaven beheld this battle
from the height of Olympus, his heart was moved by
the danger of the noble consul. He summoned Mars
and spoke thus to his son : " Son, unless thou takest
part in the strife, this will surely be the last fight of
yonder hero ; and I fear for him. Snatch him away
from the battle ; so fiery is he, and he forgets

siste ducem Libyae ; nam plus petit improbus uno
consulis exitio, tota quam strage cadentum.
praeterea, cernis, tenerae qui proelia dextrae   425
iam credit puer atque annos transcendere factis
molitur longumque putat pubescere bello,
te duce primitias pugnae, te magna magistro
audeat, et primum hoc vincat, servasse parentem."

  Haec rerum sator. at Mavors in proelia currus 430
Odrysia tellure vocat ; tum fulminis atri
spargentem flammas clipeum galeamque deorum
haud ulli facilem multoque labore Cyclopum
sudatum thoraca capit quassatque per auras
Titanum bello satiatam sanguinis hastam   435
atque implet curru campos. exercitus una
Irarum Eumenidesque simul letique cruenti
innumerae facies, frenisque operata regendis
quadriiugos atro stimulat Bellona flagello.
fertur ab immenso tempestas horrida caelo   440
nigrantesque globos et turbida nubila torquens
involvit terras ; quatitur Saturnia sedes
ingressu tremefacta dei ; ripasque relinquit,
audito curru, fontique relabitur amnis.

  Ductorem Ausonium telis Garamantica pubes 445
cinxerat et Tyrio regi nova dona parabat,
armorum spolium ac rorantia consulis ora.
stabat Fortunae non cedere certus et acri
mole retorquebat, crudescens caedibus, hastas,

---

  [a] The consul's son, P. Cornelius Scipio, the elder Africanus.
    [b] Thrace.
   [c] The vast size of the chariot is implied.
     [d] Italy : see note to i. 70.

himself in the joy of slaughter. Stop Hannibal ; for the insatiate African hopes more from the death of Scipio than from all the heaps of slain. Thou seest, moreover, that boy [a] who already relies on his youthful arm for battle, and aims at prowess beyond his years, and thinks that ripeness for war is slow to come. Thou must be his leader when he wins his maiden spurs ; thou must teach him to aspire to great deeds ; and let his first victory be the rescue of his sire."

Thus spoke the Father of all things. And straightway Mars summoned his chariot from the land of the Odrysae.[b] Then he took the shield that scatters flames of terrible lightning ; he put on the helmet too heavy for any other of the gods to wear, and the breastplate which cost the Cyclopes who wrought it much sweat ; he brandished aloft the spear that had its fill of blood in the war with the Titans ; and he filled the fields with his chariot.[c] With him went his train—Wrath accompanied by the Furies, and countless forms of bloody death ; and Bellona, busy with the reins, urged on the four coursers with her fatal scourge. A fearful storm burst from the boundless sky and shrouded the earth, driving dark masses of stormy cloud. The land of Saturn [d] trembled and shook at the approach of the god ; and the Ticinus left its banks at the sound of the chariot and flowed backwards to its source.

The Garamantian spearmen had made a ring round the Roman general ; they sought to give Hannibal what he had never got before—the dripping head of a consul, and his armour as booty. Scipio stood firm, resolved never to yield to Fortune ; made fiercer by slaughter, he hurled back spear for spear with

iamque suo, iamque hostili perfusa cruore   450
membra madent, cecidere iubae, gyroque per orbem
artato, Garamas iaculis propioribus instat
et librat saeva †coniectum†[1] cuspide ferrum.
  Hic puer ut patrio defixum corpore telum
conspexit, maduere genae, subitoque trementem 455
corripuit pallor, gemitumque ad sidera rupit.
bis conatus erat praecurrere fata parentis,
conversa in semet dextra ; bis transtulit iras
in Poenos Mavors.   fertur per tela, per hostes
intrepidus puer et Gradivum passibus aequat.   460
continuo cessere globi, latusque repente
apparet campo limes.   metit agmina tectus
caelesti clipeo et sternit super arma iacentum
corporaque auctorem teli multasque paternos
ante oculos animas, optata piacula, mactat.   465
tunc, rapta propere duris ex ossibus hasta,
innixum cervice ferens humeroque parentem,
emicat.   attonitae tanta ad spectacula turmae
tela tenent, ceditque loco Libys asper, et omnis
late cedit Hiber ; pietasque insignis et aetas   470
belligeris fecit miranda silentia campis.
tum celso e curru Mavors : " Carthaginis arces
exscindes," inquit, " Tyriosque ad foedera coges.
nulla tamen longo tanta exorietur in aevo
lux tibi, care puer : macte, o macte indole sacra, 475
vera Iovis proles ! et adhuc maiora supersunt ;
sed nequeunt meliora dari." tum nubila Mavors

----

[1] *The word obelized seems to be corrupt.*

----

  [a] For Scipio's parentage see xiii. 634 foll.
  [b] It is doubtful whether Scipio was really saved by his
son : Livy preserves a contemporary tradition, that a
Ligurian slave was the rescuer.

vehement effort. By now his limbs were drenched with his own blood and the enemy's ; the plume fell from his helmet ; the Garamantes, drawing a closer circle round him, pressed nearer with their weapons ; and one launched a dart that pierced him with its cruel point.

When the boy saw the weapon lodged in his father's body, tears wetted his cheeks, he trembled and turned pale in a moment, and his loud cry went up to heaven. Twice he sought to lay violent hands on himself and die before his father ; but twice Mars turned his fury against the Carthaginians instead. Boldly the boy rushed on through missiles and through enemies, keeping pace with Mars himself. At once the ranks gave way, and a wide passage was seen suddenly upon the plain. Protected by the god's shield, he mowed down the host ; over the armour and bodies of the slain he laid low the thrower of the dart, and many a life—the atoning sacrifice he longed for—does he immolate before his father's eyes. Then in haste he drew the spear from the tough bone, and sped away, bearing his father supported on his neck and shoulders. Amazed at such a sight, the soldiers lowered their weapons ; every fierce Libyan and every Spaniard everywhere gave ground : his youth and his noble defence of his father brought about a wondrous silence on the field of battle. Then Mars spoke from his lofty car : " Thou shalt sack the citadel of Carthage, and force her people to make peace. But the glory of this day surpasses all that a long life will offer thee, dear boy. Blessings on thy glorious promise, true child of Jupiter [a] ! Greater things are yet to come, but a better gift Heaven cannot give." [b] The sun had now completed

aetheraque, emenso terras iam sole, capessit ;
et fessas acies castris clausere tenebrae.

   Condebat noctem devexo Cynthia curru,   480
fraternis afflata rotis, et ab aequore Eoo
surgebant roseae media inter caerula flammae.
at consul, tristes campos Poenisque secundam
planitiem metuens, Trebiam collesque petebat.
iamque dies rapti cursu navoque labore,   485
et medio abruptus fluitabat in amne solutis
pons vinclis, qui Dardanium travexerat agmen,
Eridani rapidas aderat cum Poenus ad undas.
dumque vada et molles aditus per devia flexo
circuitu petit et stagni languentia quaerit,   490
interdum rapta vicinis saltibus alno
flumineam texit, qua travehat agmina, classem :
ecce aderat Trebiaeque simul vicina tenebat,
Trinacrio accitus per caerula longa Peloro,
Gracchorum proles, consul. gens inclita magno   495
atque animosa viro, multusque in imagine claris
praefulgebat avus titulis bellique domique.

   Nec Poeni, positis trans amnem in gramine castris,
deerant ; namque animos stimulabant prospera
    rerum
increpitansque super ductor : " quis tertius urbi 500
iam superest consul ? quaenam altera restat in armis
Sicania ? en omnes Latiae Daunique nepotum

---

   a The moon : her " brother " is the sun.
   b The Carthaginian cavalry was especially formidable.
The Trebia is an Apennine tributary of the Po.
   c The other consul in this year (218 B.C.), Ti. Sem-
pronius Longus. The Gracchi also belonged to the Sem-
pronian *gens*.
   d The consul had just brought reinforcements from Sicily ;

his journey over the earth, and Mars betook himself
to the clouds and the sky ; and darkness confined
the weary armies to their camps.

Cynthia[a] with downward course was ending the
night, while her brother's coursers breathed fire upon
her ; and from the eastern wave roseate lights ascended
amid the blue of heaven. Then Scipio, fearing the
fatal plain and the level ground so favourable to the
Carthaginians,[b] made for the Trebia and the hills.
The days flew by, as they marched and toiled busily ;
and, when Hannibal reached the swift stream of the
Po, the bridge by which the Roman army had crossed
was broken down and floating in midstream, with
its cables cut. While Hannibal marched round by
devious paths, seeking a ford and an easy approach
and a peaceful stretch of the river, meantime he
felled with speed the trees that grew hard by, and
built barges, to take his army across the stream. And
now, behold ! a consul, a scion of the Gracchi,[c] arrived
and encamped near his colleague beside the Trebia.
In answer to a summons he had made the long voyage
from Pelorus in Sicily. The family of this great man
was famous for its high spirit ; and, among the busts
of his ancestors, many were conspicuous for dis-
tinctions won both in war and peace.

The Carthaginians, after pitching their camp in
the fields across the river, were not backward either.
For they were encouraged by success and by their
leader, who taunted the Romans thus : " Has Rome
yet a third consul in reserve, or a second Sicily[d]
to fight her battles ? No ! all the fighting men of
Latium and all the descendants of Daunus are here
and Hannibal assumes that no further help can come from
there.

205

convenere manus.   feriant nunc foedera mecum
ductores Italum ac leges et pacta reposcant.
at tu, donata tela inter Martia luce,   505
infelix animae, sic, sic vivasque tuoque
des iterum hanc laudem nato ; nec fine sub aevi
oppetere in bello detur, cum fata vocabunt.
pugnantem   cecidisse   meum   est."   haec   personat
  ardens.
inde levi iaculo Massylumque impiger alis   510
castra sub ipsa datis irritat et elicit hostem.

 Nec Latius vallo miles debere salutem
fas putat, aut clausas pulsari cuspide portas.
erumpunt, cunctisque prior volat aggere aperto
degener haud Gracchis consul. quatit aura comantes
cassidis Auruncae cristas, humeroque refulget   516
sanguinei patrium saguli decus. agmina magno
respectans clamore vocat, quaque obvia densos
artat turba globos, rumpens iter aequore fertur.
ut torrens celsi praeceps e vertice Pindi   520
cum sonitu ruit in campos magnoque fragore
avulsum montis volvit latus ; obvia passim
armenta immanesque ferae silvaeque trahuntur ;
spumea saxosis clamat convallibus unda.

 Non, mihi Maeoniae redeat si gloria linguae,   525
centenasque pater det Phoebus fundere voces,
tot caedes proferre queam, quot dextera magni
consulis, aut contra Tyriae furor edidit irae.

---

 [a] Scipio.
 [b] " Auruncan " seems to mean " Roman " or " Italian."
The Aurunci were an ancient people of Campania.
 [c] A mountain in Thrace.
 [d] " Maeonian "=" Homeric " : Maeonia is an ancient
name of Lydia, one of the countries which claimed to be
Homer's birthplace : Maeonides, a common name for
Homer in all Latin poetry, is used by Milton also.

assembled. Now let the Roman leaders make a treaty with me; now let them insist upon their contracts and covenants! And you,[a] whose life was spared in the battle, life that was no boon, so, so may you live on and again confer this glory on your son! When life ends and Fate summons you, may death in battle be denied you! To fall fighting belongs to Hannibal." Thus he cried in his fury. Then, impatient of delay, he sent light-armed Massylian squadrons to the verge of the Roman camp, to provoke the foe and draw him forth.

The Roman soldiers too were ashamed to owe their safety to their stockade, or to let the spears strike against the closed gates of the camp. They sallied forth; and, when the rampart was levelled, the consul, worthy descendant of the Gracchi, rushed out before them all. The wind blew out the horse-hair plume of his Auruncan [b] helmet, and the scarlet cloak that had graced his ancestors was conspicuous on his shoulder. Looking back on the ranks, he summoned them with a loud voice; and wherever a mass of foemen in close formation met him, he burst his way through and sped along the plain. Even so a roaring torrent falls headlong from the summit of Pindus [c] to the plain; with a mighty noise it tears away a side of the mountain and rolls it down; all the cattle in its path, the wild beasts, and the forests, are swept along; and the foaming waters are loud in the rocky valleys.

Even if I could reproduce the glorious voice of Homer,[d] and if Father Phoebus granted me to speak with a hundred tongues, I could not set forth all the victims slain by the arm of the great consul or by the furious rage of his Carthaginian opponent. Murranus

Murranum ductor Libyae, ductorque Phalantum
Ausonius, gnaros belli veteresque laborum,   530
alter in alterius fuderunt comminus ore.
monte procelloso Murranum miserat Anxur,
Tritonis niveo te sacra, Phalante, profundo.
ut primum insigni fulsit velamine consul,
quamquam orbus partem visus unoque Cupencus 535
lumine sufficiens bellis, citat improbus hastam
et summae figit tremebundam margine parmae.
cui consul, namque ira coquit : " pone, improbe,
          quicquid
restat in ore fero et truncata fronte relucet."
sic ait, intorquens derecto turbine robur,   540
et dirum tota tramittit cuspide lumen.
nec levior dextra generatus Hamilcare saevit ;
huic cadit infelix niveis Varenus in armis,
Mevanas Varenus, arat cui divitis uber
campi Fulginia, et patulis Clitumnus in arvis   545
candentes gelido perfundit flumine tauros.
sed tristes superi, atque ingrata maxima cura
victima Tarpeio frustra nutrita Tonanti.
instat Hiber levis et levior discurrere Maurus.
hinc pila, hinc Libycae certant subtexere cornus 550
densa nube polum ; quantumque interiacet aequi
ad ripas campi, tantum vibrantia condunt
tela ; nec artatis locus est in morte cadendi.
     Allius, Argyripa Daunique profectus ab arvis

---

     [a] Also called Tarracina, a city built on a hill in the
Volscian country.
     [b] See note to iii. 322.
     [c] Hannibal.
     [d] Mevania, a town in Umbria, stands on the river Clitum-
nus, whose water was supposed to turn white the cattle that

and Phalantus were hardy veterans both ; but Hanni-
bal slew the first in close combat and Gracchus the
second, each general fighting in full view of his rival.
Murranus came from the wind-swept height of
Anxur,[a] and Phalantus from the stainless waters of the
sacred lake, Tritonis.[b] Cupencus had lost an eye, but
found the other enough to fight with ; and, when he
sighted Gracchus, conspicuous in the garb of his
rank, he boldly hurled his spear, and planted it quiver-
ing in the topmost rim of the consul's shield. Boil-
ing with rage, Gracchus cried to him : " Rash man,
leave here the sight that still remains in that fierce
face and gleams from that mutilated brow." With
these words he threw his spear with a strong straight
cast, and the whole point passed through the threat-
ening eye. Nor was the son of Hamilcar[c] less for-
midable in the fray : he slew luckless Varenus who
wore white armour and came from Mevania ; for him
fertile Fulginia ploughed her rich soil, where the
Clitumnus, flowing through the spreading fields,
bathes the white bulls in its cool stream.[d] But Heaven
was cruel, and Varenus got no recompense for the
stately victim he had bred up with fruitless care for
the Thunderer of the Capitol. The Spaniards were
nimble in attack, and the Moors yet more nimble
in their movements. Roman javelins and African
spears vied in covering the sky with a thick cloud,
and all the level ground, as far as the river-banks, was
hidden by the hurtling missiles ; and in that close-
packed throng the dead had no room to fall.

The hunter Allius had come from Argyripa[e] in the

drank of it ; and one of these white bulls was regularly
sacrificed in the course of a Roman " triumph."
  [e] Also called Arpi, a city in Apulia.

venator, rudibus iaculis et Iapyge campum   555
persultabat equo, mediosque invectus in hostes,
Apula non vana torquebat spicula dextra.
huic horret thorax Samnitis pellibus ursae,
et galea annosi vallatur dentibus apri.
verum ubi turbantem, solo ceu lustra pererret   560
in nemore aut agitet Gargano terga ferarum,
hinc Mago, hinc saevus pariter videre Maharbal,
ut subigente fame diversis rupibus ursi
invadunt trepidum gemina inter proelia taurum,
nec partem praedae patitur furor—haud secus acer
hinc atque hinc iaculo devolvitur Allius acto.   566
it stridens per utrumque latus Maurusia taxus ;
obvia tum medio sonuerunt spicula corde,
incertumque fuit, letum cui cederet hastae.
et iam, dispersis Romana per agmina signis,   570
palantes agit ad ripas, miserabile, Poenus
impellens trepidos fluvioque immergere certat.
   Tum Trebia infausto nova proelia gurgite fessis
inchoat ac precibus Iunonis suscitat undas.
haurit subsidens fugientum corpora tellus   575
infidaque soli frustrata voragine sorbet.
nec niti lentoque datur convellere limo
mersa pedum penitus vestigia ; labe tenaci
haerent devincti gressus, resolutaque ripa
implicat aut caeca prosternit fraude paludis.   580
iamque alius super atque alius per lubrica surgens,

---

^a The high wooded promontory that runs out from Apulia
into the Adriatic.

land of Daunus, and now rode over the plain ; his
horse was of Apulian breed and his weapons rude ;
yet he charged the centre of the enemy and threw
his native darts with no erring aim. His breastplate
was the bristly hide of a Samnite bear, and his helmet
was protected by tusks taken from an aged wild boar.
He fought as if he were straying through the coverts
in some lonely wood, or pursuing flying beasts on
Mount Garganus [a] ; but when Mago and fierce
Maharbal, each from his own place, sighted him at
the same moment, then, as two bears, driven by
hunger, come down from opposite cliffs, to fall upon
a bull affrighted by his two antagonists, and their
rage will not suffer them to divide the spoil—even so
brave Allius was overthrown by the javelins that
came from both his foes. The Moorish yew-wood
passed hissing through both his sides ; the points
met and clashed in the centre of his heart ; and it was
doubtful which of the two spears could claim his death.
By now the Roman standards were scattered over
the battle-field ; and Hannibal drove the frightened
stragglers towards the bank—O pitiful sight !—push-
ing them on and striving to drown them in the river.

Then, obedient to Juno's petition, the Trebia, that
river of ill omen, began a fresh assault upon the weary
Romans, and roused up its waters. The bank fell in
and swallowed up the bodies of the fugitives, and
sucked them in by the treacherous quagmire of the
soil. Nor could they move on and extract their feet
from the deep and sticky mud. For the clinging mire
held them prisoners ; the crumbling bank entangled
them, or the swampy ground trapped them without
warning and overthrew them. One after another
they struggled up the slippery sides, each trying to

dum sibi quisque viam per inextricabile litus
praeripit et putri luctatur caespite, lapsi
occumbunt seseque sua pressere ruina.
ille, celer nandi, iamiamque apprendere tuta   585
dum parat et celso connisus corpore prensat
gramina summa manu liquidisque emergit ab undis,
contorta ripae pendens affigitur hasta.
hic hostem, orbatus telo, complectitur ulnis
luctantemque vado permixta morte coercet.   590
mille simul leti facies.   Ligus occidit arvis ;
sed proiecta viri lymphis fluvialibus ora
sanguineum hauserunt longis singultibus amnem.
enabat tandem medio vix gurgite pulcher
Irpinus sociumque manus clamore vocabat,   595
cum rapidis illatus aquis et vulnere multo
impulit asper equus fessumque sub aequora mersit.
   Accumulat clades subito conspecta per undas
vis elephantorum turrito concita dorso.
namque vadis rapitur praeceps, ceu proruta cautes 600
avulsi montis, Trebiamque insueta timentem
prae se pectore agit spumantique incubat alveo.
explorant adversa viros, perque aspera duro
nititur ad laudem virtus interrita clivo.
namque inhonoratam Fibrenus perdere mortem   605
et famae nudam impatiens : " spectabimur," inquit,
" nec, Fortuna, meum condes sub gurgite letum.
experiar, sitne in terris, domitare quod ensis
non queat Ausonius, Tyrrhenave permeet hasta."

ᵃ A striking instance of the way in which Silius uses
epithets : English seems to require that both " Ausonian "
and " Tuscan " should here be rendered by " Roman."
212

outstrip the rest along the pathless bank, and battling with the crumbling turf; but they slipped and fell, buried under the rubbish that fell with them. One of them, a speedy swimmer, struggled for a safe hand-hold and forced his way upward, to grasp the turf at the top; but, just as he emerged from the water, a spear was hurled and pinned him to the bank to which he was clinging. Another, having no weapon left, clasped a foe in his arms and held him fast as he tried to swim, till they were drowned together. Death showed itself in a thousand shapes. Though Ligus fell on land, his head hung over the river and drank in the blood-stained water with long sobbing gasps. After much effort comely Irpinus had almost swum ashore from mid-stream; he was shouting to his comrades for a helping hand, when a horse, infuriated by wounds, was carried down by the swift current and struck him down and submerged the weary swimmer.

The crowning disaster came suddenly in sight, when a troop of elephants, with towers upon their backs, were driven into the river. For they rushed headlong through the water, like a cliff falling down from a shattered mountain. They drove the Trebia, dreading dangers unknown till now, before them with their forequarters, and lay down above the foaming channel. Manhood is tested by trial, and valour climbs unterrified the rocky path and difficult ascent that leads to glory. So Fibrenus disdained to die to no purpose, unhonoured and unsung. "The eyes of men shall behold me," he cried, "and Fortune shall not hide my death beneath the flood. I shall find out whether there is aught on earth which a Roman sword cannot master or a Roman spear[a] cannot

213

tum iacit assurgens dextroque in lumine sistit   610
spicula saeva ferae telumque in vulnere linquit.
stridore horrisono penetrantem cuspidis ictum
belua prosequitur laceramque cruore profuso
attollit frontem ac lapso dat terga magistro.
tum vero invadunt iaculis crebraque sagitta,   615
ausi iam sperare necem, immensosque per armos
et laterum extensus venit atra cuspide vulnus ;
stat multa in tergo et nigranti lancea dorso,
ac silvam ingentem, concusso corpore, vibrat,
donec, consumptis longo certamine telis,   620
concidit et clausit magna vada pressa ruina.

  Ecce per adversum, quamquam tardata morantur
vulnere membra virum, subit implacabilis amnem
Scipio et innumeris infestat caedibus hostem.
corporibus clipeisque simul galeisque cadentum   625
contegitur Trebia, et vix cernere linquitur undas.
Mazaeus iaculo, Gestar prosternitur ense ;
tum Pelopeus avis Cyrenes incola Thelgon.
huic torquet rapido correptum e gurgite pilum
et, quantum longo ferri tenuata rigore   630
procedit cuspis, per hiantia transigit ora.
pulsati ligno sonuere in vulnere dentes.
nec leto quaesita quies : turgentia membra
Eridano Trebia, Eridanus dedit aequoris undis.
tu quoque, Thapse, cadis, tumulo post fata negato. 635

214

pierce." Rising to his full height he threw his cruel shaft and planted it in the right eye of one great beast ; and the weapon remained in the wound. When the point of the spear went in, the monster met it with a hideous trumpeting ; then it raised its wounded and bleeding head, threw its rider, and turned in flight. But now the Romans, daring at last to hope that they might kill it, assailed it with darts and showers of arrows. Soon the vast expanse of its shoulders and sides was covered with wounds from the cruel steel ; many a lance stuck in its dusky back and rump ; and, when it shook itself, the huge forest of missiles waved. At last, when the long contest had used up all their weapons, it fell, and the huge carcass blocked the stream beneath it.

But see ! Scipio appears on the opposite bank. Though his limbs, hampered by his wound, cannot move freely, yet he enters the river, and ruthlessly deals out death to countless foes. The Trebia was covered over with close-packed bodies, and shields and helmets of the fallen, till it was scarce possible to see the water. He overthrew Mazaeus with a javelin and Gestar with his sword, and next Thelgon, a native of Cyrene whose ancestors came from the Peloponnese.[a] At him Scipio hurled a javelin which he had caught up from the running stream, and drove the whole length of the tapering iron point through his open mouth ; and the shaft made the teeth rattle in the wound. Nor did death bring him peace ; for the Trebia carried the swollen corpse to the Po, and the Po to the sea. Thapsus also fell, and a grave was denied to him after death.

[a] See note to iii. 252.

quid domus Hesperidum aut luci iuvere dearum,
fulvos aurifera servantes arbore ramos ?

   Intumuit Trebia et stagnis se sustulit imis
iamque ferox totum propellit gurgite fontem
atque omnes torquet vires ; furit unda sonoris   640
verticibus, sequiturque novus cum murmure torrens.
sensit et accensa ductor violentius ira :
" magnas, o Trebia, et meritas mihi, perfide, poenas
exsolves," inquit : " lacerum per Gallica rivis
dispergam rura atque amnis tibi nomina demam ; 645
quoque aperis te fonte, premam ; nec tangere ripas
illabique Pado dabitur. quaenam ista repente
Sidonium, infelix, rabies te reddidit amnem ? "

   Talia iactantem consurgens agger aquarum
impulit atque humeros curvato gurgite pressit.   650
arduus adversa mole incurrentibus undis
stat ductor clipeoque ruentem sustulit amnem.
necnon a tergo fluctus stridente procella
spumeus irrorat summas aspergine cristas.
ire vadis stabilemque vetat defigere gressum   655
subducta tellure deus ; percussaque longe
raucum saxa sonant ; undaeque ad bella parentis
excitae pugnant, et ripas perdidit amnis.
tum madidos crines et glauca fronde revinctum
attollit cum voce caput : " poenasne superbas   660
insuper et nomen Trebiae delere minaris,

---

   a Thapsus came from the far West, where the Hesperides
guarded the Golden Apples : see iii. 285.

   b The Trebia, being an Italian river, was treacherous when
it helped the Carthaginians.

   c To the modern reader this personification of a river
seems strange. But Silius is here imitating Homer, in whose
poem the river Scamander finds a voice and reproaches
Achilles in just the same terms as the Trebia uses here (*Iliad*
xxi. 214 foll.).

What availed him the home of the Hesperides, or the grove where the goddesses guard the ruddy branches of their gold-bearing tree ? [a]

And now the Trebia swelled high, and rose from its lowest depths, driving all its waters fiercely forward, and exerting all its might ; the stream raged with noisy eddies, and a fresh flood came roaring after. When Scipio felt this, his rage grew fiercer, and he cried : " O Trebia, you shall suffer as you deserve, and pay dearly for your treachery [b] : I shall divide your stream and make it flow in separate channels through the land of Gaul ; and I shall rob you of the name of river, and stop the spring from which you rise ; and never shall you be able to reach the banks of the Po and flow into its stream. What sudden madness has turned you, wretched Trebia, into a Carthaginian river ? "

As Scipio hurled these taunts, the rising wall of water smote him and weighed down his shoulders with its arching flood. The general, standing erect, matched his strength against the onset of the waves, and held up the rushing river with his shield. But behind him also the foaming flood with roaring blast bedewed with its spray the topmost plume of his helmet. The river-god, withdrawing the soil from beneath his feet, prevented him from wading through the water and finding firm footing ; the boulders were smitten and sent afar a hollow sound; the waves, called forth to battle by their sire, joined the fray ; and the banks of the river were lost to sight. Then the river-god raised his dripping locks and his head crowned with blue-green weed, and spoke thus [c] : " Arrogant man and enemy of my realm, do you threaten to punish me further and to wipe out my

217

o regnis inimice meis ?   quot corpora porto
dextra fusa tua !   clipeis galeisque virorum,
quos mactas, artatus iter cursumque reliqui.
caede, vides, stagna alta rubent retroque feruntur. 665
adde modum dextrae aut campis incumbe propinquis.''

   Haec, Venere adiuncta, tumulo spectabat ab alto
Mulciber, obscurae tectus caligine nubis.
ingravat ad caelum sublatis Scipio palmis :
'' di patrii, quorum auspiciis stat Dardana Roma, 670
talin me leto tanta inter proelia nuper
servastis ?   fortine animam hanc exscindere dextra
indignum est visum ?   redde o me, nate, periclis,
redde hosti !   liceat bellanti accersere mortem,
quam patriae fratrique probem.''   tum percita dictis
ingemuit Venus et rapidas direxit in amnem   676
coniugis invicti vires.   agit undique flammas
dispersus ripis ignis multosque per annos
nutritas fluvio populatur fervidus umbras.
uritur omne nemus, lucosque effusus in altos   680
immissis crepitat victor Vulcanus habenis.
iamque ambusta comas abies, iam pinus et alni ;
iam, solo restans trunco, dimisit in altum
populus assuetas ramis habitare volucres.
flamma vorax imo penitus de gurgite tractos   685
absorbet latices, saevoque urgente vapore
siccus inarescit ripis cruor.   horrida late
scinditur in rimas et hiatu rupta dehiscit
tellus, ac stagnis altae sedere favillae.

---

   [a] He regrets that his son had saved his life.
   [b] Gnaeus Scipio, consul in 222 B.C., who was now fighting
with success in Spain.
   [c] Vulcan, the fire-god.

name ? How many corpses I carry, slain by your arm ! So packed am I with the shields and helmets of your victims that I have left my proper channel ; you see how my deep pools, red with carnage, are flowing backwards. Put a limit to your deeds of arms, or else attack the plains hard by."

Vulcan was looking on meanwhile from a high hill, hidden in the darkness of a black cloud, with Venus at his side. Then Scipio raised his hands to heaven with a bitter cry : " Ye gods of our country, by whose favour Dardan Rome is preserved, did ye save my life just now in the fierce battle for such a death as this ? Did I seem unworthy to end my life by a soldier's arm ? Give me back, my son, to danger, give me back to the foe ! [a] Suffer me to fight and to welcome such a death as my country and my brother [b] would approve." Then Venus groaned, moved by his prayer, and turned against the river the devouring strength of her invincible consort. [c] Fire spread and burned all over the banks and fiercely devoured the trees that the river had nourished for many a year. All the copses were burnt up, and the victorious flame crackled as it spread in full career to the high groves. Soon the foliage of the fir-tree was seared, and the leaves of pine and alder ; soon nothing was left of the poplar but the trunk, and the tree sent off into the sky the birds that were wont to nest on its branches. The devouring flame sucked the moisture from the very bottom of the stream and licked it up ; and the blood upon the banks was dried up and caked by the fierce heat. The rugged earth everywhere split up and cracked, showing yawning chasms ; and ashes settled in heaps in the bed of the river.

Miratur pater aeternos cessare repente   690
Eridanus cursus ; Nympharumque intima maestus
implevit chorus attonitis ululatibus antra.
ter caput ambustum conantem attollere iacta
lampade Vulcanus mersit fumantibus undis,
ter correpta dei crines nudavit harundo.   695
tum demum admissae voces et vota precantis,
orantique datum ripas servare priores.
ac tandem a Trebia revocavit Scipio fessas
munitum in collem, Graccho comitante, cohortes.
at Poenus, multo fluvium veneratus honore,   700
gramineas undis statuit socialibus aras,
nescius heu, quanto superi maiora moverent,
et quos Ausoniae luctus, Thrasymenne, parares.
   Boiorum nuper populos turbaverat armis
Flaminius, facilisque viro tum gloria belli,   705
corde levem atque astus inopem contundere gentem.
sed labor haud idem Tyrio certasse tyranno.
hunc, laevis urbi genitum ad fatalia damna
ominibus, parat imperio Saturnia fesso
ductorem dignumque virum veniente ruina.   710
inde ubi prima dies iuris, clavumque regendae
invasit patriae, ac sub nutu castra fuere,
ut pelagi rudis et pontum tractare per artem
nescius, accepit miserae si iura carinae,
ventorum tenet ipse vicem cunctisque procellis   715
dat iactare ratem : fertur vaga gurgite puppis,
ipsius in scopulos dextra impellente magistri.
ergo agitur raptis praeceps exercitus armis

---

^a The Po, like all other rivers and lakes, had Nymphs of
its own.
^b The Trebia.
^c C. Flaminius, a popular leader, had been consul in
223 b.c. and now held the office again in 214 : in his first

Father Eridanus marvelled when his immemorial stream suddenly ceased to flow ; and the sorrowing company of Nymphs [a] filled their inmost caves with anguished cries. Thrice he strove to lift up his scorched head, and thrice Vulcan threw a firebrand which sent him down below the steaming water ; and thrice the reeds caught fire and left the god's head bare. At last the voice of his petition was heard, and his prayer was granted—that he might keep his former banks. And at length Scipio, accompanied by Gracchus, recalled his weary troops from the Trebia to a fortified height. But Hannibal paid high honour to the river,[b] and raised altars of turf to the friendly stream. He knew not, alas ! the much greater boon that Heaven intended for him, or the mourning that Lake Trasimene had in store for Italy.

The tribe of the Boii had formerly been attacked by an army under Flaminius [c] ; and then he had gained an easy triumph and crushed a fickle and guileless people ; but to fight the Carthaginian general was a far different task. Flaminius was born in an evil hour to inflict fatal loss upon Rome ; and Juno now chose him as ruler of an exhausted nation and a fit instrument of coming destruction. When his first day of office came, he seized the helm of the state and commanded the armies. So, if a mere landsman, with no skill to manage the sea, has got the command of a luckless vessel, he himself does the work of foul weather, and exposes the ship to be tossed by every gale ; she drifts at random over the sea, and the hand of her own captain drives her upon the rocks. So the army was equipped in haste and led toward the

consulship he had fought with success against the Gauls in N. Italy, the Boii and Insubres.

221

Lydorum in populos sedemque ab origine prisci
sacratam Corythi iunctosque a sanguine avorum 720
Maeonios Italis permixta stirpe colonos.
  Nec regem Afrorum noscenda ad coepta moratur
laude super tanta monitor deus. omnia somni
considerant aegrisque dabant oblivia curis,
cum Iuno, in stagni numen conversa propinqui 725
et madidae frontis crines circumdata fronde
populea, stimulat subitis praecordia curis
ac rumpit ducis haud spernenda voce quietem :
" o felix famae et Latio lacrimabile nomen
Hannibal, Ausoniae si te Fortuna creasset, 730
ad magnos venture deos ! cur fata tenemus ?
pelle moras : brevis est magni Fortuna favoris.
quantum vovisti, cum Dardana bella parenti
iurares, fluet Ausonio tibi corpore tantum
sanguinis, et patrias satiabis caedibus umbras. 735
nobis persolves meritos securus honores.
namque ego sum, celsis quem cinctum montibus
          ambit
Tmolo missa manus, stagnis Thrasymennus opacis."
  His agitur monitis et laetam numine pubem
protinus aërii praeceps rapit aggere montis. 740
horrebat glacie saxa inter lubrica summo
piniferum caelo miscens caput Apenninus.
conciderat nix alta trabes, et vertice celso

---

  [a] The " Lydians " are the Etruscans, who came originally
from Asia and settled in N. Italy : Maeonia is the older
name of Lydia. Cortona, a city of Etruria near Lake
Trasimene, was said to have been founded by Corythus, a
son of Paris and Oenone : the city is called " sacred,"
because Corythus was worshipped there as a " hero."
  [b] Trasimene.
  [c] A mountain in Lydia.
  [d] To reach the fertile country of Etruria, Hannibal had to

222

land of the Lydians, where stands the sacred city founded of old by Corythus, and where Maeonian settlers had mixed their blood with that of Italians in ancient times.[a]

A warning from heaven came quickly to Hannibal, that he might learn the consul's design and win great glory. Sleep had lulled all things to rest and brought to men forgetfulness of trouble, when Juno, counterfeiting the deity of the neighbouring lake,[b] appeared before him, the hair on the dripping brow crowned with poplar leaves. She stirred the general's heart with sudden anxiety, and broke his sleep with a voice he could not disregard. "Hannibal—a glorious name, though a cause of tears to Latium—had Fortune made you a Roman, you would have joined the ranks of the high gods. But why do we arrest the course of destiny ? Make haste ! The flood-tide of Fortune soon ebbs. Those rivers of blood that you vowed, when you swore to your father enmity against Rome, shall flow now from the veins of Italy, and you shall glut your father's ghost with carnage. When your troubles are over, you must pay me the honour that is my due. For I am the lake surrounded by lofty mountains, round which dwell the settlers from Tmolus[c]; I am Trasimene, the lake of shady waters."

Hannibal was encouraged by this prediction, and the soldiers rejoiced in the divine aid. At once he led them at speed over the barrier of lofty mountains.[d] The Apennines were frozen hard and lifted their pine-clad summits to heaven between slippery cliffs. The forests were buried deep in snow, and the hoary peaks

cross the Apennines, in severe winter weather. He lost the sight of one eye from ophthalmia ; and all but one of his elephants died.

canus apex structa surgebat ad astra pruina.
ire iubet : prior extingui labique videtur   745
gloria, post Alpes si stetur montibus ullis.
scandunt praerupti nimbosa cacumina saxi,
nec superasse iugum finit mulcetve laborem.
plana natant, putrique gelu liquentibus undis
invia limosa restagnant arva palude.   750
iamque ducis nudus tanta inter inhospita vertex
saevitia quatitur caeli, manante per ora
perque genas oculo. facilis sprevisse medentes,
optatum bene credit emi quocumque periclo
bellandi tempus. non frontis parcit honori,   755
dum ne perdat iter ; non cetera membra moratur
in pretium belli dare, si victoria poscat ;
satque putat lucis, Capitolia cernere victor
qua petat atque Italum feriat qua comminus hostem.
talia perpessi tandem inter saeva locorum   760
optatos venere lacus, ubi deinde per arma
sumeret amissi numerosa piacula visus.

    Ecce autem patres aderant Carthagine missi ;
causa viae non parva viris, nec laeta ferebant.
mos fuit in populis, quos condidit advena Dido,   765
poscere caede deos veniam ac flagrantibus aris,
infandum dictu ! parvos imponere natos.
urna reducebat miserandos annua casus,
sacra Thoanteae ritusque imitata Dianae.
cui fato sortique deum de more petebat   770

---

    [a] That the Phoenicians and their descendants offered
human sacrifices to their gods appears certain from modern
excavations : a Carthaginian goddess, in whose honour
children were burnt, was Tanith ; and Moloch was honoured
in the same horrid fashion.

    [b] Thoas was king of Tauris (now the Crimea) : Diana (or
Artemis) had a temple there where human sacrifices were
offered.

climbed high into the sky over snow-drifts. He bade
them march on. He thought his past glory tarnished
and lost, if any mountains barred his way after he
had crossed the Alps. They clambered up the storm-
swept heights and rocky precipices ; but even when
the mountains were crossed, there was no end and no
alleviation of their toil. The plains were flooded, the
rivers swollen with melted snow, and the pathless
fields covered with a slimy morass. And amid such
inhospitable surroundings, Hannibal's uncovered head
felt the buffetings of this savage clime, and from his eye
a discharge flowed over face and cheeks. Physicians
he laughed to scorn. He thought no danger too high
a price to pay for the coveted opportunity for war.
For the beauty of his brow he cared nothing, provided
that his march was not in vain ; if victory demanded
it, he was willing to sacrifice every limb for the sake
of war ; it seemed to him that he had sight enough, if
he could see his victorious path to the Capitol, and
a way to strike home at his foe. Such were their
sufferings in that unkind region ; but they came at
last to the lake they longed to see—the place where
Hannibal was to find on the field of battle many a
victim in atonement for his lost sight.

But behold ! senators came as envoys from Car-
thage ; they had good reason for their voyage, and
they bore heavy tidings. The nation which Dido
founded when she landed in Libya were accustomed
to appease the gods by human sacrifices [a] and to offer
up their young children—horrible to tell—upon fiery
altars. Each year the lot was cast and the tragedy
was repeated, recalling the sacrifices offered to Diana
in the kingdom of Thoas.[b] And now Hanno, the
ancient enemy of Hannibal, demanded the general's

Hannibalis prolem discors antiquitus Hannon.
sed propior metus armati ductoris ab ira
et magna ante oculos stabat genitoris imago.

Asperat haec, foedata genas lacerataque crines,
atque urbem complet maesti clamoris Imilce,   775
Edonis ut Pangaea super trieteride mota
it iuga et inclusum suspirat pectore Bacchum.
ergo inter Tyrias, facibus ceu subdita, matres
clamat : " io coniux, quocumque in cardine mundi
bella moves, huc signa refer.   violentior hic est,   780
hic hostis propior.   tu nunc fortasse sub ipsis
urbis Dardaniae muris vibrantia tela
excipis intrepidus clipeo saevamque coruscans
lampada Tarpeis infers incendia tectis.
interea tibi prima domus atque unica proles   785
heu gremio in patriae Stygias raptatur ad aras !
i nunc, Ausonios ferro populare penates
et vetitas molire vias ; i, pacta resigna,
per cunctos iurata deos !   sic praemia reddit
Carthago et tales iam nunc tibi solvit honores !   790
quae porro haec pietas, delubra aspergere tabo ?
heu primae scelerum causae mortalibus aegris,
naturam nescire deum !   iusta ite precari
ture pio caedumque feros avertite ritus.
mite et cognatum est homini deus.   hactenus, oro,
sit satis ante aras caesos vidisse iuvencos ;   796
aut si velle nefas superos fixumque sedetque,

---

[a] Hannibal's wife.
[b] The festival of Bacchus recurred at an interval of three
years.   Pangaeus is a mountain in Thrace.
[c] The crossing of the Alps is meant.

son, as the customary victim to suffer this doom
according to the lot; but the thought of the armed
general's wrath struck home to men's hearts, and the
image of the boy's father stood formidable before
their eyes.

Their fear was heightened by Imilce,[a] who tore
her cheeks and hair and filled the city with woeful
cries. As a Bacchant in Thrace, maddened by the
recurring festival,[b] speeds over the heights of Mount
Pangaeus and breathes forth the wine-god who dwells
in her breast, so Imilce, as if set on fire, cried
aloud among the women of Carthage: " O husband,
hearken! whatever the region of the world where you
are fighting now, bring your army hither; here is a
foe more furious and more pressing. Perhaps at this
moment you stand beneath the walls of Rome itself,
parrying the hurtling missiles with dauntless shield;
perhaps you are brandishing a dreadful torch and
setting fire to the Tarpeian temple. Meanwhile your
first-born and only son is seized, alas, in the heart
of his native country, for a hellish sacrifice. What
boots it to ravage the homes of Italy with the sword,
to march by ways forbidden to man,[c] and to break the
treaty which every god was called to witness? Such
is the reward you get from Carthage, and such the
honours she pays you now! Again, what sort of
religion is this, that sprinkles the temples with blood?
Alas! their ignorance of the divine nature is the chief
cause that leads wretched mortals into crime. Go ye
to the temples and pray for things lawful, and offer
incense, but eschew bloody and cruel rites. God is
merciful and akin to man. Be content with this,
I pray you—to see cattle slaughtered before the
altar. Or, if you are sure beyond all doubt that

227

me, me, quae genui, vestris absumite votis.
cur spoliare iuvat Libycas hac indole terras ?
an flendae magis Aegates et mersa profundo   800
Punica regna forent, olim si sorte cruenta
esset tanta mei virtus praerepta mariti ? "
haec dubios vario divumque hominisque timore
ad cauta illexere patres ; ipsique relictum,
abnueret sortem an superum pareret honori.   805
tum vero trepidare metu vix compos Imilce,
magnanimi metuens immitia corda mariti.

   His avide auditis, ductor sic deinde profatur :
" quid tibi pro tanto non impar munere solvat
Hannibal aequatus superis ?   quae praemia digna 810
inveniam, Carthago parens ?   noctemque diemque
arma feram ; templisque tuis hinc plurima faxo
hostia ab Ausonio veniat generosa Quirino.
at puer armorum et belli servabitur heres.
spes, o nate, meae Tyriarumque unica rerum,   815
Hesperia minitante, salus, terraque fretoque
certare Aeneadis, dum stabit vita, memento.
perge—patent Alpes—nostroque incumbe labori.
vos quoque, di patrii, quorum delubra piantur
caedibus atque coli gaudent formidine matrum,   820
huc laetos vultus totasque advertite mentes.
namque paro sacra et maiores molior aras.

---

   a See note to i. 35.
   b By leaving the decision to him.
   c Quirinus is the name given to Romulus when he was
deified after death.

wickedness is pleasing to the gods, then slay me, me
the mother, and thus keep your vows. Why rob
the land of Libya of the promise shown by this
child ? If my husband's glorious career had been
thus nipped in the bud long ago by the fatal lot,
would not that have been as lamentable a disaster
as the battle by the Aegatian islands *a* when the
power of Carthage was sunk beneath the waves ? "
The senators, hesitating between their fear of the
gods and their fear of Hannibal, were induced by
her appeal to run no risks ; and they left it to Hanni-
bal himself to decide, whether he would defy the lot
or comply with the tribute due to the gods. Then
indeed Imilce became half-frantic with terror ; for
she dreaded the stern heart of her high-souled
husband.

Hannibal listened eagerly to the message and thus
replied : " O Mother Carthage, you have set me on
a level with the gods, *b* and how shall I repay you in
full for such generosity ? What sufficient recompense
can I find ? I shall fight on, night and day, and many
a high-born victim from the people of Quirinus *c* shall
I send from this place to your temples. But the
child must be spared, to carry on my career in arms.
You, my son, on whom rest my hopes, you, who are
the only safeguard of Carthaginian power against
the menace of Italy, remember to fight against the
Aeneadae all your life long. Go forward—the Alps
lie open now—and apply yourself to my task. To
you also I call, gods of my country, whose shrines
are propitiated with bloodshed, and who rejoice in
a tribute that strikes terror to mothers' hearts, turn
hither joyful looks and your whole hearts ; for I am
preparing a sacrifice and building for you mightier

229

tu, Mago, adversi conside in vertice montis,
tu laevos propior colles accede, Choaspe,
ad claustra et fauces ducat per opaca Sychaeus.   825
ast ego te, Thrasymenne, vago cum milite praeceps
lustrabo et superis quaeram libamina belli.
namque haud parva deus promissis spondet apertis,
quae spectata, viri, patriam referatis in urbem."

---

[a] The deity of the lake, whose semblance Juno had put on.

altars. You, Mago, must encamp on the top of the mountain opposite, while Choaspes keeps closer and approaches the hills on our left; and let Sychaeus lead his men through the woods to the gorge and its mouth. I myself shall ride swiftly about Lake Trasimene with a flying force, and shall seek victims of war to offer to the gods. For the express promise of the god[a] assures me of a great victory. It is for you, ambassadors, to witness it and carry back the tale to Carthage."

LIBER QUINTUS

ARGUMENT

Hannibal lays a trap for the enemy. The name of Lake Trasimene (1-23). Flaminius makes light of evil omens

Ceperat Etruscos occulto milite colles
Sidonius ductor perque alta silentia noctis
silvarum anfractus caecis insiderat armis.
at parte e laeva, restagnans gurgite vasto,
effigiem in pelagi lacus humectabat inertis   5
et late multo foedabat proxima limo ;
quae vada, Faunigenae regnata antiquitus Arno,
nunc volvente die Thrasymenni nomina servant.
Lydius huic genitor, Tmoli decus, aequore longo
Maeoniam quondam in Latias advexerat oras   10
Tyrrhenus pubem dederatque vocabula terris ;
isque insueta tubae monstravit murmura primus
gentibus et bellis ignava silentia rupit.
nec modicus voti natum ad maiora fovebat.
verum ardens puero castumque exuta pudorem   15
(nam forma certare deis, Thrasymenne, valeres)
litore correptum stagnis demisit Agylle,

---

^a The river Arnus (now Arno) feeds the lake, and we are here told that the lake too was once called Arnus, before the Lydians came to Italy and settled in Etruria. Tmolus is a mountain in Lydia. Maeonia is an older name for Lydia.
^b See note to iv. 167.

232

BOOK V

ARGUMENT (*continued*)

and the warning of Corvinus, the soothsayer, and encourages his men to fight (24-185). The battle of Lake Trasimene (186-687).

THE Carthaginian leader had seized the Tuscan hills with an unseen force, and in the deep silence of night had occupied the winding woods with troops in ambush. But on their left hand the lake, like a sluggish sea, spread over all the region round with the overflow of its mighty waters and marred the prospect with its abundant slime. This lake was ruled over in ancient times by Arnus, son of Faunus, and now, in a later age, keeps green the name of Trasimene. The father of Trasimene was Tyrrhenus, a Lydian and the pride of Tmolus ; he had formerly brought men of Maeonia the long sea-voyage to the Latin land, and had given his own name to the country,[a] and it was he who first revealed to men the sound of the trumpet,[b] unheard till then, and broke the spiritless silence of battle. An ambitious man, he bred up his son for a higher destiny. But the nymph Agylle loved the young Trasimene ; and indeed in beauty he could contend with the gods themselves. Casting off maiden shame, she seized him on the shore and carried him down to the depths ;

flore capi iuvenem primaevo lubrica mentem
nympha nec Idalia lenta incaluisse sagitta.
solatae viridi penitus fovere sub antro   20
Naides amplexus undosaque regna trementem.
hinc dotale lacus nomen, lateque Hymenaeo
conscia lascivo Thrasymennus dicitur unda.

   Et iam curriculo nigram nox roscida metam
stringebat, nec se thalamis Tithonia coniux   25
protulerat stabatque nitens in limine primo,
cum minus abnuerit noctem desisse viator
quam coepisse diem : consul carpebat iniquas,
praegrediens signa ipsa, vias, omnisque ruebat
mixtus eques ; nec discretis levia arma maniplis 30
insertique globo pedites et inutile Marti
lixarum vulgus praesago cuncta tumultu
implere et pugnam fugientum more petebant.
tum super ipse lacus, densam caligine caeca
exhalans nebulam, late corruperat omnem   35
prospectum miseris, atque atrae noctis amictu
squalebat pressum picea inter nubila caelum.
nec Poenum liquere doli : sedet ense reposto
abditus et nullis properantem occursibus arcet.
ire datur, longeque patet, ceu pace quieta,   40
incustoditum, mox irremeabile, litus.
namque sub angustas artato limite fauces
in fraudem ducebat iter, geminumque receptis

---

   [a] Venus: she had a temple at Idalium in Cyprus.
         [b] Aurora, the Dawn.
            [c] Flaminius, one of the consuls.
234

for her young heart was quick to feel the spell of youthful beauty, nor was she slow to catch fire from the arrow of the Idalian goddess.[a] The Naiads, in their green cave far below, comforted and cherished the boy, when he shrank from his bride's embrace and that watery world. From him the lake, a gift from the bride, got its name ; and the water, aware through all its extent of the marriage joy, still bears the name of Trasimene.

And now the chariot of dewy night was close to its dusky goal, and the spouse of Tithonus,[b] not yet emerged from her marriage-chamber, stood shining on the threshold—a time when the wayfarer is less sure that day has begun than that night is ended. The Roman general [c] was marching over the uneven ground, ahead even of his standards ; all his cavalry hastened in confusion after him ; the skirmishers were not arrayed in separate companies ; the foot-men were mixed up with the body of cavalry ; and the unwarlike rabble of camp-followers filled the air with ominous uproar, and went into battle like fugitives. Then, in addition, the lake itself breathed forth a black and blinding mist, so that the doomed army could see nothing on any side ; and the sky, hidden beneath night's dark robe, was gloomy with pitch-black clouds. Nor did Hannibal forget his cunning. He lay in hiding with sword in rest ; no advance of his blocked the progress of the foe. Their course was free ; and far and wide, as in the stillness of peace, stretched the unguarded shore—the shore, from which there would soon be no returning ; for, the path narrowing as it passed into the closing gorge, their route led into the trap ; and a double doom, with the cliffs on one side and the barrier of

exitium, hinc rupes, hinc undae claustra premebant.
at cura umbroso servabat vertice montis   45
hostilem ingressum, refugos habitura sub ictu.
haud secus ac vitreas sollers piscator ad undas,
ore levem patulo texens de vimine nassam,
cautius interiora ligat mediamque per alvum,
sensim fastigans, compressa cacumina nectit   50
ac fraude artati remeare foraminis arcet
introitu facilem, quem traxit ab aequore, piscem.
   Ocius interea propelli signa iubebat
excussus consul fatorum turbine mentem,
donec flammiferum tollentes aequore currum   55
solis equi sparsere diem.   iamque, orbe renato,
diluerat nebulas Titan, sensimque fluebat
caligo in terras nitido resoluta sereno.
tunc ales, priscum populis de more Latinis
auspicium, cum bella parant mentesque deorum   60
explorant super eventu, ceu praescia luctus,
damnavit vesci planctuque alimenta refugit.
nec rauco taurus cessavit flebile ad aras
immugire sono, pressamque ad colla bipennem
incerta cervice ferens, altaria liquit.   65
signa etiam affusa certant dum vellere mole,
taeter humo lacera nitentum erupit in ora
exultans cruor, et caedis documenta futurae
ipsa parens miseris gremio dedit atra cruento ;
ac super haec divum genitor, terrasque fretumque   70

---

^a The sacred chickens, whose willingness or unwillingness
to feed was regarded by Roman generals as ominous of
victory or defeat.
   ^b See note to iii. 220.

236

the lake on the other, kept them fast in the toils.
Meanwhile on the wooded mountain-top careful watch
waited for the entrance of the Romans, ready
to strike whenever they took to flight. Even so
beside a glassy stream a cunning angler weaves
osiers to make a light and wide-mouthed weel;
the inmost part he frames with especial care, and
for the centre he makes the trap taper gradually to
a point, and fastens together the narrowed ends;
so by the contracting aperture's deceit he forbids
return to the fish which, free as they were to enter,
he has drawn in from the stream.

Meanwhile Flaminius, bereft of his senses and
swept along by destiny, ordered the standards to be
advanced with speed; and then the sun's coursers
lifted his fiery chariot from the sea and scattered day-
light abroad. Soon the sun with disk renewed had
dispelled the vapours; and the darkness, broken up
by the cloudless radiance, floated down by degrees
to earth. But now the birds,[a] which the peoples of
Latium consult by ancient custom, when they go to
war and inquire into the purpose of Heaven concerning
the issue—these birds refused to eat as if aware of
coming disaster, and fled from their food with flapping
wings. And the bull at the altar never ceased to
bellow with hoarse and mournful sound; and when
the axe was swung against him, he met the blow
with shrinking neck and ran away from the altar.
Again, when they tried to wrench the standards from
their mounds of soil,[b] noisome blood spouted forth in
their faces from the broken ground, and Mother Earth
herself sent forth from her bleeding breast dreadful
omens of coming slaughter. Moreover, the Father
of the gods, who shakes earth and sea with his thunder,

concutiens tonitru, Cyclopum rapta caminis
fulmina Tyrrhenas Thrasymenni torsit in undas ;
ictusque aetheria per stagna patentia flamma
fumavit lacus, atque arserunt fluctibus ignes.
heu vani monitus frustraque morantia Parcas   75
prodigia !   heu fatis superi certare minores !
atque hic, egregius linguae nomenque superbum,
Corvinus, Phoebea sedet cui casside fulva
ostentans ales proavitae insignia pugnae,
plenus et ipse deum et socium terrente pavore,   80
immiscet precibus monita atque his vocibus infit :
" Iliacas per te flammas Tarpeiaque saxa,
per patrios, consul, muros suspensaque nostrae
eventu pugnae natorum pignora, cedas
oramus superis tempusque ad proelia dextrum   85
opperiare.   dabunt idem camposque diemque
pugnandi ; tantum ne dedignare secundos
expectare deos : cum fulserit hora, cruentam
quae stragem Libyae portet, tum signa sequentur
nulla vulsa manu, vescique interritus ales   90
gaudebit, nullosque vomet pia terra cruores.
an te praestantem belli fugit, improba quantum
hoc possit Fortuna loco ? sedet obvius hostis
adversa fronte ; at circa nemorosa minantur
insidias iuga, nec laeva stagnantibus undis   95
effugium patet, et tenui stant tramite fauces.
si certare dolis et bellum ducere cordi est,
interea rapidis aderit Servilius armis,

---

[a] The Cyclopes worked at forges in the Lipari islands and
made thunderbolts for Jupiter.

[b] M. Valerius, when serving against the Gauls in 349 B.C.,
accepted a challenge to single combat from a gigantic Gaul.
A raven perched on his helmet and helped him to victory
by attacking his enemy. Hence he received the name of
Corvus (raven) or Corvinus.

seized thunderbolts from the forges of the Cyclopes,[a] and hurled them into the Tuscan waters of Lake Trasimene, till the lake, struck by fire from heaven, smoked all over its wide expanse, and fire burned on the water. Alas, for fruitless warnings and portents that seek in vain to hinder destiny! Alas, for gods who cannot contend against Fate! At this point Corvinus spoke, a famous orator and a noble name; his golden helmet bore the bird of Phoebus, which commemorated the glorious combat of his ancestor.[b] Himself inspired by Heaven and alarmed by the fears of the soldiers, he mingled warning with entreaty and thus began: " By the fire from Troy and by the Tarpeian rock, by the walls of Rome, by the fate of our sons that hangs on the issue of this battle—by these we entreat you, general, not to defy the gods but to await a fit time for battle. They will give us place and time for fighting; only be not too proud to wait for Heaven's favour. When comes the happy hour that shall bring death and defeat for Libya, then the standards will need no force to make them follow, the birds will take their food unterrified, and Mother Earth will vomit no blood. Do you, so skilled a soldier, fail to see how great is the power of cruel Fortune in our present position? The enemy is encamped over against us and stops our way, and the wooded heights all round threaten us with ambuscades; nor is there a way of escape on the left where the lake spreads, and the path through the gorge is narrow. If you are willing to meet guile with guile and to postpone battle, Servilius [c] will soon be here

[c] Gnaeus Servilius, the other consul, was detained at Rome for a time by necessary duties: he then started northwards and made his headquarters at Ariminum.

cui par imperium et vires legionibus aequae.
bellandum est astu : levior laus in duce dextrae."
    Talia Corvinus, primoresque addere passim   101
orantum verba, et divisus quisque timoris
nunc superos, ne Flaminio, nunc deinde precari
Flaminium, ne caelicolis contendere perstet.
acrius hoc accensa ducis surrexerat ira,   105
auditoque furens socias non defore vires :
" sicine nos," inquit, " Boiorum in bella ruentes
spectastis, cum tanta lues vulgusque tremendum
ingrueret, rupesque iterum Tarpeia paveret ?
quas ego tunc animas dextra, quae corpora fudi, 110
irata tellure sata et vix vulnere vitam
reddentes uno ! iacuere ingentia membra
per campos magnisque premunt nunc ossibus arva.
scilicet has sera ad laudes Servilius arma
adiungat, nisi diviso vicisse triumpho   115
ut nequeam et decoris contentus parte quiescam ?
quippe monent superi. similes ne fingite vobis,
classica qui tremitis, divos. sat magnus in hostem
augur adest ensis, pulchrumque et milite dignum
auspicium Latio, quod in armis dextera praestat. 120
an, Corvine, sedet, clausum se consul inerti
ut teneat vallo ? Poenus nunc occupet altos
Arreti muros, Corythi nunc diruat arcem ?
hinc Clusina petat ? postremo ad moenia Romae
illaesus contendat iter ? deforme sub armis   125

---

   [a] The army of Servilius.
   [b] Gauls had besieged the Capitol before, in 390 B.C.
   [c] He compares the Gauls, who were very big men, to the
Titans, the sons of Earth.
   [d] Cortona : see note to iv. 720.

with his hurrying troops. He has equal authority
with you, and his legions are as strong as yours.
War calls for strategy : valour is less praiseworthy
in a commander."

Thus Corvinus spoke ; and all the chief officers
added words of entreaty ; and each man, beset by
a double fear, prayed to the gods not to fight against
Flaminius, and to Flaminius not to persist in fighting
against Heaven. This roused the general's anger to
greater heat ; and, when he heard that a friendly
force *a* was near, he cried in fury : " Was it thus that
you saw me rushing to battle against the Boii, when
the great peril of that fearsome horde came against
us, and the Tarpeian rock feared a second *b* siege ?
How many I then put to death ! how many bodies
my right arm laid low !—bodies born by Earth in
anger, and men whom a single wound could hardly
kill.*c* Their huge limbs were scattered over the
plains, and now their mighty bones cover the fields.
Shall Servilius, forsooth, claim a share in my great
deeds for his belated army, so that I cannot conquer
unless I share the triumph with him, but must rest
content with half the glory ? You say that the gods
warn us. Think not that the gods are like yourselves
—men who tremble at the sound of the trumpet.
The sword is a sufficient soothsayer against the foe,
and the work of an armed right hand is a glorious
omen worthy of a Roman soldier. Is this your pur-
pose, Corvinus, that the consul should shut himself
up behind a rampart and do nothing ? Shall Hannibal
first seize the high walls of Arretium, and then destroy
the citadel of Corythus,*d* and next proceed to Clusium,
and at last march unmolested to the walls of Rome ?
Groundless superstition ill becomes an army ; Valour

vana superstitio est ; dea sola in pectore virtus
bellantum viget. umbrarum me noctibus atris
agmina circumstant, Trebiae qui gurgite quique
Eridani volvuntur aquis, inhumata iuventus.''
  Nec mora. iam medio coetu signisque sub ipsis
postrema aptabat nulli exorabilis arma.   131
aere atque aequorei tergo flavente iuvenci
cassis erat munita viro ; cui vertice surgens
triplex crista iubas effundit crine Suëvo ;
Scylla super, fracti contorquens pondera remi, 135
instabat saevosque canum pandebat hiatus,
nobile Gargeni spolium, quod rege superbus
Boiorum caeso capiti illacerabile victor
aptarat pugnasque decus portabat in omnes.
loricam induitur ; tortos huic nexilis hamos   140
ferro squama rudi permixtoque asperat auro.
tum clipeum capit, aspersum quem caedibus olim
Celticus ornarat cruor ; humentique sub antro,
ceu fetum, lupa permulcens puerilia membra
ingentem Assaraci caelo nutribat alumnum. 145
hinc ensem lateri dextraeque accommodat hastam.
stat sonipes vexatque ferox humentia frena,
Caucasiam instratus virgato corpore tigrim.
inde exceptus equo, qua dant angusta viarum,
nunc hos, nunc illos adit atque hortatibus implet : 150
" vestrum opus est vestrumque decus, suffixa per
    urbem
Poeni ferre ducis spectanda parentibus ora.

---

    [a] The Suevi were a tribe of Gauls. It seems that they
fought with the Boii against Flaminius, and that he took their
scalps as trophies.
    [b] For a similar breastplate see ii. 401 foll.
    [c] Romulus, suckled by the She-wolf. Assaracus was an
ancient king of Troy.

242

is the only deity that rules in the warrior's breast. In the darkness of night an army of ghosts stands round my bed—the unburied soldiers, whose bodies are rolling down Trebia's stream and the waters of the Po."

Straightway, surrounded by his officers and hard by the standards, he put on his armour for the last time, proof against all entreaty. His tough helmet was made of bronze and the tawny hide of a sea-calf; and above it rose a triple crest, with hair of the Suevi [a] hanging down like a mane ; and on the top stood a Scylla, brandishing a heavy broken oar and opening wide the savage jaws of her dogs. When Flaminius conquered and slew Gargenus, king of the Boii, he had fitted to his own head this famous trophy that no hand could mutilate, and proudly he bore it in all his battles. Then he put on his breastplate ; its twisted links were embossed with plates wrought of hard steel mingled with gold.[b] Next he took up his shield, formerly drenched with the slaughter of Gauls and adorned with their blood ; and on it the She-wolf, in a dripping grotto, was licking the limbs of a child, as if he were her cub, and suckling the mighty scion of Assaracus [c] for his translation to heaven. Lastly he fitted the sword to his side and the spear to his right hand. His war-horse stood by, proudly champing the foaming bit ; for saddle he bore the striped skin of a Caucasian tiger. Then the general mounted and rode from one company to another, as far as the confined space would allow, and filled their ears with his appeals : " Yours is the task, and yours the glory, to carry the head of Hannibal on a pike through the streets of Rome, for fathers and mothers to behold.

unum hoc pro cunctis sat erit caput.   aspera quisque
hortamenta sibi referat : meus, heu ! meus atris
Ticini frater ripis iacet ; at meus alta   155
metitur stagna Eridani sine funere natus.
haec sibi quisque ; sed, est vestrum cui nulla doloris
privati rabies, is vero urgentia sumat
e medio, fodiant quae magnas pectus in iras,
perfractas Alpes passamque infanda Saguntum,   160
quosque nefas vetiti transcendere flumen Hiberi,
tangere iam Thybrim.   nam dum vos augur et extis
quaesitae fibrae vanusque moratur haruspex,
solum iam superest, Tarpeio imponere castra."

   Turbidus haec, visoque artis in milibus atras   165
bellatore iubas aptante : " est, Orfite, munus,
est," ait, " hoc certare tuum, quis opima volenti
dona Iovi portet feretro suspensa cruento.
nam cur haec alia pariatur gloria dextra ? "   169
hinc praevectus equo, postquam inter proelia notam
accepit vocem : " procul hinc te Martius," inquit,
" Murrane, ostendit clamor, videoque furentem
iam Tyria te caede ; venit laus quanta ! sed, oro,
haec angusta loci ferro patefacta relaxa."
tum Soracte satum, praestantem corpore et armis,   175
Aequanum noscens, patrio cui ritus in arvo,
cum pius Arcitenens accensis gaudet acervis,

-----

   [a] The treaty made at the end of the First Punic War for-
bade the Carthaginians in Spain to advance beyond the river
Ebro : see i. 480.   [b] See note to iii. 587.
   [c] A mountain in Etruria, 25 miles from Rome, with a
temple of Apollo on the summit : the priests were supposed
to have the power of passing unharmed through fire and
treading on the hot ashes with bare feet.   Aequanus was one
of these priests.
   [d] Apollo, who defended his mother Latona by shooting
the python.

That one head will make amends for all our slain. Let each man recall the griefs that urge him on : ' My brother, alas ! my own brother is lying on the fatal banks of the Ticinus '; or ' My son, unburied, is measuring the depth of the river Po.' Let each man speak thus to himself. But, if any man feels no rage derived from private sorrow, let him find motives in the suffering of his country to sting his heart to fierce wrath—the breach made in the Alps, the awful fate of Saguntum, and those whom Heaven forbade to cross the Ebro[a] now so near to the Tiber. For, while you are held back by augurs and soothsayers vainly prying into the entrails of victims, Hannibal has but one thing more to do—to pitch his camp on the Tarpeian rock."

Thus Flaminius ranted, and then he spied in the crowded ranks a warrior fitting on his black helmet-plume. " It is your task, Orfitus," he cried, " to contend for this prize—who shall bear the spoils of honour[b] to Jupiter, a welcome offering borne aloft on a blood-stained litter. For why should this glory be won by the hand of another ? " He rode on ; and when he heard in the ranks a familiar voice, " Murranus," he cried, " your war-cry reveals your presence from afar, and I see you already frenzied as you slaughter the foe. How great the glory that awaits you ! But this is my prayer : set us free from this confinement, making a way with the sword." Next he recognized Aequanus, a son of Mount Soracte,[c] a splendid figure in splendid armour : in his native land it was his task to carry the offerings thrice in triumph over harmless fires, at the time when the Archer, the loving son,[d] takes

245

exta ter innocuos laetum portare per ignes :
" sic in Apollinea semper vestigia pruna
inviolata teras victorque vaporis ad aras   180
dona serenato referas sollemnia Phoebo :
concipe," ait, " dignum factis, Aequane, furorem
vulneribusque tuis. socio te caedis et irae
non ego Marmaridum mediam penetrare phalangem
Cinyphiaeque globos dubitarim irrumpere turmae."

   Nec iam ultra monitus et verba morantia Martem
ferre valet, longo Aeneadis quod flebitur aevo.   187
increpuere simul feralia classica signum,
ac tuba terrificis fregit stridoribus auras.
heu dolor, heu lacrimae, nec post tot saecula serae !
horresco ut pendente malo, ceu ductor ad arma   191
exciret Tyrius.   latebrosis collibus Astur
et Libys et torta Baliaris saevus habena
erumpunt multusque Maces Garamasque Nomasque;
tum, quo non alius venalem in proelia dextram   195
ocior attulerit conductaque bella probarit,
Cantaber et galeae contempto tegmine Vasco.
hinc pariter rupes, lacus hinc, hinc arma simulque
consona vox urget, signum clamore vicissim
per colles Tyria circumfundente corona.   200

   Avertere dei vultus fatoque dederunt
maiori non sponte locum ; stupet ipse tyranni
fortunam Libyci Mavors, disiectaque crinem
illacrimat Venus, et Delum pervectus Apollo
tristem maerenti solatur pectine luctum.   205

---

   a See note to iii. 687 : for Cinyphian see note to l. 288.
   b The name of this Spanish people is perhaps preserved
by the Basques.

pleasure in the blazing piles. " Aequanus," cried the general, " fill your heart with wrath that suits your prowess and your wounds ; and then may you ever tread unhurt over Apollo's fire, and conquer the flame, and carry the customary offering to the altar, while Phoebus smiles. With you as my partner in the rage of battle, I should not hesitate to pierce a phalanx of the Marmaridae [a] in their centre, or to rush upon the squares of the Cinyphian horsemen."

Flaminius no longer could endure appeals and speeches that postponed the battle. Long shall the Aeneadae lament what followed. The fatal trumpets rang forth the signal all together ; and the bugle rent the air with its awesome din. O grief ! O tears, which even after so many centuries are not belated ! I shudder, as if calamity were imminent, as if Hannibal were even now calling to arms. From the hills that hid them they rushed forth—Asturians and Libyans, fierce Balearic slingers, and swarms of Macae, Garamantians, and Numidians ; Cantabrians also, eager beyond others to hire out their swords and approve mercenary warfare ; and Vascones [b] who scorn the protection of a helmet. On this side rocks, on this the lake, on this armed men with their united cries, hem the Romans in, while the ring of Carthaginians spread the battle-cry from man to man through the hills.

The gods turned away their faces and gave way reluctantly to over-ruling Fate. Mars himself wondered at the good fortune of the Carthaginian leader ; Venus wept with dishevelled hair ; and Apollo was wafted to Delos,[c] where he soothed his grief with plaintive lyre. Juno alone remained, sit-

[c] His birthplace.

sola, Apennini residens in vertice, diras
expectat caedes immiti pectore Iuno.
    Primae Picentum, rupto ceu turbine fusa
agmina et Hannibalem ruere ut videre, cohortes
invadunt ultro, et poenas pro morte futura,   210
turbato victore, petunt accensa iuventus ;
et, velut erepto metuendi libera caelo,
manibus ipsa suis praesumpta piacula mittit.
funditur unanimo nisu et concordibus ausis
pilorum in Poenos nimbus, fixosque repulsi   215
summittunt clipeos curvato pondere teli.
acrius hoc rursum Libys—et praesentia saevi
extimulat ducis—hortantes se quisque vicissim
incumbunt pressoque impellunt pectore pectus.
    Ipsa, facem quatiens ac flavam sanguine multo
sparsa comam, medias acies Bellona pererrat.   221
stridit Tartareae nigro sub pectore divae
letiferum murmur, feralique horrida cantu
bucina lymphatas agit in certamina mentes.
his iras adversa fovent crudusque ruente   225
fortuna stimulus spem proiecisse salutis ;
hos dexter deus et laeto Victoria vultu
arridens acuit, Martisque favore fruuntur.
    Abreptus pulchro caedum Lateranus amore,
dum sequitur dextram, in medios penetraverat hostes.
quem postquam florens aequali Lentulus aevo   231

---

    [a] This weapon was the *pilum*, the characteristic weapon of
the Roman legionary ; it was over six feet long, and the iron
head was the same length as the wooden shaft. The soldier
threw it at the beginning of an attack ; if it missed the
corslet, it stuck in the shield and made it useless.
    [b] The goddess of war.

ting on a peak of the Apennines, and her cruel heart looked forward to the dreadful slaughter.

First of all, the men of Picenum, when they saw the enemy pouring forth like a cloudburst from the sky, and Hannibal in full career, anticipate the attack; the soldiers in their ardour seek a recompense for their imminent death in harassing their conqueror; and free from fear as if life was lost already, they send down before them victims to make atonement to their own ghosts. With combined effort and simultaneous action they hurled a cloud of javelins against the Carthaginians; and the foe were beaten back and lowered their shields in which the heavy curved weapons *a* stuck fast. The fiercer on that account did the Libyans press on—and the presence of their stern commander increased their efforts—while man encouraged man, till breast clashed hard against breast.

Bellona *b* herself moved through the centre of the battle, brandishing her torch, and her fair hair was spattered with abundant gore. The hoarse cry that came from the dark breast of the hellish goddess was fraught with death; and the dreadful trumpet with its mournful music drove maddened hearts into the fray. The ardour of the Romans was kindled by defeat, and despair proved a strong incentive in the hour of disaster; but the foe were encouraged by the favour of Heaven and the smiling face of Victory, and they enjoyed the favour of Mars.

Lateranus, carried away by noble love of slaughter, had gone on slaying till he pierced to the centre of the foe. While he, too eager for battle and bloodshed, defied Fortune on unequal terms among the hordes of the enemy, Lentulus, a youth of the same

conspexit, nimium pugnae nimiumque cruoris
infestas inter non aequo Marte catervas
fata irritantem, nisu se concitat acri
immitemque Bagam, qui iam vicina ferebat   235
vulnera pugnantis tergo, velocior hasta
occupat et socium duris se casibus addit.
tunc alacres arma agglomerant geminaque corusci
fronte micant, paribus fulgent capita ardua cristis.
actus in adversos casu (namque obvia ferre   240
arma quis auderet, nisi quem deus ima colentum
damnasset Stygiae nocti ?) praefracta gerebat
Syrticus excelso decurrens robora monte
et, quatiens acer nodosi pondera rami,
flagrabat geminae nequiquam caedis amore :   245
" non hic Aegates infidaque litora nautis,
o iuvenes, motumque novis sine Marte procellis
fortunam bello pelagus dabit ; aequoris olim
victores, media sit qualis, discite, terra
bellator Libys, et meliori cedite regnis."   250
ac simul infesto Lateranum pondere truncae
arboris urgebat, iungens convicia pugnae.
Lentulus huic frendens ira : " Thrasymennus in altos
ascendet citius colles, quam sanguine roret
iste pio ramus," subsidensque ilia nisu   255
conantis suspensa fodit ; tum fervidus atro
pulmone exundat per hiantia viscera sanguis.

  Nec minus accensis in mutua funera dextris
parte alia campi saevit furor. altus Iërtes
obtruncat Nerium ; Rullo ditissimus arvi   260
occumbis, generose Volunx, nec clausa repostis

---

^a See note to i. 35.

age, saw his plight and ran forward with a hasty effort against fierce Bagas, whose spear-point was close to the back of Lateranus as he fought. But Lentulus was quicker and drove his spear in first, and proved himself a friend in adversity. Then the pair eagerly joined forces ; the brows of both shone with equal light, and their heads, held high, were adorned with twin plumes. It was by chance that Syrticus, a Carthaginian, was driven to face the pair—for who would have dared to meet them in fight, unless he were condemned to nether darkness by the deity of the shades below ? He hastened down from the heights, carrying a branch broken off from an oak-tree ; and, as he fiercely brandished the heavy knotted bough, he burned with vain desire to slay the pair : " Ye Romans, here are no Aegatian islands,[a] no shore that betrays the seaman ; no sea, stirred by sudden storms and not by war, shall decide the issue of battle ; at sea ye conquered in the past ; learn now, how a Libyan can fight on dry land, and resign your power to your betters." At the same time he pressed Lateranus hard with the heavy branch, and reviled him while he attacked. But Lentulus ground his teeth with rage : " Lake Trasimene shall climb up these hills," he cried, " before his noble blood shall wet your bough." Then crouching down, he stabbed the other in the groin which the effort of his blow had lifted up, till the hot blood poured out from the black lung through the gaping entrails.

In other parts of the field the same frenzy raged, and the fighters were eager to slay and be slain. Tall Iertes slew Nerius ; and high-born Volunx, the owner of broad lands, was overthrown by Rullus.

pondera thesauris patrio nec regia quondam
praefulgens ebore et possessa mapalia soli
profuerunt.   quid rapta iuvant ?   quid gentibus auri
numquam extincta sitis ? modo quem Fortuna fovendo
congestis opibus donisque refersit opimis,   266
nudum Tartarea portabit navita cymba.

  Iuxta bellator iuvenilibus Appius ausis
pandebat campum caede atque, ubi plurima virtus
nullique aspirare vigor, decus inde petebat.   270
obvius huic Atlans, Atlans a litore Hibero,
nequicquam extremae longinquus cultor harenae,
impetit os hasta, leviterque e corpore summo
degustat cuspis generosum extrema cruorem.
intonuere minae, violentaque lumina flammis   275
exarsere novis ; furit et diffulminat omnem
obstantum turbam ; clausum sub casside vulnus
Martia commendat mananti sanguine membra.
tum vero aspiceres pavitantem et condere semet
nitentem sociis iuvenem, ceu tigride cerva   280
Hyrcana cum pressa tremit, vel territa pennas
colligit accipitrem cernens in nube columba,
aut dumis subit, albenti si sensit in aethra
librantem nisus aquilam, lepus.   ora citato
ense ferit, tum colla viri dextramque micantem   285
demetit ac mutat successu saevior hostem.

  Stabat fulgentem portans in bella bipennem
Cinyphius socerique miser Magonis inire
optabat pugnam ante oculos spe laudis Isalcas,

---

  [a] Charon.
  [b] The Cinyps is a river of N. Africa between the two
Syrtes : at its mouth there was a town of the same name.

What availed him now all his treasure locked up in secret chambers, or his kingly palace, once shining with African ivory, or whole villages belonging to him alone ? The wealth he seized could not help him, or the thirst for gold that men can never slake. The man whom Fortune favoured once and crammed with piled-up wealth and rich gifts—him now shall the Ferryman's [a] boat convey naked to Tartarus.

Near them fought the young warrior Appius, cutting a path with his sword, and seeking glory where utmost valour was needed and none else had strength to seek it. He was confronted by Atlas—Atlas from the Spanish shore ; but his distant home by the outmost sea did not save him. When he aimed his spear at the head of Appius, the point alone lightly grazed the skin and just tasted that noble blood. Like a thunder-peal were the threats of Appius ; his furious eyeballs burned with fresh fire ; the lightning of his rage scattered all in his path ; his wound was hidden by the helmet, and the flowing blood made his warlike figure more splendid. Then one might have seen his enemy striving in terror to hide behind his comrades, like a trembling hind pursued by a Hyrcanian tigress, or like a pigeon that checks her flight when she sees a hawk in the sky, or like a hare that dives into the thicket at sight of the eagle hovering with outstretched wings in the cloudless sky. He was wounded in the face by the furious sword ; then Appius cut off his head and quivering right hand, and sought a fresh victim, made fiercer by his victory.

Isalcas stood near ; he came from Cinyps,[b] and his weapon was a shining axe ; his ambition, poor wretch, was to fight and win glory under the eyes of Mago,

Sidonia tumidus sponsa vanoque superbus   290
foedere promissae post Dardana proelia taedae.
huic immittit atrox violentas Appius iras
conantique gravem fronti librare securim,
altior insurgens, galeam super exigit ictum.
at fragilis valido conamine solvitur ensis   295
aere in Cinyphio ; nec dispar sortis Isalcas
umbonem incerto detersit futilis ictu.
tum quod humo haud umquam valuisset tollere saxum,
ni vires trux ira daret, contorquet anhelans
Appius et lapsu resupino in terga cadentem   300
mole premit scopuli perfractisque ossibus urget.
vidit coniuncto miscens certamina campo
labentem socer, et lacrimae sub casside fusae
cum gemitu, rapidusque ruit ; data foedera nuper
accendunt animos expectatique nepotes.   305
iamque aderat clipeumque viri atque immania membra
lustrabat visu, propiorque a fronte coruscae
lux galeae saevas paulum tardaverat iras.
haud secus, e specula praeceps delatus opaca,
subsidens campo summissos contrahit artus,   310
cum vicina trucis conspexit cornua tauri,
quamvis longa fames stimulet, leo ; nunc ferus alta
surgentes cervice toros, nunc torva sub hirta
lumina miratur fronte ac iam signa moventem
et sparsa pugnas meditantem spectat harena.   315
hic prior intorquens telum sic Appius infit :
" si qua tibi pietas, ictum ne desere foedus

---

a That is, his prospective father-in-law. Mago was
Hannibal's brother and one of his chief officers.
254

his father-in-law [a]; for he was proud of his Carthaginian bride-to-be, and flattered by the vain promise that, when war with Rome was over, they should be wedded. Fierce Appius turned his furious rage against Isalcas, and, rising to his full height, delivered his stroke at the helmet, while the other sought to aim his heavy axe at the forehead. But the brittle sword broke against the helmet of the Cinyphian, so sturdy was the stroke. Nor was Isalcas more fortunate : he missed his mark and only cut off the boss of the Roman's shield. Then Appius, breathing hard, swung aloft a stone, which he could never have lifted from the ground but for the strength that anger gave him, and crushed his foe as he fell backwards with the heavy boulder, and rammed it down upon the shattered bones. Mago, who was fighting not far away, groaned when he saw his son-in-law fall, and the tears fell behind his helmet. Then he rushed up in haste ; the marriage he had lately approved, and his hope of grandchildren, stirred his rage. On he came and surveyed the shield and the huge limbs of Appius ; and the light that shone from the front of the gleaming helmet, seen at close quarters, cooled his fierce wrath for a space. So a lion, that has rushed down from a wooded height, crouches down upon the plain and gathers his limbs under him, when he sees hard by the horns of a fierce bull, even though long fasting urges him on ; the beast stares now at the starting muscles on the great neck, and now at the savage eyes beneath the shaggy forehead, and watches the bull preparing for action and pawing the dust in readiness for fight. And now Appius was first to brandish his spear, and thus he spoke : " If you feel the ties of kindred, then be true to the

et generum comitare socer." per tegmina velox
tunc aerisque moras laevo stetit hasta lacerto.
at contra non dicta Libys, sed fervidus hastam   320
perlibrat, magni donum memorabile fratris,
caeso quam victor sub moenibus ille Sagunti
abstulerat Durio ac spectatae nobile pugnae
germano dederat portare in proelia pignus.
telum ingens perque arma viri perque ora, doloris 325
adiutum nisu, letalem pertulit ictum ;
exsanguesque viri conantis vellere ferrum
in vulnus cecidere manus. iacet aequore nomen
clarum Maeonio atque Italae pars magna ruinae
Appius ; intremuere lacus, corpusque refugit   330
contractis Thrasymennus aquis ; telum ore cruento
expirans premit atque admorsae immurmurat hastae.
   Nec fati melior Mamercus corpore toto
exsolvit poenas, nulli non saucius hosti.
namque per adversos, qua Lusitana ciebat   335
pugnas dira manus, raptum cum sanguine caesi
signiferi magna vexillum mole ferebat
et trepida infelix revocabat signa suorum.
sed furiata cohors ausisque accensa superbis,
quodcumque ipsa manu gestabat missile, quicquid
praebebat tellus, sparsis vix pervia telis,   341
iniecit pariter, pluresque in corpore nullum
invenere locum perfossis ossibus hastae.
   Advolat interea, fraterni vulneris ira
turbatus, Libyae ductor ; visoque cruore,   345

---

   a Maeonian = Lydian = Etruscan : see note to iv. 721.
            b Portuguese.

alliance you have formed, and go where your son-in-law has gone." The weapon flew through the shield and the brazen armour, and stuck fast in the left shoulder. Mago made no reply, but fiercely levelled his spear, the famous gift that his great brother gave him ; for beneath the walls of Saguntum Hannibal had taken it from Durius whom he had conquered and slain, and had given it to his brother to bear in battle, the glorious token of a famous contest. The huge weapon, made more formidable by the rage of the thrower, passed through the helmet and the head of Appius, dealing a fatal wound. His bloodless hands, seeking to pluck forth the weapon, fell helpless upon the wound. Low on the Maeonian [a] plain lies Appius, that famous name ; and much of Italy's might fell with him. The lake shivered, and Trasimene withdrew its waters from contact with the body. The bleeding mouth of the dying man closed on the weapon and muttered as it bit the spear.

Nor was Mamercus more fortunate : he suffered in every limb and was wounded by every foe. He had killed a standard-bearer and seized the heavy standard ; and now he was carrying it through the enemy's ranks, where a fierce company of Lusitanians [b] were fighting. He was rallying the wavering eagles of the Romans, when the Lusitanians, maddened to fury by his bold action, hurled at the unhappy man every weapon they carried themselves or that they could pick up from the ground, covered so thick with missiles that movement was scarce possible. Even his bones were pierced ; and scarce could half of the spears find room in his body.

Meanwhile Hannibal came up in haste, stirred to anger by his brother's wound. Distracted at sight

num lateri cuspis, num toto pondere telum
sedisset, fratremque amens sociosque rogabat.
utque metum leti procul et leviora pavore
cognovit, proprio tectum gestamine praeceps
ex acie rapit et tutis a turbine pugnae   350
constituit castris.   medicas hinc ocius artes
et senioris opem Synhali vocat ; unguere vulnus
herbarum hic sucis ferrumque e corpore cantu
exigere et somnum tacto misisse chelydro,
anteibat cunctos, nomenque erat inde per urbes 355
perque Paraetoniae celebratum litora Syrtis.
ipse olim antiquo primum Garamanticus Hammon
scire pater dederat Synhalo, morsusque ferarum
telorumque graves ictus sedare medendo.
atque is deinde suo moriens caelestia dona   360
monstravit nato, natusque heredis honori
tramisit patrias artes ; quem deinde secutus
haud levior fama Synhalus Garamantica sollers
monstrata augebat studio multaque vetustum
Hammonis comitem numerabat imagine patrem. 365
tum, proavita ferens leni medicamina dextra,
ocius, intortos de more astrictus amictus,
mulcebat lympha purgatum sanguine vulnus.
at Mago, exuvias secum caesique volutans
hostis mente necem, fraternas pectore curas   370
pellebat dictis et casum laude levabat :
" parce metu, germane.   meis medicamina nulla
adversis maiora feres ; iacet Appius hasta

---

   a See i. 412.
   b See note to iii. 225.
   c See note to i. 415.
   d The first Synhalus was so famous that busts of him were
often to be seen.
   e The object was presumably to leave their hands free.

of the blood, he kept asking Mago and his companions whether the wound was in the body, and whether the spear had struck home with all its weight. When he heard better news than he dreaded, and that danger of death was remote, he covered Mago with his own shield, and hurried him off the field, and lodged him in the camp, safe from the storm of battle. Next he made haste to summon the skill of the healer and the aid of ancient Synhalus. Synhalus surpassed all men in anointing a wound with the juices of simples ; he could draw a weapon forth from the body by incantation and send snakes to sleep by stroking them.[a] Hence his fame was great through the cities of Libya and the shores of Egyptian [b] Syrtis. In ancient days the first Synhalus had learnt from his father, Ammon[c] himself, the deity of the Garamantes, how to give relief and healing to men bitten by wild beasts or sore wounded in battle ; and he, when dying, revealed the divine gift to his son ; and the son bequeathed his father's skill, to make his heir glorious ; and next in succession came this Synhalus, no less famous than his sires. By his sagacity and by study he added to the lore of Ammon, and could point to his ancestor, the ancient comrade of Ammon, on many a bust.[d] Now with healing hand he brought the remedies his ancestors had used ; his garments were wound tightly about his loins, as the custom of physicians is [e] ; and quickly he cleansed the wound of blood and soothed it by washing. But Mago, reflecting on the death and spoiling of his foe, comforted his brother by his words, and made light of a mishap so glorious : " Fear nothing, brother," he said. " You can apply no more potent remedy to my suffering than this—that Appius

259

ad manes pulsus nostra. si vita relinquat,
sat nobis actum est, sequar hostem laetus ad umbras."
  Quae dum turbatos avertunt aequore campi   376
ductores valloque tenent, ex agmine Poenum
cedentem consul tumulo speculatus ab alto
atque atram belli castris se condere nubem,
turbidus extemplo trepidantes milite lecto[1]   380
invadit cuneos subitoque pavore relaxat
iam rarescentes acies ; tum voce feroci
poscit equum ac mediae ruit in certamina vallis.
sic ubi torrentem crepitanti grandine nimbum
illidit terris molitus Iupiter altas   385
fulmine nunc Alpes, nunc mixta Ceraunia caelo,
intremuere simul tellus et pontus et aether,
ipsaque commoto quatiuntur Tartara mundo.
incidit attonitis inopino turbine Poenis
haud secus improvisa lues, gelidusque sub ossa   390
pervasit miseris conspecti consulis horror.
it medius ferroque ruens densissima latum
pandit iter. clamor vario discrimine vocum
fert belli rabiem ad superos et sidera pulsat.
ceu pater Oceanus cum saeva Tethye Calpen   395
Herculeam ferit atque exesa in viscera montis
contortum pelagus latrantibus ingerit undis :
dant gemitum scopuli, fractasque in rupibus undas
audit Tartessus latis distermina terris,
audit non parvo divisus gurgite Lixus.   400
  Ante omnes iaculo tacitas fallente per auras

---

[1] lecto *Heinsius* : laeto *edd.*

---

[a] Hannibal is the cloud.
[b] A mountain-range on the west coast of Epirus.
[c] Calpe (Gibraltar) is one of the Pillars of Hercules.
[d] See note to vi. 1

lies low, sent to the nether world by my spear. Even if I lose my life, I have done enough and shall gladly follow my foe to the shades."

While this mischance disturbed the leaders, taking them from the battle-field and penning them in the camp, Flaminius, watching from a high mound, saw Hannibal leave the fighting-line and the black cloud of war [a] disappear within the camp. At once in fury he attacked the wavering enemy with a picked force, and the sudden alarm opened up the ranks that were already growing thin ; then he called fiercely for his horse, and rushed into the conflict in the centre of the valley. So, when Jupiter smites the earth with pouring rain and crackling hail, and stirs with his thunderbolt now the Alpine heights and now the Ceraunian [b] mountains that reach to heaven, earth and sea and sky all quake together, and Tartarus itself is shaken in the convulsion of the universe. Even so the sudden storm of unforeseen destruction fell upon the startled Carthaginians, and cold terror made its way into their bones, when they saw the consul. He rode through their midst, making a wide passage and hewing down with his sword the ranks where they were thickest. The shouting with all its discordant cries carried the madness of war to heaven, and struck the stars. So Father Ocean together with raging Tethys beats on Calpe,[c] a Pillar of Hercules, and drives the churned-up sea with its roaring waves into the hollow interior of the mountain; the cliffs bellow ; and the crash of the breakers on the rocks is heard by Tartessus[d] far-parted by broad lands, and heard by Lixus [e] across a great space of sea.

Bogus [f] was the first to fall, by a javelin that came

[e] A river and town in Morocco. [f] See iv. 131.

occumbit Bogus, infaustum qui primus ad amnem
Ticini rapidam in Rutulos contorserat hastam.
ille sibi longam Clotho turbamque nepotum
crediderat, vanis deceptus in alite signis.   405
sed non augurio Parcarum impellere metas
concessum cuiquam : ruit inter tela cruentis
suspiciens oculis caelum superosque reposcit
tempora promissae media iam morte senectae.
nec Bagaso exultare daturve impune relictum,   410
consulis ante oculos vita spoliasse Libonem.
laurigeris decus illud avis navaque iuventa
florebat ; sed Massylus succiderat ensis
pubescente caput mala, properoque virentes
delerat leto bellator barbarus annos.   415
Flaminium implorasse tamen iam morte suprema
haud frustra fuit ; avulsa est nam protinus hosti
ore simul cervix ; iuvit punire feroci
victorem exemplo et monstratum reddere letum.

Quis deus, o Musae, paribus tot funera verbis   420
evolvat ?   tantisque umbris in carmine digna
quis lamenta ferat ?   certantes laude cadendi
primaevos iuvenes mortisque in limine cruda
facta virum et fixis rabiem sub pectore telis ?
sternitur alternus vastis concursibus hostis,   425
nec spoliare vacat praedaeque advertere mentem.
urget amor caedum, clausis dum detinet hostem
fraternum castris vulnus, funditque ruitque
nunc iaculis, nunc ense, modo inter milia consul
bellantum conspectus equo, modo Marte feroci   430
ante aquilas et signa pedes.   fluit impia rivis

stealing noiselessly through the sky. He had launched the first flying spear against the Romans by the ill-omened river of Ticinus. Beguiled by deceitful omens from birds, he had believed that he would live long and see many children of his children. But no man may postpone by augury the date that Fate has fixed. He fell in the battle, looking up to heaven with blood-shot eyes, and calling upon the gods, even as he died, to redeem their promise of old age. Nor might Bagasus triumph or escape unpunished, when he had slain Libo in the consul's sight. Libo's ancestors had won laurels, and he was glorious in his vigorous youth ; but the sword of the Massylian cut off the head on which the beard was just growing, and the savage warrior cut down by an early death the blossom of youth. But he cried to Flaminius, even as life left him, and his cry was not vain; for, head and all, the foeman's neck was instantly shorn away : glad was he to imitate the conqueror's cruelty and to slay him even as he had slain.

Ye Muses, what god could narrate so many deaths in fitting language ? What poet could utter a dirge worthy of the mighty dead ? Who could tell of the striplings contending with one another for the prize of death ; of the brave deeds done on the brink of the grave ; of the fury that filled breasts pierced with wounds ? Foe clashed furiously against foe and fell ; and none found time to spoil his victim or think of plunder. They were driven on by thirst for blood, while Hannibal was kept close in camp by his brother's wound. Among the myriad warriors Flaminius, spreading destruction with javelin or sword, was now conspicuous on horseback, and now fought fiercely on foot, in front of the eagles and standards. The

sanguineis vallis, tumulique et concava saxa
armorum sonitus flatusque imitantur equorum.
  Miscebat campum, membrorum in proelia portans
celsius humano robur, visaque paventes   435
mole gigantei vertebat corporis alas
Othrys Marmarides ; lati super agmen utrumque
ingens tollebant humeri caput, hirtaque torvae
frontis caesaries et crinibus aemula barba
umbrabat rictus ; squalore hic hispida diro   440
et villosa feris horrebat pectora saetis.
aspirare viro propioremque addere Martem
haud ausum cuiquam : laxo ceu belua campo
incessebatur tutis ex agmine telis.
tandem vesanos palantum in terga ferenti   445
cum fremitu vultus tacita per nubila penna
intravit torvum Gortynia lumen harundo
avertitque virum.   fugientis ad agmina consul
intorquet tergo iaculum, quod tegmine nudas
irrupit costas hirtoque a pectore primum   450
mucronem ostendit.   rapidus convellere tentat,
qua nasci ferrum fulgenti cuspide cernit,
donec, abundanter defuso sanguine, late
procubuit moriens et telum vulnere pressit.
spiritus exundans vicinum pulvere moto   455
perflavit campum et nubem dispersit in auras.
  Nec minor interea tumulis silvisque fremebat
diversis Mavors, variaque per ardua pugna
et saxa et dumi rorantes caede nitebant.
exitium trepidis letique et stragis acerbae   460

---

accursed valley ran with blood ; and the hills and hollow rocks echoed the clashing of arms and the snorting of horses.

The combatants were scattered by Othrys of Marmarica, who brought to battle superhuman strength and stature ; and the mere sight of his huge frame turned the Roman troops to flight. His giant head rose on broad shoulders high over both armies, and his mouth was hidden by the shaggy locks that grew on his grim forehead, and by a beard that rivalled his hair ; a matted growth of bristles, like a wild beast's fell, covered his hairy chest. None dared to challenge him or fight him at close quarters : like a wild beast in the open plain, he was assailed by missiles thrown from a safe distance by the host. At last as, shouting loud, he rushed with furious face against the backs of the straggling Romans, a Cretan *a* arrow, flying noiselessly through the air, pierced his threatening eye and stopped his course. As he fled to the main body, Flaminius cast a javelin at his back ; and it pierced the undefended ribs and revealed its point sticking out beyond the shaggy breast. Quickly he strove to pluck it forth, where he saw the bright steel point protrude. At last, after losing much blood, he fell forward in death, covering much ground, and hid the weapon with his wounded breast. His breath, as it poured forth, stirred the dust, blowing over the plain beside him and raising a cloud into the sky.

Meanwhile, fighting as fierce went raging on, over the scattered hills and woods ; and rocks and thickets were wet and red with manifold encounters fought over the rough ground. Sychaeus was the destroyer of the fugitives, bringing death upon them

causa Sychaeus erat ; Murranum ille eminus hasta
perculerat, quo non alius, cum bella silerent,
dulcius Oeagrios pulsabat pectine nervos.
occubuit silva in magna patriosque sub ipso
quaesivit montes leto ac felicia Baccho   465
Aequana et Zephyro Surrentum molle salubri.
addiderat misero comitem pugnaeque ferocis
gaudebat tristi victor novitate Sychaeus.
palantes nam dum sequitur, pervaserat altam
in silvam et priscae reclinis ab ictibus ulmi   470
terga tuebatur trunco frustraque relictos
Tauranus comites suprema voce ciebat.
transegit iuvenem, ac perfossis incita membris
haesit in opposito cuspis Sidonia ligno.
    Quid vobis ?   quaenam ira deum, vel mente sinistra
quae sedit formido, viri ? qui, Marte relicto,   476
ramorum quaesistis opem.   non aequus in artis
nimirum rebus suasor metus ; arguit asper
exitus eventu pravi consulta timoris.
annosa excelsos tendebat in aethera ramos   480
aesculus, umbrosum magnas super ardua silvas
nubibus insertans altis caput, instar, aperto
si staret campo, nemoris lateque tenebat
frondosi nigra tellurem roboris umbra.
par iuxta quercus, longum molita per aevum   485
vertice canenti proferre sub astra cacumen,
diffusas patulo laxabat stipite frondes
umbrabatque coma summi fastigia montis.
huc Hennaea cohors, Triquetris quam miserat oris

---

   [a] Oeagrus, a Thracian, was father of Orpheus.
   [b] Now Sorrento, on the coast of Campania.
   [c] Hiero II., king of Syracuse, a staunch ally of Rome :
Arethusa is a fountain in Syracuse.   For Henna see note to
i. 93.

and untimely slaughter. His spear struck down from
afar Murranus, who, in times of peace, was surpassed
by none in drawing sweet strains from the lyre of
Orpheus.[a] He fell in a great forest and even in death
recalled the mountains of his home, the vine-clad
Aequan hills and soft Surrentum [b] with its healthful
breezes. Then Sychaeus sent another to keep com-
pany with Murranus ; and the conqueror rejoiced in
the strange manner of that cruel death. For Tau-
ranus, while following the stragglers, had found his
way to a high wood, where he leant his back against
an ancient elm-tree and tried to shield himself with
its trunk against attack ; and there with his last
words he summoned the comrades he had left behind.
In vain ; for the spear of Sychaeus pierced him, and,
after swiftly passing through his body, lodged in the
tree that stood in its path.

What ailed ye, O men ? Was it divine wrath or
disastrous panic that possessed your minds, when you
gave up fighting and sought help in trees ? Fear is
indeed an evil counsellor in danger : the stern issue
proved that cowardice gives bad advice. An ancient
oak grew there, which shot its tall branches to the
sky, thrusting its shady top into the clouds and
towering over the forest ; had it grown on the open
plain, it would have looked like a whole grove ; and
it covered a wide space of ground with the dark shade
of its foliage. Beside it grew another oak of equal
size, that had striven for centuries to exalt its hoary
head to the sky ; the spreading trunk was crowned
with a vast circle of leafage that overshadowed the
top of the mountain. Hither flew in haste men of
Henna, whom the king of Arethusa [c] had sent from

rex, Arethusa, tuus, defendere nescia morti   490
dedecus et mentem nimio mutata pavore,
certatim sese tulit ascendensque vicissim
pressit nutantes incerto pondere ramos.
mox alius super atque alius consistere tuto
dum certant, pars excussi (nam fragmine putri   495
ramorum et senio male fida fefellerat arbor)
pars trepidi celso inter tela cacumine pendent.
turbatos una properans consumere peste,
corripit aeratam iam dudum in bella bipennem,
deposito clipeo mutatus tela, Sychaeus.   500
incumbunt sociae dextrae, magnoque fragore
pulsa gemit, crebris succumbens ictibus, arbos.
fluctuat infelix concusso stipite turba,
ceu Zephyrus quatit antiquos ubi flamine lucos,
fronde super tremuli vix tota cacuminis haerens 505
iactatur, nido pariter nutante, volucris.
procubuit tandem multa devicta securi
suffugium infelix miseris et inhospita quercus
elisitque virum spatiosa membra ruina.
    Inde aliae cladum facies.   contermina caedis   510
collucet rapidoque involvitur aesculus igni.
iamque inter frondes, arenti robore gliscens
verticibus saevis, torquet Vulcanus anhelos
cum fervore globos flammarum et culmina torret.
nec tela interea cessant.   semusta gementum   515
atque amplexa cadunt ardentes corpora ramos.
    Haec inter miseranda virum certamina consul
ecce aderat, volvens iram exitiumque Sychaeo.
at iuvenis dubio tantae discrimine pugnae
occupat eventum telo tentare priorem ;   520

---

^a The fire-god is represented as doing the work of fire :
see iv. 681.

Sicily; they knew not how to preserve death from disgrace, and they were mad with terror. One after another they climbed aloft and bent the swaying branches with their shifting weight. Then, as one climbed above another in his eagerness to reach a place of safety, some fell to the ground, deceived by the rotten boughs and decay of the treacherous tree, while others hung in terror in the lofty tree-top, a mark for missiles. Eager to destroy them all in their distress by the same death, Sychaeus changed his weapon: he laid down his shield and caught up at once his brazen battle-axe. His comrades lent a hand, and the tree, yielding to repeated blows, creaked with a crashing sound. The wretched fugitives toss to and fro when the trunk is smitten; as, when the blast of the West-wind rocks ancient groves, the bird and her nest also are tossed about, and she can scarce find foothold on the swaying tree-top. At last the unfriendly oak, a sorry refuge in trouble, fell under the blows of many axes, and crushed the men's limbs in its far-spreading downfall.

Other forms of disaster followed. The other oak, close to the scene of slaughter, took fire and was soon wrapped in flames. And now among the leaves, spreading with fierce eddies over the dry wood, Vulcan *a* brandished tongues of fire with panting heat and scorched the topmost branches. And all the time the shooting went on; and half-burnt bodies, clutching at blazing branches, fell shrieking to the ground.

In the midst of these pitiful conflicts, see! Flaminius arrives, with wrath in his heart and destruction for Sychaeus. The young man, fearing the danger of so mighty a duel, was first to try his fortune with his

cui medio leviter clipeo stetit aeris in ora
cuspis et oppositas vetita est tramittere crates.
sed non et consul misso concredere telo
fortunam optatae caedis parat ac latus ense
haurit ; nec crudae tardarunt tegmina parmae.   525
labitur infelix atque appetit ore cruento
tellurem expirans.   tum, diffundente per artus
frigore se Stygio, manantem in viscera mortem
accipit et longo componit lumina somno.

Atque ea dum variis permixtus tristia Mavors   530
casibus alternat, iam castris Mago relictis,
iam Libyae ductor properantia signa citato
raptabant cursu et cessata reponere avebant
tempora caede virum ac multo pensare cruore.
it globus intorquens nigranti turbine nubem   535
pulveris, et surgit sublatis campus harenis ;
quaque ferens gressum flectit vestigia ductor,
undanti circum tempestas acta procella
volvitur atque altos operit caligine montes.
occubuere femur Fontanus, Buta canorum   540
transfixi guttur, pressoque e vulnere cuspis
prospexit terga : hunc tristes luxere Fregellae
multiplicem proavis, hunc mater Anagnia flevit.
haud dispar fortuna tibi, Laevine, sed auso
non eadem ; neque enim Tyrio concurrere regi   545
tentas, sed lectus par ad certamen Ithemon,
Autololum moderator, erat ; quem poplite caeso
dum spoliat, gravis immiti cum turbine costas
fraxinus irrupit, collapsaque membra sub ictu
hoste super fuso subita cecidere ruina.   550

ª Fregellae was an ancient Volscian town : Anagnia was
the chief town of the Hernici : both were near Rome.

spear; but the weapon lodged lightly on the brazen plate in the centre of the shield, unable to pierce the wicker-work in its path. The consul, unlike his rival, was not willing to trust to his spear for success in the victory he desired: he stabbed Sychaeus in the body with his sword; and the round shield of raw leather failed to stop it. The victim fell and, as he died, bit the earth with bleeding mouth. Then, as the fatal chill spread through his frame, and death made its way to his vital parts, he suffered it, and closed his eyes in eternal sleep.

While the battle went on thus, with varying fortune and such scenes of horror, Mago and Hannibal had already left the camp, and were hurrying their troops on with speedy march, eager to make up for lost time by slaying Romans, and to make it good by much bloodshed. On came their troops, raising a black cloud of whirling dust; the sand rose and lifted the soil with it; and, wherever Hannibal moved and turned his steps, the storm of war, driven by a billowy tempest, rolled in all directions and veiled the high mountains with darkness. Fontanus fell, pierced in the thigh; pierced was the throat of Buta, the minstrel, and the spear-point stuck out beyond the sore wound and beheld his back. The first, a man of long descent, was mourned by Fregellae [a]; and his native Anagnia wept for the other. Laevinus fared no better, though he had been less bold; not daring to challenge Hannibal, he had chosen Ithemon, a captain of Autololes, as a fitting rival. Him he had hamstrung and was stripping him, when the heavy ashen spear with furious force broke in his ribs; and he collapsed under the blow and fell instantly on the corpse of his prostrate foe.

SILIUS ITALICUS

Nec Sidicina cohors defit. Viriasius armat
mille viros, nulli victus vel ponere castra,
vel iunxisse ratem duroque resolvere muros
ariete et in turrim subitos immittere pontes.
quem postquam Libyae ductor virtute feroci   555
exultare videt (namque illi vulnere praeceps
terga dabat levibus diffisus Arauricus armis)
acrius hoc, pulchro Mavorte accensus in iram
et dignum sese ratus in certamina saevo
comminus ire viro, referenti e corpore telum   560
advolat et fodiens pectus : " laudande laborum,
quisquis es, haud alia decuit te occumbere dextra.
ad manes leti perfer decus.   Itala gentis
ni tibi origo foret, vita donatus abires."
hinc Fadum petit et veterem bellare Labicum,   565
cui Siculis quondam terris congressus Hamilcar
clarum spectato dederat certamine nomen.
immemor annorum seniumque oblitus, in arma
ille quidem cruda mente et viridissimus irae
ibat, sed vani frigentem in Marte senectam   570
prodebant ictus ; stipula crepitabat inani
ignis iners cassamque dabat sine robore flammam.
quem postquam accepit patrio monstrante superbus
armigero Poenum ductor : " certamina primae
hic lue nunc," inquit, " pugnae ; te notus Hamilcar
hac trahit ad manes dextra." tum librat ab aure   576
intorquens iaculum et versantem in vulnere sese
transigit.   extracta foedavit cuspide sanguis
canitiem et longos finivit morte labores.

ᵃ Teanum Sidicinum is the full name of this Campanian
city.
ᵇ This must have been in the First Punic War.

Nor were the men of Sidicinum [a] backward. A thousand of them served under Viriasius, who had no superior in pitching a camp or building a raft or battering walls with the tough ram or planting improvised gangways against a tower. But Hannibal saw him exulting in his prowess, because Arauricus, distrusting his light armour, fled wounded before him in hot haste ; and his ardour was kindled by the prospect of a glorious combat ; and he thought it not beneath him to close in conflict with the fierce warrior. As Viriasius drew his spear forth from the body of Arauricus, Hannibal rushed up and stabbed him in the breast, crying : " Famous fighter, whoever you are, you deserved to fall by no hand but mine ; carry down to the shades the glory of your death ; had not the land of Italy given you birth, I should have suffered you to depart alive." Next he attacked Fadus and the veteran Labicus, whom Hamilcar had once fought in Sicily [b] and made famous by a memorable contest. Unmindful of his years and forgetting his age, he came forth now to battle. He kept his youthful ardour and all the passion of youth ; but his feeble blows betrayed the weakness of the aged warrior : so a fire of straw crackles to no purpose and blazes up with no strength and no effect. When Hannibal learnt his name from Hamilcar's armour-bearer, he cried exultingly : " Here and now you shall pay the penalty for the first battle in which you fought : the famous Hamilcar uses my arm to send you down to the shades." Then he raised a javelin to his ear and threw it, and then ran him through as he lay writhing upon his wound. When the weapon was drawn forth, the blood defiled his grey hairs, and death ended his long service. Herminius likewise was

nec minus Herminium primis obtruncat in armis, 580
assuetum, Thrasymenne, tuos praedantibus hamis
exhaurire lacus patriaeque alimenta senectae
ducere suspenso per stagna iacentia lino.

Interea exanimum maesti super arma Sychaeum
portabant Poeni corpusque in castra ferebant.   585
quos ubi conspexit tristi clamore ruentes
ductor, praesago percussus pectora luctu :
" quinam," inquit, " dolor, o socii, quemve ira deorum
eripuit nobis ?   num te, dulcedine laudis
flagrantem et nimio primi Mavortis amore,   590
atra, Sychaee, dies properato funere carpsit ? "
utque dato gemitu lacrimae assensere ferentum,
et dictus pariter caedis maerentibus auctor :
" cerno," ait, " adverso pulchrum sub pectore vulnus
cuspidis Iliacae.   dignus Carthagine, dignus   595
Hasdrubale ad manes ibis ; nec te optima mater
dissimilem lugebit avis, Stygiave sub umbra
degenerem cernens noster vitabit Hamilcar.
at mihi Flaminius, tam maesti causa doloris,
morte sua minuat luctus.   haec pompa sequetur 600
exequias, seroque emptum volet impia Roma,
non violasse mei corpus mucrone Sychaei."

Sic memorans torquet fumantem ex ore vaporem,
iraque anhelatum proturbat pectore murmur,
ut multo accensis fervore exuberat undis,   605
clausus ubi exusto liquor indignatur aeno.
tum praeceps ruit in medios solumque fatigat
Flaminium incessens ; nec dicto segnius ille

slain in his first battle by Hannibal—Herminius who
was wont to pillage Lake Trasimene and draw forth
the fish with his hook, pulling out food for his ancient
father with a line that hung over the motionless pools.

Meanwhile the sorrowing Carthaginians raised the
lifeless body of Sychaeus upon his shield and bore it
to the camp. When Hannibal saw them hasting with
loud lament, his heart was stricken with foreboding
grief. "Why mourn ye thus, comrades?" he asked:
"Whom have the angry gods taken from us? Is it
you, Sychaeus, burning with desire of glory and too
eager in your first battle, whom the black death-day
has cut off before your time?" When the tears of
the mourners answered his question, and when they
told at the same time the name of the slayer, Hanni-
bal spoke thus: "I see the glorious wound of the
Roman spear on the front of your body. You will
go down to the shades, worthy of Carthage, worthy
of Hasdrubal; your good mother will mourn you as
a true descendant of your ancestors; and, when my
father Hamilcar meets you in the darkness of Hades,
he will not shun you as degenerate. My own grief
shall be lessened by the death of Flaminius, the
author of our sorrow. He shall be the escort that
follows you to the grave; and wicked Rome shall
dearly repent too late the stroke that robbed my
beloved Sychaeus of life."

While he spoke thus, a reeking steam issued from
his mouth, and a hoarse inarticulate sound came forth
from his furious breast, as water overflows with fire-
heated waves, when it rages angrily, confined in the
burnt cauldron. Then he rushed headlong into the
fray, and singled out Flaminius for attack, taunt-
ing him; and Flaminius was ready for battle on

bella capessebat ; propiorque insurgere Mavors
coeperat, et campo iunctus iam stabat uterque,   610
cum subitus per saxa fragor, motique repente,
horrendum, colles et summa cacumina totis
intremuere iugis ; nutant in vertice silvae
pinifero, fractaeque ruunt super agmina rupes.
immugit penitus convulsis ima cavernis   615
dissiliens tellus nec parvos rumpit hiatus,
atque umbras late Stygias immensa vorago
faucibus ostendit patulis ; manesque profundi
antiquum expavere diem.   lacus ater, in altos
sublatus montes et sede excussus avita,   620
lavit Tyrrhenas ignota aspergine silvas.
iamque eadem populos magnorumque oppida regum
tempestas et dira lues stravitque tulitque.
ac super haec reflui pugnarunt fontibus amnes,
et retro fluctus torsit mare ; monte relicto   625
Apenninicolae fugere ad litora Fauni.
    Pugnabat tamen (heu belli vecordia !) miles,
iactatus titubante solo, tremebundaque tela,
subducta tellure ruens, torquebat in hostem,
donec pulsa vagos cursus ad litora vertit   630
mentis inops stagnisque illata est Daunia pubes.
quis consul terga increpitans, nam turbine motae
ablatus terrae inciderat : " quid deinde, quid, oro,
restat, io, profugis ?   vos en ad moenia Romae
ducitis Hannibalem ; vos in Tarpeia Tonantis   635
tecta faces ferrumque datis.   sta, miles, et acres

---

a This earthquake is not a poetic fiction : the historian
Livy vouches for it (xxii. c. 5) and assures his readers that
not one of the combatants was aware of it ; so taken up
were they with the business in hand.

the instant. The War-god towered up closer, and now the pair stood face to face on the field, when suddenly there came an awful crash along the cliffs, and the heights were shaken and the high peaks rocked all along the range; on the pine-clad summit the trees swayed, and fragments of rock rushed down upon the armies. Splitting asunder in its lowest depths, the earth rumbled in its tortured hollows and opened up great chasms; and the vast gulf, yawning wide, revealed the shades below; and the dead in the depths were terrified by the daylight they once had known. The dark lake, forced from its ancient seat, rose to the height of the mountains, and bathed the Tuscan woods with moisture unfelt before. And now that same storm and dire catastrophe overthrew and destroyed nations and the cities of mighty kings. And rivers also flowed backwards and fought against their sources; the sea-waves reversed their course; and the Fauns who dwell on the Apennines left the hills and fled towards the coast.[a]

Yet—alas for the frenzy of war !—the battle still went on; and the soldiers, though staggering on the unsteady ground and falling when the earth withdrew beneath them, kept hurling their uncertain missiles against the foe. At last the Romans were defeated and turned their random flight to the lake-shore, and were driven distracted into the water. The consul had been separated from them by the earthquake; but now he overtook them and reproached them from behind: " What still remains, if you fly now? what, I beseech you? *You* are leading Hannibal against the walls of Rome; *you* are giving him fire and sword, to use against the Tarpeian shrine of the Thunderer. Stand firm, soldiers, and

disce ex me pugnas ; vel, si pugnare negatum,
disce mori.   dabit exemplum non vile futuris
Flaminius ; ne terga Libys, ne Cantaber umquam
consulis aspiciat.   solus, si tanta libido   640
est vobis rabiesque fugae, tela omnia solus
pectore consumo et moriens, fugiente per auras
hac anima, vestras revocabo ad proelia dextras."
   Dumque ea commemorat densosque obit obvius
      hostes,
advolat ora ferus mentemque Ducarius. acri   645
nomen erat gentile viro, fusisque catervis
Boiorum quondam patriis antiqua gerebat
vulnera barbaricae mentis ; noscensque superbi
victoris vultus : " tune," inquit, " maximus ille
Boiorum terror ?   libet hoc cognoscere telo,   650
corporis an tanti manet de vulnere sanguis.
nec vos paeniteat, populares, fortibus umbris
hoc mactare caput : nostros hic curribus egit
insistens victos alta ad Capitolia patres.
ultrix hora vocat."   pariter tunc undique fusis   655
obruitur telis, nimboque ruente per auras
contectus, nulli dextra iactare reliquit
Flaminium cecidisse sua.   nec pugna perempto
ulterior ductore fuit ; namque agmine denso
primores iuvenum, laeva ob discrimina Martis   660
infensi superis dextrisque et cernere Poenum
victorem plus morte rati, super ocius omnes
membra ducis stratosque artus certamine magno

---

   a See iv. 704 foll.   Livy says that Ducarius, belonging to
the Gallic tribe of the Insubres, himself killed Flaminius.
   b He suggests in mockery that the general is not, after all,
invulnerable.
   c When he celebrated a triumph over the Boii : the captives

learn from me to fight bravely ; or, if fight is impossible, learn how to die. Flaminius shall set a worthy example to coming generations. No Libyan, no Spaniard, shall ever behold the back of a consul. If you are possessed by such a mad passion for flight, then single-handed I shall intercept every weapon with my own breast ; and, dying, as my soul departs through the sky, I shall call your swords back to the battle."

While Flaminius spoke thus and plunged into the thickest of the enemy, Ducarius rode up, savage in mind as in aspect. That fierce warrior bore a name familiar in his tribe, and his savage heart had long cherished resentment for the defeat suffered in time past by his countrymen, the Boii.[a] Recognizing the face of their proud conqueror, he cried : " Art *thou* he whom the Boii so much dreaded? I intend this weapon to decide whether blood will flow, when such a hero is wounded.[b] And you, my countrymen, shrink not from offering up this victim to our noble dead. This is the man who stood in the chariot[c] and drove our defeated sires to the Capitol. Now the hour of vengeance summons him." Then the consul was overwhelmed with missiles that rained from all sides alike; and, covered by the shower that hurtled through the sky, he left to none the power of boasting that his hand had slain Flaminius. When the leader was slain, the fighting ceased. For the foremost soldiers closed their ranks ; and then, enraged against Heaven and themselves for their defeat, and thinking it worse than death to see the Carthaginians conquer, they hastened eagerly to pile over the body of Flaminius and walked in front of their conqueror's chariot to the temple of Jupiter.

telaque corporaque et non fausto Marte cruentas
iniecere manus.   sic densae caedis acervo,   665
ceu tumulo, texere virum.   tum, strage per undas,
per silvas sparsa perque altam sanguine vallem,
in medias fratre invectus comitante catervas
caesorum iuvenum Poenus : " quae vulnera cernis !
quas mortes ! " inquit. " premit omnis dextera
      ferrum,   670
armatusque iacet servans certamina miles.
hos, en, hos obitus nostrae spectate cohortes !
fronte minae durant, et stant in vultibus irae.
et vereor, ne, quae tanta creat indole tellus
magnanimos fecunda viros, huic fata dicarint   675
imperium, atque ipsis devincat cladibus orbem."
    Sic fatus cessit nocti ; finemque dedere
caedibus infusae, subducto sole, tenebrae.

his prostrate limbs their weapons, their bodies, and their hands red with the blood of defeat. Thus they covered him with a close-packed heap of corpses for a tomb. The dead lay scattered in the water, in the woods, and in the valley where the blood ran deep, when Hannibal rode up with his brother to the centre of the carnage : " Do you see these wounds, these deaths ? " he said to Mago : " each hand grasps its sword, and the warrior lies in his armour, and still maintains the strife. Let our soldiers look and see how these men died ! Their brows still frown, and martial ardour is fixed upon their faces. It misgives me that this land, the fertile mother of such noble heroes, may be destined to hold empire, and may, even by its lost battles, conquer the world."

Thus Hannibal spoke and then gave way to night ; for the sun had vanished, and the coming on of darkness ended the slaughter.

LIBER SEXTUS

ARGUMENT

Scenes on the field of the lost battle. Flight of the Romans (1-61). Serranus, a son of the famous Regulus, is one of the fugitives : he reaches the dwelling of Marus, who had been his father's squire in Africa : Marus dresses his wounds (62-100), and tells the story of Regulus as conqueror and as captive (101-551). Mourning and consternation at Rome after the defeat. Serranus returns to his mother, Marcia

Iam, Tartessiaco quos solverat aequore Titan
in noctem diffusus, equos iungebat Eois
litoribus, primique novo Phaëthonte retecti
Seres lanigeris repetebant vellera lucis,
et foeda ante oculos strages, propiusque patebat   5
insani Mavortis opus : simul arma virique
ac mixtus sonipes dextraeque in vulnere caesi
haerentes hostis ; passim clipeique iubaeque
atque artus trunci capitum fractusque iacebat
ossibus in duris ensis ; nec cernere deerat   10
frustra seminecum quaerentia lumina caelum.
tum spumans sanie lacus et fluitantia summo
aeternum tumulis orbata cadavera ponto.
  Nec tamen adversis ruerat tota Itala virtus.

---

a Tartessus, identified by some scholars with the Tarshish of Scripture, was a town on the west coast of Spain : the name is often used by the Roman poets to denote the Far West and the setting sun : see iii. 399.

BOOK VI

ARGUMENT (*continued*)

(552-589).   *The Senate discuss plans of campaign.   Jupiter
prevents Hannibal from marching on Rome.   Q. Fabius is
chosen Dictator (590-618).   His wisdom (619-640).   Hanni-
bal marches through Umbria and Picenum to Campania : at
Liternum he sees on the temple-walls pictures of scenes in the
First Punic War, and orders them all to be burnt (641-716).*

Now on Eastern shores the Sun was yoking the
steeds that he had freed in the sea of Tartessus [a]
when he scattered his fires for the night ; and the
Seres, first disclosed by the sunrise, began again to
pluck fleeces from their wool-bearing trees.[b]   Then
hideous havoc was revealed, and the work of War's
madness was seen clearer—a medley of arms and men
and horses, and hands that still clung to the wound
of a slain enemy.   The ground was littered with
shields and helmet-plumes, with headless corpses and
swords that had broken against tough bones ; and
one might see the eyes of half-dead men looking in
vain for the light.   Then there was the lake foaming
with gore, and the corpses floating on its surface, for
ever deprived of a grave.

Yet Roman courage had not utterly collapsed in

[b] The Seres (Chinese) were regarded by the ancients as an
Indian people ; and it was long believed that silk, like cotton,
was a vegetable product and grew on trees.

Bruttius ingenti miserandae caedis acervo,   15
non aequum ostentans confosso corpore Martem,
extulerat vix triste caput truncosque trahebat
per stragem, nervis interlabentibus, artus ;
tenuis opum, non patre nitens linguave, sed asper
ense ; nec e Volsca quisquam vir gente redemit   20
plus aevi nece magnanima.   puer addere sese
pubescente gena castris optarat et acri
Flaminio spectatus erat, cum Celtica victor
obrueret bello divis melioribus arma.
inde honor ac sacrae custodia Marte sub omni   25
alitis ; hinc causam nutrivit gloria leti.
namque necis certus, captae prohibere nequiret
cum Poenos aquilae, postquam subsidere fata
viderat et magna pugnam inclinare ruina,
occulere interdum et terrae mandare parabat.   30
sed, subitis victus telis, labentia membra
prostravit super atque iniecta morte tegebat.
verum ubi lux nocte e Stygia miseroque sopore
reddita, vicini de strage cadaveris hasta
erigitur, soloque vigens conamine, late   35
stagnantem caede et facilem discedere terram
ense fodit, clausamque aquilae infelicis adorans
effigiem, palmis languentibus aequat harenas.
supremus fessi tenues tum cessit in auras
halitus et magnam misit sub Tartara mentem.   40
   Iuxta cernere erat meritae sibi poscere carmen
virtutis sacram rabiem.   Laevinus, ab alto
Priverno, vitis Latiae praesignis honore,

ᵃ The eagle, the principal ensign of the Roman legion.
   ᵇ " Death " must here mean " a dying man."

the hour of defeat. Bruttius, whose wounded body showed his ill-fortune in the battle, slowly raised his head from a huge pile of hapless corpses, and dragged his mutilated limbs through the carnage with muscles that failed him from time to time. He had not wealth or noble birth or eloquence ; but his sword was keen, and none of the Volscian people gained more glory than he by a heroic death. As a boy, before his beard grew, he had chosen to join the army, and his prowess had been witnessed by brave Flaminius, when with better fortune he fought the Celtic armies and crushed them. Thus Bruttius won honour and guarded the sacred bird [a] in every battle ; and this distinction was the cause of his death. He was sure to die ; and, when he could not prevent the Carthaginians from taking the eagle, he tried to bury it in the ground for the time ; for he saw that fate was adverse and the battle was turning into a great disaster. But a sudden wound made him throw his failing limbs over his charge ; and death [b] lay over it to hide it. But, when day returned after a dreadful night of distressful slumber, he raised himself on a spear taken from the nearest corpse ; then, exerting all his strength for the effort, he dug a hole in the earth with his sword ; and the ground, drenched in blood all round, parted easily. Next he bowed before the buried effigy of the luckless eagle, and smoothed the sand over it with strengthless palms. Then his last feeble breath went forth into thin air, and sent a brave heart to Tartarus.

Near by one might see an awful frenzy of valour that deserves to claim the poet's verse. Laevinus, a native of Privernum [c] on the hill, who had earned

[c] A town of Latium.

285

exanimum Nasamona Tyren super ipse iacebat
exanimis ; non hasta viro, non ensis ; in artis   45
abstulerat Fors arma ; tamen certamine nudo
invenit Marti telum dolor. ore cruento
pugnatum, ferrique vicem dens praebuit irae.
iam lacerae nares foedataque lumina morsu,
iam truncum raptis caput auribus, ipsaque diris   50
frons depasta modis, et sanguine abundat hiatus ;
nec satias, donec mandentia linqueret ora
spiritus, et plenos rictus mors atra teneret.
    Talia dum praebet tristis miracula virtus,
diverso interea fugientes saucia turba   55
iactantur casu silvisque per avia caecis
ablati furtim multo cum vulnere solos
per noctem metantur agros : sonus omnis et aura
exterrent pennaque levi commota volucris.
non sopor aut menti requies : agit asper acerba   60
nunc Mago attonitos, nunc arduus Hannibal hasta.
    Serranus, clarum nomen, tua, Regule, proles,
qui, longum semper fama gliscente per aevum,
infidis servasse fidem memorabere Poenis,
flore nitens primo, patriis heu Punica bella   65
auspiciis ingressus erat ; miseramque parentem
et dulces tristi repetebat sorte penates
saucius. haud illi comitum super ullus, et atris

---

^a Each centurion carried a rattan made of vine-wood and
applied it to the backs of soldiers who were negligent in
performing their military duties.

^b Serranus was a name borne by many members of the
Atilian *gens*, to which Regulus belonged.   Here Silius begins
a digression of nearly 500 lines (it ends at l. 551), in which he
describes the doings and sufferings of Regulus in the First
Punic War.   Regulus was taken prisoner in Africa in 255
B.C., thirty-eight years before the battle of Lake Trasimene.

the distinction of the Roman vine-staff,[a] lay there
on the top of Tyres, a Nasamonian ; and both were
dead. He had neither spear nor sword : Fortune
had robbed him of his weapons in the hard fight ;
yet in the unarmed contest rage found a weapon to
fight with. He had fought with savage mouth, and
his teeth did the work of steel, to gratify his rage.
Already the nose of Tyres was torn and the eyes
marred by the cruel jaws ; the ears were bitten off
and the head mutilated ; the forehead itself was
horribly gnawed, and blood streamed from the open
lips ; nor was Laevinus satisfied, until the breath left
those champing jaws and dark death arrested the
crammed mouth.

While hideous valour displayed such portentous
deeds, the stricken mob of fugitives were harassed
meanwhile by a different fate. Covered with wounds,
they slunk away along pathless tracks in the dark
forests, and traversed the deserted fields all night.
They were terrified by every sound, by the breeze,
and by the stirring of a bird on its light wings.
Sleep or peace of mind was impossible. Panic-
stricken, they were driven on now by fierce Mago,
and now by Hannibal prancing on with relentless
spear.

Serranus [b] bore a glorious name : he was the son
of Regulus, whose fame ever increases with the pass-
age of time, and of whom it will never be forgotten,
that he kept faith with the faithless Carthaginians.
Serranus was in the flower of his youth ; but, alas,
he had begun the war against Carthage with his
father's ill-fortune, and now, sore-wounded, he sought
in sad plight to return to his unhappy mother and
the home he loved. Of his comrades none was left,

vulneribus qui ferret opem ; per devia, fractae
innitens hastae furtoque ereptus opacae   70
noctis, iter tacitum Perusina ferebat in arva.
ac fessus parvi, quaecumque ibi fata darentur,
limina pulsabat tecti, cum membra cubili
evolvens non tarda Marus (vetus ille parentis
miles et haud surda tractarat proelia fama)   75
procedit, renovata focis et paupere Vesta
lumina praetendens. utque ora agnovit et aegrum
vulneribus diris ac, lamentabile visu,
lapsantes fultum truncata cuspide gressus,
funesti rumore mali iam saucius aures :   80
" quod scelus, o nimius vitae nimiumque ferendis
adversis genitus, cerno ? te, maxime, vidi,
ductorum, cum captivo Carthaginis arcem
terreres vultu, crimen culpamque Tonantis,
occidere atque hausi, quem non Sidonia tecta   85
expulerint eversa meo de corde, dolorem.
estis ubi en iterum, superi ? dat pectora ferro
Regulus, ac tantae stirpem periura recidit
surgentem Carthago domus." inde aegra reponit
membra toro ; nec ferre rudis medicamina (quippe 90
callebat bellis) nunc purgat vulnera lympha,
nunc mulcet sucis : ligat inde ac vellera molli
circumdat tactu et torpentes mitigat artus.
exin cura seni, tristem depellere fesso
ore sitim et parca vires accersere mensa.   95
quae postquam properata, sopor sua munera tandem

---

    [a] A city of Etruria, now Perugia.
    [b] In humble households an image of Vesta generally stood
on or near the hearth.
    [c] Regulus.
    [d] Jupiter ought to have defended such a Roman as Regulus
from such a dreadful fate.

and there was none to dress his grievous wounds.
Leaning on a broken spear, and rescued from doom
by the connivance of dark night, he crept silently
through bypaths towards the fields of Perusia.[a]
Worn out, he knocked at the door of a humble dwell-
ing, whatever fate might meet him there ; and
Marus was not slow to rise from his bed. Long
ago Marus had served under Regulus, and the ear of
Fame had heard of his prowess. Now he came forth,
holding up a light he had kindled at the poor hearth
where he worshipped Vesta.[b] He recognized Ser-
ranus and saw him suffering from dreadful wounds,
and supporting himself on his halting feet by the
broken spear—a piteous sight to behold. Rumour of
the fatal disaster had already wounded his ears ;
and now he cried : "What horror is this I see !—
I have lived too long and was born to suffer too
much adversity. I saw you,[c] greatest of generals,
when, though you were a prisoner, your aspect terri-
fied the citadel of Carthage ; I witnessed your death,
a scandal and a shame to the Thunderer [d] ; and even
the destruction of Carthage could never expel from
my heart the grief I suffered then. And now once
more, where are ye, ye gods ? A Regulus offers his
breast to the sword, and perjured Carthage lops off
the hopeful scion of that mighty house." Next he
laid the sick man on the bed, and, with the skill in
medicine which he had learnt in war, now cleansed
the wounds with water and now applied healing
simples, binding them up and wrapping them in
wool with gentle hand, and warming the stiffened
limbs. The old man's next care was to slake the sick
man's grievous thirst, and to recall his strength by a
sparing meal. When all this was quickly done, sleep

applicat et mitem fundit per membra quietem.
necdum exorta dies, Marus instat vulneris aestus
expertis medicare modis gratumque teporem,
exutus senium, trepida pietate ministrat.　　　100
　Hic iuvenis, maestos tollens ad sidera vultus,
cum gemitu lacrimisque simul : " si culmina nondum
Tarpeia exosus damnasti sceptra Quirini,
extremas Italum res Ausoniamque ruentem
aspice," ait, " genitor ; tandemque adverte procellis
aequos Iliacis oculos. amisimus Alpes,　　　106
nec deinde adversis modus est : Ticinus et ater
stragibus Eridanus, tuque insignite tropaeis
Sidoniis Trebia, et tellus lacrimabilis Arni.
sed quid ego haec ? gravior quanto vis ecce malorum !
vidi crescentes Thrasymenni caedibus undas　　111
prostrataque virum mole ; inter tela cadentem
vidi Flaminium. testor, mea numina, manes
dignam me poenae tum nobilitate paternae
strage hostis quaesisse necem, ni tristia letum,　115
ut quondam patri, nobis quoque fata negassent."
　Cetera acervantem questu lenire laborans
effatur senior : " patrio, fortissime, ritu,
quicquid adest duri, et rerum inclinata feramus.
talis lege deum clivoso tramite vitae　　　120
per varios praeceps casus rota volvitur aevi ;
sat tibi, sat magna et totum vulgata per orbem
stant documenta domus : sacer ille et numine nullo
inferior, tuus ille parens decora alta paravit
restando adversis nec virtutem exuit ullam　　125

---

　　[a] Jupiter.　　　　　　　[b] See note to iv. 813.
　　　　[c] Etruria : see note to v. 11.
　　　　[d] Regulus, his famous father, is meant.

290

at last did its kindly office and diffused gentle rest through all his limbs. Before day dawned Marus, forgetful of his years, made haste to treat the fever of the wound with tried remedies, and provided a pleasant coolness with eager loyalty.

Now Serranus, raising his sorrowful eyes to heaven, cried out amid groans and tears : " O Father,[a] if thou hast not yet condemned the realm of Quirinus,[b] and dost not hate the Tarpeian citadel, then look down on the desperate plight of Italy and the ruin of Rome ; turn at last a merciful eye upon our troubles. We lost the Alps ; nor is there any limit to our sufferings since then—the Ticinus, the river Po dark with our dead, the Trebia made famous by Punic triumph, and the lamentable country of the Arnus.[c] But why speak of all this when, behold ! a far heavier weight of calamity is ours ? I saw the level of Lake Trasimene raised by the multitude of the slain ; I saw Flaminius fall amid the missiles. I swear by the dead,[d] whom I worship, that I sought death then in striking down the foe—a death befitting the famous sufferings of my father ; but cruel fate, which denied him a soldier's death, denied it to me also."

As he still heaped complaint upon complaint, the old man strove to comfort him, saying : " In your father's fashion, brave youth, let us bear reverses of fortune and all the troubles that beset us. Such is the law of Heaven : the wheel of our existence, as it moves on along the steep track of life, is subject to many a slip. Great enough and famous throughout the world are the title-deeds of your house ; your father, that sacred figure whom no deity excels, gained his high renown by defying ill-fortune ; and he discarded none of the virtues until the time when

ante reluctantes liquit quam spiritus artus.
vix puerile mihi tempus confecerat aetas,
cum primo malas signabat Regulus aevo.
accessi comes, atque omnes sociavimus annos,
donec dis Italae visum est extinguere lumen   130
gentis, in egregio cuius sibi pectore sedem
ceperat alma Fides mentemque amplexa tenebat.
ille ensem nobis magnorum hunc instar honorum
virtutisque ergo dedit et, sordentia fumo
quae cernis nunc, frena, sed est argenteus ollis   135
fulgor ; nec cuiquam Marus est post talia dona
non praelatus eques.   verum superavit honores
omnes hasta meos.   cui me libare Lyaei
quod cernis latices, dignum cognoscere causam.
     "Turbidus arentes lento pede sulcat harenas   140
Bagrada, non ullo Libycis in finibus amne
victus limosas extendere latius undas
et stagnante vado patulos involvere campos.
hic studio laticum, quorum est haud prodiga tellus,
per ripas laeti saevis consedimus arvis.   145
lucus iners iuxta Stygium pallentibus umbris
servabat sine sole nemus, crassusque per auras
halitus erumpens taetrum expirabat odorem.
intus dira domus curvoque immanis in antro
sub terra specus et tristes sine luce tenebrae.   150
horror mente redit.   monstrum exitiabile et ira
telluris genitum, cui par vix viderit aetas
ulla virum, serpens centum porrectus in ulnas

---

 a The warrior treats his weapon as a sacred thing.
   b This river flows into the Mediterranean not far from
Carthage and Utica.
   c This monstrous serpent was not invented by Silius :

his spirit fled from the unwilling body. I had hardly outgrown the years of boyhood, when the first beard was growing on the face of Regulus. I became his comrade, and we spent all our years together, till Heaven saw fit to put out the light of the Roman people—the man in whose noble breast kindly Loyalty had fixed her seat and remained the tenant of his heart. He gave me this sword for valour—an honour second to none—and the bridle which you see now blackened by smoke, though the sheen of the silver still remains ; and, when Marus had received such gifts, there was no horseman who took precedence of him. But the chief of all my distinctions was my lance. You see me pour wine in its honour [a] ; and it is worth your while to learn the reason.

" The turbid stream of Bagrada [b] furrows the sandy desert with sluggish course ; and no river in the land of Libya can boast that it spreads its muddy waters further, or covers the wide plains with greater floods. Here, in that savage land, we were glad to encamp upon its banks ; for we needed water, which is scarce in that country. Hard by stood a grove whose trees were ever motionless and sunless, with shade dark as Erebus ; and from it burst thick fumes that spread a noisome stench through the air. Within it was a dreadful dwelling, a vast subterranean hollow in a winding cavern, where the dismal darkness let in no light. I shudder still to think of it. A deadly monster [c] lived there, spawned by Earth in her wrath, whose like scarce any generation of men can see again ; a serpent, a hundred ells in length,

Livy described the battle of the army against the reptile, and says that its skin, 120 feet long, was sent to Rome.

letalem ripam et lucos habitabat Avernos.
ingluviem immensi ventris gravidamque venenis   155
alvum deprensi satiabant fonte leones,
aut acta ad fluvium torrenti lampade solis
armenta et tractae foeda gravitate per auras
ac tabe afflatus volucres.   semesa iacebant
ossa solo, informi dape quae repletus et asper   160
vastatis gregibus nigro ructarat in antro.
isque ubi ferventi concepta incendia pastu
gurgite mulcebat rapido et spumantibus undis,
nondum etiam toto demersus corpore in amnem
iam caput adversae ponebat margine ripae.   165
imprudens tantae pestis gradiebar, Aquino
Apenninicola atque Umbro comitatus Avente ;
scire nemus pacemque loci explorare libebat.
iamque propinquantum tacitus penetravit in artus
horror, et occulto riguerunt frigore membra.   170
intramus tamen et Nymphas numenque precamur
gurgitis ignoti trepidosque et multa paventes
arcano gressus audemus credere luco.
ecce e vestibulo primisque e faucibus antri
Tartareus turbo atque insano saevior Euro   175
spiritus erumpit, vastoque e gurgite fusa
tempestas oritur, mixtam stridore procellam
Cerbereo torquens.   pavefacti clade vicissim
aspicimus : resonare solum, tellusque moveri,
atque antrum ruere, et visi procedere manes.   180
quantis armati caelum petiere Gigantes

---

a The word has here, and often, the sense of " deadly."
b The mention of Cerberus implies that a passage to the
nether world was opened up.

294

haunted that fatal bank and the Avernian [a] grove.
He filled his vast maw and poison-breeding belly
with lions caught when they came for water, or with
cattle driven to the river when the sun was hot, and
with birds brought down from the sky by the foul
stench and corruption of the atmosphere. On the
floor lay half-eaten bones, which he had belched up
in the darkness of his cave after filling his maw with
a hideous meal on the flocks he had laid low. And,
when he was fain to bathe in the foaming waters of
the running stream and cool the heat engendered
by his fiery food, before he had plunged his whole
body in the river, his head was already resting on
the opposite bank. Unwitting of such a danger I
went forth ; and with me went Aquinus, a native of
the Apennines, and Avens, an Umbrian. We sought
to examine the grove and find out whether the place
was friendly. But as we drew near, an unspoken
dread came over us, and a mysterious chill paralysed
our limbs. Yet we went on and prayed to the
Nymphs and the deity of the unknown river, and
then ventured, though anxious and full of fears,
to trust our feet to the secret grove. Suddenly
from the threshold and outer entrance of the cave
there burst forth a hellish whirlwind and a blast
fiercer than the frantic East-wind ; and a storm
poured forth from the vast hollow, a hurricane in
which the baying of Cerberus [b] was heard. Horror-
struck we gazed at one another. A noise came from
the ground, the earth was shaken, the cave fell in
ruins, and the dead seemed to come forth. Huge
as the snakes that armed the Giants [c] when they

[c] The Giants who tried to storm heaven are often repre-
sented in later Greek art as having serpents for feet.

anguibus, aut quantus Lernae lassavit in undis
Amphitryoniaden serpens, qualisque comantes
auro servavit ramos Iunonius anguis :
tantus disiecta tellure sub astra coruscum   185
extulit assurgens caput atque in nubila primam
dispersit saniem et caelum foedavit hiatu.
diffugimus tenuemque metu conamur anheli
tollere clamorem frustra ; nam sibila totum
implebant nemus. ac subita formidine caecus   190
et facti damnandus Avens (sed fata trahebant)
antiquae quercus ingenti robore sese
occulit, infandum si posset fallere monstrum.
vix egomet credo ; spiris ingentibus altae
arboris abstraxit molem penitusque revulsam   195
evertit fundo et radicibus eruit imis.
tum trepidum ac socios extrema voce cientem
corripit atque haustu sorbens et faucibus atris
(vidi respiciens) obscaena condidit alvo.
infelix fluvio sese et torrentibus undis   200
crediderat celerique fuga iam nabat Aquinus.
hunc medio invasit fluctu ripaeque relatos
(heu genus infandum leti) depascitur artus.

" Sic dirum nobis et lamentabile monstrum
effugisse datur. quantum mens aegra sinebat,   205
appropero gressum et ductori singula pando.
ingemuit, casus iuvenum miseratus acerbos.
utque erat in pugnas et Martem et proelia et hostem
igneus et magna audendi flagrabat amore,
ocius arma rapi et spectatum Marte sub omni   210

---

^a The dragon that guarded the golden apples in the
Garden of the Hesperides : see note to iii. 282.

296

stormed heaven, or as the hydra that wearied Hercules by the waters of Lerna, or as Juno's snake [a] that guarded the boughs with golden foliage—even so huge he rose up from the cloven earth and raised his glittering head to heaven, and first scattered his slaver into the clouds and marred the face of heaven with his open jaws. Hither and thither we fled and tried to raise a feeble shout, though breathless with terror ; but in vain ; for the sound of his hissing filled all the grove. Then Avens, blind with sudden fear—blameworthy was his act, but Fate had him in the toils—hid in the huge trunk of an ancient oak, hoping that the horrible monster might not see him. I can scarce believe it myself ; but the serpent, clinging with its huge coils, removed the great tree bodily, tearing it from the ground, and wrenching it up from the roots. Then, as the trembling wretch called on his companions with his latest utterance, the serpent seized him and swallowed him down with a gulp of its black throat—I looked back and saw it—and buried him in its beastly maw. Unhappy Aquinus had entrusted himself to the running stream of the river, and was swimming fast away. But the serpent attacked him in midstream, carried his body to the bank, and there devoured it—a dreadful form of death !

"Thus I alone was suffered to escape from the monster so terrible and deadly. I ran as fast as grief would let me, and told all to the general. He groaned aloud, in pity for the cruel fate of his men. Then, eager as he ever was for war and battle and conflict with the foe, and burning with a passion for great achievements, he ordered his men to arm instantly, and his cavalry, well tried in many a fight, to

ire iubet campis equitem.   ruit ipse, citatum
quadrupedem planta fodiens, scutataque raptim
consequitur iusso manus et muralia portat
ballistas tormenta graves suetamque movere
excelsas turres immensae cuspidis hastam.   215
iamque ubi feralem strepitu circumtonat aulam
cornea gramineum persultans ungula campum,
percitus hinnitu serpens evolvitur antro
et Stygios aestus fumanti exsibilat ore.
terribilis gemino de lumine fulgurat ignis ;   220
at nemus arrectae et procera cacumina saltus
exsuperant cristae ; trifido vibrata per auras
lingua micat motu atque assultans aethera lambit.
ut vero strepuere tubae, conterritus alte
immensum attollit corpus tergoque residens   225
cetera sinuatis glomerat sub pectore gyris.
dira dehinc in bella ruit rapideque resolvens
contortos orbes derecto corpore totam
extendit molem subitoque propinquus in ora
lato distantum spatio venit ; omnis anhelat   230
attonitus serpentis equus, frenoque teneri
impatiens crebros expirat naribus ignes.
arduus ille super tumidis cervicibus altum
nutat utroque caput ; trepidos inde incitus ira
nunc sublime rapit, nunc vasto pondere gaudet   235
elisisse premens.   tunc fractis ossibus atram
absorbet saniem et, tabo manante per ora,
mutat hians hostem semesaque membra relinquit.
cedebant iam signa retro, victorque catervas
longius avectas afflatus peste premebat,   240
cum ductor, propere revocatam in proelia turmam
vocibus impellens : ' serpentine Itala pubes

---

a This engine was the *falarica*, for which see note to i. 351.

take the field. He galloped forward himself, spurring his flying steed ; and at his command there followed a body of shieldsmen, bringing the heavy catapults used in sieges and the weapon [a] whose huge point can batter down high towers. And now, when the horses speeding over the grassy plain surrounded the fatal spot with the thunder of their hoofs, the serpent, aroused by the neighing, glided forth from his cave and hissed forth a hellish blast from his reeking jaws. Both his eyes flashed horrible fire ; his erected crest towered over the tall tree-tops ; and his three-forked tongue darted and flickered through the air and rose up till it licked the sky. But, when the trumpets sounded, he was startled and reared aloft his huge bulk ; then, couching on his rear, he gathered the rest of his body beneath his front in circling coils. Then he began a fearsome conflict, quickly un-winding his coils and stretching his body out to its full length, till he reached in a moment the faces of men far away. All the horses snorted, in their terror of the serpent, refusing to obey the rein and breathing frequent fire from their nostrils. The monster, tower-ing above the frightened men with swollen neck, waved his high head to right and left and, in his rage, now hoisted them on high, and now delighted in crushing them beneath his huge weight. Then he breaks their bones and gulps down the black gore ; with his open jaws wet with blood, he leaves the half-eaten body and seeks a fresh foe. The soldiers fell back, and the victorious serpent attacked the squadrons from a distance with his pestilential breath. But then Regulus speedily recalled the troops to battle and encouraged them thus : ' Shall we, the men of Italy, retreat before a serpent, and admit

terga damus Libycisque parem non esse fatemur
anguibus Ausoniam ?   si debellavit inertes
halitus, ac viso mens aegra effluxit hiatu,   245
ibo alacer solusque manus componere monstro
sufficiam.'   clamans haec atque interritus hastam
fulmineo volucrem torquet per inane lacerto.
venit in adversam non vano turbine frontem
cuspis et, haud paulum vires adiuta ruentis   250
contra ardore ferae, capiti tremebunda resedit.
clamor ad astra datur, vocesque repente profusae
aetherias adiere domos.   furit ilicet ira
terrigena, impatiens dare terga novusque dolori
et chalybem longo tum primum passus in aevo.   255
nec frustra rapidi, stimulante dolore, fuisset
impetus, ablato ni Regulus arte regendi
instantem elusisset equo rursusque secutum
cornipedis gyros flexi curvamine tergi
detortis laeva celer effugisset habenis.   260
   " At non spectator Marus inter talia segni
torpebat dextra.   mea tanto in corpore monstri
hasta secunda fuit.   iam iamque extrema trisulca
lambebat lingua fessi certamine terga
quadrupedis ; torsi telum atque urgentia velox   265
in memet saevi serpentis proelia verto.
hinc imitata cohors certatim spicula dextris
congerit alternasque ferum diducit in iras,
donec murali balista coercuit ictu.
tum fractus demum vires, non iam amplius aegra 270
consuetum ad nisus spina praestante rigorem
et solitum in nubes tolli caput.   acrius instant,

that Rome is no match for the snakes of Libya ? If his breath has conquered your feeble strength, and your courage has oozed away at sight of his open mouth, then I will go boldly forward and cope with the monster single-handed.' Thus he shouted and undismayed hurled his flying spear through the air with lightning speed. The weapon rushed on and did its work : it struck the serpent fairly on the head, gaining not a little force from the fierceness of the creature's charge, and stuck there quivering. A shout of triumph rose, and the sudden noise of it went up to Heaven. At once the earth-born monster went mad with rage : he spurned defeat and was a stranger to pain ; for never before in his long life had he felt the steel. Nor would the swift charge, prompted by his pain, have failed, had not Regulus, skilled horseman that he was, eluded the onset with wheeling steed, and then, when the serpent, with a bend of its supple back, once again followed the turning horse, pulled the rein with his left hand and soon got out of reach.

" But Marus did not merely look on at such a scene and take no part : my spear was the second to transfix the great body of the monster. His three-forked tongue was now licking the rump of the general's tired horse ; I threw my weapon and quickly turned on myself the serpent's fierce assault. The men followed my example and hurled their darts together with a will, making the creature shift its rage from one foe to another; and at length he was restrained by a blow from a catapult that would level a wall. Then at last his strength was broken ; for his injured spine could no longer stand up stiff for attack, and the head had no strength to rear up to the sky. We

iamque alvo penitus demersa falarica sedit,
et geminum volucres lumen rapuere sagittae.
iam patulis vasto sub vulnere faucibus ater   275
tabificam expirat saniem specus ; ultima iamque
ingestis cauda et iaculis et pondere conti
haeret humi ; lassoque tamen minitatur hiatu ;
donec tormentis stridens magnoque fragore
discussit trabs acta caput, longoque resolvens   280
aggere se ripae tandem exhalavit in auras
liventem nebulam fugientis ab ore veneni.
erupit tristi fluvio mugitus et imis
murmura fusa vadis ; subitoque et lucus et antrum
et resonae silvis ulularunt flebile ripae.   285
heu quantis luimus mox tristia proelia damnis !
quantaque supplicia et quales exhausimus iras !
nec tacuere pii vates famulumque sororum
Naiadum, tepida quas Bagrada nutrit in unda,
nos violasse manu seris monuere periclis.—   290
haec tunc hasta decus nobis pretiumque secundi
vulneris a vestro, Serrane, tributa parente,
princeps quae sacro bibit e serpente cruorem.''
    Iamdudum vultus lacrimis atque ora rigabat
Serranus medioque viri sermone profatur :   295
'' huic si vita duci nostrum durasset in aevum,
non Trebia infaustas superasset sanguine ripas,
nec, Thrasymenne, tuus premeret tot nomina gurges.''
    Tum senior : '' magnas,'' inquit, '' de sanguine
        poenas

---

    [a] This refers to the defeat and capture of Regulus, which
soon followed.
    [b] The spear which Marus showed to Serranus was not the
spear which he himself threw : it had belonged to Regulus
and was given by him to Marus as a reward for valour.
302

attacked more fiercely ; and soon a huge missile was
lodged deep in the monster's belly, and the sight of
both his eyes was destroyed by flying arrows. Now
the dark pit of the gaping wound sent forth a
poisonous slaver from the open jaws ; and now the
end of the tail was held fast to the ground by showers
of darts and heavy poles ; and still he threatened
feebly with open mouth. At last a beam, discharged
from an engine with a loud hissing sound, shattered
his head ; and the body lay at last relaxed far along
the raised bank, and discharged into the air a dark
vapour of poison that escaped from its mouth. Then
a cry of sorrow burst from the river, and the sound
spread through the depths ; and suddenly both grove
and cave sent forth a noise of wailing, and the banks
replied to the trees. Alas, how great were our losses,
and how dearly we paid in the end for our luckless
battle ! [a] How much we suffered, and what a cup of
retribution we had to drink ! Our soothsayers were
not silent : they warned us that we had laid profane
hands on the servant of the Naiads, the sisters who
dwell in the warm stream of the Bagrada, and that
we should suffer for it later.—Then it was, Serranus,
that your father gave me this spear as my reward
and prize for dealing the second wound ; this was
the first weapon to draw blood from the sacred
serpent." [b]

The eyes and cheeks of Serranus had long been wet
with tears, and now he interrupted Marus and said :
" Had Regulus lived on to our time, the Trebia would
never have overflowed its fatal banks with blood, nor
would the waters of Lake Trasimene hide so many
famous dead."

The older man replied : " The Carthaginians paid

percepit Tyrio et praesumpta piacula mortis.　　300
nam, defecta viris et opes attrita, supinas
Africa tendebat palmas, cum sidere diro
misit Agenoreis ductorem animosa Therapne.
nulla viro species decorisque et frontis egenum
corpus ; in exiguis vigor, admirabile, membris　　305
vividus, et nisu magnos qui vinceret artus.
iam Martem regere atque astus adiungere ferro
et duris facilem per inhospita ducere vitam
haud isti, quem nunc penes est sollertia belli,
cederet Hannibali.　vellem hunc, o tristia nobis　310
Taygeta, hunc unum non durassetis opacis
Eurotae ripis !　vidissem moenia flammis
Phoenissae ruere, aut certe non horrida fata
flevissem ducis et, nulla quos morte nec igni
exutos servans portabo in Tartara, luctus.　　315
consertae campis acies, multusque per arva
fervebat Mavors ; nec mens erat ulla sine ira.
hic inter medios memorandis Regulus ausis
laxabat ferro campum inque pericla ruebat
nec repetenda dabat letali vulnera dextra.　　320
sic ubi nigrantem torquens stridentibus austris
portat turbo globum piceaque e nube ruinam
pendentem terris pariter pontoque minatur,
omnis et agricola et nemoroso vertice pastor
et pelago trepidat subductis navita velis.　　325
at fraudem nectens, socios ubi concava saxa
claudebant, vertit subito certamina Graius

---

a Xanthippus : see note to ii. 305.　" Therapne " is here
and often used as equivalent to " Sparta " : it was close to
that city : it is called " brave " because of the military
training which Spartans underwent.　Taygetus and Eurotas
mentioned below are the mountain and river of Sparta.

b Carthage.

dearly with their blood, and he, while he yet lived, took vengeance for his death. For Africa, with her armies thinned and her treasure exhausted, was holding out her hands in supplication, when brave Therapne in an evil hour sent a leader [a] to the Carthaginians. His aspect was mean : no beauty or noble brow was his ; but with his low stature there went a tireless activity to marvel at—an activity whose effort could conquer giants. In the art of war, in combining the sword with stratagem, in enduring hardship and contriving to exist in an unfriendly country, he was not inferior to yonder Hannibal, who is now supreme for skill in war. Glad had I been if Taygeta, so cruel to us, had made an exception of Xanthippus, and not hardened him on the shady banks of the Eurotas. Then I should have seen the walls of Dido [b] overthrown in flames ; or at least I should not have mourned the dreadful doom of Regulus—a sorrow which no death or funeral fire can ever take from me, but I shall keep it and carry it with me to Tartarus. The armies met in the field ; war raged fiercely throughout the land ; and every heart was full of martial ardour. Here, in the midst of his men, Regulus did memorable deeds, opening a path in the field with his sword, dashing into danger, and dealing out with his deadly arm strokes that needed not to be struck again. So, when a hurricane sweeps along a whirling mass of dark cloud with shrieking southwinds, and the pitch-dark heaven threatens earth and sea alike with destruction from above, all tillers of the soil and herdsmen on their wooded heights are terrified, and every seaman on the deep furls his sails. But the Greek general devised a trick : hiding a force behind rocky hollows, he suddenly ceased fighting

et dat terga celer ficta formidine ductor.
haud secus ac stabulis procurans otia pastor
in foveam parco tectam velamine frondis   330
ducit nocte lupos positae balatibus agnae.
abripuit traxitque virum fax mentis honestae
gloria et incerti fallax fiducia Martis.
non socios comitumve manus, non arma sequentum
respicere, insano pugnae tendebat amore   335
iam solus, nubes subito cum densa Laconum
saxosis latebris intento ad proelia circum
funditur, et pone insurgit vis saeva virorum.
o diram Latio lucem fastisque notandam !
dedecus o, Gradive, tuum ! tibi dextera et urbi 340
nata tuae tristi damnatur sorte catenae.
haud umquam absistam gemitu.   te, Regule, vidit
Sidonius carcer ! tuque huic sat magna triumpho
visa es, Carthago, superis ! quae poena sequetur
digna satis tali pollutos Marte Laconas ?   345
    " At nova Elissaei iurato foedera patres
consultant mandare duci pacisque sequestrem
mittere, poscentes vinctam inter proelia pubem
captivamque manum ductore rependere nostro.
nec mora, iam stabat primis in litoris undis   350
navali propulsa ratis, iam nautica pubes
aut silvis stringunt remos, aut abiete secta
transtra novant ; his intortas aptare rudentes,
his studium erecto componere carbasa malo.
unca locant prora curvati pondera ferri.   355
ante omnes doctus pelagi rectorque carinae

---

and beat a hasty retreat in pretended fear. Even so a shepherd, seeking safety for his flock, lures the wolves at night by the bleating of a tethered lamb into the pitfall masked by a slender covering of leafage. Regulus was caught and carried away by the desire of fame that fires the noble heart, and by mistaken trust in the fickle god of war. To no companions or helpers or troops did he look back but was pressing on alone in his wild desire for battle, when suddenly a cloud of Spartans issued from their ambush in the rocks and surrounded the eager warrior, while behind him rose up a great army. O fearful day for Rome, that she must mark with black on her calendar! What disgrace to Mars, that a warrior born to serve the god and the god's city [a] was doomed to the sad lot of a captive! Never shall I cease to mourn over it. Did Carthage behold Regulus a prisoner? Did Carthage seem to Heaven to deserve so great a triumph? What fitting punishment shall attend the Spartans for their foul manner of warfare?

" But now the senate of Carthage resolved to take an oath of Regulus and send him to Rome as mediator with new conditions of peace; they sought to exchange Regulus for their own soldiers who had been taken prisoners in the course of the war. With no delay, a ship was launched from the arsenal and rode already on the waters close to the shore; and already the crew were shaping oars in the woods or felling pines to make new thwarts; some were busily engaged in fitting the twisted cordage, and others in fixing the canvas upon the high mast. They laid upon the prow the heavy iron anchor with its curved flukes. Chief of all Cothon, a skilful seaman and

puppim aptat clavumque Cothon.   micat aereus alta
fulgor aqua trifidi splendentis in aequore rostri.
tela simul variamque ferunt contra aspera ponti
rerum ad tempus opem.   mediae stat margine puppis,
qui voce alternos nautarum temperet ictus   361
et remis dictet sonitum pariterque relatis
ad numerum plaudat resonantia caerula tonsis.

   "Postquam confectum nautis opus, horaque cursus,
atque armata ratis ventique dedere profundum,   365
omnis turba ruit, matres puerique senesque.
per medios coetus trahit atque inimica per ora
spectandum Fortuna ducem.   fert lumina contra
pacatus frontem, qualis cum litora primum
attigit appulsa rector Sidonia classe.   370
accessi comes, haud ipso renuente, ratique
impositus maestus socium me casibus addo.
illuviem atque inopes mensas durumque cubile
et certare malis urgentibus hoste putabat
devicto maius ; nec tam fugisse cavendo   375
adversa egregium, quam perdomuisse ferendo.
spes tamen una mihi (quamquam bene cognita et
          olim
atrox illa fides) urbem murosque domumque
tangere si miseris licuisset, corda moveri
posse viri et vestro certe mitescere fletu.   380
claudebam sub corde metus lacrimasque putabam
esse viro et nostrae similem inter tristia mentem.
cum tandem patriae Tiberino allabimur amni,

308

steersman of the ship, saw to the vessel and its
rudder; the shining brass of the triple beak was
reflected on the deep and glittered over the sea.
Weapons also were brought on board, and much else
to help them against the dangers of the sea in time
of need. Amidships by the gunwale the coxswain
stood, to regulate the rowers' successive strokes, to
set their cadence to the oars, and, as the blades were
drawn back together, to make the water echo to the
rhythm.

"When the sailors had done their work, and the
time for starting came, and the ship was fitted out,
and the wind made sailing possible, then all the people
hastened to the shore—women and boys and old men.
Through the midst of the crowd and before their un-
friendly eyes Regulus was brought along by Fortune,
for them to look at. His calm brow met their gaze—
calm as when he first brought the fleet under his
command to the Carthaginian shore. I went with
him, and he made no objection; sadly I went on
board, to share his ill-fortune. To contend with
pressing evils—squalid attire and meagre fare and
a hard bed—this he thought more glorious than to
win a battle; and he held it a nobler thing to conquer
adversity by endurance than to avoid it by pre-
caution. One hope I still cherished—although I knew
well, and had long known, the inflexible conscience
of the man—that, if we wretches were permitted to
reach the walls of Rome and our homes, his resolu-
tion might give way and be melted at least by the
tears of his wife and children. I hid my fears in
my breast, and believed that Regulus could weep
and feel misfortune like other men. When at last
our ship glided into the Tiber, our native river, I

servabam vultus ducis ac prodentia sensum
lumina et obtutu perstabam intentus eodem.   385
si qua fides, unum, puer, inter mille labores,
unum etiam in patria saevaque in Agenoris urbe
atque unum vidi poenae quoque tempore vultum.
obvia captivo cunctis simul urbibus ibat
Ausonia, et, campum turba vincente, propinqui   390
implentur colles ; strepit altis Albula ripis.
ipsi Poenorum proceres immitia corda
ad patrios certant cultus revocare, togaeque
addebatur honos. stetit, illacrimante senatu
et matrum turba iuvenumque dolore profuso,   395
inter tot gemitus immobilis ; aggere consul
tendebat dextram et patria vestigia primus
ponentem terra occursu celebrabat amico.
collegit gressum ; monitusque recedere consul
nec summum violare decus ; cingente superba   400
Poenorum turba captivoque agmine saeptus
ibat et invidiam caelo divisque ferebat.

    " Ecce trahens geminum natorum Marcia pignus,
infelix nimia magni virtute mariti,
squalentem crinem et tristis lacerabat amictus.   405
(agnoscisne diem ? an teneris non haesit in annis ?)
atque ea, postquam habitu iuxta et velamine Poeno
deformem aspexit, fusis ululatibus aegra
labitur, et gelidos mortis color occupat artus.
si qua deis pietas, tales, Carthago, videre   410
dent tibi Sidonias matres. me voce quieta

    ᵃ Carthage : Agenor, father of Cadmus, was a king of the
Phoenicians.   ᵇ The ancient name of the Tiber.
    ᶜ The toga, the white woollen gown characteristic of the
Roman citizen.
    ᵈ Romans who were to be exchanged for Carthaginians
if the embassy from Carthage succeeded in their object.

watched his face and the eyes that reveal the mind, and never did I take my gaze off him. If you can believe me, young man, his expression was unchanged amid a thousand dangers, unchanged in Rome and in the cruel city of Agenor,[a] and unchanged even when he was tortured. From all the cities of Italy men came to meet the prisoner; and, when the plain could not contain the crowd, the neighbouring hills were thronged, and the high banks of the Albula[b] resounded. Even the Carthaginian senators pleaded with that stern heart to resume his native dress, and the dignity of the gown[c] was offered him. He stood there unmoved, while the senators shed tears, and the crowd of matrons and the young men wept for sorrow. On the river bank the consul first held out his hand, in friendly welcome to the exile as he set foot upon his native soil. Regulus stepped back; he bade the consul withdraw and not dishonour his high office; only the haughty Carthaginians and the company of prisoners[d] were round him when he moved on, causing men to reproach Heaven and the gods.

"Now Marcia came up, leading two boys, the pledges of their love—Marcia made unhappy by the too lofty virtue of her great husband; in her sorrow she tore her disordered hair and rent her garments. (Do you remember that day, Serranus, or has it slipped from your boyish memory?) When she saw him near, changed in mien and wearing the unsightly dress of Carthage, with a loud cry she fell fainting, and the hue of death covered her cold limbs. (If the gods have any pity, let them make Carthage witness mothers suffering like Marcia.) Regulus

311

affatus, iubet et vestros et coniugis una
arcere amplexus ; patet impenetrabilis ille
luctibus et numquam summissus colla dolori."
    Hic alto iuvenis gemitu lacrimisque coortis :   415
" magne parens," inquit, " quo maius numine nobis
Tarpeia nec in arce sedet, si iura querelis
sunt concessa piis, cur hoc matrique mihique
solamen, vel cur decus hoc, o dure, negasti,
tangere sacratos vultus atque oscula ab ore   420
libavisse tuo ? dextram mihi prendere dextra
non licitum ? leviora forent haec vulnera quantum,
si ferre ad manes infixos mente daretur
amplexus, venerande, tuos. sed vana recordor
ni, Mare,—nam primo tunc haerebamus in aevo—
humana maior species erat ; horrida cano   426
vertice descendens ingentia colla tegebat
caesaries, frontique coma squalente sedebat
terribilis decor atque animi venerabile pondus.
nil posthac oculis simile incidit." excipit inde   430
iam Marus atque, inhibens convellere vulnera questu :
" quid, cum praeteritis invisa penatibus," inquit,
" hospitia et sedes Poenorum intravit acerbas ?
affixi clipei currusque et spicula nota
aedibus in parvis, magni monumenta triumphi,   435
pulsabant oculos, coniuxque in limine primo
clamabat : ' quo fers gressus ? non Punicus hic est,
Regule, quem fugias, carcer. vestigia nostri
casta tori domus et patrium sine crimine servat
inviolata larem. semel hic iterumque (quid, oro,   440

spoke to me in a calm voice and bade me keep from
him the embraces of you two, his children, and of
his wife ; he remained obdurate against grief and
never bowed his neck to pain."

Then Serranus spoke with a deep groan and start-
ing tears : " Noble father," he said, " not less divine
to me than even the deity who dwells on the Tarpeian
rock, if love has a right to complain, why did you so
sternly deny my mother and me this consolation
and this glory—to touch your sacred face and take
kisses from your lips ? Was I forbidden to clasp
your hand in mine ? How much lighter my present
wounds would be, had I been allowed to carry
to the grave the undying memory of your embrace,
O worshipful father ! But, Marus, unless memory
deceives me—and I was but a child then—his stature
was more than human ; the unkempt hair fell down
from his white head and hid the great shoulders ;
and on his brow with its disordered locks sat an awful
majesty and reverend dignity. None like him have
I seen since." But here Marus took up the tale and
prevented him from making his wounds worse by com-
plaining : " And what," he cried, " when he passed
by his own house and sought the hateful hospitality
of the Carthaginians and their unfriendly lodging ?
Shields and chariots and javelins were fastened at his
doors—famous trophies of a great victory adorning
a humble dwelling ; these struck on his sight, and
his wife was crying out from the threshold : ' Whither
are you going, Regulus ? This is no Carthaginian
prison, for you to shun. This house preserves the
prints on our chaste marriage-bed, and our hereditary
household gods are stained by no guilt. In it once
and again—what, I ask, have I done to dishonour the

pollutum est nobis ?) prolem, gratante senatu
et patria, sum enixa tibi.   tua, respice, sedes
haec est, unde ingens humeris fulgentibus ostro
vidisti Latios consul procedere fasces ;
unde ire in Martem, quo capta referre solebas   445
et victor mecum suspendere postibus arma.
non ego complexus et sanctae foedera taedae
coniugiumve peto : patrios damnare penates
absiste ac natis fas duc concedere noctem.'

    " Hos inter fletus iunctus vestigia Poenis   450
limine se clusit Tyrio questusque reliquit.
vixdum clara dies summa lustrabat in Oeta
Herculei monumenta rogi, cum consul adire
accirique iubet Libyas.   tum limina templi
vidimus intrantem.   quae consultata senatus,   455
quasve viri voces extremum curia maerens
audierit, placido nobis ipse edidit ore.
intulit ut gressus, certatim voce manuque
ad solitam sedem et vestigia nota vocabant.
abnuit antiquumque loci aspernatur honorem.   460
at circumfusi non secius undique dextram
prensare ac, patriae ductorem nomine tanto
redderet, orabant ; captiva posse redemptum
pensari turba, ac Tyrias tum iustius arces
arsuras dextra, fuerit quae vincta catenis.   465

    " Tum palmas simul attollens ac lumina caelo :
' iustitiae rectique dator, qui cuncta gubernas,
nec levior mihi diva Fides Sarranaque Iuno,

    ᵃ These would be the quarters provided by the State for the
accommodation of the Carthaginian envoys.
    ᵇ An elaborate way of saying that the sun was rising : for
Oeta see note to iii. 43.
    ᶜ The Senate-house is often called a temple ; and also meet-
ings of the Senate were often held in the temple of some god.

house ?—I bore you a child, and the Senate and people wished us joy. Look back ! this is your own dwelling, from which, in all a consul's state, your shoulders gleaming with purple, you saw the Roman lictors march forth. From it you went to the wars ; and to it you often brought back the victor's spoils, and we hung them up together on the threshold. No embraces do I ask, no union that the hallowed torch of wedlock brings ; but do not persist in shunning the house of your fathers, and count it no crime to pass one night here for the sake of your sons.'

' While thus she lamented, he passed along with the Carthaginians and shut himself up in their lodging,[a] deaf to her appeal. Scarce was the daylight shining on the famous pyre of Hercules upon Oeta's height,[b] when the consul ordered the Carthaginians to be summoned. Then we saw Regulus entering the temple.[c] How the Senate debated, and how Regulus at last addressed the sorrowing house—this he reported to me himself with calm utterance. When he entered, all eagerly called on him with voice and gesture to take his wonted seat and former place. He refused and declined the seat of honour that once was his. None the less they gathered round, all seeking to grasp his hand and begging him not to deprive his country of so great a general ; he, they said, might be exchanged for the crowd of Carthaginian prisoners ; and then the hand which once wore fetters at Carthage would more fitly set fire to the Carthaginian citadel.

"Then he lifted hand and eye together to heaven : 'O Ruler of the universe, source of justice and truth ; and O Loyalty, no less divine to me, and Juno of Tyre, ye

315

quos reditus testes iurata mente vocavi,
si mihi fas me digna loqui Latiosque tueri   470
voce focos, ibo ad Tyrios non segnior,' inquit,
' stante fide reditus et salvo foedere poenae.
sic nobis rerum exitio desistite honorem
tendere.   tot bellis totque annis fregimus aevum ;
nunc etiam vinclis et longo carcere torpent   475
captivo in senio vires.   fuit ille nec umquam,
dum fuit, a duro cessavit munere Martis
Regulus : exsangui spectatis corpore nomen.
at non Carthago, fraudum domus, inscia quantum
e nobis restet, iuvenes parat, aspera ferro   480
pectora, captivos nostra pensare senecta.
ite dolos contra, gensque astu fallere laeta
discat, me capto quantum tibi, Roma, supersit.
nec vero placeat, nisi quae de more parentum
pax erit.   exposcunt Libyes nobisque dedere   485
haec referenda, pari libeat si pendere bellum
foedere et ex aequo geminas conscribere leges.
sed mihi sit Stygios ante intravisse penates,
talia quam videam ferientes pacta Latinos.'

    " Haec fatus Tyriae sese iam reddidit irae,   490
nec monitus spernente graves fidosque senatu,
Poenorum dimissa cohors, quae maesta repulsa
ac minitans capto patrias properabat ad oras.
prosequitur vulgus patres, ac planctibus ingens

---

    [a] The imprisonment of Regulus at Carthage lasted eight
years, from 258 to 250 B.C.: Silius says little about this long
interval.
    [b] The Carthaginians asked for the restitution of the *status
quo* before the war ; and this would have involved the

gods whom I invoked to witness my oath that I would return, if I am permitted to speak words that befit me, and by my voice to protect the hearths of Rome, not unwillingly shall I go to Carthage, keeping my promise to return and enduring the prescribed penalty. Therefore cease to honour me and thus ruin the state. So many years, so many wars, have broken down my strength ; and also long captivity [a] in fetters has sapped the energy of an old man and a prisoner. Regulus is not the man he was once, when he never rested from the hard task of war ; what you see now is a mere name, a bloodless body. But Carthage, that home of treachery, knows well what a wreck I am, and is scheming to get in exchange for my worn-out body our prisoners who are young and eager for battle. Foil their knavish tricks, and teach a nation that delights in deceit how much, though I be a prisoner, is still left to Rome. Accept no peace that is not concluded in the fashion of our fathers. The Carthaginians demand—and this is the message they gave me to carry—that you should weigh this war in equal scales, and frame conditions of peace that shall favour neither nation.[b] But I would rather go down to the house of Hades than see the Romans strike so base a bargain.'

"Thus he spoke and at once gave himself up again to the anger of Carthage. Nor did the Senate reject a warning so serious and so honest, but sent off the Carthaginian envoys, who made haste for home, vexed by their failure and threatening their prisoner. The Roman populace accompanied the senators, beating their breasts and mourning, till the vast Field

surrender of Sicily, and the recognition of Carthaginian independence.

personat et luctu campus : revocare libebat   495
interdum et iusto raptum retinere dolore.

    " At trepida et subito ceu stans in funere coniux
ut vidit puppi properantem intrare, tremendum
vociferans, celerem gressum referebat ad undas :
' tollite me, Libyes, comitem poenaeque necisque.
hoc unum, coniux, uteri per pignora nostri   501
unum oro : liceat tecum quoscumque ferentem
terrarum pelagique pati caelique labores.
non ego Amyclaeum ductorem in proelia misi,
nec nostris tua sunt circumdata colla catenis.   505
cur usque ad Poenos miseram fugis ?   accipe mecum
hanc prolem.   forsan duras Carthaginis iras
flectemus lacrimis, aut, si praecluserit aures
urbs inimica suas, eadem tunc hora manebit
teque tuosque simul ; vel, si stat rumpere vitam,   510
in patria moriamur.   adest comes ultima fati.'

    " Has inter voces vinclis resoluta moveri
paulatim et ripa coepit decedere puppis.
tum vero infelix, mentem furiata dolore,
exclamat, fessas tendens ad litora palmas :   515
' en, qui se iactat Libyae populisque nefandis
atque hosti servare fidem !   data foedera nobis
ac promissa fides thalamis ubi, perfide, nunc est ? '
ultima vox duras haec tunc penetravit ad aures ;
cetera percussi vetuerunt noscere remi.   520

    " Tum fluvio raptim ad pelagi devolvimur oras
ac legimus pontum pinuque immane cavata
aequor et immensas curva trabe findimus undas.

---

    ^a The chief public park in Rome, used for many purposes :
it stretched along the banks of the Tiber.
    ^b Xanthippus : see note to ll. 304 foll.   Amyclae was a
town in Laconia, on the Eurotas.

of Mars [a] was filled with the sound. They were eager at times to call him back and to rescue him by force in their righteous indignation.

"But when Marcia saw him hastening on board, she was bewildered and uttered a terrible cry, as if she stood suddenly by his death-bed. Hurrying to the shore, 'Take me, ye Carthaginians,' she cried, 'to share his punishment and his death. Husband, I ask but one thing in the name of the children I bore you : suffer me to endure along with you whatever earth and sea and sky can inflict. It was not I who sent the Spartan leader [b] forth to battle ; nor mine were the chains that were riveted round your neck. Why do you go all the way to Carthage, to escape unhappy me ? Take me and these children with you. Perhaps our tears will melt the hard hearts of the Carthaginians ; or, if that hostile city turns a deaf ear, then the same hour will await you and yours together. Or, if you are resolved to end your life, let us die in our own country. Here is one to share your fate to the end.'

"While she spoke, the ship was cast loose from her moorings and began to move slowly from the shore. Then indeed the unhappy wife, frantic with grief, stretched forth her weary hands over the bank with a loud cry : 'See him ! He boasts of keeping faith with the enemy and the abominable people of Libya. But where is now the compact made with me, and the troth you plighted at our marriage, unfaithful husband ? ' These were the last words that reached the inflexible ear of Regulus ; the rest was drowned by the plashing of the oars.

"Then we went swiftly down the river to the sea-shore, and sailed over the deep, cleaving the vast expanse of water and the great waves with our hollow

ludibrium necis horrescens, vis aspera ponti
obrueret, scopulisque ratem furor improbus Euri   525
frangeret, optabam ; letum id commune fuisset.
sed nos ad poenam moderato flamine lenes
vexerunt Zephyri Tyrioque dedere furori.
    " Infelix vidi patriamque remissus in urbem
narrator poenae dura mercede reverti.   530
nec tibi nunc ritus imitantem irasque ferarum
Pygmalioneam tentarem expromere gentem,
si maius quicquam toto vidisset in orbe
gens hominum, quam quod vestri veneranda parentis
edidit exemplum virtus : pudet addere questus   535
suppliciis, quae spectavi placido ore ferentem.
tu quoque, care puer, dignum te sanguine tanto
fingere ne cessa atque orientes comprime fletus.
praefixo paribus ligno mucronibus omnes
armantur laterum crates, densumque per artem   540
texitur erecti stantisque ex ordine ferri
infelix stimulus, somnisque hac fraude negatis
quocumque inflexum producto tempore torpor
inclinavit iners, fodiunt ad viscera corpus.
absiste, o iuvenis, lacrimis : patientia cunctos   545
haec superat currus. longo revirescet in aevo
gloria, dum caeli sedem terrasque tenebit
casta Fides ; dum virtutis venerabile nomen,
vivet ; eritque dies, tua quo, dux inclite, fata
audire horrebunt a te calcata minores."   550
haec Marus et maesta refovebat vulnera cura.

---

    [a] For Pygmalion see note to i. 21.
    [b] The digression which began on p. 287 ends here. Silius
was determined to include the history of Regulus in his poem,
though it was no part of the Second Punic War. But it is
not easy to see why Serranus should not have heard all these

ship. Dreading a shameful death, I prayed that the
violence of the sea might sink our vessel, or that the
wild fury of the wind might dash her upon the rocks ;
then we should have died together. But the mild
breath of gentle zephyrs carried us on to the torture,
and gave us over to the rage of Carthage.

"I, alas, witnessed his punishment, and was sent
back to Rome to tell the tale ; and dearly did I pay for
my release. Nor would I now essay to tell you how
the people of Carthage[a] behaved with the cruelty of
wild beasts, if mankind had ever seen in any part
of the world a nobler example than was set by the
splendid courage of your father. I am ashamed to
complain of tortures which I saw him endure with
cheerfulness. You too, dear youth, must still think
yourself worthy of such a glorious descent, and check
those starting tears. A frame all round him was
faced with planking studded with points of equal
length, and there was artfully compacted a painful
system of puncture consisting of rows of projecting
iron spikes. By this device sleep was denied him ;
for to whichever side passive drowsiness made him
lean as time dragged on, these spikes pierced deep
into his flesh. Weep no more, young man. That
endurance is greater than all triumphs. His laurels
will be green throughout the ages, as long as unstained
Loyalty keeps her seat in heaven and on earth, and
will last as long as virtue's name is worshipped. The
day will come when posterity will shudder to hear
of the death which thou, O famous leader, madest
light of." Thus Marus spoke, while he tended the
young man's wounds with sorrowful care.[b]

details many years earlier, either from his mother, Marcia,
or from Marus himself.

Interea, rapidas perfusa cruoribus alas,
sicut sanguinea Thrasymenni tinxerat unda,
vera ac ficta simul spargebat Fama per urbem.
Allia et infandi Senones captaeque recursat   555
attonitis arcis facies : excussit habenas
luctificus Pavor, et tempestas aucta timendo.
hic raptim ruit in muros.   vox horrida fertur,
hostis adest, iaciuntque sudes et inania tela.
ast aliae, laceris canentes crinibus, alta   560
verrunt tecta deum et seris post fata suorum
sollicitant precibus.   requiem tenebraeque diesque
amisere ; iacent portis ululante dolore
dispersum vulgus, remeantumque ordine longo
servat turba gradus ; pendent ex ore loquentum, 565
nec laetis sat certa fides, iterumque morantur
orando et, vultu interdum sine voce precati,
quod rogitant, audire pavent.   hinc fletus, ubi aures
percussae graviore malo ; metus inde, negatum
si scire, et dubius responsi nuntius haesit.   570
iamque ubi conspectu redeuntum visa propinquo
corpora, sollicite laeti funduntur et ipsis
oscula vulneribus figunt superosque fatigant.

  Hic inter trepidos, curae venerandus, agebat
Serranum Marus ; atque olim post fata mariti   575
non egressa domum vitato Marcia coetu
et lucem causa natorum passa, ruebat
in luctum similem antiquo ; turbata repente

---

a See note to i. 624.

Meanwhile Rumour, her swift wings dyed with blood—she had dipped them in the blood-stained waters of Lake Trasimene—spread tidings true and false throughout Rome. In their terror men recalled the battle of the Allia, the accursed Senones, and the sight of the captured citadel.[a] Woeful Fear shook off all restraint, and the calamity was made worse by apprehension. Some rush to the walls. A dreadful cry is raised—" The enemy is upon us." They hurl stakes and javelins at an imaginary foe. Women also, with their grey hair torn, lay their heads in the dust of the lofty temples, and besiege the gods with prayer for their dear ones whom death has already taken. Neither day nor night brings relief. The people, vociferous in their grief, lie scattered round the different gates ; and they follow, step by step, the long procession of fugitives, and hang upon their lips. Good news they can hardly believe ; they stop a man, to ask a second time ; some beg for tidings with dumb looks, and dread the answer to their question. Some weep, when they hear of a grievous loss ; others are affrighted, when the messenger professes ignorance and hesitates to answer. But when the fugitives came close and were clearly seen, then their friends crowded round them with a fearful joy, kissing their very wounds, and wearying Heaven with prayers.

Now Marus came through the anxious crowd, leading Serranus with praiseworthy care ; and then Marcia, who had never left the house since her husband's death, but shunned society and endured life only for the sake of her sons—she too rushed forth, to mourn as she had mourned long ago. Startled by

323

agnoscensque Marum : " fidei comes inclite magnae,
hunc certe mihi reddis," ait.   " leve vulnus ? an alte
usque ad nostra ferus penetravit viscera mucro ? 581
quicquid id est, dum non vinctum Carthago catenis
abripiat poenaeque instauret monstra paternae,
gratum est, o superi.   quotiens heu, nate, petebam,
ne patrias iras animosque in proelia ferres,   585
neu te belligeri stimularet in arma parentis
triste decus.   nimium vivacis dura senectae
supplicia expendi.   quaeso, iam parcite, si qua
numina pugnastis nobis."

                     At cladis acerbae
discussa ceu nube, patres conquirere fessis   590
iam rebus meditantur opem, atque ad munera belli
certatur, pulsusque timor graviore periclo.
maxima curarum, rectorem ponere castris,
cui Latium et moles rerum quassata recumbat,
spectante occasum patria.   Iovis illa ruenti   595
Ausoniae atque Italis tempus protendere regnis
cura fuit ; nam Tyrrhenos Poenumque secundis
Albana surgens respexerat arce tumentem,
qui ferre in muros victricia signa parabat.
tum quassans caput : " haud umquam tibi Iupiter,"
    inquit,
" o iuvenis, dederit portas transcendere Romae   601
atque inferre pedem.   Tyrrhenas sternere valles
caedibus, et ripas fluviorum exire Latino
sanguine fas fuerit : Tarpeium accedere collem
murisque aspirare veto."   quater inde coruscum   605
contorsit dextra fulmen, quo tota reluxit

---

[a] He had a famous temple on the Alban mount, where
the Roman consuls had to offer sacrifice once a year.
324

the sudden sight and recognizing Marus, she spoke to him : " Famous comrade of one most faithful, one at least you bring back to me alive. Is his wound slight ? Or did the cruel point pierce deep, to my very vitals ? In either case, I thank the gods, if only Carthage does not carry him off in fetters, and repeat the tortures that his father endured. Alas, my son, how often I begged you not to carry into battle the impetuous ardour of your sire, and not to be urged on to feats of arms by his crown of thorns ! I have lived too long and paid a heavy penalty for my long life. Spare me henceforth, ye gods, if any gods have fought against us."

And now, as if the thunder-cloud of cruel disaster had dispersed, the Senate discussed the means of mending their desperate plight ; each did his utmost to carry on the war ; and fear was dispelled by the terrible danger. Their chief task was to appoint a commander, who could support Rome and the shattered edifice of the state, now that destruction was in sight. It was Jupiter who took in hand to grant a reprieve from ruin to Italy and to Roman rule. For aloft on the Alban mount [a] he had seen the land of Tuscany, and Hannibal puffed up with success and ready to carry his victorious standards against the walls of Rome. Shaking his head in anger, he spoke : " Never shall Jupiter permit you, young man, to pass the gates of Rome and walk her streets. To cover the valleys of Tuscany with the slain, and to make the rivers brim with Roman blood—these things you may do ; but I forbid you to approach the Tarpeian hill and to raise your hopes to the walls of Rome." Then four times he hurled his flashing bolt with his right arm, till all Tuscany was lighted up ; and rolling a

Maeonidum tellus, atramque per aethera volvens
abrupto fregit caelo super agmina nubem.
nec Poenum avertisse satis ; dat numine magno
Aeneadis mentem, gremio deponere tuto   610
Romuleam sedem Fabioque salutis habenas
credere ductori. cui postquam tradita belli
iura videt : " non hunc," inquit, " superaverit unquam
invidia aut blando popularis gloria fuco ;
non astus fallax, non praeda aliusve cupido.   615
bellandi vetus ac laudum cladumque quieta
mente capax ; par ingenium castrisque togaeque."
sic genitor divum recipitque ad sidera gressum.

Hic, circumspectis nulli deprensus in armis
laudatusque Iovi, Fabius mirabile quantum   620
gaudebat reducem patriae annumerare reversus,
duxerat egrediens quam secum in proelia, pubem.
nec membris quisquam natove pepercit amato
acrius, aut vidit socium per bella cruorem
tristior. atque idem, perfusus sanguine victor   625
hostili, plenis repetebat moenia castris.
stirpe genus clarum caeloque affinis origo.
nam remeans longis olim Tirynthius oris
et triplicis monstri famam et spectacula captas
mira boves hac, qua fulgent nunc moenia Romae,   630
egit ovans. tunc Arcadius, sic fama, locabat

---

a Quintus Fabius Maximus, surnamed *Cunctator* (Dawdler,
Slow-coach), was elected Dictator after the defeat of Trasi-
mene. He is one of the most famous of old Roman worthies ;
and to his cautious strategy his countrymen attributed their
ultimate defeat of Hannibal. See note to ii. 3.

b Geryon : see note to i. 277.

c Evander, a son of Mercury and Carmentis, brought a
band of colonists from Arcadia to Italy : with the consent of
King Faunus, he founded a city, called Pallantium after his
326

black cloud through the sky, he broke it and made a
rift in the heavens over the head of the Carthaginian
army.   Nor was he content with turning Hannibal
away : his divine power inspired the Aeneadae to
place a sure shield before the seat of Romulus, and
to entrust to Fabius *a* as general the control of their
deliverance ;   and when he saw the supreme com-
mand handed over to him, " This man," he said,
" will never yield to jealousy or the sweet poison of
popular applause ;   he will be proof against artful
devices and desire of plunder and all other passions.
A veteran soldier, he can meet success and disaster
with a quiet mind ;   neither war nor peace is beyond
his capacity."   Thus spoke the Father of the gods,
and went back to his heaven.

This Fabius, so praised by Jupiter, was never sur-
prised by any foe ;   so wary a campaigner was he.
Marvellous was his joy, when he came home and
brought the soldiers he had led forth to war back to
their country without one missing.   No man was ever
more eager to guard his own life, or the life of a
beloved son, than he to spare his soldiers ;   and no
man was sadder to see the blood of his comrades shed
in battle ;   and yet he ever returned to Rome red with
the slaughter of foemen, a conqueror with undepleted
ranks.   His birth was noble, and the founder of his
family was akin to the gods.   For Hercules long ago,
when he came back from a far country, drove his
booty in triumph to the place where glorious Rome
now stands.   He had taken the kine that were the
pride of the triple monster *b* ; and men marvelled to
see them.   Legend tells that a man from Arcadia *c*

birthplace, on one of the Seven Hills which was afterwards
called the Palatine.

inter desertos fundata Palatia dumos
paupere sub populo ductor ; cum regia virgo,
hospite victa sacro, Fabium de crimine laeto
procreat et magni commiscet seminis ortus   635
Arcas in Herculeos mater ventura nepotes.
ter centum domus haec Fabios armavit in hostem,
limine progressus uno ; pulcherrima quorum
cunctando Fabius superavit facta ducemque
Hannibalem aequando.   tantus tunc, Poene, fuisti !

   Dum se perculsi renovant in bella Latini,   641
turbatus Iove et exuta spe moenia Romae
pulsandi, colles Umbros atque arva petebat
Hannibal, excelso summi qua vertice montis
devexum lateri pendet Tuder, atque ubi latis   645
proiecta in campis nebulas exhalat inertes,
et sedet ingentem pascens Mevania taurum,
dona Iovi ; tum Palladios se fundit in agros
Picenum dives praedae atque errantibus armis,
quo spolia invitant, transfert populantia signa ;   650
donec pestiferos mitis Campania cursus
tardavit bellumque sinu indefensa recepit.

   Hic dum stagnosi spectat templumque domosque
Literni ductor, varia splendentia cernit
pictura belli patribus monumenta prioris   655
exhausti—nam porticibus signata manebant—
quis inerat longus rerum et spectabilis ordo.
primus bella truci suadebat Regulus ore,

---

   ^a See vii. 39 foll.
   ^b That he was not defeated by Fabius is the best proof of
Hannibal's genius for war.
   ^c Also called Tudertum (now Todi) : a town in Umbria.
   ^d For the bulls of Mevania see iv. 544 foll.
   ^e A town on the Campanian coast, where Scipio Africanus

was then building a house on the Palatine among
uninhabited thorn-brakes, a king with needy sub-
jects ; and the king's daughter, unable to resist the
divine stranger, gave birth to a Fabius—a sin that
brought no sorrow ; and thus the Arcadian woman
blended with her own the blood of that mighty sire,
to become the ancestress of the stock of Hercules.
Three hundred Fabii once went forth to war from a
single household [a] ; but this Fabius surpassed their
glorious deed by delay and by proving himself a match
for Hannibal. So great wert thou then, O Hannibal ! [b]

While the defeated Romans were preparing for
a fresh campaign, Hannibal, rebuffed by Jupiter's
warning and hopeless of battering the walls of Rome,
made for the hills and fields of Umbria, where Tuder [c]
hangs on a high mountain-top and slopes down its
side ; and where Mevania, lying low on the wide
plains, breathes forth sluggish mists and feeds mighty
bulls for Jupiter's altar.[d] Next he passed on over the
land of Picenum, rich in olives, and took much booty ;
then he moved his plundering forces from place to
place, wherever spoil attracted them, till mild Cam-
pania stopped his destructive raids and harboured the
war in her undefended breast.

Here, at Liternum [e] in the marshes, while Hannibal
viewed the temple and buildings of the city, he saw,
painted in divers colours on the temple-cloisters, a
record of the former war, which the past generation
had fought to a finish ; and these pictures remained
upon the walls, representing a long succession of
notable events. First there was Regulus, speaking
with fierce aspect in favour of war—war that he

died, having withdrawn from Rome in disgust with the state
of public affairs.

329

bella neganda, viro si noscere fata daretur.
at princeps Poenis indicta more parentum   660
Appius astabat pugna lauroque revinctus
iustum Sarrana ducebat caede triumphum.
aequoreum iuxta decus et navale tropaeum,
rostra gerens nivea surgebat mole columna ;
exuvias Marti donumque Duilius, alto   665
ante omnes mersa Poenorum classe, dicabat.
cui, nocturnus honos, funalia clara sacerque
post epulas tibicen adest ; castosque penates
insignis laeti repetebat murmure cantus.
cernit et extremos defuncti civis honores :   670
Scipio ductoris celebrabat funera Poeni,
Sardoa victor terra.   videt inde ruentem
litoribus Libycis dispersa per agmina pubem ;
instabat crista fulgens et terga premebat
Regulus ; Autololes Nomadesque et Maurus et
    Hammon   675
et Garamas positis dedebant oppida telis.
lentus harenoso spumabat Bagrada campo
viperea sanie, turmisque minantibus ultro
pugnabat serpens et cum duce bella gerebat.
necnon proiectum puppi frustraque vocantem   680
numina Amyclaeum mergebat perfida ponto
rectorem manus, et seras tibi, Regule, poenas
Xanthippus digni pendebat in aequore leti.

---

[a] That is, his own defeat and captivity.

[b] Appius Claudius Caudex, consul in 264 B.C., led a Roman
army to Sicily and defeated the Carthaginians.

[c] In 260 B.C. C. Duilius, consul in that year, defeated a
Carthaginian fleet at Mylae, on the N.E. coast of Sicily : he
received a triumph as well as the peculiar honours mentioned
here, which he seems to have conferred upon himself.

should have spoken against, could he have foretold the future.[a] Next Appius [b] was seen ; he was first to declare war in the ancient fashion against Carthage ; and crowned with laurel he led along a triumphal procession, earned by slaughter of Carthaginians. Hard by was seen a tall column of white marble, adorned with the beaks of ships, a naval trophy for a victory at sea ; Duilius,[c] the first to sink a Carthaginian fleet, was dedicating his spoils to Mars and offering sacrifice. (He had honour in the night ; for flaming torches and a temple-piper attended him home from the banquet ; and he walked back to his modest dwelling to the sound of a merry tune.) Here Hannibal saw too the last honours paid to a dead countryman ; for Scipio, victorious over Sardinia, was conducting the funeral of a Carthaginian general. Next he saw the Roman soldiers on the African coast rushing on through a routed army ; and in hot pursuit of the rear came Regulus with glittering plume : Autololes, Numidians, Moors, Ammonians, Garamantes — all laid down their arms and gave up their towns. Bagrada, the sluggish river that passes over a sandy desert, was shown there also, foaming with the monster's slime, when the serpent challenged the threatening squadrons and fought a battle against Regulus.[d] Elsewhere, the Spartan general, hurled overboard and appealing to the gods in vain, was being drowned by a treacherous crew ; and thus Xanthippus at last paid the penalty to Regulus by a deserved death in the sea.[e] The artists

[d] See ll. 146 foll.
[e] Several ancient writers report that the Carthaginians, being jealous of the fame of Xanthippus, caused him to be thrown overboard while he was returning to Sparta.

addiderant geminas medio consurgere fluctu
Aegates ; lacerae circum fragmenta videres   685
classis et effusos fluitare in gurgite Poenos.
possessor pelagi pronaque Lutatius aura
captivas puppes ad litora victor agebat.
haec inter iuncto religatus in ordine Hamilcar,
ductoris genitor, cunctarum ab imagine rerum   690
totius in sese vulgi converterat ora.
sed Pacis faciem et pollutas foederis aras
deceptumque Iovem ac dictantes iura Latinos
cernere erat.   strictas trepida cervice secures
horrebat Libys, ac summissis ordine palmis   695
orantes veniam iurabant irrita pacta.
haec Eryce e summo spectabat laeta Dione.

   Quae postquam infesto percensuit omnia vultu
arridens Poenus, lenta proclamat ab ira :
" non leviora dabis nostris inscribere tectis   700
acta meae dextrae : captam, Carthago, Saguntum
da spectare, simul flamma ferroque ruentem ;
perfodiant patres natorum membra ; nec Alpes
exiguus domitas capiet locus ; ardua celsis
persultet iuga victor equis Garamasque Nomasque.
addes Ticini spumantes sanguine ripas   706
et nostrum Trebiam et Thrasymenni litora Tusci
clausa cadaveribus.   ruat ingens corpore et armis
Flaminius ; fugiat consul manante cruore
Scipio et ad socios nati cervice vehatur.   710
haec mitte in populos, et adhuc maiora dabuntur.

---

   [a] See note to i. 35.
   [b] Venus, who had a famous temple upon Mount Eryx in
Sicily.
   [c] See iv. 454 foll.

had painted also the two Aegatian islands [a] rising in mid-sea ; and the remnants of a shattered fleet were visible all round, and shipwrecked Carthaginians adrift on the water, while Lutatius, lord of the sea, drove the captured ships ashore before the wind. And there too was Hamilcar, the father of Hannibal ; fettered in a long row of prisoners, he turned the eyes of the whole throng away from all the painted scenes upon himself alone. But there one might see the form of Peace, and the profaned altars at which the treaty was sworn, and the mockery of Jupiter, and the Romans dictating terms. With bowed necks the Libyans shrank from the bare axes, and held out their hands together begging for pardon, and swore to a treaty which they did not observe, while Dione [b] looked on the scene rejoicing, from the heights of Eryx.

All these pictures Hannibal surveyed with a face of anger and contempt, and then cried out with rising passion : " Deeds as great as these, the work of my right arm, shall Carthage yet display upon her walls. Let us see there the capture of Saguntum, overthrown by fire and sword together ; let fathers be shown stabbing their own children ; the conquest of the Alps will claim no little space ; let Garamantes and Numidians, riding on their horses, trample on the high peaks.   Add the banks of the Ticinus foaming with blood, and my victory on the Trebia, and the shore of Lake Trasimene covered deep with the Roman dead. Let us see Flaminius, a giant in giant armour, crash to the ground, and the consul Scipio a wounded fugitive, borne on his son's shoulders back to their camp.[c] Show these sights to the people, Carthage ; and greater sights shall be forthcoming in future : you

flagrantem effinges facibus, Carthago, Libyssis
Romam et deiectum Tarpeia rupe Tonantem.
interea vos, ut dignum est, ista, ocius ite,
o iuvenes, quorum dextris mihi tanta geruntur,   715
in cineres monumenta date atque involvite flammis."

shall display Rome blazing with Libyan fire-brands,
and the Thunderer cast down from the Tarpeian rock.
For the present, ye soldiers, by whose valour my great
deeds are accomplished, make haste to do what is
right to be done : throw these pictures into the fire
and wrap them in flames."

LIBER SEPTIMUS

ARGUMENT

Fabius determines to take no risks in the field (1-19).
*Cilnius, one of his prisoners, informs Hannibal concerning
the family history and character of Fabius* (20-73). *Re-
ligious observances at Rome* (74-89). *Fabius restores dis-
cipline in the army. Hannibal cannot tempt him to fight*
(90-122). *Hannibal moves to Apulia and tries to provoke
Fabius by various devices. He returns to Campania and
ravages the Falernian country* (123-161). *The visit of Bacchus
to the aged peasant, Falernus* (162-211). *Fabius explains his
policy of inaction to his discontented soldiers* (212-259). *A
trick of Hannibal's, to make the Dictator more unpopular*

Interea trepidis Fabius spes unica rebus.
ille quidem socios atque aegram vulnere praeceps
Ausoniam armabat viridique ad dura laborum
bellator senio iam castra movebat in hostem.
sed mens humana maior non tela nec enses   5
nec fortes spectabat equos : tot milia contra
Poenorum invictumque ducem, tot in agmina solus
ibat et in sese cuncta arma virosque gerebat.
ac ni sacra seni vis impressumque fuisset,
sistere Fortunam cunctando adversa foventem,   10
ultima Dardanii transisset nominis aetas.
ille modum superis in Punica castra favoris

336

BOOK VII

MEANWHILE Fabius was the one beacon-light in that dark hour. He made haste to arm sore-wounded Italy and her allies ; his green old age faced the hardships of war, and he soon marched against the foe. But that more than human genius recked little of spears and swords and strong steeds. He went forth alone against an army of so many thousand Carthaginians and their invincible leader ; and all the men and arms of Italy were comprised in his person. But for that old man's godlike power, but for his fixed resolve to check by delay Fortune's favour for the enemy, the Roman name would have passed away for ever. He it was who made the gods withdraw their favour from the Punic host, and put a stop to

addidit et Libyae finem inter prospera bella
vincendi statuit ; tumefactum cladibus ille
Hesperiis lento Poenum moderamine lusit.   15
summe ducum, qui regna iterum labentia Troiae
et fluxas Latii res maiorumque labores,
qui Carmentis opes et regna Evandria servas,
surge, age et emerito sacrum caput insere caelo.

   At Libyae ductor, postquam nova nomina lecto 20
dictatore vigent, raptim mutata Latinis
imperia haud frustra reputans, cognoscere avebat,
quae fortuna viro, quodnam decus ; ultima fessis
ancora cur Fabius, quem post tot Roma procellas
Hannibali putet esse parem.   fervore carentes   25
angebant anni fraudique inaperta senectus.
ocius accitum captivo ex agmine poscit
progeniem ritusque ducis dextraeque labores.
Cilnius, Arreti Tyrrhenis ortus in oris,
clarum nomen erat ; sed laeva adduxerat hora   30
Ticini iuvenem ripis, fususque ruentis
vulnere equi, Libycis praebebat colla catenis.
hic ardens exire malis et rumpere vitam :
" non cum Flaminio tibi res, nec fervida Gracchi
in manibus consulta," inquit.   " Tirynthia gens est ;
quam si fata tuis genuissent, Hannibal, oris,   36
terrarum imperium Carthaginis arce videres.
non ego te longa serie per singula ducam.
hoc sat erit, nosces Fabios certamine ab uno :
Veientum populi violata pace negabant   40
acceptare iugum, ac vicino Marte furebat

---

   ^a For Evander and Carmentis see note to vi. 631.
   ^b A noble Etruscan name, borne later by C. Cilnius
Maecenas, the patron and friend of the Augustan poets.
   ^c He expected to suffer death for his bold answer.

the victorious campaign of the African invaders ; it was his wise policy of delay that baffled Hannibal elated with conquest. O greatest of generals, who didst save the realm of Troy from falling a second time, preserver of perishing Italy and the great deeds of our ancestors, of Carmentis's treasure and the throne of Evander[a]—arise and lift up thy sacred head to the heaven which is thy due !

But, when the dictator had been chosen and new names came to the front, Hannibal, reflecting that the Romans had not so quickly changed the supreme command without good reason, was eager to learn the dictator's rank and reputation ; he wondered why Fabius was the sole remaining anchor of the storm-tossed state, and why Rome thought him a match for Hannibal. He was troubled by his rival's age, free from youthful passion and proof against stratagem. Quickly he summoned one of his prisoners and questioned him concerning the dictator's family, his manner of life, and his martial exploits. Cilnius,[b] born in the Tuscan land of Arretium, bore a famous name ; but an evil hour had brought him to the banks of the Ticinus, where he was thrown from his wounded horse and taken prisoner by the Libyans. He was eager to end his troubles by a violent death [c] and answered thus : "You have not now to do with a Flaminius or a hot-headed Gracchus. Hercules is the ancestor of his house ; and if Fate had made them your countrymen, Hannibal, you would have seen Carthage mistress of the world. I shall not detain you with a long list of separate achievements : one will suffice, and from one battle you shall learn what the Fabii are. The people of Veii had broken the peace and refused to submit to the Roman yoke, war

ad portas bellum, consulque ciebat ad arma.
dilectus vetiti, privataque castra penates
Herculei implevere ; domo, mirabile, ab una
patricius iunctis exercitus ibat in armis.   45
ter centum exiluere duces ; quocumque liberet,
uno non pavidus rexisses bella magistro.
sed (dirum egressis omen) Scelerata minaci
stridentis sonitu tremuerunt limina portae,
maximaque Herculei mugivit numinis ara.   50
invasere hostem, numerarique aspera virtus
haud est passa viros, et plures milite caedes.
saepe globo densi, saepe et per devia passim
dispersi subiere vices ; meritique labore
aequato nulli quisquam virtute secundus,   55
ducere ter centum Tarpeia ad templa triumphos.
spes heu fallaces oblitaque corda caducum,
mortali quodcumque datur ! grex ille virorum,
qui Fabia gente incolumi deforme putabat
publica bella geri, pariter cecidere deorum   60
invidia, subitis circumvenientibus armis.
nec tamen occisos est cur laetere ; supersunt,
quot tibi sint Libyaeque satis ; certaverit unus
ter centum dextris. tam vivida membra laborque
providus et cauta sollertia tecta quiete.   65
nec vero, calidi, nunc tu, cui sanguinis aetas,
foderis in pugna velocius ilia planta
bellatoris equi frenisque momorderis ora."
quem cernens avidum leti post talia Poenus :

---

^a The Porta Carmentalis, between the Capitoline Hill and
the Tiber, was called *Scelerata* after the destruction of the
Fabii, who had marched out of Rome by that gate. The
date assigned is 478 B.C.
  ^b The Great Altar of Hercules stood in the cattle-market at
Rome.

340

was raging close to the gates of Rome, and the consul gave the call to arms. No levy was held : the clan of Hercules, unhelped by the State, made up an army. From a single house—marvellous to tell !—there went forth an army of patricians to fight side by side. Three hundred leaders sprang to arms, and with any one of them in command you might have fought a campaign with confidence. But they went forth with evil omens : the Bloody Gate [a] creaked with inauspicious sound, and a moaning came from the Great Altar of divine Hercules.[b] When they attacked the foe, their fierce valour suffered them not to count the enemy, and they slew more than their own number. Often in close array, and often scattered afar over uneven ground, they endured the changing chances of battle ; and by their equal effort and equal valour they deserved to lead three hundred triumphs to the temple of Jupiter. But alas for hope deceived ! They forgot that no boon granted to mortal man is lasting. That band of heroes, who thought shame that the Fabian clan should not hazard their lives when their country was at war, were suddenly surrounded and slain all together, because of the jealousy of Heaven. But you, Hannibal, have no reason to rejoice at their death : enough of them is left to cope with you and Libya : one Fabius will match the three hundred warriors. Such life is there in his limbs ; so painstaking is his foresight ; such shrewdness does he hide beneath calmness and caution. Though you are of the age when blood is hot, you will not be swifter than Fabius to spur the flanks of your war-horse and tear his mouth with the bridle." Such a speech showed Hannibal that Cilnius was eager for death. " Fool ! " he cried :

341

" nequicquam nostras, demens," ait, " elicis iras   70
et captiva paras moriendo evadere vincla.
vivendum est. arta serventur colla catena."
haec iuvenis, divisque tumens ausisque secundis.
  At patres Latiasque nurus raptabat ad aras
cura deum. maesto suffusae lumina vultu   75
femineus matres graditur chorus ; ordine longo
Iunoni pallam conceptaque vota dicabant :
" huc ades, o regina deum, gens casta precamur
et ferimus, digno quaecumque est nomine, turba
Ausonidum pulchrumque et, acu et subtemine fulvo 80
quod nostrae nevere manus, venerabile donum.
ac dum decrescit matrum metus, hoc tibi, diva,
interea velamen erit. si pellere nostris
Marmaricam terris nubem dabis, omnis in auro
pressa tibi varia fulgebit gemma corona."   85
necnon et proprio venerantur Pallada dono
Phoebumque   armigerumque   deum   primamque
    Dionen.
tanta adeo, cum res trepidae, reverentia divum
nascitur ; at rarae fumant felicibus arae.
  Dum Roma antiquos templis indicit honores,   90
iam Fabius, tacito procedens agmine et arte
bellandi lento similis, praecluserat omnes
Fortunaeque hostique vias. discedere signis
haud licitum, summumque decus, quo tollis ad astra
imperii, Romane, caput, parere docebat.   95
verum ubi prima satis conspecta in montibus altis
signa procul, fulsitque novis exercitus armis,
arrectae spes Sidonii, fervetque secundis
fortunae iuvenis. vincendi sola videtur,
quod nondum steterint acies, mora : " Pergite,"
    clamat,   100

" in vain you seek to rouse my wrath and to escape captivity by death. You must go on living. Let him be guarded in close fetters." Thus he spoke, proud of victory and the favour of Heaven.

But the senators and matrons of Rome repaired in haste to the temples, to worship the gods. With sad looks and streaming eyes, the band of women marched in long procession, and offered a robe to Juno and solemn vows. " Be present, O Queen of Heaven, we, thy chaste people, pray ; and we, all the Roman women of noble name, bring thee a gift wondrous fair, which our own hands have woven and embroidered with threads of gold. This robe thou shalt wear for the present, O goddess, until mothers grow less fearful for their sons. But if thou dost grant us to drive the African storm-cloud away from our land, divers jewels, set in gold, shall adorn thy glittering crown." They made special offerings also to Pallas and Phoebus, to the War-god, and to Dione *a* above all. So great is the sudden piety of men in time of trouble ; but altars seldom smoke in prosperous times.

While Rome in ancient fashion appointed sacrifices for the temples of the gods, Fabius, moving quietly forwards, by his strategy which might be mistaken for inaction, had barred every approach against Fortune and the foe. He suffered none to leave the ranks, and taught his men discipline—discipline, the chief glory that raises the imperial head of Rome to heaven. But, when the first Roman ensigns were distinctly seen on the heights, and the new weapons of the army glittered in the distance, Hannibal's hopes rose high. Intoxicated by success, he made sure of victory as soon as the armies met : " On ! on ! "

a Venus, the ancestress of the Roman nation.

" ite citi, ruite ad portas, propellite vallum
pectoribus.   quantum campi distamus, ad umbras
tantum hosti superest.   resides ad bella vocantur,
quis pudeat certare, senes : quodcumque videtis,
hoc reliquum est, primo damnatum ut inutile bello.
en, ubi nunc Gracchi atque ubi nunc sunt fulmina
              gentis   106
Scipiadae ? pulsi Ausonia non ante paventem
dimisere fugam, quam terror ad ultima mundi
Oceanumque tulit ; profugus nunc errat uterque,
nomina nostra tremens, et ripas servat Hiberi.   110
est etiam, cur Flaminio mihi gloria caeso
creverit, et titulis libeat cur figere nostris
crudum Marte viri nomen : quot demere noster
huic annos Fabio gladius valet !   at tamen audet.
audeat.   haud ultra faxo spectetur in armis."   115
   Talia vociferans volucri rapit agmina cursu
ac, praevectus equo, nunc dextra provocat hostem,
nunc voce increpitat, missa nunc eminus hasta
fertur ovans pugnaeque agitat simulacra futurae.
ut Thetidis proles Phrygiis Vulcania campis   120
arma tulit, clipeo amplexus terramque polumque
maternumque fretum totumque in imagine mundum.
   Cassarum sedet irarum spectator et alti
celsus colle iugi domat exultantia corda
infractasque minas dilato Marte fatigat   125
sollers cunctandi Fabius.   ceu nocte sub atra
munitis pastor stabulis per ovilia clausum

---

   [a] Ti. Sempronius Gracchus, consul in 213 B.C., is meant:
see iv. 495 foll. The Scipios are the brothers, Publius
Cornelius and Gnaeus Cornelius Scipio, the father and uncle
of Africanus : they had been sent to fight Hasdrubal,
Hannibal's brother, in Spain, and both fell there in battle.
   [b] See note to i. 270.   [c] The Ebro.

he cried; " make haste! Rush to the gates of Rome!
Knock down the ramparts with your breasts! The
space between the hosts is all that separates the
enemy from death. They summon to arms the old
and feeble, unworthy antagonists for us. All whom
you see now are the refuse—men discarded as useless
when the war began. Where are now the Gracchi,
and where are the two Scipios,[a] the thunderbolts of
their nation? Behold! Hunted out of Italy, they
never paused in their cowardly flight until terror
drove them to the Ocean and the World's End [b]; each
is now a wandering exile, and keeps to the banks of
the Iberus,[c] in dread of my name. With good reason
my fame was increased when Flaminius fell; with
good reason I rejoice to add to the list of my exploits
the name of that doughty warrior; but how few
years can my sword cut off from the life of this
Fabius! And yet he dares. Let him dare! Never
again, I warrant, shall he be seen in arms."

Thus he shouted, and pushed his army on with
flying speed. Riding in advance, now he shook his
fist at the foe, and now taunted them, and again
hurled his spear from far and rode on triumphant, re-
hearsing the impending battle. So the son of Thetis [d]
bore on the plains of Troy the armour that Vulcan
forged—the shield on which the whole world was
depicted—earth and sky and his mother's sea.

Fabius sat and watched this fruitless rage from a
lofty mountain-top; by refusing battle he tamed their
proud hearts, and wore out their baffled boasting
by masterly delay. So through the dark night
the shepherd sleeps secure who keeps his flock

---

[d] Achilles: Thetis was a marine goddess.

345

impavidus somni servat pecus ; effera saevit
atque impasta truces ululatus turba luporum
exercet morsuque quatit restantia claustra.　　130
　　Irritus incepti movet inde atque Apula tardo
arva Libys passu legit ac nunc valle residit
conditus occulta, si praecipitare sequentem
atque inopinata detur circumdare fraude ;
nunc nocturna parat caecae celantibus umbris　　135
furta viae retroque abitum fictosque timores
assimulat ; tum castra citus deserta relicta
ostentat praeda atque invitat prodigus hostem.
qualis Maeonia passim Maeandrus in ora,
cum sibi gurgitibus flexis revolutus oberrat.　　140
nulla vacant incepta dolis ; simul omnia versat
miscetque exacuens varia ad conamina mentem.
sicut aquae splendor, radiatus lampade solis,
dissultat per tecta, vaga sub imagine vibrans
luminis, et tremula laquearia verberat umbra.　　145
iamque dolore furens ita secum immurmurat irae :
" obvia si primus nobis hic tela tulisset,
nullane nunc Trebiae et Thrasymenni nomina ?　nulli
lugerent Itali ? numquam Phaëthontius amnis
sanguinea pontum turbasset decolor unda ?　　150
inventum, dum se cohibet, terimurque sedendo,
vincendi genus ; en quotiens, velut obvius iret,
discinxit ratione dolos fraudesque resolvit ! "
haec secum, mediam insomni cum bucina noctem
divideret, iamque, excubias sortitus iniquas,　　155

---

　a Of provoking a battle.
　b The Eridanus, the river Po : Phaëthon fell into this river
when he made his ill-fated attempt to drive the chariot of the
Sun.
　c In a Roman camp both day and night were divided into
four watches of three hours each; and Hannibal's army may
have observed the same routine.

penned in the fold behind iron bars, while the pack
of wolves rage outside, mad with hunger, howling in
their fury and rattling with their teeth at the unyield-
ing barriers.

Foiled in his design,[a] Hannibal moved away and
marched slowly through the land of Apulia. Some-
times he halted and hid in some remote valley, hoping
for a chance to hurry on the foe behind him and
surround them with an unexpected ambush; or
again he planned secret marches under cover of
night, and pretended to retreat in panic; and again
he suddenly abandoned in sight of the enemy a
camp filled with booty, and set a trap for them,
careless of the cost. Thus the Maeander, as it flows
through the land of Lydia, turns back in its crooked
course and wanders till it rejoins its own stream.
All his attempts are full of guile; he tries every
trick at once, and sharpens his ingenuity for every
kind of enterprise. Even so, when a sunbeam is
reflected in water, the light flits to and fro through
the room, quivering as the reflection moves, and
strikes the ceiling with flickering shadow. And now,
wild with rage, Hannibal thus complained in his
wrath : " If I had met Fabius at first in battle, would
the Trebia and Lake Trasimene never have become
famous ? would no Italians be mourning their dead ?
would the river of Phaëthon [b] never have darkened
the sea with its blood-stained waters? He has in-
vented a new method of conquest : he holds his hand,
and we are weakened by inaction. How often, pre-
tending an attack, has he skilfully unmasked our plots
and disclosed our stratagems ! " Thus the sleepless
general pondered, when the bugle sounded the mid-
night hour, and when the third watch,[c] to whom the

tertius abrupta vigil iret ad arma quiete.
vertit iter Daunique retro tellure relicta
Campanas remeat notus populator in oras.
hic vero, intravit postquam uberis arva Falerni—
dives ea et numquam tellus mentita colono—   160
addunt frugiferis inimica incendia ramis.
    Haud fas, Bacche, tuos tacitum tramittere honores,
quamquam magna incepta vocent. memorabere, sacri
largitor laticis, gravidae cui nectare vites
nullum dant prelis nomen praeferre Falernis.   165
Massica sulcabat meliore Falernus in aevo,
ensibus ignotis, senior iuga. pampinus umbras
nondum uvae virides nudo texebat in arvo,
pocula nec norant sucis mulcere Lyaei.
fonte sitim et pura soliti defendere lympha.   170
attulit hospitio pergentem ad litora Calpes
extremumque diem pes dexter et hora Lyaeum,
nec pigitum parvosque lares humilisque subire
limina caelicolam tecti : cepere volentem
fumosi postes et ritu pauperis aevi   175
ante focos mensae ; laetus nec senserat hospes
advenisse deum ; sed enim de more parentum
grato cursabat studio instabatque senectae,
donec opes festas puris nunc poma canistris
composuit, nunc irriguis citus extulit hortis   180
rorantes humore dapes. tum lacte favisque
distinxit dulces epulas nulloque cruore

---

^a Apulia.
^b The best wine known to the Romans was produced there.
^c A legendary figure who gave his name to the place :
Mount Massicus is in Campania.
^d A name for Bacchus : he made a triumphal progress
from India to Spain, from the Far East to the Far West.
^e Bread.

unwelcome duty was allotted, were roused from sleep to take up their arms. He now changed his route : he left the land of Daunus *a* behind him and returned to Campania which had felt the spoiler's hand before ; but this time when he reached the fertile district of Falernus *b*—a rich soil it is, that never deceived the husbandman—they flung destroying fire on the fruitful branches.

Though called away by my great theme, I may not pass over the honours of Bacchus without mention. I must tell of the god who bestowed on man the divine drink, and whom the nectar-bearing vines forbid to set any brand above the presses of Falernus. In the good old days before swords were known, Falernus,*c* a man in years, used to plough the high ground of Mount Massicus. Then the fields were bare, and no vine-plant wove a green shade for the clusters ; nor did men know how to mellow their draught with the juice of Lyaeus,*d* but were wont to slake their thirst with the pure water of a spring. But when Lyaeus was on his way to the shore of Calpe and the setting sun, a lucky foot and a lucky hour brought him hither as a guest ; nor did the god disdain to enter the cottage and pass beneath its humble roof. The smoke-grimed door welcomed a willing guest ; the meal was set, in the fashion of that simple age, in front of the hearth ; nor was the happy host aware that he entertained a god ; but, as his fathers used to do, he ran hither and thither with kindly zeal, tasking his failing strength. At last the feast was set—fruit in clean baskets, and dainties dripping dew which he hastened to cull from his well-watered garden. Then he adorned the toothsome meal with milk and honeycomb, and heaped the gifts of Ceres *e*

polluta castus mensa cerealia dona
attulit, ac primum Vestae detersit honorem
undique et in mediam iecit libamina flammam.   185
deesse tuos latices, hac sedulitate senili
captus, Iacche, vetas.   subito, mirabile dictu,
fagina pampineo spumarunt pocula suco,
pauperis hospitii pretium ; vilisque rubenti
fluxit mulctra mero, et quercu in cratera cavata   190
dulcis odoratis humor sudavit ab uvis.
" en cape," Bacchus ait, " nondum tibi nota, sed olim
viticolae nomen pervulgatura Falerni
munera "—et haud ultra latuit deus.   inde nitentem
lumine purpureo frontem cinxere corymbi,   195
et fusae per colla comae, dextraque pependit
cantharus, ac vitis, thyrso delapsa virenti,
festas Nysaeo redimivit palmite mensas.
nec facilis laeto certasse, Falerne, sapori,
postquam iterata tibi sunt pocula, iam pede risum,
iam lingua titubante moves, patrique Lyaeo   201
tempora quassatus grates et praemia digna
vix intellectis conaris reddere verbis,
donec composuit luctantia lumina Somnus,
Somnus, Bacche, tibi comes additus.   hic ubi primo
ungula dispersit rores Phaëthontia Phoebo,   206
uviferis late florebat Massicus arvis,
miratus nemora et lucentes sole racemos.
it monti decus, atque ex illo tempore dives
Tmolus et ambrosiis Ariusia pocula sucis   210
ac Methymna ferox lacubus cessere Falernis.

---

   [a] The thyrsus was the staff carried by Bacchus and his
votaries : the top of it was decked with vine-leaves or ivy-
leaves.
   [b] Nysa, some undetermined place in the East, was the
birthplace of Bacchus.

on a chaste board which no blood defiled. And from each dish he first plucked a portion in honour of Vesta, and threw what he had plucked into the centre of the fire. Pleased by the old man's willing service, Bacchus decreed that his liquor should not be lacking. Suddenly a miracle was seen : to pay the poor man for his hospitality, the beechen cups foamed with the juice of the grape ; a common milk-pail ran red with wine ; and the sweet moisture of fragrant clusters sweated in the hollow oaken bowl. " Take my gift," said Bacchus ; " as yet it is strange to you, but hereafter it will spread abroad the name of Falernus, the vine-dresser " ; and the god was no longer disguised. Straightway ivy crowned his brows that glowed and flushed ; his locks flowed down over his shoulders ; a beaker hung down from his right hand ; and a vine-plant, falling from his green thyrsus,[a] clothed the festive board with the leaves of Nysa.[b] Falernus found it hard to strive against the cheerful draught : when he had drunk once again of the cup, his stammering tongue and staggering feet roused mirth. With splitting head he tried, though he could not speak plain, to render thanks and praise to Father Lyaeus ; and at last Sleep, who goes ever in the train of Bacchus, closed his reluctant eyes. And when the sun rose and the hoofs of Phaëthon's horses dispelled the dews, all Mount Massicus was green with vine-bearing fields, and marvelled at the leafage and the bunches shining in the sunlight. The fame of the mountain grew, and from that day fertile Tmolus and the nectar of Ariusia and the strong wine of Methymna [c] have all yielded precedence to the vats of Falernus.

[c] The best Greek wines came from Mount Tmolus in Lydia, Ariusa in Chios, and Methymna in Lesbos.

Haec tum vasta dabat terrisque infestus agebat
Hannibal, et sicci stimulabant sanguinis enses,
ludificante ducem Fabio. iamque improba castris
Ausoniis vota et pugnandi prava libido   215
gliscebat ; proni decurrere monte parabant.
    Da famae, da, Musa, virum, cui vincere bina
concessum castra et geminos domitare furores.
" fervida si nobis corda abruptumque putassent
ingenium patres et si clamoribus," inquit,   220
" turbari facilem mentem, non ultima rerum
et deplorati mandassent Martis habenas.
stat pensata diu belli sententia : vincam
servare invitos urgentesque ultima fata.
nulli per Fabium e vobis cecidisse licebit.   225
si lucis piget, et supremis esse cupido est
nominis Ausonii, taedetque in tempore tali
nullum clade nova claraeque fragore ruinae
insignem fecisse locum, revocandus ab atris
Flaminius nobis est sedibus.   ille ruendi   230
iam dudum properans signum auspiciumque dedisset.
an nondum praeceps vicinaque fata videtis ?
una, ut debellet, satis est victoria Poeno.
state, viri, et sentite ducem.   cum optabile tempus
deposcet dextras, tunc ista ferocia dicta   235
aequentur factis.   non est, mihi credite, non est
arduus in pugnas ferri labor : una reclusis
omnes iam portis in campum effuderit hora :
magnum illud solisque datum, quos mitis euntes
Iupiter aspexit, magnum est, ex hoste reverti.   240

---

^a His own and that of Hannibal.   ^b See iv. 708 foll.

This was the land which Hannibal then ravaged and fiercely persecuted. He was impatient, because the blood on his swords was dry, while Fabius still foiled him. But now over-confidence and a perverse desire for battle grew strong in the Roman camp, and the men were ready to rush down from their position on the heights.

Muse, make famous the man who was enabled to master two armies [a] and to quell the fury of them both. Fabius spoke thus : " If the Senate had considered me a man of hot blood and violent temper, a man easily upset by clamour, they would not have trusted me in the last resort with the control of a war already all but lost. My plan of campaign has long been weighed and is fixed : I will persist in saving you, though you protest against it and court your doom. Not one of you shall be allowed to perish, if I can help it. If you are tired of life, and wish to be the last bearers of the Roman name, and if at this crisis you are not content unless you have made some spot famous for fresh disaster and resounding defeat, then we must call Flaminius [b] back from the realm of darkness. Long ago he would have given the order and the signal to attack. Or are you still blind to the yawning precipice and imminent destruction ? One victory more for Hannibal, and the war is over. Stay where you are, my men, and learn to understand your leader. When a favourable moment calls for action, then let your deeds match your present vaunting words. It is not, I assure you, it is not a hard thing to rush to battle : when the gates of the camp are opened, a single hour will see you all pour out into the field. But it is a great thing—and none get it, unless Jupiter has smiled on them as they went forth—to

fortunae Libys incumbit flatuque secundo
fidit agens puppim. dum desinat aura, sinusque
destituat tumidos subducto flamine ventus,
in rem cunctari fuerit. non ulla perenni
amplexu Fortuna fovet. iam copia quanto   245
artior, et—nullo Tyriis certamine—quantum
detritum est famae ! quin inter cetera nostra
haud laude afuerit, modo qui—sed parcere dictis
sit melius. iam vos acies et proelia et hostem
poscitis ? o maneat, superi, fiducia talis !   250
interea, exclusa maioris sorte pericli,
me solum, quaeso, toti me opponite bello.''
his dictis fractus furor, et rabida arma quierunt.
ut cum turbatis placidum caput extulit undis
Neptunus totumque videt totique videtur   255
regnator ponto, saevi fera murmura venti
dimittunt nullasque movent in frontibus alas ;
tum, sensim infusa tranquilla per aequora pace,
languentes tacito lucent in litore fluctus.

Sensit cura sagax Poeni fraudisque veneno   260
aggreditur mentes. pauca atque haec ruris aviti
iugera nec multis Fabius vertebat aratris ;
Massicus uviferis addebat nomina glebis.
hinc pestem placitum moliri et spargere causas
in castra ambiguas : ferro flammisque pepercit   265

---

[a] Modesty prevents him from saying that he hopes to beat
Hannibal in the end. Or Fabius may have meant to add,
" if only I am not prevented by Minucius."
[b] Ancient sculptors and painters represented winds as
354

come back after the battle. Hannibal is following up
his good fortune, and driving his ship with confidence
before a favouring wind. Until the breeze falls and
the flagging wind deserts his swelling sails, to delay
will prove our gain. Fortune never clings to any man
with a lasting embrace. Already, how much reduced
are their forces, and how much reputation they have
lost! And yet we have fought no battle against
them. Indeed, my titles to fame may include him
who not long ago—but it may be better to say no
more.[a] Do you call for immediate action and battle
with the foe? I pray to Heaven that your confident
spirit may be lasting. In the meantime, avert the
risk of a great disaster, and set me, me only, in
opposition to the whole war." His words tamed their
frenzy and calmed their angry weapons. So, when
Neptune, the ruler of the sea, raises his serene brow
above the stormy waves, and sees the whole ocean
and is seen by it, the angry winds stop their fierce
howling and cease to ply the wings[b] on their fore-
heads; then peace and quiet spread gradually over
the deep, and gentle waves reflect the light along the
silent shore.

Hannibal, watchful and shrewd, was aware of this,
and tried to poison men's minds by a trick. Fabius
owned a small estate inherited from his ancestors,
which needed but few ploughs to till it; but the
fields grew vines that Mount Massicus made famous.
Hence Hannibal resolved to stir up mischief and sow
disaffection in the camp: with wicked cunning he
refrained from fire and sword and left that land in

winged creatures: their practice was imitated by the later
poets; and the winds bore wings not only on their shoulders
and feet but also on their temples, as here.

suspectamque loco pacem dedit arte maligna,
ceu clandestino traheretur foedere bellum.
　Intellectus erat Fabio, Tyriosque videbat
dictator saevire dolos ; sed non vacat aegram
invidiam gladios inter lituosque timere　　　　　　270
et dubia morsus famae depellere pugna,
donec reptantem, nequiquam saepe trahendo
huc illuc castra ac scrutantem proelia Poenum,
qua nemorosa iuga et scopulosi vertice colles
exsurgunt, clausit sparsa ad divortia turma.　　　275
hinc Laestrygoniae saxoso monte premebant
a tergo rupes, undosis squalida terris
hinc Literna palus. nec ferri aut militis usum
poscebat regio. saeptos sed fraude locorum
arta fames, poenas miserae exactura Sagunti,　　280
urgebat, finisque aderat Carthaginis armis.
　Cuncta per et terras et lati stagna profundi
condiderat somnus, positoque labore dierum
pacem nocte datam mortalibus orbis agebat.
at non Sidonium curis flagrantia corda　　　　　285
ductorem vigilesque metus haurire sinebant
dona soporiferae noctis. nam membra cubili
erigit et fulvi circumdat pelle leonis,
qua super instratos proiectus gramine campi
presserat ante toros. tunc ad tentoria fratris　　290
fert gressus vicina citos ; nec degener ille
belligeri ritus, taurino membra iacebat
effultus tergo et mulcebat tristia somno.
haud procul hasta viri terrae defixa propinquae,
et dira e summa pendebat cuspide cassis ;　　　295

　ᵃ People might suspect Fabius of saying to Hannibal,
“ If you spare my land, I will be slack in the conduct of the
war.”
　ᵇ Laestrygonians were found in Sicily and also round

peace ; thus men might suspect that the war was
prolonged by a secret understanding.[a]

The dictator saw through the trick of the Cartha-
ginian and perceived its danger. But he was too
busy, amid the clashing of swords and the sound of
bugles, to fear morbid jealousy, and to parry the
tooth of calumny by fighting a hazardous battle. At
last, as Hannibal crept about, shifting his camp with-
out result and spying out any chance of battle, Fabius
posted cavalry where cross-roads met, and shut him
in, where there were wooded heights and steep rising
cliffs. The high rocks of Laestrygonia [b] hemmed
in his rear ; in front were the marshes of Liternum,
a dismal stretch of flooded fields. The ground made
the soldier's sword useless ; they were trapped by
the treacherous position ; Famine, soon to claim the
penalty for the tragedy of Saguntum, held them in
her grip ; and the army of Carthage came near to
destruction.

Sleep had lulled all things to rest over the earth
and the calm wide sea ; the labour of the day was
done, and the world enjoyed the peace that night
brings to all mankind. But restless anxiety and
watchful fear prevented Hannibal from tasting the
bounty of drowsy night. Rising from his bed, he
put on the tawny lion-skin which had served him as
bedding when he lay stretched upon the grassy sward.
Then he went in haste to his brother's [c] tent which
was pitched near his own. Mago too was no effeminate
soldier : his limbs rested on an ox-hide, as he lay
there soothing trouble with sleep. His spear was
planted in the ground beside him, and from the spear-

Formiae, a town of Latium on the borders of Campania :
the latter place is meant here.   [c] Mago.

at clipeus circa loricaque et ensis et arcus
et telum Baliare simul tellure quiescunt.
iuxta lecta manus, iuvenes in Marte probati ;
et sonipes strato carpebat gramina dorso.
ut pepulere levem intrantis vestigia somnum :   300
" heus ! " inquit pariterque manus ad tela ferebat,
" quae te cura vigil fessum, germane, fatigat ? "
ac iam constiterat sociosque in caespite fusos
incussa revocat castrorum ad munera planta,
cum Libyae ductor : " Fabius me noctibus aegris,
in curas Fabius nos excitat ; illa senectus,   306
heu fatis quae sola meis currentibus obstat !
cernis, ut armata circumfundare corona,
et vallet clausos collectus miles in orbem.
verum, age, nunc quoniam res artae, percipe porro
quae meditata mihi.   latos correpta per agros   311
armenta assueto belli de more secuntur.
cornibus arentes edicam innectere ramos
sarmentique leves fronti religare maniplos,
admotus cum fervorem disperserit ignis,   315
ut passim exultent stimulante dolore iuvenci
et vaga per colles cervice incendia iactent.
tum terrore novo trepidus laxabit iniquas
custos excubias maioraque nocte timebit.
si cordi consulta (moras extrema recusant)   320
accingamur," ait.   gemino tentoria gressu
inde petunt.   ingens clipeo cervice reposta
inter equos interque viros interque iacebat
capta manu spolia et rorantia caede Maraxes
ac dirum, in somno ceu bella capesseret, amens   325
clamorem tum forte dabat dextraque tremente

----

[a] See note to i. 314.

point his dreadful helmet hung down ; and his shield
and breastplate, his sword and bow and Balearic
sling [a] lay on the ground beside him. A chosen band
of veteran soldiers attended him ; and his war-horse
wore the saddle as it grazed. When his light slumber
was broken by the sound of entering footsteps, " Ha,
brother ! " he cried, and at the same time reached
out for his weapons ; " what sleepless anxiety forbids
you to rest your weary limbs ? " Already he stood
erect, and a stamp of his foot summoned to attention
his men who lay stretched upon the sward, when
Hannibal thus began : " It is Fabius who breaks my
rest, Fabius who excites my fears ; that old man,
alas, alone withstands the tide of my fortunes. You
see how you are surrounded by a ring of warriors,
trapped and encircled by the army he has placed
there. But, come, since we are in this strait, hear
further a plan I have devised. The cattle we have
seized up and down the land are with us now, after
the custom of war. I shall order dry branches to be
tied to their horns, and bundles of light faggots
to be fixed to their foreheads ; then, when fire is
applied and spreads its heat, the beasts, driven mad
by pain, will run wild and spread a blaze over the
hills with tossing heads. Then our jailers, surprised
and alarmed, will relax their strict guard, and will
fear worse dangers in the darkness. If my plan
pleases you, let us set to work—the crisis forbids
delay." Together they went at once to the camp.
There lay huge Maraxes, his head pillowed on his
shield ; around him were horses and men and blood-
dripping spoils that he had taken in battle ; and,
as if fighting in dreams, he uttered just then a frantic
cry, while his shaking hand felt eagerly for his

arma toro et notum quaerebat fervidus ensem.
huic Mago, inversa quatiens ut dispulit hasta
bellantem somnum : " tenebris, fortissime ductor,
iras compesce atque in lucem proelia differ.   330
ad fraudem occultamque fugam tutosque receptus
nunc nocte utendum est.   arentes nectere frondes
cornibus et latis accensa immittere silvis
armenta, oppositi reserent quo claustra manipli,
germanus parat atque obsessa evellere castra.   335
emergamus, et hic Fabio persuadeat astus,
non certare dolis."   nihil hinc cunctante sed acris
incepti laeto iuvene, ad tentoria Acherrae
festinant ; cui parca quies minimumque soporis,
nec notum somno noctes aequare ; feroci   340
pervigil inservibat equo fessumque levabat
tractando et frenis ora exagitata fovebat.
at socii renovant tela arentemque cruorem
ferro detergent et dant mucronibus iras.
quid fortuna loci poscat, quid tempus, et ipsi   345
quaenam agitent, pandunt et coeptis ire ministrum
haud segnem hortantur.   discurrit tessera castris ;
intentique docent, quae sint properanda, monentque
quisque suos ; instat trepidis stimulatque ruentes
navus abire timor, dum caeca silentia dumque   350
maiores umbrae.   rapida iam subdita peste
virgulta atque altis surgunt e cornibus ignes.
hic vero ut, gliscente malo et quassantibus aegra
armentis capita, adiutae pinguescere flammae
coepere, et vincens fumos erumpere vertex :   355

360

good sword and the weapons on his bed. With a blow from the butt of his spear Mago awoke him from his unpeaceful slumber. " Control your ardour in the hours of darkness, brave captain," he said, " and postpone your fighting till day comes. We must make use of to-night for a stratagem, for a secret flight and safe retreat. My brother intends to fix dry branches to the horns of the cattle and to turn them loose when lighted all through the woods, that the foe may relax his grasp ; and he hopes thus to wrench the beleaguered army from their clutches. Let us make our way out, and teach Fabius that he is no match for us in cunning." Rejoicing in this bold stroke, the warrior tarried not. The pair next hastened to the quarters of Acherras, a man content with brief slumbers who never slept the whole night through. He was awake now and attending to a mettlesome steed, rubbing him down after exercise and bathing the mouth which the bit had chafed. His men were furbishing their weapons, washing the dry blood from the steel and sharpening their swords. The pair explained their business and the requirements of the place and time, and bade Acherras go with speed and further the plan. The word was passed round through the camp ; the captains zealously instructed their men and explained the work to be done ; fear beset them and quickened their pace, urging them to depart in the silence and darkness, before the shadow of night grew lighter. The brushwood was quickly kindled, and fire rose high from the horns of the cattle. But when the mischief spread and the beasts tossed their tortured heads, the flames, so helped, grew thicker, and their crest burst upwards through the smoke and conquered it. All

SILIUS ITALICUS

per colles dumosque (lues agit atra) per altos
saxosi scopulos montis lymphata feruntur
corpora anhela boum, atque obsessis naribus igni
luctantur frustra rabidi mugire iuvenci.
per iuga, per valles errat Vulcania pestis,   360
nusquam stante malo ; vicinaque litora fulgent.
quam multa, affixus caelo sub nocte serena,
fluctibus e mediis sulcator navita ponti
astra videt ; quam multa videt, fervoribus atris
cum Calabros urunt ad pinguia pabula saltus,   365
vertice Gargani residens incendia pastor.
   At facie subita volitantum montibus altis
flammarum, quis tunc cecidit custodia sorti,
horrere atque ipsos, nullo spargente, vagari
credere et indomitos pasci sub collibus ignes.   370
caelone exciderint, et magna fulmina dextra
torserit Omnipotens, an caecis rupta cavernis
fuderit egestas accenso sulphure flammas
infelix tellus, media in formidine quaerunt.
iamque abeunt ; faucesque viae citus occupat armis
Poenus et in patulos exultans emicat agros.   376
huc tamen usque vigil processerat arte regendi
dictator Trebiam et Tusci post stagna profundi,
esset ut Hannibali Fabium Romanaque tela
evasisse satis.   quin et vestigia pulsi   380
et gressus premeret castris, ni sacra vocarent
ad patrios veneranda deos.   tum, versus ad urbem,
alloquitur iuvenem, cui mos tramittere signa
et belli summam primasque iubebat habenas,

---

    [a] See note to iv. 561.   [b] Lake Trasimene.
    [c] As the head of the Fabian family, he was obliged to offer
sacrifice yearly to Diana on the Quirinal Hill.

over the hills and thickets, over the high cliffs of
the rocky mountain, the maddened cattle rushed on
panting, driven by that dreadful scourge ; and the
steers, their nostrils stopped by the fire, tried in vain
to bellow. Nothing can check the destroying fire :
it runs from place to place over hill and valley ; and
the sea, not far away, reflects it. It was like the
multitude of stars which the seaman beholds from
his ship as he ploughs the deep on a clear night, with
his gaze fixed upon the sky ; or like the multitude
of fires that the shepherd sees from his seat on Mount
Garganus,[a] when the uplands of Calabria are burnt
and blackened, to improve the pasture.

But the Roman sentries whose turn it was to be on
guard were horror-struck by the sudden sight of flames
moving about on the mountain-tops : they believed that
no hand of man had sent forth fire, but that it spread of
itself and flourished unrestrained beneath the hills.
"Did it fall from heaven ?" they asked in their fear;
"had the Almighty launched thunderbolts with his
strong arm? or had the vexed earth burst asunder and
sent forth flames, vomited from hidden hollows with
burning sulphur?" Quickly they fled; and the Cartha-
ginian army made haste to seize the narrow pass and
dashed forth triumphant into the open country. Yet
by his skilful management the watchful Dictator had
succeeded so far, that Hannibal, even after the Trebia
and the Tuscan lake,[b] was content now to have escaped
Fabius and the Roman attack. Indeed Fabius would
have followed with his army the retreating foe, had
he not been summoned to pay worship to the gods
of his family.[c] As he turned his face to Rome, he
addressed the younger man, who took over, as custom
required, the colours and the supreme command, and

atque his praeformat dictis fingitque monendo :　385
" si factis nondum, Minuci, te cauta probare
erudiit Fortuna meis, nec ducere verba
ad verum decus ac pravis arcere valebunt.
vidisti clausum Hannibalem ; nil miles et alae
iuvere aut densis legio conferta maniplis.　390
testor te, solus clausi, nec deinde morabor.
dis sine me libare dapem et sollemnia ferre.
hunc iterum atque iterum vinctum vel montibus altis
amnibus aut rapidis—modo pugna absistite—tradam.
interea (crede experto, non fallimus) aegris　395
nil movisse salus rebus.　sit gloria multis
et placeat, quippe egregium, prosternere ferro
hostem ; sed Fabio sit vos servasse triumphus.
plena tibi castra atque intactus vulnere miles
creditur ; hos nobis (erit haec tibi gloria) redde.　400
iam cernes Libycum huic vallo assultare leonem,
iam praedas offerre tibi, iam vertere terga,
respectantem adeo atque iras cum fraude coquentem.
claude, oro, castra et cunctas spes eripe pugnae.
haec monuisse satis ; sed si compescere corda　405
non datur oranti, magno te iure pioque
dictator capere arma veto." sic castra relinquens
vallarat monitis ac se referebat ad urbem.
　Ecce autem flatu classis Phoenissa secundo
litora Caietae Laestrygoniosque recessus　410

---

　[a] M. Minucius Rufus was Master of the Knights to the
Dictator, and second in command of the army.
　[b] A seaport town on the borders of Latium and Campania:
for the Laestrygonians see note to l. 276.

spoke thus, instructing him beforehand and schooling him with warning : " Minucius,[a] if you have not yet learned from my actions to approve caution, then words also will be too weak to attract you to true glory and to guard you from mistakes. You have seen Hannibal entrapped : his footmen and his horsemen and his army with its serried ranks were all useless. I alone entrapped him, I call you to witness. Nor shall I be slow to do it again. Suffer me to make a feast for the gods and offer the customary sacrifices. Again and again—do you but refrain from battle—I shall show you Hannibal penned in by lofty mountains or rapid rivers. For the present (take the word of experience, I speak the truth) inaction is safety in peril. Let many generals feel joy and pride when they have laid low the enemy in battle —and it is indeed a glorious thing ; but let Fabius regard this as his height of glory, that he has saved the lives of you all. I hand over to you an undepleted force and unwounded men ; give them back to me unharmed, and that shall be your boast. Soon you will see the Libyan lion charging our ramparts ; at one time he will offer you spoil, and at another he will retreat, looking ever backwards and nursing wrath in his guileful heart. Shut the gates of the camp, I entreat you, and rob him of all hope of fighting. This is sufficient warning ; but, if my entreaties cannot restrain your ardour, then by my high office of dictator and by my duty I forbid you to take up arms." Thus he defended the camp by his warnings ere he left it and returned to Rome.

But now, before a favouring wind, Carthaginian ships were seen ploughing with their beaks the sea by the shore of Caieta[b] and the bay of the Laestry-

sulcabat rostris portusque intrarat apertos,
ac totus multo spumabat remige pontus,
cum trepidae fremitu vitreis e sedibus antri
aequoreae pelago simul emersere sorores
ac possessa vident infestis litora proris.   415
tum magno perculsa metu Nereia turba
attonitae propere refluunt ad limina nota,
Teleboum medio surgunt qua regna profundo
pumiceaeque procul sedes.   immanis in antro
conditur abrupto Proteus ac spumea late   420
cautibus obiectis reiectat caerula vates.
is postquam (sat gnarus enim rerumque metusque)
per varias lusit formas et terruit atri
serpentis squamis horrendaque sibila torsit,
aut fremuit torvo mutatus membra leone :   425
" dicite," ait, " quae causa viae ?   quisve ora repente
pervasit pallor ?   cur scire futura libido ? "
    Ad quae Cymodoce, Nympharum maxima natu
Italidum :   " nosti nostros, praesage, timores.
quid Tyriae classes ereptaque litora nobis   430
portendunt ?   num migrantur Rhoeteia regna
in Libyam superis ?   aut hos Sarranus habebit
navita iam portus ?   patria num sede fugatae
Atlantem et Calpen extrema habitabimus antra ? "
    Tunc sic, evolvens repetita exordia, retro   435
incipit ambiguus vates reseratque futura :
" Laomedonteus Phrygia cum sedit in Ida
pastor et, errantes dumosa per avia tauros
arguta revocans ad roscida pascua canna,

---

^a Nereids.
  ^b The island of Capri : the residence of Proteus, the
prophet and god of the sea, is generally placed elsewhere by
the poets.
  ^c The epithet perhaps refers to the power of Proteus to
change his shape.

gonians. They had entered the undefended harbour, and the number of their oarsmen churned all the sea to foam. The noise startled the Sea Sisters,[a] and they rose up together from the crystal seats of their grotto, and saw the shore occupied by hostile vessels. Then in great fear and consternation the train of Nereids swam off quickly to a familiar haunt, where the realm of the Teleboans [b] rises far off in mid-sea, and there are rocky caves. Proteus, the monstrous [c] seer, hides here in his cavern among the rocks, and keeps the foaming deep at a distance by a barrier of cliffs. He knew well the cause of their alarm ; but first he eluded them by taking various shapes : he frightened them in the likeness of a black and scaly snake, and hissed horribly ; again he changed into a fierce lion and roared. At last he spoke : " Tell me the cause of your coming, and why have your faces suddenly turned pale ? Why seek ye to know the future ? "

Cymodoce replied, the eldest of the Italian nymphs: " Prophet," she said, " you know why we are afraid. What mean these ships of Carthage that have robbed us of our shore ? Are the gods removing the empire of Rome [d] to Libya ? Or shall the seamen of Tyre possess these harbours in future ? Must we leave our native seat and dwell in the caves of uttermost Atlas and Calpe ? "

Then the prophet, the deity of many forms, thus began to reveal the future, beginning his tale far back in the distant past. " When the shepherd son [e] of Laomedon sat on Phrygian Ida, and his sweet piping recalled to the dewy pastures his bulls that strayed

---

[d] Lit. " of Rhoeteum " : this was a promontory near Troy : see note to ii. 51.

[e] Paris.

audivit sacrae lectus certamina formae,   440
tum matris currus niveos agitabat olores,
tempora sollicitus litis servasse, Cupido.
parvulus ex humero gorytos et aureus arcus
fulgebat, nutuque vetans trepidare parentem,
monstrabat gravidam telis se ferre pharetram.   445
ast alius nivea comebat fronte capillos,
purpureos alius vestis religabat amictus,
cum sic suspirans roseo Venus ore decoros
alloquitur natos : ' testis certissima vestrae
ecce dies pietatis adest.   quis credere salvis   450
hoc ausit vobis ?   de forma atque ore (quid ultra
iam superest rerum ?) certat Venus.   omnia parvis
si mea tela dedi blando medicata veneno,
si vester, caelo ac terris qui foedera sancit,
stat supplex, cum vultis, avus : victoria nostra   455
Cypron Idumaeas referat de Pallade palmas,
de Iunone Paphos centum mihi fumet in aris.'
dumque haec aligeris instat Cytherea, sonabat
omne nemus gradiente dea.   nam bellica virgo,
aegide deposita atque assuetum casside crinem   460
involvi tunc compta tamen pacemque serenis
condiscens oculis, ibat lucoque ferebat
praedicto sacrae vestigia concita plantae.
parte alia intrabat iussis Saturnia silvis,
iudicium Phrygis et fastus pastoris et Iden   465
post fratris latura toros.   postrema nitenti
affulsit vultu ridens Venus.   omnia circa
et nemora et penitus frondosis rupibus antra

---

[a] Jupiter.
[b] The birthplace of Venus : Paphos in Cyprus was one of
the seats of her worship.   For Idume see note to iii. 600.
[c] Pallas.   [d] Juno.

through pathless thickets, he was chosen to witness
the contest of the goddesses for the prize of beauty.
Then a Cupid drove the snow-white swans harnessed
to his mother's car, and feared to be too late for the
contest.   A tiny quiver and a golden bow glittered at
his shoulder, and he signed to his mother to have no
fear, and showed her the quiver that he carried loaded
with arrows.   Another Cupid combed the tresses on
her snow-white brow, and a third put the girdle round
the folds of her purple robe.   Then Venus sighed, and
her rosy lips thus addressed her pretty children : ' See,
the day has come that will prove beyond all doubt
your love for your mother.   Who would dare to
believe, that while you still live, the claim of Venus
to the prize for beauty is contested ?   What worse
remains behind ?   If I gave to my children all my
arrows steeped in delicious poison—if your grandsire,[a]
the Lawgiver of heaven and earth, stands a suppliant
before you when so you please, then let my triumph
bear back to Cyprus [b] the palm of Edom won from
Pallas, and let the hundred altars of Paphos smoke for
my conquest of Juno.'   And, while Cytherea thus
charged her winged children, all the grove re-echoed
the footsteps of a goddess.   For now came the Warrior
Maid.[c]   She had laid aside her aegis ; the hair which
the helmet was wont to hide was braided now, and
her clear eyes wore a studied look of peace ; and her
sacred feet bore her quickly to the appointed grove.
From another quarter obedient to the call came the
daughter of Saturn [d] ; though wedded to her brother,
Jupiter, she must endure to be judged and rejected
by the Trojan shepherd on Mount Ida.   Last came
Venus with smiling face, glorious in her beauty.   All
the surrounding groves and all the hollows of the

spirantem sacro traxerunt vertice odorem.
nec iudex sedisse valet ; fessique nitoris   470
luce cadunt oculi, ac metuit dubitasse videri.
sed victae fera bella deae vexere per aequor,
atque excisa suo pariter cum iudice Troia.
tum pius Aeneas, terris iactatus et undis,
Dardanios Itala posuit tellure penates.   475
dum cete ponto innabunt, dum sidera caelo
lucebunt, dum sol Indo se litore tollet,
hic regna et nullae regnis per saecula metae.
at vos, o natae, currit dum immobile filum,
Hadriaci fugite infaustas Sasonis harenas.   480
sanguineis tumidus ponto miscebitur undis
Aufidus et rubros impellet in aequora fluctus ;
damnatoque deum quondam per carmina campo
Aetolae rursus Teucris pugnabitis umbrae.
Punica Romuleos quatient mox spicula muros,   485
multaque Hasdrubalis fulgebit strage Metaurus.
hinc ille in furto genitus patruique piabit
idem ultor patrisque necem ; tum litus Elissae
implebit flammis avelletque Itala Poenum
viscera torrentem et propriis superabit in oris.   490
huic Carthago armis, huic Africa nomine cedet.
hic dabit ex sese, qui tertia bella fatiget
et cinerem Libyae ferat in Capitolia victor."

---

^a The prophet foretells the battle of Cannae : the Roman
blood shed there will flow down the river Aufidus into the
sea : Saso is an island on the coast of Epirus.
^b The Sibyl of Cumae : cp. ix. 57.
^c See note to i. 125.   ^d Romans.
^e Scipio Africanus, the conqueror of Hannibal : see xiii.
615 foll.
^f The Scipio brothers both fell in Spain in 212 B.C.
^g He assumed the name of Africanus.
^h In 146 B.C. P. Cornelius Scipio Africanus Aemilianus

leaf-clad heights drank in deeply the fragrance that breathed from that divine head. The judge could not sit still ; his eyes, dazzled by the brilliance of her beauty, sank to the ground ; and he feared lest he might seem ever to have been in doubt. But the defeated goddesses brought a fierce army across the sea, and Troy was demolished together with the Trojan who had judged them. Then good Aeneas, after much suffering on land and sea, established the gods of Troy on the soil of Italy. So long as sea-monsters shall swim the deep and stars shine in the sky and the sun rise on the Indian shore, Rome shall rule, and there shall be no end to her rule throughout the ages. But you, my daughters, while the thread of Fate that none may change still runs on, avoid the ill-omened sands of Saso [a] in the Adriatic sea. For Aufidus will fall into that sea, his stream swollen with gore, and will pour incarnadined waters into the main ; and on a field condemned long ago by the oracles of Heaven,[b] the ghosts of Aetolia [c] shall fight the Trojans [d] once more. Later the missiles of Carthage shall batter the walls of Romulus, and the Metaurus shall be famous for the utter defeat of Hasdrubal. Next the offspring of stolen love [e] shall duly avenge his father and his uncle [f] as well ; then he shall spread fire over the coast of Dido, and tear Hannibal away from the vitals of Italy on which he is preying, and defeat him in his own country. To him Carthage shall surrender her arms, and Africa her name.[g] And his son's son shall finish a third war with victory and bring back the ashes of Libya to the Capitol." [h]

destroyed Carthage and ended the Third Punic War : he was, by adoption, the grandson of the first Africanus.

Quae dum arcana deum vates evolvit in antro,
iam monita et Fabium bellique equitumque magister
exuerat mente ac praeceps tendebat in hostem.   496
pascere nec Poenus pravum ac nutrire furorem
deerat et, ut parvo maiora ad proelia damno
eliceret, dabat interdum simulantia terga.
non aliter, quam qui sparsa per stagna profundi 500
evocat e liquidis piscem penetralibus esca,
cumque levem summa vidit iam nare sub unda,
ducit sinuato captivum ad litora lino.

Fama furit versos hostes, Poenumque salutem
invenisse fuga ; liceat si vincere, finem   505
promitti cladum ; sed enim dicione carere
virtutem, et poenas vincentibus esse repostas.
clausurum iam castra ducem rursusque referri
vaginae iussurum enses, reddatur in armis
ut ratio, et purget miles, cur vicerit hostem.   510
haec vulgus ; necnon patrum Saturnia mentes
invidiae stimulo fodit et popularibus auris.
tunc indigna fide censent optandaque Poeno,
quae mox haud parvo luerent damnata periclo.

Dividitur miles, Fabioque equitumque magistro
imperia aequantur geminis. cernebat, et expers 516
irarum senior, magnas ne penderet alti
erroris poenas patria inconsulta, timebat.
ac tum, multa putans secum, ut remeavit ab urbe,
partitus socias vires, vicina propinquis   520

---

^a Juno.

While the prophet in his grotto revealed these secret things of the gods, the Master of the Knights and commander of the army had put from his mind the warnings of Fabius, and was pressing forward against the enemy. And Hannibal was not slow to feed and encourage this folly : he feigned at times to retreat, that by a trifling loss he might tempt Minucius to a pitched battle. So the fisherman tempts a fish forth from the watery depths by scattering bait in the pools, and then, when he sees his nimble prey swimming close to the surface, draws it captive to the shore in his bellying net.

Wild rumours ran—that the enemy was routed, and Hannibal had saved himself by flight ; an end of defeats was certain, if the Romans were allowed to conquer ; but the brave had no authority, and punishment was in store for the victorious. Soon would Fabius keep the army in camp and order the sword to be sheathed once more, that the warrior might be called to account and clear himself of the crime of conquering. Thus the people murmured ; and even the hearts of the Senators were stirred up by the daughter of Saturn [a] with the sting of jealousy and with the desire for popular favour. Then they passed a decree unworthy of belief, a decree that Hannibal might have prayed for ; they were soon to repent it and to pay for it with great disaster.

The army was divided, and the Master of the Knights was given equal powers with the Dictator. The older man looked on without resentment ; but he feared that the ill-advised government might pay a heavy penalty for their grievous error. And then, revolving many things in his breast, he returned from Rome and, after dividing the forces with Minucius,

signa iugis locat et specula sublimis ab alta
non Romana minus servat, quam Punica castra.
nec mora ; disiecto Minuci vecordia vallo
perdendi simul et pereundi ardebat amore.

Quem postquam rapidum vidit procedere castris
hinc Libys, hinc Fabius, simul accendere sagaces 526
in subitum curas.   propere capere arma maniplis
edicit valli tenet munimine turmas
Ausonius ; torquet totas in proelia vires
Poenorum ductor propellitque agmina voce :   530
" dum dictator abest, rape, miles, tempora pugnae.
non sperata diu plano certamina campo
offert ecce deus.   quoniam data copia, longum
detergete situm ferro multoque cruore
exsatiate, viri, plenos rubiginis enses."   535

Atque ea Cunctator pensabat ab aggere valli,
perlustrans campos oculis, tantoque periclo
discere, quinam esset Fabius, te, Roma, dolebat.
cui natus, iuncta arma ferens : " dabit improbus,"
      inquit,
" quas dignum est, poenas ; qui per suffragia caeca
invasit nostros haec ad discrimina fasces.   541
insanae spectate tribus !   pro lubrica rostra
et vanis fora laeta viris !   nunc munera Martis
aequent imperio et solem concedere nocti
sciscant imbelles : magna mercede piabunt   545
erroris rabiem et nostrum violasse parentem."
tum senior, quatiens hastam lacrimisque coortis :

ᵃ The nickname which Fabius made a title of honour.
ᵇ It was a meeting of the plebs, voting by tribes, which
carried the proposal that Minucius should have equal
authority with Fabius.
ᶜ The *Rostra* (the orators' platform) stood in the market-
place.

encamped on a neighbouring height, where from his
lofty watch-tower he kept an eye on the Roman army
as much as on the army of Hannibal. Minucius in
his folly at once dismantled the rampart of his
camp; he was burning with eagerness to destroy
and, at the same time, to be destroyed.

When Hannibal from one point and Fabius from
another saw him hurrying forth from his camp, each
instantly conceived wise plans to meet the emergency.
The Roman general ordered his foot-soldiers to arm
with speed, and kept his cavalry behind the protec-
tion of the ramparts, while Hannibal threw every
man into the fighting-line, and called on them thus
to go forward: "Soldiers, seize the opportunity for
battle, while Fabius is absent. See! Heaven offers
us the chance so long denied of fighting on the open
plain. Since the opportunity is given, cleanse the
steel from the mould of long disuse, my men, and glut
your rusty swords with much bloodshed."

The Delayer [a] surveyed the country from the high
rampart, and weighed these things in his heart. He
was grieved that Rome should learn the value of a
Fabius at so great a cost. His son who served at his
side said: "That rash man will suffer as he deserves
—the man who by the votes of the blind populace
usurped our authority and has brought things to this
pass. Look on now, ye senseless Tribes! [b] Shame
on the rhetoric that leads to ruin, and on the market-
place [c] that approves worthless men! Let them now,
in their ignorance of war, divide the command over
the army and vote that light shall give place to
darkness! Dearly shall they pay for their mad mis-
take, and for their insult to my father." As the old
man answered him, he shook his spear, and the tears

" sanguine Poenorum, iuvenis, tam tristia dicta
sunt abolenda tibi.   patiarne ante ora manusque
civem deleri nostras ?   aut vincere Poenum,   550
me spectante, sinam ?   non aequavisse minorem
solventur culpa, si sunt mihi talia cordi ?
iamque hoc, ne dubites, longaevi, nate, parentis
accipe et aeterno fixum sub pectore serva :
succensere nefas patriae ; nec foedior ulla   555
culpa sub extremas fertur mortalibus umbras.
sic docuere senes.   quantus qualisque fuisti,
cum pulsus lare et extorris Capitolia curru
intrares exul !   tibi corpora caesa, Camille,
damnata quot sunt dextra !   pacata fuissent   560
ni consulta viro mensque impenetrabilis irae,
mutassentque solum sceptris Aeneia regna,
nullaque nunc stares terrarum vertice, Roma.
pone iras, o nate, meas.   socia arma feramus
et celeremus opem."   iamque intermixta sonabant
classica, procursusque viros colliserat acer.   566
    Primus claustra manu portae dictator et altos
disiecit postes rupitque in proelia cursum.
non graviore movent venti certamina mole
Odrysius Boreas et Syrtim tollere pollens   570
Africus : obnixi cum bella furentia torquent,
distraxere fretum ac diversa ad litora volvunt
aequor quisque suum ; sequitur stridente procella
nunc huc, nunc illuc, raptum mare et intonat undis.

---

    [a] Camillus, the hero of his age, returned from exile to
inflict a crushing defeat upon the Gauls who had burnt
Rome in 390 B.C. When the Romans planned to migrate
from the burnt city to Veii, his eloquence prevented the
design.
    [b] See note to i. 408. Africus is the S.W. wind.

rose to his eyes : " My son, you must wash away that harsh speech in Punic blood. Shall I suffer my countryman to be slain before my eyes, and not move a hand, or allow Hannibal to conquer while I look on ? If such were my feeling, will not those who set me on a level with my subordinate be acquitted of all blame ? And now, my son, take this for certain from your aged father, and keep it ever engraved upon your heart : to harbour wrath against your country is a sin; and no more heinous crime can mortal man carry down to the shades below. Such was the doctrine of our fathers. How great and noble was Camillus,ᵃ when, exiled from home and country, he returned from banishment to drive his triumphal car to the Capitol ! How many enemies were slain by that right hand which Romans had condemned ! But for the placid wisdom of Camillus and his refusal to harbour wrath, the realm of Aeneas would have changed its seat of empire,ᵃ and Rome would not stand now at the summit of the world. Be not angry for your father's sake, my son ; but let us fight side by side and make haste to help." Already the trumpets were sounding together with the trumpets of the foe ; and men had charged forward, to clash in conflict.

The Dictator was the foremost man to knock down the bars and tall gate-posts of the camp, and to rush into the fray. No mightier are the winds when they war against one another, Boreas from Thrace and Africus that has power to lift the Syrtis ᵇ ; when they rage in stubborn conflict, they divide the sea and each rolls his own part to an opposite shore ; as the tempest howls, the tide is swept after it hither and thither, and the waves thunder. No possible achievement—not

377

haud prorsus daret ullus honos tellusque subacta 575
Phoenicum et Carthago ruens, iniuria quantum
orta ex invidia decoris tulit ; omnia namque
dura simul devicta viro, metus, Hannibal, irae,
invidia, atque una fama et fortuna subactae.

Poenus ab excelso rapidos decurrere vallo   580
ut vidit, tremuere irae, ceciditque repente
cum gemitu spes haud dubiae praesumpta ruinae ;
quippe aciem denso circumvallaverat orbe,
hausurus clausos coniectis undique telis.
atque hic Dardanius pravo certamine ductor   585
iam Styga et aeternas intrarat mente tenebras
(nam Fabium auxiliumque viri sperare pudebat)
cum senior, gemino complexus proelia cornu,
ulteriore ligat Poenorum terga corona
et modo claudentes aciem nunc, extima cingens, 590
clausos ipse tenet.   maiorem surgere in arma
maioremque dedit cerni Tirynthius : altae
scintillant cristae et, mirum, velocibus ingens
per subitum membris venit vigor ; ingerit hastas
aversumque premit telorum nubibus hostem.   595
qualis post iuvenem, nondum subeunte senecta,
rector erat Pylius bellis aetate secunda.

Inde ruens Thurin et Buten et Narin et Arsen
dat leto fisumque manus conferre Mahalcen,
cui decus insigne et quaesitum cuspide nomen. 600
tum Garadum largumque comae prosternit Adherben
et geminas acies superantem vertice Thulin,
qui summas alto prensabat in aggere pinnas.

---

^a *i.e.* Minucius had given himself up for lost.
^b Nestor, the aged hero of the Homeric epic.

the conquest of Africa and the fall of Carthage—could confer on Fabius such glory as he reaped from the wrong done him by envy ; for he conquered at the same time every obstacle—danger and Hannibal, resentment and jealousy—and he trod underfoot calumny and Fortune together.

When Hannibal saw the Romans rushing down from their high rampart, his ardour was shaken : he groaned, and his sanguine hopes of a crushing victory sank in a moment. For he had surrounded the army of Minucius with a serried ring of soldiers and hoped to destroy them by a shower of missiles from every side. And now the Roman general in that ill-judged battle had already in thought crossed the Styx to the place of eternal darkness ^a—for he was ashamed to look to Fabius for help—when the Dictator, surrounding the battle-field with his two flanks, hemmed in the Carthaginian rear with an outer circle, and now, from his outside position, blockaded those who had lately been blockaders. By grace of Hercules he seemed to rise higher as he fought and to grow in stature. The plume of his helmet flashed on high ; and his frame was suddenly endued with marvellous strength and activity ; he hurled spear after spear and assailed the enemy in their rear with clouds of darts. Thus the King of Pylus ^b fought in his second stage of life, when youth was gone and old age not yet come.

On he rushed and slew Thuris and Butes, Naris and Arses, and Mahalces who had dared to face him, a famous warrior who had gained glory by his spear. Then he laid low Garadus and Adherbes of the long hair, and Thulis who towered above both armies and could grasp the topmost battlements on a lofty wall.

eminus hos : gladio Sapharum gladioque Monaesum
et Morinum pugnas aeris stridore cientem,   605
dexteriore gena cui sedit letifer ictus,
perque tubam fixae decurrens vulnere malae,
extremo fluxit propulsus murmure sanguis.
proximus huic iaculo Nasamonius occidit Idmon.
namque super tepido lapsantem sanguine et aegra
lubrica nitentem nequicquam evadere planta   611
impacto prosternit equo trepideque levantem
membra afflicta solo pressa violentius hasta
implicuit terrae telumque in caede reliquit.
haeret humi cornus motu tremefacta iacentis   615
et campo servat mandatum affixa cadaver.

    Necnon exemplo laudis furiata iuventus,
Sullaeque Crassique simul iunctusque Metello
Furnius ac melior dextrae Torquatus, inibant
proelia et unanimi vel morte emisse volebant   620
spectari Fabio.   miser hinc vestigia retro
dum rapit et molem subducto corpore vitat
intorti Bibulus saxi atque in terga refertur,
strage super lapsus socium, qua fibula morsus
loricae crebro laxata resolverat ictu,   625
accepit lateri penitusque in viscera adegit,
exstabat fixo quod forte cadavere, ferrum.
heu sortem necis ! evasit Garamantica tela
Marmaridumque manus, ut inerti cuspide fusus
occideret, telo non in sua vulnera misso.   630
volvitur exanimis, turpatque decora iuventa

These he slew from a distance; and his sword accounted for Sapharus and Monaesus, and for Morinus, as he stirred the hearts of the combatants with the trumpet's blare; the fatal blow struck his right cheek, and the blood, running down through the trumpet from the wound in his face, flowed forth, expelled by his dying breath. Close by him fell Idmon, a Nasamonian, slain by a javelin. For as he slipped on the warm blood and was vainly striving to plant his unsteady feet on firm ground, the Dictator's horse struck him down; and, when he tried in haste to lift his bruised limbs from the ground, Fabius pinned him to the earth by a strong thrust of his spear and left the weapon in the deadly wound. Sticking in the ground, the spear quivered as the dying man moved, and kept guard on the plain over the corpse consigned to it.

This glorious example inflamed the younger men: a Sulla and a Crassus with him, Furnius and his comrade Metellus, and Torquatus, a more practised warrior, entered the battle; and all alike were willing even to die, if they might have the eyes of Fabius upon them. Unhappy Bibulus was stepping quickly backwards and swerving aside, to elude a huge stone hurled at him, when he stumbled on a heap of Roman corpses in his movement to the rear; and an iron point, which happened to project from a dead body, entered his side where many a blow had loosened the clasps of the buckle on his corslet; and his fall drove the weapon home to his vitals. Alas, for so strange a death! He was spared by the missiles of the Garamantes and the swords of the Marmaridae, in order to be laid low by a senseless weapon—a weapon aimed at a different victim. Down he fell in death; a

ora novus pallor ; membris dimissa solutis
arma fluunt, erratque niger per lumina somnus.
   Venerat ad bellum Tyria Sidone, nepotum
excitus prece, et auxilio socia arma ferebat,   635
Eoa tumidus pharetrati militis ala,
gens Cadmi, Cleadas ; fulva cui plurima passim
casside et aurato fulgebat gemma monili.
qualis ubi Oceani renovatus Lucifer unda
laudatur Veneri et certat maioribus astris.   640
ostro ipse ac sonipes ostro totumque per agmen
purpura Agenoreis saturata micabat aënis.
hic avidum pugnae et tam clarum excidere nomen
Brutum exoptantem, varie nunc laevus in orbem,
nunc dexter levibus flexo per devia gyris   645
ludificatus equo, volucrem post terga sagittam
fundit, Achaemenio detractans proelia ritu.
nec damnata manus, medio sed, flebile, mento
armigeri Cascae penetrabilis haesit harundo,
obliquumque secans surrecta cuspide vulnus   650
umenti ferrum admovit tepefacta palato.
at Brutus, diro casu turbatus amici,
ausum multa virum et spargentem in vulnera saevos
fraude fugae calamos, iam nullis cursibus instat
prendere cornipedis, sed totam pectoris iram   655
mandat atrox hastae telumque volatile nodo
excutit, et summum, qua laxa monilia crebro
nudabant versu, tramittit cuspide pectus.

---

   ^a The planet Venus, called by the Romans Lucifer as a
morning star, and Hesperus as an evening star.
   ^b The purple dye of Sidon, made from the *murex* or purple-
fish, was the most famous in the ancient world.

strange pallor disfigured his youthful beauty; his shield fell from his loosened grasp, and the sleep of darkness stole over his eyes.

Cleadas, a descendant of Cadmus, had come to the wars from Tyrian Sidon, summoned by the entreaty of the daughter-city, and fought side by side with the Carthaginians, proud of his troop of archers from the East; jewels sparkled all over his golden helmet and golden collar. So sparkles Lucifer,[a] when, refreshed by the waters of Ocean, he is approved by Venus and outshines the greater stars. Purple was his dress, and purple the housings of his steed; and on all his company glittered the precious dye that is steeped in the vats of Sidon.[b] Brutus, eager for the fray, was burning to blot out such a famous name; but Cleadas mocked him, wheeling his horse lightly round in mazy circles, now to the right and now to the left; and then he shot a winged arrow over his shoulder, refusing in Persian[c] fashion to face his foe. Nor did he fail to hit: the keen arrow lodged, alas, right in the chin of Casca, the squire of Brutus; warmed with blood the point passed upwards, leaving a jagged wound, and forced the steel into the moist palate. But Brutus, troubled by the grievous plight of his friend, no longer tried to ride down Cleadas, as he ranged at large and sent out a shower of deadly arrows while pretending flight: he entrusted to his spear all the fierce anger of his heart, and launched the flying weapon with a thong[d]; and the point pierced his breast, where the collar with its row of pendants hung loose and left the neck exposed.

[c] The Parthian archers are meant: it was their regular practice to shoot their arrows while retreating.

[d] See note to i. 318.

labitur intento cornu transfossus, et una
arcum laeva cadens dimisit, dextra sagittam.　　660
　At non tam tristi sortitus proelia Marte
Phoebei Soractis honor Carmelus agebat ;
sanguine quippe suo iam Bagrada tinxerat ensem,
dux rectorque Nubae populi ; iam fusus eidem
Zeusis, Amyclaei stirps impacata Phalanti,　　665
quem tulerat mater claro Phoenissa Laconi.
talia dum metuit, nec pugnae fisus in hoste
tam rapido nec deinde fugae, suadente pavore,
per dumos miser in vicina cacumina quercus
repserat atque alta sese occultabat in umbra　　670
Hampsicus, insistens tremulis sub pondere ramis.
hunc longa multa orantem Carmelus et altos
mutantem saltu ramos transverberat hasta ;
ut, qui viscata populatur harundine lucos,
dum nemoris celsi procera cacumina sensim　　675
substructa certat tacitus contingere meta,
sublimem calamo sequitur crescente volucrem.
effudit vitam, atque alte manante cruore
membra pependerunt curvato exsanguia ramo.
　Iamque in palantes ac versos terga feroces　　680
pugnabant Itali, subitus cum mole pavenda
terrificis Maurus prorumpit Tunger in armis.
nigra viro membra, et furvi iuga celsa trahebant
cornipedes, totusque novae formidinis arte
concolor aequabat liventia currus equorum　　685
terga ; nec erectis similes imponere cristis
cessarat pennas, aterque tegebat amictus.

---

　　[a] See note to v. 175.　　　　[b] The founder of Tarentum.
　　[c] The ancient bird-catcher used a cane-rod tipped with
bird-lime and made in separate joints, like our fishing-rods,
so that he could lengthen it out by degrees till it reached the
bird.

Cleadas' bow was bent when he was laid low by the spear ; the bow slipped from his left hand and the arrow from his right, as down he fell.

But better fortune in battle befell Carmelus, the pride of Soracte *a* sacred to Apollo. For he had already dyed his sword with the blood of Bagrada, lord and leader of a Nubian people ; and he had slain Zeusis also, a warlike son of Spartan Phalantus, *b* whom a Punic mother had borne to a famous Lacedaemonian. Then fearing the same fate, Hampsicus had not confidence to engage so active a foe, nor even to fly : urged by terror, the poor wretch had passed through thickets and climbed to the top of a neighbouring oak, where he hid in the thick leafage, standing on boughs that shook under his weight. But Carmelus ran him through with his long spear, as he begged hard for mercy and sprang from branch to branch overhead. Thus the fowler who dispeoples the grove with his cane-rod tipped with birdlime, pursues the bird over his head with a lengthening reed, and silently tries to reach at last the topmost branches by adding a joint to his tapering rod. *c* Hampsicus poured forth his life ; his blood streamed down from above, and his lifeless limbs bent down the branch on which they hung.

And now the Romans were fighting fiercely against the straggling and fleeing foe, when suddenly Tunger, the Moor, a terrible giant, rushed forward to battle. His body was black, and his lofty chariot was drawn by black horses ; and the chariot — a new device to strike terror—was the same colour all over as the dusky backs of the steeds ; and on his lofty crest he had been careful to set a plume of the same hue ; and the garment he wore was black also.

ceu quondam aeternae regnator noctis, ad imos
cum fugeret thalamos, Hennaea virgine rapta,
egit nigrantem Stygia caligine currum. 690
at Cato, tum prima sparsus lanugine malas,
quod peperere decus Circaeo Tuscula dorso
moenia, Laërtae quondam regnata nepoti,
quamquam tardatos turbata fronte Latinos
collegisse gradum videt, imperterritus ipse 695
ferrata calce atque effusa largus habena
cunctantem impellebat equum. negat obvius ire
et trepidat cassa sonipes exterritus umbra.
tum celer in pugnam dorso delatus ab alto
alipedem planta currum premit atque volanti 700
assilit a tergo : cecidere et lora repente
et stimuli ; ferrumque super cervice tremiscens
palluit infelix subducto sanguine Maurus.
ora rapit gladio praefixaque cuspide portat.
    At saevo Mavorte ferox perrumpit anhelum 705
dictator cum caede globum. miserabile visu,
vulneribus fessum ac multo labente cruore
ductorem cernit suprema ac foeda precantem.
manavere genis lacrimae, clipeoque paventem
protegit et natum stimulans : " fortissime, labem 710
hanc pellamus," ait, " Poenoque ob mitia facta,
quod nullos nostris ignes disperserit arvis,
dignum expendamus pretium." tunc, arte paterna
ac stimulis gaudens, iuvenis circumdata Poenum

---

    [a] Pluto (or Dis), when he carried off Proserpina from
Henna, to be his queen in the nether world, came up to earth
in a black chariot.
    [b] The famous Censor, M. Porcius Cato : born in 234 B.C.,
he was now seventeen years old.
    [c] Telegonus, a son of Ulysses and Circe, and therefore

So the Ruler of the eternal darkness, when he carried off the maiden from Henna long ago and hastened to their bridal chamber in the lower world, drove a chariot black with the darkness of Hell.[a] But Cato,[b] on whose cheeks the down of manhood was just appearing, was undismayed. He was the pride of his native Tusculum, which lies on Circe's height and was once ruled by the grandson of Laërtes.[c] Though he saw that the Roman van was checked and had withdrawn in confusion, he drove on his hesitating steed with iron heel and freely loosened rein. The horse refused to go forward and stood trembling, terrified by the harmless shadow that Tunger cast. Then quickly dismounting from his tall horse to fight, he followed the flying chariot on foot, and sprang upon it from behind as it sped on. Reins and whip were dropped in a moment; and the ill-fated Moor lost courage and turned pale, dreading the sword that hung over his neck. Cato cut off his head with the sword and carried it away, stuck on the point of his spear.

Meanwhile the Dictator, exulting in fierce battle, burst his way through a mass of exhausted men, and carried death with him. Then he saw a pitiful sight —Minucius weary, wounded, and bleeding, and asking for a shameful death. Fabius shed tears, and protected the frightened general with his shield. Then he encouraged his son to battle thus : " Brave son, let us wipe off the stain upon us and repay Hannibal in full for his kind treatment in dropping no fire upon our fields." [d] Then, rejoicing in the encouragement of his wise father, the young man drove

grandson of Laërtes, was the legendary founder of Tusculum (now Frascati). $\qquad$ [d] See ll. 260 foll.

agmina deturbat gladio campumque relaxat,   715
donec Sidonius decederet aequore ductor ;
ceu, stimulante fame, rapuit cum Martius agnum
averso pastore lupus fetumque trementem
ore tenet presso ; tum, si vestigia cursu
auditis celeret balatibus obvia pastor,   720
iam sibimet metuens, spirantem dentibus imis
reiectat praedam et vacuo fugit aeger hiatu.
tum demum, Tyrium quas circumfuderat atra
tempestas, Stygiae tandem fugere tenebrae.
torpebant dextrae, et sese meruisse negabant   725
servari, subitisque bonis mens aegra natabat.
ut, qui collapsa pressi iacuere ruina,
eruta cum subito membra et nox atra recessit,
conivent solemque pavent agnoscere visu.

   Quis actis, senior, numerato milite laetus,   730
colles et tuto repetebat in aggere castra.
ecce autem e media iam morte renata iuventus,
clamorem tollens ad sidera et ordine longo
ibat ovans Fabiumque decus Fabiumque salutem
certatim et magna memorabant voce parentem.   735
tum, qui partitis dissederat ante maniplis :
" sancte," ait, " o genitor, revocato ad lucis honorem
si fas vera queri, cur nobis castra virosque
dividere est licitum ? patiens cur arma dedisti,
quae solus rexisse vales ? hoc munere lapsi   740
aeternas multo cum sanguine vidimus umbras.

---

   [a] They were unable at first to use their hands in greeting
their deliverer.   [b] Minucius.

off with the sword the surrounding ranks of Carthage, and cleared the plain ; and Hannibal at last withdrew from the field. So, when the shepherd's back is turned, the wolf that Mars loves, urged by hunger, snatches up a lamb and holds the frightened young-ling fast in its jaws ; but, if the shepherd hears a bleating and runs to face the wolf, then it fears for itself, and casts up the still breathing prey from between its teeth, and makes off in wrath with empty jaws. Not till then was the Stygian darkness, with which the black cloud of the Carthaginian attack had surrounded the army of Minucius, at last dispelled. Their hands were numbed ;[a] they said they were not worthy to be rescued ; they were stunned and confused by sudden good fortune. Even so, men buried beneath a falling house, when dug out and suddenly released from darkness, blink with their eyes and fear to see the sun again.

When all this was done, Fabius numbered his army and was glad, and marched back to the heights where they were safe in camp. But, behold, the soldiers, recalled to life from the very jaws of death, raised a shout to the sky and marched triumphantly in long procession, all with one acclaim loudly hailing Fabius as their glory, Fabius as their saviour, and Fabius as their father. Then the general[b] who had lately parted from him, taking half the army with him, spoke thus : " O worshipful father, if I, thus restored to the blessing of light, may make a just complaint, why were we permitted to have separate camps and separate armies ? Why did you submit to hand over a force which you alone are fit to command ? To that generous act we owed our fall and looked on the darkness of death, and much blood was spilt.

ocius huc aquilas servataque signa referte.
hic patria est, murique urbis stant pectore in uno.
tuque dolos, Poene, atque astus tandem exue notos ;
cum solo tibi iam Fabio sunt bella gerenda."   745
   Haec ubi dicta dedit, mille hinc, venerabile visu,
caespite de viridi surgunt properantibus arae.
nec prius aut epulas aut munera grata Lyaei
fas cuiquam tetigisse fuit, quam multa precatus
in mensam Fabio sacrum libavit honorem.   750

---

^a Wine.

Make haste, ye soldiers, to bring back hither the eagles and standards which Fabius saved! Fabius is our country, and the walls of Rome rest on the shoulders of a single man! And you, Hannibal, have done with your stale tricks and stratagems; in future you have to fight Fabius and him alone."

When Minucius had spoken thus, an imposing sight then was seen—a thousand altars of green turf raised in haste; and no man dared to touch food or the pleasant gift of Lyaeus,[a] till he had offered many a prayer and poured out wine upon the board in honour of Fabius.

LIBER OCTAVUS

ARGUMENT

. *Hannibal's anxiety (1-24). Juno sends Anna to comfort him : Anna, the sister of Dido, is now a nymph of the river Numicius : she tells her own history, and encourages Hannibal by foretelling the battle of Cannae (25-241). C. Terentius Varro is elected consul at Rome : his boastful*

Primus Agenoridum cedentia terga videre
Aeneadis dederat Fabius. Romana parentem
solum castra vocant, solum vocat Hannibal hostem
impatiensque morae fremit : ut sit copia Martis,
expectanda viri fata optandumque sub armis   5
Parcarum auxilium ; namque, hac spirante senecta,
nequicquam sese Latium sperare cruorem.
iam vero concors miles signisque relatis
indivisus honos, iterumque et rursus eidem
soli obluctandum Fabio, maioribus aegrum   10
angebant curis.   lentando fervida bella
dictator cum multa adeo, tum miles egenus
cunctarum ut rerum Tyrius foret, arte sedendi
egerat ; et, quamquam finis pugnaque manuque
hauddum partus erat, iam bello vicerat hostem.   15
quin etiam ingenio fluxi, sed prima feroces,
vaniloquum Celtae genus ac mutabile mentis,

BOOK VIII

FABIUS had been the first to show the Romans the
retreating backs of the Carthaginians. Him alone his
soldiers called their father, and him alone Hannibal
called his foe. The Carthaginian leader raged,
impatient of delay : for a chance of fighting, he must
wait for the death of Fabius and summon the Fates
as allies in war ; for, so long as that old man lived, he
had no hope of shedding Italian blood. Further, the
united army, serving with standards restored under
a single commander, and the necessity of wrestling
again and again with Fabius alone—all this weighed
still more heavily on his anxious spirit. By skilful
inaction and by slackening the pace of war, the
Dictator had effected much ; and, above all, he
had deprived the Tyrian army of all supplies ; and,
though a fight to a finish was still in the future, he
was already the master of the foe. Moreover, the
Gauls, a boastful and unstable people, bold at the
start but infirm of purpose, were turning their eyes

393

respectare domos ; maerebant caede sine ulla
(insolitum sibi) bella geri, siccasque cruore
inter tela siti Mavortis hebescere dextras.   20
his super internae labes et civica vulnus
invidia augebant : laevus conatibus Hannon
ductoris non ulla domo summittere patres
auxilia aut ullis opibus iuvisse sinebat.

   Quis lacerum curis et rerum extrema paventem 25
ad spes armorum et furialia vota reducit
praescia Cannarum Iuno atque elata futuris.
namque hac accitam stagnis Laurentibus Annam
affatur voce et blandis hortatibus implet :
" sanguine cognato iuvenis tibi, diva, laborat   30
Hannibal, a vestro nomen memorabile Belo.
perge, age et insanos curarum comprime fluctus.
excute sollicito Fabium.   sola illa Latinos
sub iuga mittendi mora iam discingitur armis :
cum Varrone manus et cum Varrone serenda   35
proelia, nec desit fatis ad signa movenda.
ipsa adero.   tendat iamdudum in Iapyga campum.
huc Trebiae rursum et Thrasymenni fata sequentur."

   Tum diva, indigetis castis contermina lucis :
" haud," inquit, " tua ius nobis praecepta morari. 40
sit fas, sit tantum, quaeso, retinere favorem

---

   [a] See ii. 276 foll.
   [b] The Numicius was a little river which flowed into the
sea between Lavinium and Ardea.   Anna Perenna, a
tutelary nymph of the river, was identified by the Roman
poets with Anna, the sister of Dido.
   [c] C. Terentius Varro, the popular leader of the day, was
elected consul for 216 B.C. together with L. Aemilius Paulus.

homewards : unaccustomed to a bloodless campaign,
they grieved that their hands, unwetted with gore in
time of war, should be enfeebled by thirst for conflict.
Nor was this all : his troubles were increased by
dangers at home—the jealousy of his fellow-citizens
and the opposition of Hanno [a] to the enterprise ; for
Hanno would not suffer their senate to send reinforce-
ments or supplies of any kind.

Though tortured by these anxieties and fearing the
worst, Hannibal regained hope of victory and renewed
his insane ambition, by help of Juno ; the goddess
foresaw the field of Cannae, and coming events filled
her with pride. Summoning Anna from the river
of Laurentum [b] she thus addressed her, pressing her
with flattering appeal : " Goddess, a youth akin to
you is in sore straits—even Hannibal, a famous name,
descended from Belus the Phoenician. Arise, hasten,
and assuage his raging sea of troubles. Dislodge
Fabius from his mind. Fabius alone stands between
the Romans and subjugation ; but he is now putting
off his armour, and Hannibal will have to fight
against Varro [c] and meet Varro in battle. Let him
move his standards forward and take advantage of
Fortune. I myself shall be there. Let him march
instantly to the plain of Iapygia.[d] The doom of
the Trebia and Lake Trasimene shall be repeated
there."

Then the nymph, who dwells near the sacred grove
of the native god,[e] thus replied : " It is my duty to
do your bidding without delay. One thing only I
beg : suffer me to keep the goodwill of my former

[d] Apulia : see note to iii. 707.

[e] Aeneas : he was believed to have been drowned in the
river Numicius and was worshipped in a temple there.

antiquae patriae mandataque magna sororis,
quamquam inter Latios Annae stet numen honores."
  Multa retro rerum iacet atque ambagibus aevi
obtegitur densa caligine mersa vetustas,   45
cur Sarrana dicent Oenotri numina templo,
regnisque Aeneadum germana colatur Elissae.
sed pressis stringam revocatam ab origine famam
narrandi metis breviterque antiqua revolvam.
  Iliaco postquam deserta est hospite Dido,   50
et spes abruptae, mediam in penetralibus atram
festinat furibunda pyram : tum corripit ensem
certa necis, profugi donum exitiale mariti.
despectus taedae regnis se imponit Iarbas,
et tepido fugit Anna rogo : quis rebus egenis   55
ferret opem, Nomadum late terrente tyranno ?
Battus Cyrenen molli tum forte fovebat
imperio, mitis Battus lacrimasque dedisse
casibus humanis facilis.   qui, supplice visa,
intremuit regum eventus dextramque tetendit.   60
atque ea, dum flavas bis tondet messor aristas,
servata interea sedes ; nec longius uti
his opibus Battoque fuit ; nam ferre per aequor
exitium miserae iam Pygmaliona docebat.
ergo agitur pelago, divis inimica sibique,   65
quod se non dederit comitem in suprema sorori,
donec iactatam laceris, miserabile, velis
fatalis turbo in Laurentes expulit oras.
non caeli, non illa soli, non gnara colentum

---

  a Dido bequeathed vengeance against Rome.
  b Aeneas.   *c* An African prince.
        d She stayed there two years.
            e See note to i. 21.

country and to carry out the solemn behests of my
sister,[a] although the deity of Anna is among those
honoured by the Romans."

Far back in history, and hidden in deep darkness
by the uncertain report of antiquity, lies the answer
to this question : why should the Italians consecrate
a temple to a Phoenician deity, and why should Dido's
sister be worshipped in the country of the Aeneadae ?
But I shall repeat the legend from the beginning,
keeping my tale within strict limits, and briefly re-
calling the past.

When Dido was deserted by her Trojan guest [b] and
hope was utterly dead, she hastened in frenzy to
the fatal pyre within the palace. Then, resolved
on death, she seized the sword which her runagate
husband had given her for her destruction. Iarbas,[c]
whose hand she had refused in marriage, usurped the
throne, and Anna fled before her sister's pyre was
cold. Who would help her in her need, when that
king of the Numidians spread terror far and wide ?
It chanced that Battus then ruled Cyrene with gentle
sway—Battus, a kindly man and ready to give a tear
to human suffering. When he saw the suppliant, he
trembled at the thought of what princes may suffer,
and stretched forth his hand to her. And there she
stayed for a time, till the golden ears were twice cut
down by the reapers.[d] Then she could no longer
avail herself of Battus and his friendship ; for he
told her that Pygmalion [e] was sailing thither, intent
on her destruction. So she was driven to the sea,
angry with Heaven, and with herself for not dying
together with her sister, and was pitifully tossed with
tattered sails, till at last a fateful storm wrecked her
upon the coast of Laurentum. A stranger to that

Sidonis in Latia trepidabat naufraga terra.   70
ecce autem Aeneas, sacro comitatus Iulo,
iam regni compos, noto sese ore ferebat.
qui terrae defixam oculos et multa timentem
ac deinde allapsam genibus lacrimantis Iuli
attollit mitique manu intra limina ducit.   75
atque ubi iam casus adversorumque pavorem
hospitii lenivit honos, tum discere maesta
exposcit cura letum infelicis Elissae.
cui sic, verba trahens largis cum fletibus, Anna
incipit et blandas addit pro tempore voces :   80
" nate dea, solus regni lucisque fuisti
germanae tu causa meae ; mors testis et ille
(heu cur non idem mihi tum !) rogus.   ora videre
postquam est ereptum miserae tua, litore sedit
interdum, stetit interdum ; ventosque secuta   85
infelix oculis, magno clamore vocabat
Aenean comitemque tuae se imponere solam
orabat paterere rati.   mox turbida anhelum
rettulit in thalamos cursum subitoque tremore
substitit et sacrum timuit tetigisse cubile.   90
inde amens nunc sideream fulgentis Iuli
effigiem fovet amplexu, nunc tota repente
ad vultus conversa tuos, ab imagine pendet
conqueriturque tibi et sperat responsa remitti.
non umquam spem ponit amor.   iam tecta domumque
deserit et rursus portus furibunda revisit,   96
si qui te referant converso flamine venti.
ad magicas etiam fallax atque improba gentis
Massylae levitas descendere compulit artes.
heu sacri vatum errores !   dum numina noctis   100

398

clime and soil and to its inhabitants, the Phoenician
princess was afraid when shipwrecked upon the land
of Italy. But see! Aeneas, having now gained a
kingdom, came with godlike Iulus, and his face she
knew. In great fear she gazed upon the ground and
then knelt down before weeping Iulus; but Aeneas
raised her up and led her gently within the palace.
And when a courteous reception had lightened her
troubles and dispelled her fear of danger, with anxious
sorrow he asked to hear about the death of unhappy
Dido. And Anna thus began, sighing and weeping
abundantly as she spoke, and used soft words too to
suit the occasion: "O goddess-born, my sister's
throne and her life depended upon you alone; bear
witness her death and that funeral-pyre, which would
that I then had shared! When the sight of your face
was taken from her, she sometimes sat, sometimes
stood, on the shore in her misery; watching the
course of the winds, she called Aeneas back with a
great cry, and prayed that you would deign to take
her alone on board your ship. Then in confused
haste she hurried back to her chamber, and suddenly
trembled and stood still, fearing to touch that sacred
couch. Next in her distraction, she first clasps the
beauteous image of radiant Iulus, and then, quickly
turning her whole mind to your likeness, hangs upon
your image, making her plaint to you and hoping for
an answer. Love never abandons hope. Now she
leaves the palace and goes back in frenzy to the
harbour, in case some wind may shift its course and
blow you back. She stooped even to magic arts,
driven to this by the wicked deceitfulness and folly of
the Massylian race. But, out upon wizards and their
accursed delusions! While they called up the infernal

eliciunt spondentque novis medicamina curis
(quod vidi decepta nefas !) congessit in atram
cuncta tui monumenta pyram et non prospera dona.''
   Tunc sic Aeneas dulci repetitus amore :
'' tellurem hanc iuro, vota inter nostra frequenter
auditam vobis ; iuro caput, Anna, tibique   106
germanaeque tuae dilectum mitis Iuli,
respiciens aegerque animi tum regna reliqui
vestra, nec abscessem thalamo, ni magna minatus
meque sua ratibus dextra imposuisset et alto   110
egisset rapidis classem Cyllenius Euris.
sed cur (heu seri monitus !) cur tempore tali
incustodito saevire dedistis amori ? ''
   Contra sic infit, volvens vix murmur anhelum
inter singultus labrisque trementibus Anna :   115
'' nigro forte Iovi, cui tertia regna laborant,
atque atri sociae thalami nova sacra parabam,
quis aegram mentem et trepidantia corda levaret
infelix germana tori, furvasque trahebam
ipsa manu, properans ad visa pianda, bidentes ; 120
namque super somno dirus me impleverat horror :
terque suam Dido, ter cum clamore vocarat
et laeta exultans ostenderat ora Sychaeus.
quae dum abigo menti et, sub lucem ut visa secundent,
oro caelicolas ac vivo purgor in amni,   125
illa, cito passu pervecta ad litora, mutae
oscula, qua steteras, bis terque infixit harenae ;
deinde amplexa sinu late vestigia fovit,
ceu cinerem orbatae pressant ad pectora matres.

---

   ^a See note to iii. 168.
   ^b Jupiter was king of heaven and earth, Neptune of the sea,
and Pluto of the nether world.   ^c Proserpina.
   ^d The dead husband of Dido.
   ^e A common ceremony of purification.

gods and promised relief for her strange trouble—
what a dreadful sight did I, who believed them,
witness !—she heaped upon a fatal pyre all memorials
of you and your ill-starred gifts."

Then Aeneas answered, revisited by passion with
all its sweetness : " I swear by this land, to which
you both often heard me appeal when we exchanged
vows ; I swear by the head of gentle Iulus, once so
dear to you and to your sister : in sorrow and with a
longing look behind I left your kingdom ; nor would
I have broken off the marriage, had not the god of
Cyllene,[a] with dreadful threats, set me on board
with his own hand, and driven the fleet out to sea
with swift winds. But why—too late, alas, is my
warning—why at such a moment did ye allow passion
to run wild unwatched ? "

Anna thus replied with quivering lips and in a
breathless voice between her sobs : " I chanced to
be preparing strange offerings for the sable King
whom the third realm obeys,[b] and for the partner of
his gloomy bed,[c] in order to relieve my love-lorn sister
of her sorrow and unrest ; and I was myself bringing
black-fleeced sheep, and making haste, to avert an
evil dream. For, in my sleep, an awful fear had filled
my heart ; and thrice, thrice over with a loud cry,
had Sychaeus [d] claimed Dido as his own and shown
a face of pride and joy. I drove this from my
thoughts and prayed to the gods to give a favourable
turn to the dream, when day came ; and I bathed in
a running stream.[e] Meanwhile, Dido went quickly
to the beach and kissed many times the dumb sand
where you had stood ; and then she fondly embraced
all your foot-prints, even as a mother strains to her
breast the ashes of a lost son. Then she rushed back

tum rapido praeceps cursu resolutaque crinem   130
evasit propere in celsam, quam struxerat ante
magna mole, pyram ; cuius de sede dabatur
cernere cuncta freta et totam Carthaginis urbem.
hic Phrygiam vestem et bacatum induta monile,
postquam illum infelix hausit, quo munera primum
sunt conspecta, diem et convivia mente reduxit   136
festasque adventu mensas teque ordine Troiae
narrantem longos, se pervigilante, labores,
in portus amens rorantia lumina flexit :
' di longae noctis, quorum iam numina nobis   140
mors instans maiora facit, precor,' inquit, ' adeste
et placidi victos ardore admittite manes.
Aeneae coniux, Veneris nurus, ulta maritum,
[1]vidi constructas nostrae Carthaginis arces.
nunc ad vos magni descendet corporis umbra.   145
me quoque fors dulci quondam vir notus amore
expectat, curas cupiens aequare priores.'
haec dicens ensem media in praecordia adegit,
ensem Dardanii quaesitum in pignus amoris.
viderunt comites tristique per atria planctu   150
concurrunt ; magnis resonant ululatibus aedes.
accepi infelix dirisque exterrita fatis,
ora manu lacerans, lymphato regia cursu
tecta peto celsosque gradus evadere nitor.
ter diro fueram conata incumbere ferro,   155
ter cecidi exanimae membris revoluta sororis.
iamque ferebatur vicina per oppida rumor :
arma parant Nomadum proceres et saevus Iarbas.   157 a

---

[1] *For the lacuna that begins here see Introd. p. xvii.*

headlong with hair unbound and came to the great high pyre she had raised already ; and from its site all the sea was visible and the whole city of Carthage. Next she put on the robe from Troy and the necklace of pearls ; she drank in, poor wretch, the memory of that day when she first saw those gifts ; she recalled the banquet and the feast that greeted your arrival, when you told in order the long agony of Troy, and she sat late to hear you. Then in distraction she turned her weeping eyes to the harbour. ' Ye gods of endless night,' she cried, ' whose power seems greater to one at the point of death, help me, I pray, and give a kindly welcome to a spirit that love has conquered. The wife of Aeneas, the daughter-in-law of Venus, I avenged my husband,[a] I saw the towers of my city Carthage rise ; and now the shade of a great queen shall go down to your domain. Perhaps my husband, whose love was sweet to me long ago, is waiting for me there, eager to love me no less than before.' Thus speaking she drove a sword into the centre of her breast—the sword which she had received as a pledge of the Trojan's love. Her attendants saw it, and rushed together through the halls with mourning and beating of breasts ; the palace resounded with their loud cries. I, unhappy, heard the tidings ; terror-stricken by that dreadful death, I tore my cheeks with my nails, as I rushed in frenzy to the palace and struggled to climb the lofty steps. Thrice I strove to throw myself on the accursed sword, and thrice I fell prostrate on the body of my dead sister. Soon the rumour spread through the neighbouring cities ; the Numidian chiefs and fierce Iarbas [b] prepared for war ; and I, driven by

[a] Sychaeus.   [b] See l. 54.

tum Cyrenaeam fatis agitantibus urbem
devenio ; hinc vestris pelagi vis appulit oris."
   Motus erat placidumque animum mentemque
     quietam   160
Troius in miseram rector susceperat Annam.
iamque omnes luctus omnesque e pectore curas
dispulerat, Phrygiis nec iam amplius advena tectis
illa videbatur.   tacito nox atra sopore
cuncta per et terras et lati stagna profundi   165
condiderat, tristi cum Dido aegerrima vultu
has visa in somnis germanae effundere voces :
" his, soror, in tectis longae indulgere quieti,
heu nimium secura, potes ? nec, quae tibi fraudes
tendantur, quae circumstent discrimina, cernis ?   170
ac nondum nostro infaustos generique soloque
Laomedonteae noscis telluris alumnos ?
dum caelum rapida stellas vertigine volvet,
lunaque fraterno lustrabit lumine terras,
pax nulla Aeneadas inter Tyriosque manebit.   175
surge, age, iam tacitas suspecta Lavinia fraudes
molitur dirumque nefas sub corde volutat.
praeterea (ne falsa putes haec fingere somnum)
haud procul hinc parvo descendens fonte Numicus
labitur et leni per valles volvitur amne.   180
huc rapies, germana, viam tutosque receptus.
te sacra excipient hilares in flumina Nymphae,
aeternumque Italis numen celebrabere in oris."
sic fata in tenuem Phoenissa evanuit auram.
   Anna novis somno excutitur perterrita visis,   185
itque timor totos gelido sudore per artus.

---

^a The Trojans : Laomedon was a king of Troy, and the
father of Priam.

fate, came to the city of Cyrene; and at last the violence of the sea brought me to your coast."

Aeneas was touched: he had admitted to his heart a gentle and kindly feeling towards Anna in her troubles. Soon she had put away all grief and sorrow from her heart, and she no longer seemed a stranger in the palace of the Trojan. When black night had wrapped all things in silent sleep, over all the earth and the still expanse of sea, she dreamed that her sister, Dido, with a face of sorrow and utmost grief, spoke to her thus: "Sister, too heedless sister, how can you bear to sleep long under this roof? Are you blind to the snares laid for you and the dangers that surround you? Do you not yet understand that the people of Laomedon *a* bring doom upon our nation and our land? As long as the sky makes the stars revolve with rapid course, and the moon lights up the earth with her brother's radiance, no lasting peace shall there be between the Aeneadae and the men of Tyre. Rise in haste; I distrust Lavinia *b*—already she is laying snares in secret, and ponders some horrible outrage. Further—nor deem this message the idle coinage of sleep — not far from here the river Numicus *c* flows down from a little spring and runs with gentle current through the valleys. Hasten, sister, to a harbour of safety there. The Nymphs will gladly admit you to their sacred stream; and your deity shall be for ever honoured in the land of Italy." So Dido spoke and vanished into thin air.

Terrified by her strange dream, Anna started up from sleep; and fear covered her limbs with a cold

---

b The wife whom Aeneas had married in Italy: it is implied that she was jealous of Anna and intended to kill her.

c This river was called either Numicus or Numicius.

tunc, ut erat tenui corpus velamine tecta,
prosiluit stratis humilique egressa fenestra
per patulos currit plantis pernicibus agros,
donec harenoso, sic fama, Numicius illam   190
suscepit gremio vitreisque abscondidit antris.
orta dies totum radiis impleverat orbem,
cum nullam Aeneadae thalamis Sidonida nacti
et Rutulum magno errantes clamore per agrum,
vicini ad ripas fluvii manifesta secuntur   195
signa pedum ; dumque inter se mirantur, ab alto
amnis aquas cursumque rapit ; tum sedibus imis
inter caeruleas visa est residere sorores
Sidonis et placido Teucros affarier ore.
ex illo primis anni celebrata diebus   200
per totam Ausoniam venerando numine culta est.

　Hanc postquam in tristes Italum Saturnia pugnas
hortata est, celeri superum petit aethera curru,
optatum Latii tandem potura cruorem.
diva deae parere parat magnumque Libyssae   205
ductorem gentis nulli conspecta petebat.
ille, virum coetu tum forte remotus ab omni,
incertos rerum eventus bellique volutans,
anxia ducebat vigili suspiria corde.[1]
cui dea sic dictis curas solatur amicis :   210
" quid tantum ulterius, rex o fortissime gentis
Sidoniae, ducis cura aegrescente dolorem ?
omnis iam placata tibi manet ira deorum,
omnis Agenoridis rediit favor.　eia, age, segnes
rumpe moras, rape Marmaricas in proelia vires.   215

[1] corde *Bentley* : voce *edd.*

---

[a] They were now on the way to become Romans.

406

sweat. Then, just as she was, with one thin garment to cover her, she sprang from her bed and, climbing out by the low window, ran swiftly over the open fields, until the river Numicius—so the legend runs—received her in his sandy depths and hid her in his crystal grottoes. Dawn had filled the whole world with radiance, when the Aeneadae found that the stranger from Carthage had vanished from her chamber. With loud shouts they went to and fro through the country, and followed the plain footprints to the river-bank. And while they marvelled, one to another, the river stopped the seaward course of its waters ; and then the stranger was seen sitting among her sister Naiads, and she addressed the Trojans *a* with friendly speech. Ever since, Anna's feast has been held on the first days of the year, and she has been worshipped as divine throughout Italy.

When Juno had appealed to Anna to stir up battle and sorrow for Italy, her swift car carried her back to heaven ; she hoped at last to gain her wish and drink the blood of Latium. Anna, obedient to the goddess, made her way in invisible shape to the great leader of the Libyan people. He, as it chanced, had banished all company from him ; he was pondering the uncertain issues of fortune and of war, and sighed in his perplexity, while his mind kept watch. Thus the goddess soothed his troubles with friendly speech : " Mightiest ruler of the Phoenicians, why do you persist in nursing this great grief in sick anxiety ? All the wrath of the gods against you has now been appeased, all their goodwill has come back to the children of Agenor. Rise up, then, without loitering or delay ! Speed on the forces of Marmarica

mutati fasces : iam bellum atque arma senatus
ex inconsulto posuit Tirynthius heros ;
cumque alio tibi Flaminio sunt bella gerenda.
me tibi, ne dubites, summi matrona Tonantis
misit : ego Oenotris aeternum numen in oris   220
concelebror, vestri generata e sanguine Beli.
haud mora sit ; rapido belli rape fulmina cursu,
celsus Iapygios ubi se Garganus in agros
explicat. haud longe tellus ; huc dirige signa."
dixit et in nubes humentia sustulit ora.   225
   Cui dux, promissae revirescens pignore laudis :
" nympha, decus generis, quo non sacratius ullum
numen," ait, " nobis, felix oblata secundes.
ast ego te, compos pugnae, Carthaginis arce
marmoreis sistam templis iuxtaque dicabo   230
aequatam gemino simulacri munere Dido."
haec fatus socios stimulat tumefactus ovantes :
" Pone graves curas tormentaque lenta sedendi,
fatalis Latio miles : placavimus iras
caelicolum ; redeunt divi. finita maligno   235
hinc Fabio imperia et mutatos consule fasces
nuntio. nunc dextras mihi quisque atque illa referto,
quae Marte exclusus promittere magna solebas.
en, numen patrium spondet maiora peractis.
vellantur signa, ac diva ducente petamus   240
infaustum Phrygibus Diomedis nomine campum."

---

^a Fabius, the Dictator.
^b The rash general defeated at Lake Trasimene.
^c See note to iv. 561.
^d She had now become a river-nymph.

to battle! The consuls are changed. By the un-
wisdom of the Senate the heroic scion of Hercules [a]
has laid down his arms, and you have to fight against
a second Flaminius.[b] I was sent to you—doubt it not—
by the consort of the almighty Thunderer. Though
I am honoured in the land of Italy as an immortal
goddess, I was born of the seed of Belus, your ancestor.
Make no delay; launch the thunderbolts of war with
utmost speed, where Mount Garganus [c] sinks down to
the fields of Iapygia; the land is not far distant;
straight to that point send your standards." She
ended, and her watery [d] image rose up to the clouds.

The general, revived by this pledge of glory to
come, addressed her thus: "Nymph, glory of our
nation, as sacred to me as any deity, be propitious
and give a favourable issue to your promises. If I
may fight a battle, I will set your image in a marble
shrine on the citadel of Carthage, and dedicate beside
it an image of Dido, and both shall be honoured
alike." Thus he spoke, and then swollen with pride
encouraged his triumphant comrades. "Soldiers!
messengers of death to Italy! Here is an end to heavy
hearts and the lingering torture of inaction. We
have appeased the anger of the gods, and they turn
again to us. I announce to you that the command of
Fabius, that pettifogger, is now at an end, and that
the rods are borne before a new consul. Now let
each of you renew his pledges to me, and make good
the deeds of valour which you used to promise
when debarred from fighting. See! a goddess of our
country promises a future greater than our past.
Pull up the standards, and let us follow the goddess
to the field where the name of Diomede is of ill omen
to Trojans."

Dumque Arpos tendunt instincti pectora Poeni,
subnixus rapto plebei muneris ostro,
saevit iam rostris Varro, ingentique ruinae
festinans aperire locum, fata admovet urbi.   245
atque illi sine luce genus surdumque parentum
nomen, at immodice vibrabat in ore canoro
lingua procax. hinc auctus opes largusque rapinae,
infima dum vulgi fovet oblatratque senatum,
tantum in quassata bellis caput extulit urbe,   250
momentum ut rerum et fati foret arbiter unus,
quo conservari Latium victore puderet.
hunc Fabios inter sacrataque nomina Marti
Scipiadas interque Iovi spolia alta ferentem
Marcellum fastis labem suffragia caeca   255
addiderant, Cannasque malum exitiale fovebat
ambitus et Graio funestior aequore Campus.
idem, ut turbarum sator atque accendere sollers
invidiam pravusque togae, sic debilis arte
belligera Martemque rudis versare nec ullo   260
spectatus ferro, lingua sperabat adire
ad dextrae decus atque e rostris bella ciebat.
ergo alacer Fabiumque morae increpitare professus,
ad vulgum in patres, ut ovans iam, verba ferebat:
" vos, quorum imperium est, consul praecepta modum-
              que   265
bellandi posco. sedeone an montibus erro,
dum mecum Garamas et adustus corpora Maurus

---

a The city founded by Diomede in Apulia : see note to
iv. 554.
  b The purple-bordered toga of the consul.
  c A register which preserved the names of the consuls and
other high magistrates.
  d See note to i. 133.
  e By bribing the electors who voted in the Field of Mars,
410

Thus encouraged, the Carthaginians made for
Arpi.[a]   Meanwhile Varro, relying on the purple [b] that
he had seized by gift of the people, was already
ranting on the Rostrum, and, by his haste to prepare
the way for a mighty downfall, brought Rome near to
destruction.   His birth was obscure ; the name of his
ancestors was never heard ; but his impudent tongue
wagged unceasingly, and his voice was loud.   Thus he
got wealth, and he was liberal with his plunder ; and
so, by courting the dregs of the people and railing at
the Senate, he rose so high in the war-stricken city
that he alone could turn the scale of events and
settle the course of destiny, though Italy might
blush to owe even victory and safety to such a man.
Blind voters had given to him, that blot upon the
Calendar,[c] a place among such men as Fabius, and the
Scipios, whose names are sacred to Mars, and Mar-
cellus, who presented his glorious spoils to Jupiter.[d]
The holocaust of Cannae was due to bribery, and to
the Field of Mars, more fatal than the field of Dio-
mede.[e]   Also, though a bad citizen, skilful to stir up
trouble and kindle hatred, he was helpless in the field,
unpractised in the conduct of war, and not approved
by any deed of valour ; but he hoped to gain martial
glory by his tongue and sounded the war-cry from the
Rostrum.   Therefore he bestirred himself ; and, pro-
fessing to blame Fabius for delay, he attacked the
Senate in a speech to the people, as if he were already
victorious : " The supreme power is yours," he said,
" and from you I, the consul, ask directions for the
conduct of the war.   Am I to do nothing, or to move
from height to height, while Garamantians and dark-

Varro had been elected consul. The " field of Diomede " is
the battle-field of Cannae.

dividit Italiam ?   an ferro, quo cingitis, utor ?
exaudi, bone dictator, quid Martia plebes
imperitet : pelli Libyas Romamque levari   270
hoste iubent.   num festinant, quos plurima passos
tertius exurit lacrimosis casibus annus ?
ite igitur, capite arma, viri : mora sola triumpho
parvum iter est : quae prima dies ostenderit hostem,
et patrum regna et Poenorum bella resolvet.   275
ite alacres ; Latia devinctum colla catena
Hannibalem Fabio ducam spectante per urbem."

   Haec postquam increpuit, portis arma incitus effert
impellitque moras, veluti cum carcere rupto
auriga indocilis totas effudit habenas   280
et, praeceps trepida pendens in verbera planta,
impar fertur equis ; fumat male concitus axis,
ac frena incerto fluitant discordia curru.
cernebat Paulus (namque huic communia Campus
iura atque arma tulit) labi, mergente sinistro   285
consule, res pessumque dari ; sed mobilis ira est
turbati vulgi, signataque mente cicatrix
undantes aegro frenabat corde dolores.
nam cum perdomita est armis iuvenilibus olim
Illyris ora viri, nigro allatraverat ore   290
victorem invidia et ventis iactarat iniquis.
hinc inerat metus et durae reverentia plebis.
sed genus admotum superis summumque per altos

---

   [a] Fabius.
   [b] L. Aemilius Paulus, Varro's colleague, had been consul in
219 B.C. and had celebrated a triumph for victories in Illyri-
cum ; but he was afterwards prosecuted for embezzlement
and narrowly escaped condemnation : since then he had
lived in retirement.

skinned Moors share Italy with me, or am I to use
the sword which you gird about me ? Listen, O
worthy Dictator,[a] to the order issued by the people
of Mars : this is their demand, that the Libyans be
driven out and Rome relieved of her enemy. Are
they impatient ? No ! They have endured countless
woes, and a third year is now consuming them with its
suffering and sorrow. Rise then and arm, citizens !
A short march is all that divides you from victory.
The first day that reveals the enemy to your view will
end the tyranny of the Senate and the war with
Carthage. Go forward with good courage ; I shall
yet lead Hannibal through the city with Roman chains
about his neck, and Fabius shall look on.''

After this invective he led the army in haste outside
the gates, and swept away all obstacles. So, when
the starting-gate is broken down, the unskilful
charioteer loses all control of the reins : bending for-
ward with unsteady foothold to flog his team, he is
borne on headlong at the mercy of the horses ; the
axles smoke with the excessive speed, and the tangled
reins of the unsteady car swing from side to side.
Paulus,[b] to whom the voters had given equal power
and authority with Varro, saw that the state was
rushing on to ruin, destroyed by the ill-omened consul.
But the anger of a turbulent mob is easily stirred ;
and the scar of an ancient wrong, imprinted on his
memory, checked the wave of resentment in his
troubled breast. For, when formerly as a younger
man he had conquered Illyricum, the foul mouth of
envy had barked at the conqueror and persecuted
him with cruel slander. Hence he feared the people
and bowed before their enmity. Yet his race was
akin to the gods, and he was related to the lords of

413

attingebat avos caelum : numerare parentem
Assaracum retro praestabat Amulius auctor   295
Assaracusque Iovem ; nec, qui spectasset in armis,
abnueret genus.   huic Fabius iam castra petenti :
" si tibi cum Tyrio credis fore maxima bella
ductore (invitus vocem hanc e pectore rumpam)
frustraris, Paule.   Ausonidum te proelia dira   300
teque hostis castris gravior manet, aut ego multo
nequiquam didici casus praenoscere Marte.
spondentem audivi (piget heu taedetque senectae,
si, quas prospicio, restat passura ruinas !)
cum duce tam fausti Martis, qua viderit hora,   305
sumpturum pugnam.   quantum nunc, Paule, supremo
absumus exitio, vocem hanc si consulis ardens
audierit Poenus !   iam latis obvia credo
stat campis acies, expectaturque sub ictu
alter Flaminius.   quantos, insane, ciebis   310
Varro viros, tu (pro superi !) tam pronus in arma !
tu campum noscas ante exploresque trahendo,
qui ritus hostis ?   tu non, quae copia rerum,
quae natura locis, quod sit, rimabere sollers,
armorum genus, et stantem super omnia tela   315
fortunam aspicies.   fer, Paule, indevia recti
pectora ;   cur, uni patriam si affligere fas est,
uni sit servare nefas ?   eget improbus arto
iam victu Libys, et, belli fervore retuso,
laxa fides socium est.   non hic domus hospita tecto
invitat patrio, non fidae moenibus urbes   321
excipiunt renovatque pari se pube iuventus.

---

heaven through his ancestors. For through Amulius, the founder of his line, he could trace descent from Assaracus, and through Assaracus to Jupiter ; and none who saw him fight would dispute his pedigree. Now, when he was going to the camp, Fabius addressed him thus : " Paulus, though I shrink from saying this thing, you are mistaken if you regard Hannibal as your chief opponent. Sore strife with Romans lies ahead of you, and a more grievous foe in your own camp ; or else long experience of war has not taught me to predict disaster. I heard Varro promise—irksome, alas ! and burdensome is my old age, if it lasts on to endure the destruction I foresee—yes, promise that he would fight Hannibal, that favourite of Fortune, the very hour he saw him. How near we are now, Paulus, to utter ruin, if this boast of the consul's comes to the eager ear of Hannibal ! Already, I doubt not, his army is arrayed on the wide plains to meet us, and waiting with uplifted swords for a second Flaminius.[a] What mighty opponents will you rouse, Varro—you, God help us !—in your mad desire for battle ! Are you the man to study the ground beforehand and examine at leisure the ways of the enemy ? You have no skill to investigate his supplies or the strength of his position or his method of warfare ; you will not keep an eye on Fortune which matters more than any weapon. But you, Paulus, keep to the path of duty unswervingly. If a single arm may destroy our country, why should not a single arm preserve it ? Bold Hannibal now lacks food for his army, and his allies are lukewarm and have lost their keenness for battle. No house in Italy offers him the hospitality due from kindred, no loyal cities welcome him, and his army is not renewed with recruits of

415

tertia vix superest, crudo quae venit Hibero,
turba virum.   persta et cauti medicamina belli
lentus ama.   si qua interea irritaverit aura   325
annueritque deus, velox accede secundis."

   Cui breviter maesto consul sic ore vicissim :
" mecum erit haec prorsus pietas, mentemque feremus
in Poenos, invicte, tuam.   nec me unica fallit
cunctandi ratio, qua te grassante senescens   330
Hannibal oppressum vidit considere bellum.
sed quaenam ira deum ?   consul datus alter, opinor,
Ausoniae est, alter Poenis.   trahit omnia secum
et metuit demens, alio ne consule Roma
concidat.   e Tyrio consortem accite senatu,   335
non tam saeva volet.   nullus, qui portet in hostem,
sufficit insano sonipes ;   incedere noctis,
quae tardent cursum, tenebras dolet ; itque superbus
tantum non strictis mucronibus, ulla retardet
ne pugnas mora, dum vagina ducitur ensis.   340
Tarpeiae rupes cognataque sanguine nobis
tecta Iovis, quaeque arce sua nunc stantia linquo
moenia felicis patriae, quocumque vocabit
summa salus, testor, spreto discrimine iturum.
sed si surda mihi pugnabunt castra monenti,   345
haud ego vos ultra, nati, dulcemque morabor
Assaraci de gente domum, similemve videbit
Varroni Paulum redeuntem saucia Roma."

---

^a Rome.
^b He means that in case of defeat he will not return alive.

equal value. Scarce a third part survives of the army that started from the banks of the cold Ebro. Persevere, and keep to the cautious methods that alone can heal the wounds of war. But if meanwhile some favourable turn encourages you and Heaven approves, then be quick to follow up good fortune."

Brief and sad was the reply of Paulus : " I shall surely follow that path of duty, and in your spirit I shall meet the Carthaginians, O undefeated Fabius. And I realize our one resource—the resource of delay, which you used till an enfeebled Hannibal saw the war arrested and crushed. But what means this anger of Heaven ? Of the two consuls one, I believe, is their gift to Rome and the other their gift to Carthage. Varro drags all things in his train, and the madman fears that some other consul than himself may witness the fall of Rome. If a Carthaginian senator were summoned as my colleague, he would be less ruthless in his purpose. No war-horse is swift enough to carry that madman against the enemy ; when the darkness of night comes on, he resents the hindrance to his activity ; he marches proudly on, with swords that are all but drawn, that the drawing of the blade from the sheath may not delay the battle. I swear by the Tarpeian rock, by the temple of Jupiter with whom I claim kindred, and by the walls of my glorious native city,[a] which I leave still standing with their citadel—I swear that whithersoever the safety of the state summons me, thither I will go and despise the danger. But if the soldiers, deaf to my warning, engage in battle, then I shall think no longer of my sons, the dear descendants of Assaracus ; and never shall a stricken Rome see me like Varro returning home." [b]

Sic tum diversa turbati mente petebant
castra duces. at praedictis iam sederat arvis   350
Aetolos Poenus servans ad proelia campos.
non alias maiore virum, maiore sub armis
agmine cornipedum concussa est Itala tellus.
quippe extrema simul gentique urbique timebant,
nec spes certandi plus uno Marte dabatur.   355
　Faunigenae socio bella invasere Sicano
sacra manus Rutuli, servant qui Daunia regna
Laurentique domo gaudent et fonte Numici ;
quos Castrum Phrygibusque gravis quondam Ardea
　misit,
quos, celso devexa iugo Iunonia sedes,   360
Lanuvium atque altrix casti Collatia Bruti ;
quique immite nemus Triviae, quique ostia Tusci
amnis amant tepidoque fovent Almone Cybelen.
hinc Tibur, Catille, tuum sacrisque dicatum
Fortunae Praeneste iugis Antemnaque, prisco   365
Crustumio prior, atque habiles ad aratra Labici ;
necnon sceptriferi qui potant Thybridis undam,
quique Anienis habent ripas gelidoque rigantur
Simbruvio rastrisque domant Aequicula rura.
his Scaurus monitor, tenero tunc Scaurus in aevo,   370
sed iam signa dabat nascens in saecula virtus.
non illis solitum crispare hastilia campo,
nec mos pennigeris pharetram implevisse sagittis ;

ᵃ If defeated at Cannae, the Romans could not hope to
put another army in the field.
　ᵇ Daunus, an ancient king, migrated from Apulia to
Latium, and there founded Ardea, the chief city of the
Rutulians. An old tradition said that Sicanians (also called
Sicilians) had migrated from Latium to Sicily.
　ᶜ The avenger of chaste Lucretia, surnamed Collatinus.
　ᵈ See note to iv. 769.　　　　ᵉ The Tiber.
　ᶠ A lake formed by the river Anio.

418

So then the two commanders set off for the camp, disquieted by discordant purposes. Hannibal had already encamped where Anna had foretold, keeping to the plains of Diomede for a battle-ground. Never was the soil of Italy trampled by a greater concourse of men or by a larger body of cavalry in arms. For men dreaded the destruction of nation and capital alike ; and there was no prospect of ever fighting a second battle.[a]

The Rutulians, descendants of Faunus, aided by Sicanians, came to battle ; these are a sacred band, who dwell in the realm of Daunus,[b] and rejoice in the dwellings of Laurentum and the stream of the Numicius ; they were sent forth by Castrum and by Ardea once hostile to Trojans, and by Lanuvium, the home of Juno that lies on the side of a steep hill ; and by Collatia, the nurse of chaste Brutus.[c] They also came who love the grove of pitiless [d] Diana and the mouths of the Tuscan river,[e] and wash Cybele's image in the warm stream of Almo. Next came Tibur, the city of Catillus ; and Praeneste, whose sacred hill is dedicated to Fortune ; and Antemna, more ancient than even Crustumium ; and the men of Labicum, handy with the plough ; and also those who drink the water of imperial Tiber ; and those who dwell on the banks of the Anio, and draw water from chill Simbruvius,[f] and harrow the fields of Aequicola. All these were led by Scaurus[g] ; and though Scaurus was but youthful then, his youth already gave promise of undying fame ; his men were not wont to hurl the spear-shaft in battle, or to fill quivers

[g] This is a tribute to members of the family who gained distinction later, especially M. Aemilius Scaurus, consul in 115 and 108 B.C., and censor.

pila volunt brevibusque habiles mucronibus enses ;
aere caput tecti surgunt super agmina cristis.   375
    At, quos ipsius mensis seposta Lyaei[a]
Setia et e celebri[1] miserunt valle Velitrae,
quos Cora, quos spumans immiti Signia musto,
et quos pestifera Pomptini uligine campi,
qua Saturae nebulosa palus restagnat, et atro   380
liventes coeno per squalida turbidus arva
cogit aquas Ufens atque inficit aequora limo,
ducit avis pollens nec dextra indignus avorum
Scaevola, cui dirae caelatur laudis honora
effigie clipeus : flagrant altaribus ignes,   385
Tyrrhenum valli medio stat Mucius ira
in semet versa, saevitque in imagine virtus :
tanta ictus specie finire hoc bella magistro
cernitur effugiens ardentem Porsena dextram.[b]
    Quis Circaea iuga et scopulosi verticis Anxur[c]   390
Hernicaque impresso raduntur vomere saxa,
quis putri pinguis sulcaris Anagnia gleba,
Sulla Ferentinis Privernatumque maniplis
ducebat simul excitis ; Soraeque iuventus
addita fulgebat telis.   hic Scaptia pubes,   395
hic Fabrateriae vulgus ; nec monte nivoso
descendens Atina aberat detritaque bellis
Suessa atque a duro Frusino haud imbellis aratro.[d]
at, qui Fibreno miscentem flumina Lirim
sulphureum tacitisque vadis ad litora lapsum   400

<hr>

    [1] e celebri *Heinsius* : incelebri *edd.*

<hr>

    [a] Bacchus.
    [b] Mucius Scaevola, having failed to stab Lars Porsena,
burnt his own hand in the fire ; and his action made the
invader retreat from Rome.   [c] Formiae.
    [d] Suessa Pometia, the chief town of the Volscians, was
repeatedly sacked by the early Romans.

with feathered arrows ; they prefer the pilum and
handy short-bladed sword ; they wear helmets of
bronze, and their plumes wave above the ranks.

Setia, whose vintage is reserved for the table of
Lyaeus [a] himself, sent her men, and so did the valley
of Velitrae well known to fame, and Cora, and Signia
whose foaming wine is bitter ; and the Pomptine
marshes that breed disease, where the misty swamp
of Satura covers the land, and the dark Ufens drives
his black and muddy current through unsightly
fields and dyes the sea with slime. These were led
by Scaevola, nobly born and in courage not unworthy
of his ancestors. Carved upon his shield was a
picture of that dreadful deed of heroism [b] : the fire
blazed on the altar, and Mucius stood in the centre
of the Tuscan camp and turned his rage against him-
self ; and his ruthless courage was seen in the carving.
Cowed by such a sight, and taught by such an ex-
ample, Porsena was shown, abandoning the war and
flying from that burning hand.

Sulla led to war the men who till the heights of Circe [c]
and the steep hill of Anxur, and the Hernicans who
drive the ploughshare deep into their stony ground, and
those who furrow the rich crumbling soil of Anagnia ;
and he summoned also the men of Ferentinum
and Privernum ; and the fighting men of Sora were
there too with glittering arms. Here were the men
of Scaptia and of Fabrateria ; nor did Atina fail
to come down from its snow-clad height, nor Suessa,
lessened by wars, [d] nor Frusino, trained to battle by
the labour of the plough. Then the hardy men of
Arpinum, dwellers by the Liris, which mingles its
sulphurous waters with the Fibrenus and runs with
silent course to the sea, rose up in arms, bringing

accolit, Arpinas, accita pube Venafro
ac Larinatum dextris, socia hispidus arma
commovet atque viris ingens exhaurit Aquinum.
Tullius aeratas raptabat in agmina turmas,
regia progenies et Tullo sanguis ab alto.   405
indole pro quanta iuvenis quantumque daturus
Ausoniae populis ventura in saecula civem !
ille, super Gangen, super exauditus et Indos,
implebit terras voce et furialia bella
fulmine compescet linguae nec deinde relinquet   410
par decus eloquio cuiquam sperare nepotum.

   Ecce inter primos Therapnaeo a sanguine Clausi
exultat rapidis Nero non imitabilis ausis.
hunc Amiterna cohors et Bactris nomina ducens
Casperia, hunc Foruli magnaeque Reate dicatum   415
caelicolum Matri necnon habitata pruinis
Nursia et a Tetrica comitantur rupe cohortes.
cunctis hasta decus clipeusque retortus in orbem
conique implumes et laevo tegmina crure.
ibant et laeti pars Sancum voce canebant,   420
auctorem gentis, pars laudes ore ferebat,
Sabe, tuas, qui de proprio cognomine primus
dixisti populos magna dicione Sabinos.

   Quid, qui Picenae stimulat telluris alumnos,
horridus et squamis et equina Curio crista,   425
pars belli quam magna venit !   non aequore verso
tam creber fractis albescit fluctus in undis,
nec coetu leviore, ubi mille per agmina virgo

-----

   ^a Tullus Attius was an ancient king of the Volscians.
   ^b M. Tullius Cicero was a native of Arpinum.
   ^c A reference to Cicero's speeches against Catiline and
against M. Antonius.
   ^d Attus Clausus, supposed to be of Spartan descent, mi-
grated from the Sabine country to Rome, and founded the
famous Claudian family : see xiii. 466 ; xvii. 33.

with them fighters from Venafrum and Larinum, and
draining mighty Aquinum of its men. Their mail-
clad squadrons were sped to battle by Tullius, the
son of kings and descended from Tullus [a] of old.
How noble was his youthful promise! and how
great the immortal descendant [b] he was to give
to Italy! That voice shall fill the earth and be
heard beyond the Ganges and the peoples of India;
with the thunders of his tongue Cicero shall quell
the frenzy of war, [c] and shall leave behind him
a renown that no orator of after times can hope to
equal.

But lo! Nero rides proudly among the foremost,
with the Spartan blood of Clausus [d] in his veins, and
unrivalled in swift deeds of valour. With him come
the soldiers of Amiterna, and Casperia that takes
its name from Bactra, [e] and Foruli, and Reate sacred
to the great Mother of the Gods, and Nursia the
abode of snow, and warriors from rocky Tetricus.
All these carry spears and rounded shields; their
helmets have no plume, and they wear greaves on
the left leg. As they marched, some of them raised
a song in honour of Sancus, the founder of their race,
while others praised Sabus, who first gave his name
to the wide dominion of the Sabines.

And what of Curio, bristling with scale-armour and
plume of horse-hair—Curio, a host in himself, who
urged on the men of Picenum? Thick and fast they
come, like the billows on a stormy sea that whiten
amid the breaking waves; less active are the riders,
when the Warrior Maid [f] with the crescent-shaped

---

[e] Bactra stands for the East: there was a town and district
in India, whose name was not unlike Casperia.

[f] Penthesilea, the queen of the Amazons: see note to ii. 73.

lunatis acies imitatur Martia peltis,
perstrepit et tellus et Amazonius Thermodon.   430
hic et, quos pascunt scopulosae rura Numanae,
et quis litoreae fumant altaria Cuprae,
quique Truentinas servant cum flumine turres,
cernere erat ; clipeata procul sub sole corusco
agmina sanguinea vibrant in nubila luce.   435
stat fucare colus nec Sidone vilior Ancon
murice nec Libyco ; statque humectata Vomano
Hadria et inclemens hirsuti signifer Ascli.
hoc Picus quondam, nomen memorabile ab alto
Saturno, statuit genitor, quem carmine Circe   440
exutum formae volitare per aethera iussit
et sparsit croceum plumis fugientis honorem.
ante, ut fama docet, tellus possessa Pelasgis,
quis Aesis regnator erat fluvioque reliquit
nomen et a sese populos tum dixit Asilos.   445
    Sed non ruricolae firmarunt robore castra
deteriore, cavis venientes montibus, Umbri.
hos Aesis Sapisque lavant rapidasque sonanti
vertice contorquens undas per saxa Metaurus,
et lavat ingentem perfundens flumine sacro   450
Clitumnus taurum Narque, albescentibus undis
in Thybrim properans, Tiniaeque inglorius humor
et Clanis et Rubico et Senonum de nomine Sena.
sed pater ingenti medios illabitur amne
Albula et admota perstringit moenia ripa.   455
his urbes Arna et laetis Mevania pratis,
Hispellum et duro monti per saxa recumbens

---

[a] A river of Pontus that flows into the Black Sea.
[b] Picus was an ancient king of Italy with prophetic
powers, whom Circe turned into a woodpecker, because he
refused her love.   [c] See note to iv. 545.
[d] The ancient name of the Tiber.
424

shield reviews her thousand squadrons in mimic war-
fare, till the earth resounds, and Thermodon [a] too, the
river of the Amazons. Here might be seen the men
whom the fields of rocky Numana feed, and those
for whom the altar of Cupra smokes by the shore, and
those who guard the towers and rivers of Truentum;
their shielded ranks glitter afar in the sunlight and
throw a blood-red radiance skyward. Here stood
Ancona, which rivals Sidon and the purple of Libya in
the dyeing of cloth; and here stood Hadria washed
by the Vomanus, and here the fierce standard-
bearers of wooded Asculum. Picus,[b] the famous son
of ancient Saturn, was the father and founder of
Asculum long ago—Picus whom Circe by her spells
deprived of human shape, and sentenced to fly about
in the sky; and she speckled his feathers with bright
saffron colour as he fled from her. Legend tells that
the land was possessed earlier by Pelasgians, the
subjects of Aesis who left his name to a river and
called his people after himself by the name of Asili.

But the Umbrians, dwellers in the country, brought
no less strength to the Roman army, when they came
from their hills and valleys. Their rivers are the
Aesis and the Sapis, and the Metaurus which drives
its rapid stream over rocks in noisy eddies; and there
Clitumnus bathes in its sacred waters the mighty
bull[c]; and there is the Nar whose pale waves hasten
to the Tiber, and the Tinia unknown to fame, and the
Clanis, and the Rubicon, and the Sena named after
the Senones. But Father Albula[d] flows through
their midst with his mighty stream and grazes
their walls and brings near his banks. The
Umbrian towns are Arna, Mevania of rich pastures,
Hispellum, Narnia that lies among the rocks on the

Narnia et infestum nebulis humentibus olim
Iguvium patuloque iacens sine moenibus arvo
Fulginia ; his populi fortes : Amerinus et, armis 460
vel rastris laudande Camers, his Sassina, dives
lactis, et haud parci Martem coluisse Tudertes.
ductor Piso viros spernaces mortis agebat,
ora puer pulcherque habitum, sed corde sagaci
aequabat senium atque astu superaverat annos. 465
is primam ante aciem pictis radiabat in armis,
Arsacidum ut fulvo micat ignea gemma monili.
  Iamque per Etruscos legio completa maniplos
rectorem magno spectabat nomine Galbam.
huic genus orditur Minos illusaque tauro 470
Pasiphaë, clarique dehinc stant ordine patres.
lectos Caere viros, lectos Cortona, superbi
Tarchonis domus, et veteres misere Graviscae.
necnon Argolico dilectum litus Halaeso
Alsium et obsessae campo squalente Fregenae. 475
affuit et, sacris interpres fulminis alis,
Faesula et, antiquus Romanis moenibus horror,
Clusinum vulgus ; cum, Porsena magne, iubebas
nequiquam pulsos Romae imperitare Superbos.
tunc, quos a niveis exegit Luna metallis, 480
insignis portu, quo non spatiosior alter
innumeras cepisse rates et claudere pontum,
Maeoniaeque decus quondam Vetulonia gentis.
bissenos haec prima dedit praecedere fasces
et iunxit totidem tacito terrore secures ; 485

---

  [a] The name of Arsaces was borne by a long succession
of Parthian kings ; and the Parthian people are often called
Arsacidae.
  [b] One bearer of the name was Roman emperor for a few
weeks A.D. 69.

rough mountain-side, Iguvium that damp mists
formerly made unhealthy, and Fulginia that stands
unwalled on the open plain. These sent good soldiers
—Amerians, Camertes famous alike with sword or
plough, men of Sassina rich in flocks, and men of
Tuder, no laggards in war. These death-defying
warriors were led by Piso, with the face of a boy and
fair to see ; but he had all the wisdom of age and wit
beyond his years. In the front rank he stood, a
splendid figure in shining armour, even as a fiery
jewel glitters on the golden collar of a Parthian king.[a]

Another army manned by Etruscan warriors obeyed
Galba [b] of glorious name. Minos, and Pasiphaë
whom the bull deceived, were the authors of his line,
and his ancestors who followed in order were famous
too. The choicest of their men were sent by Caere
and Cortona, the seat of proud Tarchon,[c] and by
ancient Graviscae. Alsium too sent men, the city
by the sea that Halaesus the Argive loved ; and
Fregenae, girt about by a barren plain. Faesula also
was present—Faesula that can interpret the winged
lightning of heaven ; and the people of Clusium,
terrible once to the walls of Rome, when great Porsena
in vain required of the Romans to obey the tyrants
they had expelled. Then Luna sent out fighters from
her marble quarries—Luna, whose famous harbour, as
large as any, shuts out the sea and shelters countless
vessels ; and Vetulonia, once the pride of the Lydian [d]
race. From that city came the twelve bundles of
rods that are borne before the consul, and also the
twelve axes with their silent menace ; she adorned

---

[c] Tarchon was said to have come with Telephus from Asia
to Italy, where he founded the Twelve Cities of Etruria.

[d] i.e. Etruscan : see note to iv. 721.

haec altas eboris decoravit honore curules
et princeps Tyrio vestem praetexuit ostro ;
haec eadem pugnas accendere protulit aere.
his mixti Nepesina cohors Aequique Falisci,
quique tuos, Flavina, focos, Sabatia quique   490
stagna tenent Ciminique lacum, qui Sutria tecta
haud procul et sacrum Phoebo Soracte frequentant.
spicula bina gerunt ; capiti cudone ferino
sat cautum ; Lycios damnant hastilibus arcus.

   Hae bellare acies norant ; at Marsica pubes   495
et bellare manu et chelydris cantare soporem
vipereumque herbis hebetare et carmine dentem.
Aeëtae prolem, Angitiam mala gramina primam
monstravisse ferunt tactuque domare venena
et lunam excussisse polo, stridoribus amnes   500
frenantem, ac silvis montes nudasse vocatis.
sed populis nomen posuit metuentior hospes,
cum fugeret Phrygias trans aequora Marsya Crenas,
Mygdoniam Phoebi superatus pectine loton.
Marruvium, veteris celebratum nomine Marri,   505
urbibus est illis caput, interiorque per udos
Alba sedet campos pomisque rependit aristas.
cetera in obscuro famae et sine nomine vulgi
sed numero castella valent.   coniungitur acer
Pelignus, gelidoque rapit Sulmone cohortes.   510

   Nec cedit studio Sidicinus sanguine miles,
quem genuere Cales : non parvus conditor urbi,

---

    a The Lycians, like the Cretans, were famous archers.
     b See i. 412.
     c A sister of Circe's and possessing like powers.
    d He was defeated by Apollo in a musical contest.
      e Phrygian.

the high curule chairs with the beauty of ivory, and first bordered the robe of office with Tyrian purple ; and the brazen trumpet which inflames the warrior was her invention also. Together with these came the men of Nepete, and the Aequi of Falerium, and the inhabitants of Flavina, and men who dwell by the Sabatian lakes and the Ciminian mere, and their neighbours from Sutrium, and those who haunt Soracte, the sacred hill of Phoebus. Each carries two spears ; a wild beast's skin is protection enough for their heads ; their spears despise the bow of Lycia.[a]

All these knew how to make war ; but the Marsi could not only fight but could also send snakes to sleep by charms,[b] and rob a serpent's tooth of its venom by simples and spells. They say that Angitia,[c] daughter of Aeetes, first revealed to them magic herbs, and taught them to tame vipers by handling them, to drive the moon from the sky, to arrest the course of rivers by their muttering, and to strip the hills by calling down the forests. But this people got their name from Marsyas,[d] the settler who fled in fright across the sea from Phrygian Crenai, when the Mygdonian[e] pipe was defeated by Apollo's lyre. Marruvium, which bears the famous name of ancient Marrus, is the chief of their cities ; and further inland lies Alba in water-meadows, and compensates by its orchards for the lack of corn. Their other strongholds, though unknown to fame and with no name among the people, are formidable by their number. The Pelignians were forward to join the rest, and brought their troops in haste from chilly Sulmo.

No less zealous were the natives of Sidicinum, whose mother-city is Cales. Cales had no mean

ut fama est, Calais, Boreae quem rapta per auras
Orithyia vago Geticis nutrivit in antris.
haud ullo levior bellis Vestina iuventus   515
agmina densavit, venatu dura ferarum ;
quae, Fiscelle, tuas arces Pinnamque virentem
pascuaque haud tarde redeuntia tondet Aveiae ;
Marrucina simul, Frentanis aemula pubes,
Corfini populos magnumque Teate trahebat.   520
omnibus in pugnam fertur sparus, omnibus alto
assuetae volucrem caelo demittere fundae.
pectora pellis obit caesi venatibus ursi.

   Iam vero, quos dives opum, quos dives avorum
e toto dabat ad bellum Campania tractu,   525
ductorum adventum vicinis sedibus Osci
servabant ; Sinuessa tepens fluctuque sonorum
Vulturnum, quasque evertere silentia, Amyclae
Fundique et regnata Lamo Caieta domusque
Antiphatae, compressa freto, stagnisque palustre 530
Liternum et quondam fatorum conscia Cyme.
illic Nuceria et Gaurus, navalibus acta
prole Dicarchea ; multo cum milite Graia
illic Parthenope ac Poeno non pervia Nola,
Allifae et Clanio contemptae semper Acerrae.   535
Sarrastes etiam populos totasque videres
Sarni mitis opes ; illic, quos sulphure pingues

----

   [a] A daughter of Erechtheus, king of Athens, she was
carried off by Boreas to his northern kingdom.
   [b] This applies not to a Campanian city but to the mother-
city, Amyclae in Laconia. After many false alarms, they
passed a law that no one should mention the subject of in-
vasion. Hence, when the Spartans came, no one dared
announce their approach, and the town was taken (about 800
B.C.).
   [c] The Greek name of Cumae, where the Sibyl had her
cave.

founder—even Calais, who, as legend tells, was
nurtured in Thracian caves by Orithyia,[a] when she
was carried off by the blast of wanton Boreas through
the sky. The Vestini, inferior to none as fighters, and
hardened by hunting wild animals, came in serried
ranks ; their flocks graze on the heights of Fiscellus
and green Pinna, and in the meadows of Aveia that
are quick to grow again. The Marrucini likewise,
in rivalry with Frentani, brought with them the in-
habitants of Corfinium, and great Teate. All these
carried a pike to battle, and all carried slings that
had struck down many a bird high in air. For
corslets they wore the skins of bears slain by the
hunters.

Moreover the Oscans, whom Campania, rich in
wealth and ancient blood, sent to battle from all her
wide domain, were waiting close by for the coming
of their leaders : Sinuessa of warm springs, and Vul-
turnum within sound of the sea, and Amyclae which
silence once destroyed[b] ; Fundi, and Caieta where
Lamus once was king, and the home of Antiphates
shut in by the sea ; Liternum with its marshy
pools, and Cyme[c] which could once foretell the
future. There were seen Nuceria and Gaurus ; and
the sons of Dicaearchus were sent forth from their
arsenal[d] ; Greek Parthenope[e] was there, with many
a man-at-arms, and Nola, barred against Hannibal[f] ;
Allifae also, and Acerrae, ever mocked at[g] by the
Clanius. One might have seen too the Sarrastian
men and all the assembled might of the gentle Sarnus.
There were the chosen men from the Phlegraean

---

[a] Puteoli.   [e] Naples.
[f] He was beaten off from Nola in 215 B.C.
[g] The river threatened always to submerge the town.

Phlegraei legere sinus, Misenus et ardens
ore giganteo sedes Ithacesia Bai ;
non Prochyte, non ardentem sortita Typhoea   540
Inarime, non antiqui saxosa Telonis
insula, nec parvis aberat Calatia muris ;
Surrentum et pauper sulci cerealis Abella ;
in primis Capua, heu rebus servare serenis
inconsulta modum et pravo peritura tumore !   545
    Laetos rectoris formabat Scipio bello.
ille viris pila et ferro circumdare pectus
addiderat ; leviora domo de more parentum
gestarant tela, ambustas sine cuspide cornos ;
aclydis usus erat factaeque ad rura bipennis.   550
ipse inter medios venturae ingentia laudis
signa dabat, vibrare sudem, tramittere saltu
murales fossas, undosum frangere nando
indutus thoraca vadum ; spectacula tanta
ante acies virtutis erant.   saepe alite planta   555
ilia perfossum et campi per aperta volantem,
ipse pedes, praevertit equum ; saepe arduus idem
castrorum spatium et saxo tramisit et hasta ;
Martia frons facilesque comae nec pone retroque
caesaries brevior ; flagrabant lumina miti   560
aspectu, gratusque inerat visentibus horror.
    Affuit et Samnis, nondum vergente favore
ad Poenos, sed nec veteri purgatus ab ira :

---

^a The volcanic district on the Campanian coast.
^b Baiae on that coast, famous for its hot springs, was sup-
posed to have got its name from Baius, one of the crew of
Ulysses.   Prochyta (now Procida) and Inarime (now Ischia)
are islands on the same coast.   The volcanic eruptions were
attributed to the giants imprisoned below the islands.
^c Capri.
^d The capital city of Campania.

bays rich in sulphur,[a] and from Misenus, and from
the seat of Baius the Ithacan with its mighty red-hot
crater. Prochyte was not absent, nor Inarime, the
place appointed for ever-burning Typhoeus,[b] nor the
rocky isle [c] of ancient Telo, nor Calatia of the little
walls. Surrentum was there, and Abella ill-provided
with corn-fields ; and Capua [d] above all ; but she, alas,
knew not how to observe moderation in prosperity,
and her wicked pride went before a fall.[e]

Scipio [f] trained the Campanians for war, and they
were proud of their leader. He had given them
javelins and iron corslets ; at home they had carried
lighter weapons after the fashion of their fathers—
made of wood hardened in the fire and with no iron
point ; they used the club and the axe, the country-
man's tool. In their midst Scipio gave splendid
promise of his future fame, hurling stakes, leaping
trenches under city-walls, and stemming the billows
of the sea with his breastplate on ; such the display of
vigour he gave before the ranks. Often his flying
feet outstripped a courser as it flew, cruelly spurred,
over the open plain ; often, rising to his full height, he
threw stone or spear beyond the limits of the camp.
He had a martial brow and flowing hair ; nor was the
hair at the back of his head shorter. His eyes burned
bright, but their regard was mild ; and those who
looked upon him were at once awed and pleased.

The Samnites [g] too there were ; their allegiance
was not yet turning towards the Carthaginians, but
they still cherished their ancient grudge. Here were

[e] Capua, having revolted to Hannibal, was captured by
the Romans in 211 B.C.   [f] Africanus.
[g] A Sabine people, inveterate enemies of Rome in her
early history : after Cannae they joined Hannibal.

qui Batulum Nucrasque metunt, Boviania quique
exagitant lustra, aut Caudinis faucibus haerent,   565
et quos aut Rufrae, quos aut Aesernia, quosve
obscura incultis Herdonia misit ab agris.

  Bruttius, haud dispar animorum, unaque iuventus
Lucanis excita iugis Hirpinaque pubes
horrebat telis et tergo hirsuta ferarum.   570
hos venatus alit : lustra incoluere sitimque
avertunt fluvio, somnique labore parantur.

  Additur his Calaber Sallentinaeque cohortes
necnon Brundisium, quo desinit Itala tellus.
parebat legio audaci permissa Cethego.   575
qui socias vires atque indiscreta maniplis
arma recensebat : nunc sese ostendere miles
Leucosiae e scopulis, nunc, quem Picentia Paesto
misit et exhaustae mox Poeno Marte Cerillae,
nunc Silarus quos nutrit aquis, quo gurgite tradunt
duritiem lapidum mersis inolescere ramis.   581
ille et pugnacis laudavit tela Salerni,
falcatos enses, et, quae Buxentia pubes
aptabat dextris, irrasae robora clavae.
ipse, humero exsertus gentili more parentum,   585
difficili gaudebat equo roburque iuventae
flexi cornipedis duro exercebat in ore.

  Vos etiam, accisae desolataeque virorum
Eridani gentes, nullo attendente deorum
votis tunc vestris, casura ruistis in arma.   590
certavit Mutinae quassata Placentia bello ;

---

    [a] The Caudine Forks was a narrow pass in which a Roman
army suffered an ignominious defeat at the hands of the
Samnites in 321 B.C.

    [b] It was a custom with the family of the Cethegi to wear no
tunic under the toga, so that the arms were bare.

    [c] The inhabitants of Cisalpine Gaul, on both sides of the

the reapers of Batulum and Nucrae, the hunters of Bovianum, the dwellers in the gorge of Caudium,[a] and those whom Rufrae or Aesernia or unknown Herdonia sent from her untilled fields.

The Bruttians, inferior to none in spirit, and also the men called forth from the Lucanian hills, and the Hirpini, carried pointed weapons and were shaggy with the hides of beasts. They get their living by hunting ; they live in the forest, and slake their thirst in the rivers, and earn their sleep by toil.

To these were added the Calabrians, and the troops of Sallentia, and of Brundisium where Italy comes to an end. These troops were given to bold Cethegus as commander ; and he reviewed their united strength, not broken up into companies. Here men from the rocks of Leucosia showed themselves, and those whom Picentia sent from Paestum ; and men of Cerillae, which was afterwards depopulated by the enemy ; and people fed by the water of the Silarus, which has power, men say, to turn into stone branches dipped in it. Cethegus praised the sickle-shaped swords with which the fighting Salernians are armed, and the rough oaken clubs which the men of Buxentum suited to their grasp. He himself, with his shoulder bared in the manner of his fathers,[b] took pleasure in his unruly steed, and exerted his youthful strength in forcing the hard-mouthed horse to turn in circles.

Ye too, the peoples of the river Po, though sore smitten and bereft of your men,[c] rushed forth now to battle and defeat, and no god hearkened to your prayers. Placentia, though crippled by the war, vied

Po, had suffered severely from Hannibal on his first arrival in Italy.

Mantua mittenda certavit pube Cremonae,
Mantua, Musarum domus atque ad sidera cantu
evecta Aonio et Smyrnaeis aemula plectris.
tum Verona, Athesi circumflua, et undique sollers 595
arva coronantem nutrire Faventia pinum.
Vercellae fuscique ferax Pollentia villi
et, quondam Teucris comes in Laurentia bella,
Ocni prisca domus parvique Bononia Rheni.
quique gravi remo, limosis segniter undis,   600
lenta paludosae proscindunt stagna Ravennae.
tum Troiana manus, tellure antiquitus orti
Euganea profugique sacris Antenoris oris.
necnon cum Venetis Aquileia superfluit armis.
tum pernix Ligus et sparsi per saxa Vagenni 605
in decus Hannibalis duros misere nepotes.
maxima tot populis rector fiducia Brutus
ibat et hortando notum accendebat in hostem.
laeta viro gravitas ac mentis amabile pondus
et sine tristitia virtus : non ille rigoris   610
ingratas laudes nec nubem frontis amabat
nec famam laevo quaerebat limite vitae.

  Addiderat ter mille viros, in Marte sagittae
expertos, fidus Sicula regnator ab Aetna.

---

  a Mantua was the birthplace of Virgil, for whom Silius
had a special devotion. Smyrna was one of the seven cities
which claimed to be the birthplace of Homer.
  b Aeneas and his men.
  c The people of Patavium (now Padua) are meant here :
legend said that Patavium was founded after the Trojan war
by Antenor, who expelled the original inhabitants, the
Euganeans.
  d Inhabitants of the Riviera are meant.

with Mutina; and Cremona sent forth her sons in
rivalry with Mantua—Mantua, the home of the
Muses, raised to the skies by immortal verse, and a
match for the lyre of Homer.[a] Men came from
Verona too, round which flows the Athesis; from
Faventia, skilful to nurture the pine-trees that grow
everywhere round her fields; and Vercellae, with
Pollentia rich in dusky fleeces; and Bononia of the
little Rhine; the ancient seat of Ocnus, which went
to war long ago with the Trojans[b] against Laurentum.
Then came the men of Ravenna, who paddle slowly
with heavy oars over muddy waters, as they cleave
the stagnant pools of their marshes. There was also
a band of Trojans, coming from the Euganean country
in ancient times and driven forth from the sacred soil
of Antenor.[c] Aquileia too together with the Veneti
was full to overflowing with troops. The active
Ligurians, and the Vagenni[d] who dwell scattered
among rocks, sent their hardy sons to swell the triumph
of Hannibal. All these peoples had Brutus for their
leader and relied entirely upon him; and his appeals
roused their spirit against a foe they knew already.
Though dignified, Brutus was genial; his powerful
intellect won men's hearts, and there was nothing
forbidding in his virtue. To wear a frowning brow,
or win a thankless reputation for severity, was not
his way; nor did he court notoriety by a perverse
course of life.[e]

Three thousand men, skilled archers, had also been
sent by the loyal king[f] from Etna in Sicily; and

---

[e] It is a plausible suggestion that Silius here describes a
later Brutus, the friend of Cicero and conspirator against
Caesar: he was a Stoic without the asperities of Stoicism.

[f] Hiero II., king of Syracuse.

non totidem Ilva viros, sed laetos cingere ferrum   615
armarat patrio, quo nutrit bella, metallo.
  Ignosset, quamvis avido committere pugnam,
Varroni, quicumque simul tot tela videret.
tantis agminibus Rhoeteo litore quondam
fervere, cum magnae Troiam invasere Mycenae,   620
mille rates vidit Leandrius Hellespontus.
  Ut ventum ad Cannas, urbis vestigia priscae,
defigunt diro signa infelicia vallo.
nec, tanta miseris iamiam impendente ruina,
cessarunt superi vicinas prodere clades.   625
per subitum attonitis pila exarsere maniplis,
et celsae toto ceciderunt aggere pinnae,
nutantique ruens prostravit vertice silvas
Garganus, fundoque imo mugivit anhelans
Aufidus, et magno late distantia ponto   630
terruerunt pavidos accensa Ceraunia nautas.
quaesivit Calaber, subducta luce repente
immensis tenebris, et terram et litora Sipus ;
obseditque frequens castrorum limina bubo.
nec densae trepidis apium se involvere nubes   635
cessarunt aquilis ; non unus crine corusco,
regnorum eversor, rubuit letale cometes.
castra quoque et vallum rabidae sub nocte silenti
irrupere ferae raptique ante ora paventum
adiunctos vigilis sparserunt membra per agros.   640
ludificante etiam terroris imagine somnos,
Gallorum visi bustis erumpere manes ;

---

  [a] The island of Elba, to which Napoleon was banished.
  [b] The royal city of Agamemnon.
  [c] So called because Leander swam across it.
  [d] See note to iv. 561.   [e] See note to v. 386.
  [f] The Greek name of Sipontum, a harbour south of
Mt. Garganus.

Ilva [a] had armed with her native iron, on which war
thrives, fewer men, but all of them eager to gird on
the sword.

Any man who had seen so great an army mustered
might have pardoned Varro's eagerness to fight a
battle. In ancient times when great Mycenae [b]
attacked Troy, Leander's [c] Hellespont saw a thousand
ships swarm with as huge a host on the shore of
Rhoeteum.

When the Romans reached Cannae, built on the
site of a former city, they planted their doomed
standards on a rampart of evil omen. Nor, when
such destruction was hanging over their unhappy
heads, did the gods fail to reveal the coming disaster.
Javelins blazed up suddenly in the hands of astounded
soldiers ; high battlements fell down along the length
of the ramparts ; Mount Garganus, [d] collapsing with
tottering summit, overset its forests; the Aufidus
rumbled in its lowest depths and roared ; and
far away across the sea seamen were scared by
fire burning on the Ceraunian [e] mountains. Light
was suddenly withdrawn, and the Calabrian mariners,
plunged in darkness, looked in vain for the shore and
land of Sipus [f] ; and many a screech-owl beset the
gates of the camp. Thick swarms of bees constantly
twined themselves about the terrified standards, and
the bright hair of more than one comet, the portent
that dethrones monarchs, showed its baleful glare.
Wild beasts also in the silence of night burst through
the rampart into the camp, snatched up a sentry
before the eyes of his frightened comrades, and
scattered his limbs over the adjacent fields. Sleep
also was mocked by terrible images : men dreamt
that the ghosts of the Gauls were breaking forth from

terque quaterque solo penitus tremuere revulsae
Tarpeiae rupes, atque atro sanguine flumen
manavit Iovis in templis, lacrimaeque vetusta   645
effigie patris large fluxere Quirini.
maior et horrificis sese extulit Allia ripis.
non Alpes sedere loco, non nocte dieve
ingentes inter stetit Apenninus hiatus.
axe super medio, Libyes a parte, coruscae   650
in Latium venere faces, ruptusque fragore
horrisono polus, et vultus patuere Tonantis.
Aetnaeos quoque contorquens e cautibus ignes
Vesvius intonuit, scopulisque in nubila iactis
Phlegraeus tetigit trepidantia sidera vertex.   655
   Ecce inter medios belli praesagus, et ore
attonito sensuque simul, clamoribus implet
miles castra feris et anhelat clade futura :
" parcite, crudeles superi ; iam stragis acervis
deficiunt campi ; video per densa volantem   660
agmina ductorem Libyae currusque citatos
arma virum super atque artus et signa trahentem.
turbinibus furit insanis et proelia ventus
inque oculos inque ora rotat. cadit, immemor aevi,
nequicquam, Thrasymenne, tuis Servilius oris   665
subductus. quo, Varro, fugis ? pro Iupiter ! ictu
procumbit saxi, fessis spes ultima, Paulus.
cesserit huic Trebia exitio. pons ecce cadentum
corporibus struitur, ructatque cadavera fumans
Aufidus, ac victrix insultat belua campis.   670

---

    a The deified Romulus.
    b See note to i. 547.
    c For Phlegra see note to iv. 275 : Phlegraean = volcanic.
    d The dust of Cannae is historical : blown by a fierce wind
in the faces of the Romans, it contributed to their defeat:
see note to ix. 495.

their graves. Again and again the Tarpeian rock was shaken and wrenched from its very base; a dark stream of blood flowed in the temples of Jupiter; and the ancient image of Father Quirinus [a] shed floods of tears. The Allia [b] rose high above its fatal banks. The Alps did not keep their place, and the Apennines were never still day or night among their vast gorges. In the southern sky, bright meteors shot against Italy from the direction of Africa; and the heavens burst open with a fearful crash, and the countenance of the Thunderer was revealed. Vesuvius also thundered, hurling flames worthy of Etna from her cliffs; and the fiery [c] crest, throwing rocks up to the clouds, reached to the trembling stars.

But lo! in the midst of the army a soldier foretells the battle. With distraction in his aspect and his brain, he fills the camp with his wild shouting, and gasps as he reveals coming disaster: " Spare us, ye cruel gods! The heaps of dead are more than the fields can contain; I see Hannibal speeding through the serried ranks and driving his furious chariot over armour and human limbs and standards. The wind rages in wild gusts, and drives the dust [d] of battle in our faces and eyes. Servilius,[e] careless of his life, is down; his absence from the field of Trasimene does not help him now. Whither is Varro fleeing? Ye gods! Paulus, the last hope of despairing men, is struck down by a stone. Trebia cannot rival this destruction. See! the bodies of the slain form a bridge, and reeking Aufidus belches forth corpses, and the huge beast [f] treads the plain victorious.

[e] As consul in the previous year (217 B.C.) he had imitated the caution of Fabius.
[f] The elephant.

gestat Agenoreus nostro de more secures
consulis, et sparsos lictor fert sanguine fasces.
in Libyam Ausonii portatur pompa triumphi.
o dolor !   hoc etiam, superi, vidisse iubetis ?
congesto, laevae quodcumque avellitur, auro   675
metitur Latias victrix Carthago ruinas."

---

[a] To prove the greatness of his victory, Hannibal sent
home the gold rings taken from the corpses of the Roman

The Carthaginian copies us and carries the consul's axes, and his lictors bear blood-stained rods. The triumphal procession of the Roman passes from Rome to Libya. And, O grief!—do the gods force us to witness this also ? — victorious Carthage measures the downfall of Rome by all the heap of gold that was torn from the left hands of the slain." [a]

nobles : these were poured out in the Carthaginian senate, and filled three peck-measures, according to some authorities (Livy xxiii. 12. 1). See xi. 532 foll.

Printed in Great Britain by R. & R. CLARK, LIMITED, *Edinburgh.*

THE LOEB CLASSICAL LIBRARY

VOLUMES ALREADY PUBLISHED

LATIN AUTHORS

APULEIUS. THE GOLDEN ASS (METAMORPHO-SES). Trans. by W. Adlington (1566). Revised by S. Gaselee. (*5th Impression.*)

AULUS GELLIUS. Trans. by J. C. Rolfe. 3 Vols.

AUSONIUS. Trans. by H. G. Evelyn White. 2 Vols.

BEDE: HISTORICAL WORKS. Trans. by J. King. 2 Vols.

BOETHIUS: TRACTATES AND DE CONSOLATIONE PHILOSOPHIAE. Trans. by the Rev. H. F. Stewart and E. K. Rand. (*2nd Impression.*)

CAESAR: CIVIL WARS. Trans. by A. G. Peskett. (*3rd Impression.*)

CAESAR: GALLIC WAR. Trans. by H. J. Edwards. (*6th Impression.*)

CATULLUS. Trans. by F. W. Cornish; TIBULLUS. Trans. by J. P. Postgate; PERVIGILIUM VENERIS. Trans. by J. W. Mackail. (*9th Impression.*)

CICERO: DE FINIBUS. Trans. by H. Rackham. (*3rd Impression revised.*)

CICERO: DE NATURA DEORUM AND ACADEMICA. Trans. by H. Rackham.

CICERO: DE OFFICIIS. Trans. by Walter Miller. (*3rd Impression.*)

CICERO: DE REPUBLICA AND DE LEGIBUS. Trans. by Clinton Keyes.

CICERO: DE SENECTUTE, DE AMICITIA, DE DIVINATIONE. Trans. by W. A. Falconer. (*3rd Imp.*)

CICERO: LETTERS TO ATTICUS. Trans. by E. O. Winstedt. 3 Vols. (Vols. I. *4th*, II. *3rd*, III. *2nd Imp.*)

CICERO: LETTERS TO HIS FRIENDS. Trans. by W. Glynn Williams. 3 Vols.

CICERO: PHILIPPICS. Trans. by W. C. A. Ker.

CICERO: PRO ARCHIA POETA, POST REDITUM IN SENATU, POST REDITUM AD QUIRITES, DE DOMO SUA, DE HARUSPICUM RESPONSIS, PRO PLANCIO. Trans. by N. H. Watts.

1

THE LOEB CLASSICAL LIBRARY

CICERO: PRO CAECINA, PRO LEGE MANILIA, PRO CLUENTIO, PRO RABIRIO. Trans. by H. Grose Hodge.

CICERO: PRO MILONE, IN PISONEM, PRO SCAURO, PRO FONTEIO, PRO RABIRIO, PRO MARCELLO, PRO LIGARIO, PRO DEIOTARO. Trans. by N. H. Watts.

CICERO: PRO QUINCTIO, PRO ROSCIO AMERINO, PRO ROSCIO COMOEDO, CONTRA RULLUM. Trans. by J. H. Freese.

CICERO: TUSCULAN DISPUTATIONS. Trans. by J. E. King.

CICERO: VERRINE ORATIONS. Trans. by L. H. G. Greenwood. 2 Vols. Vol. I.

CLAUDIAN. Trans. by M. Platnauer. 2 Vols.

FLORUS. Trans. by E. S. Forster; CORNELIUS NEPOS. Trans. by J. C. Rolfe.

FRONTINUS: STRATAGEMS AND AQUEDUCTS. Trans. by C. E. Bennett.

FRONTO: CORRESPONDENCE. Trans. by C. R. Haines. 2 Vols.

HORACE: ODES AND EPODES. Trans. by C. E. Bennett. (9th Impression revised.)

HORACE: SATIRES, EPISTLES, ARS POETICA. Trans. by H. R. Fairclough. (3rd Impression revised.)

JUVENAL AND PERSIUS. Trans. by G. G. Ramsay. (5th Impression.)

LIVY. Trans. by B. O. Foster. 13 Vols. Vols. I.-V. (Vol. I. 2nd Impression revised.)

LUCAN. Trans. by J. D. Duff.

LUCRETIUS. Trans. by W. H. D. Rouse. (3rd Imp. rev.)

MARTIAL. Trans. by W. C. A. Ker. 2 Vols. (3rd Impression revised.)

MINUCIUS FELIX: cf. TERTULLIAN.

OVID: THE ART OF LOVE AND OTHER POEMS. Trans. by J. H. Mozley.

OVID: FASTI. Trans. by Sir James G. Frazer.

OVID: HEROIDES, AMORES. Trans. by Grant Shower-man. (3rd Impression.)

OVID: METAMORPHOSES. Trans. by F. J. Miller. 2 Vols. (5th Impression.)

OVID: TRISTIA AND EX PONTO. Trans. by A. L. Wheeler.

2

THE LOEB CLASSICAL LIBRARY

PETRONIUS. Trans. by M. Heseltine: SENECA:
APOCOLOCYNTOSIS. Trans. by W. H. D. Rouse.
(*5th Impression revised.*)

PLAUTUS. Trans. by Paul Nixon. 5 Vols. Vols. I.-IV.
(Vols. I.-III. *3rd Impression.*)

PLINY: LETTERS. Melmoth's trans. revised by W. M. L.
Hutchinson. 2 Vols. (Vol. I. *4th*, Vol. II. *3rd Imp.*)

PROPERTIUS. Trans. by H. E. Butler. (*4th Impression.*)

QUINTILIAN. Trans. by H. E. Butler. 4 Vols. (Vol. I.
2nd Impression.)

ST. AUGUSTINE: CONFESSIONS OF. Trans. by W.
Watts (1631). 2 Vols. (*4th Impression.*)

SAINT AUGUSTINE: SELECT LETTERS. Trans. by
J. H. Baxter.

SAINT JEROME: SELECT LETTERS. Trans. F. A.
Wright.

SALLUST. Trans. by J. C. Rolfe. (*2nd Impression revised.*)

SCRIPTORES HISTORIAE AUGUSTAE. Trans. by
D. Magie. 3 Vols. (Vol. I. *2nd Impression revised.*)

SENECA: EPISTULAE MORALES. Trans. by R. M.
Gummere. 3 Vols. (Vols. I. and II. *2nd Impression,*
Vol. II. *revised.*)

SENECA: MORAL ESSAYS. Trans. by J. W. Basore.
3 Vols. Vols. I.-II.

SENECA: TRAGEDIES. Trans. by F. J. Miller.
2 Vols. (*2nd Impression revised.*)

SILIUS ITALICUS: PUNICA. Trans. by J. D. Duff.
2 Vols.

STATIUS. Trans. by J. H. Mozley. 2 Vols.

SUETONIUS. Trans. by J. C. Rolfe. 2 Vols. (*4th Im-
pression revised.*)

TACITUS: DIALOGUS. Trans. by Sir Wm. Peterson;
and AGRICOLA AND GERMANIA. Trans. by Maurice
Hutton. (*4th Impression.*)

TACITUS: HISTORIES AND ANNALS. Trans. by
C. H. Moore and J. Jackson. 3 Vols. Vols. I and II.

TERENCE. Trans. by John Sargeaunt. 2 Vols. (*5th Imp.*)

TERTULLIAN: APOLOGIA AND DE SPECTACULIS.
Trans. by T. R. Glover. MINUCIUS FELIX. Trans.
by G. H. Rendall.

VELLEIUS PATERCULUS AND RES GESTAE DIVI
AUGUSTI. Trans. by F. W. Shipley.

VIRGIL. Trans. by H. R. Fairclough. 2 Vols. (Vol. I. 11*th Impression*, Vol. II. 8*th Impression*.)

VITRUVIUS: DE ARCHITECTURA. Trans. by F Granger. 2 Vols.

GREEK AUTHORS

ACHILLES TATIUS. Trans. by S. Gaselee.

AENEAS TACTICUS, ASCLEPIODOTUS AND ONA-SANDER. Trans. by The Illinois Greek Club.

AESCHINES. Trans. by C. D. Adams.

AESCHYLUS. Trans. by H. Weir Smyth. 2 Vols. (Vol. I. 3*rd Impression*, Vol. II. 2*nd Impression revised*.)

APOLLODORUS. Trans. by Sir James G. Frazer. 2 Vols.

APOLLONIUS RHODIUS. Trans. by R. C. Seaton. (4*th Impression*.)

THE APOSTOLIC FATHERS. Trans. by Kirsopp Lake. 2 Vols. (Vol. I. 5*th Impression*, Vol. II. 4*th Impression*.)

APPIAN'S ROMAN HISTORY. Trans. by Horace White. 4 Vols. (Vol. I. 3*rd*, Vols. II.-IV. 2*nd Impression*.)

ARATUS: *cf.* CALLIMACHUS.

ARISTOPHANES. Trans. by Benjamin Bickley Rogers. 3 Vols. (Verse translation.) (3*rd Impression*.)

ARISTOTLE: THE " ART " OF RHETORIC. Trans. by J. H. Freese.

ARISTOTLE: THE METAPHYSICS. Trans. by H. Tredennick; OECONOMICA AND MAGNA MORALIA. Trans. by W. G. Armstrong. 2 Vols. Vol. I.

ARISTOTLE: THE NICOMACHEAN ETHICS. Trans. by H. Rackham. (2*nd Impression revised*.)

ARISTOTLE: THE PHYSICS. Trans. by the Rev. P. Wicksteed and F. M. Cornford. 2 Vols. Vol. I.

ARISTOTLE: POETICS; " LONGINUS ": ON THE SUBLIME. Trans. by W. Hamilton Fyfe; DEMETRIUS: ON STYLE. Trans. by W. Rhys Roberts. (2*nd Imp. rev.*)

ARISTOTLE: THE POLITICS. Trans. by H. Rackham.

ARRIAN: HISTORY OF ALEXANDER AND INDICA. Trans. by the Rev. E. Iliffe Robson. 2 Vols.

ATHENAEUS: THE DEIPNOSOPHISTS. Trans. by C. B. Gulick. 7 Vols. Vols. I.-V.

CALLIMACHUS AND LYCOPHRON. Trans. by A. W. Mair; ARATUS. Trans. by G. R. Mair.

CLEMENT OF ALEXANDRIA. Trans. by the Rev. G. W. Butterworth.

THE LOEB CLASSICAL LIBRARY

COLLUTHUS : *cf.* OPPIAN.

DAPHNIS AND CHLOE. Thornley's translation revised by J. M. Edmonds : AND PARTHENIUS. Trans. by S. Gaselee. (*2nd Impression.*)

DEMOSTHENES : DE CORONA AND DE FALSA LEGATIONE. Trans. by C. A. Vince and J. H. Vince.

DEMOSTHENES : OLYNTHIACS, PHILIPPICS, LEPTINES, AND MINOR SPEECHES. Trans. by J. H. Vince.

DIO CASSIUS : ROMAN HISTORY. Trans. by E. Cary. 9 Vols. (Vol. II. *2nd Impression.*)

DIO CHRYSOSTOM. 4 Vols. Vol. I. Trans. by J. W. Cohoon.

DIODORUS SICULUS. Trans. by C. H. Oldfather. 9 Vols. Vol. I.

DIOGENES LAERTIUS. Trans. by R. D. Hicks. 2 Vols. (Vol. I. *2nd Impression.*)

EPICTETUS. Trans. by W. A. Oldfather. 2 Vols.

EURIPIDES. Trans. by A. S. Way. 4 Vols. (Verse trans.) (Vols. I. and II. *5th,* Vol. III. *3rd,* Vol. IV. *4th Imp.*)

EUSEBIUS : ECCLESIASTICAL HISTORY. Trans. by Kirsopp Lake and E. L. Oulton. 2 Vols.

GALEN : ON THE NATURAL FACULTIES. Trans. by A. J. Brock. (*2nd Impression.*)

THE GREEK ANTHOLOGY. Trans. by W. R. Paton. 5 Vols. (Vol. I. *3rd,* Vols. II. and III. *2nd Impression.*)

THE GREEK BUCOLIC POETS (THEOCRITUS, BION, MOSCHUS). Trans. by J. M. Edmonds. (*5th Imp. rev.*)

GREEK ELEGY AND IAMBUS WITH THE ANACREONTEA. Trans. by J. M. Edmonds. 2 Vols.

HERODES, ETC. Trans. by A. D. Knox : *cf.* THEOPHRASTUS, CHARACTERS.

HERODOTUS. Trans. by A. D. Godley. 4 Vols. (Vol. I. *3rd Impression,* Vols. II.-IV. *2nd Impression.*)

HESIOD AND THE HOMERIC HYMNS. Trans. by H. G. Evelyn White. (*4th Impression.*)

HIPPOCRATES AND HERACLEITUS. Trans. by W. H. S. Jones and E. T. Withington. 4 Vols.

HOMER : ILIAD. Trans. by A. T. Murray. 2 Vols. (Vol. I. *3rd Impression,* Vol. II. *2nd Impression.*)

HOMER : ODYSSEY. Trans. by A. T. Murray. 2 Vols. (*4th Impression.*)

ISAEUS. Trans. by E. S. Forster.

ISOCRATES. Trans. by G. Norlin. 3 Vols. Vols. I. and II.

JOSEPHUS. Trans. by H. St. J. Thackeray. 8 Vols.
Vols. I.-IV.
JULIAN. Trans. by Wilmer Cave Wright. 3 Vols. (Vol. I.
2nd Impression.)
LUCIAN. Trans. by A. M. Harmon. 8 Vols. Vols. I.-IV.
(Vols. I. and II. 3rd Impression.)
LYCOPHRON : cf. CALLIMACHUS.
LYRA GRAECA. Trans. by J. M. Edmonds. 3 Vols. (Vol.
I. 2nd Edition revised and enlarged, Vol. II. 2nd Imp.)
LYSIAS. Trans. by W. R. M. Lamb.
MARCUS AURELIUS. Trans. by C. R. Haines. (3rd
Impression revised.)
MENANDER. Trans. by F. G. Allinson. (2nd Imp. rev.)
OPPIAN, COLLUTHUS AND TRYPHIODORUS. Trans.
by A. W. Mair.
PAPYRI, SELECT. Trans. by A. S. Hunt and C. C.
Edgar. 2 Vols. Vol. I.
PARTHENIUS : cf. DAPHNIS AND CHLOE.
PAUSANIAS : DESCRIPTION OF GREECE. Trans.
by W. H. S. Jones. 4 Vols. and Companion Vol. Vols.
I.-III. (Vol. I. 2nd Impression.)
PHILO. Trans. by F. H. Colson and the Rev. G. H.
Whitaker. 10 Vols. Vols. I.-V.
PHILOSTRATUS : THE LIFE OF APOLLONIUS OF
TYANA. Trans. by F. C. Conybeare. 2 Vols. (Vol. I.
3rd Impression, Vol. II. 2nd Impression.)
PHILOSTRATUS AND EUNAPIUS : LIVES OF THE
SOPHISTS. Trans. by Wilmer Cave Wright.
PHILOSTRATUS. IMAGINES ; CALLISTRATUS.
DESCRIPTIONS. Trans. by A. Fairbanks.
PINDAR. Trans. by Sir J. E. Sandys. (5th Imp. rev.)
PLATO : CHARMIDES, ALCIBIADES I. AND II.,
HIPPARCHUS, THE LOVERS, THEAGES, MINOS,
EPINOMIS. Trans. by W. R. M. Lamb.
PLATO : CRATYLUS, PARMENIDES, GREATER AND
LESSER HIPPIAS. Trans. by H. N. Fowler.
PLATO : EUTHYPHRO, APOLOGY, CRITO, PHAEDO,
PHAEDRUS. Trans. by H. N. Fowler. (7th Impression.)
PLATO : LACHES, PROTAGORAS, MENO, EUTHY-
DEMUS. Trans. by W. R. M. Lamb.
PLATO : LAWS. Trans. by the Rev. R. G. Bury. 2 Vols.
PLATO : LYSIS, SYMPOSIUM, GORGIAS. Trans. by
W. R. M. Lamb. (2nd Impression revised.)

THE LOEB CLASSICAL LIBRARY

PLATO: REPUBLIC. Trans. by Paul Shorey. 2 Vols. Vol. I.

PLATO: STATESMAN, PHILEBUS. Trans. by H. N. Fowler; ION. Trans. by W. R. M. Lamb.

PLATO: THEAETETUS, SOPHIST. Trans. by H. N. Fowler. (2nd Impression.)

PLATO: TIMAEUS, CRITIAS, CLITOPHO, MENEXENUS, EPISTULAE. Trans. by the Rev. R. G. Bury.

PLUTARCH: THE PARALLEL LIVES. Trans. by B. Perrin. 11 Vols. (Vols. I., II., III. and VII. 2nd Imp.)

PLUTARCH: MORALIA. Trans. by F. C. Babbitt. 14 Vols. Vols. I.-III.

POLYBIUS. Trans. by W. R. Paton. 6 Vols.

PROCOPIUS; HISTORY OF THE WARS. Trans. by H. B. Dewing. 7 Vols. Vols. I.-V. (Vol. I. 2nd Imp.)

QUINTUS SMYRNAEUS. Trans. by A. S. Way. (Verse.)

ST. BASIL: THE LETTERS. Trans. by R. Deferrari. 4 Vols.

ST. JOHN DAMASCENE: BARLAAM AND IOASAPH. Trans. by the Rev. G. R. Woodward and Harold Mattingly.

SEXTUS EMPIRICUS. Trans. by the Rev. R. G. Bury. 3 Vols. Vol. I. OUTLINES OF PYRRHONISM.

SOPHOCLES. Trans. by F. Storr. 2 Vols. (Verse translation.) (Vol. 1. 6th Impression, Vol. II. 4th Impression.)

STRABO: GEOGRAPHY. Trans. by Horace L. Jones. 8 Vols. (Vol. I. 2nd Impression.)

THEOPHRASTUS: CHARACTERS. Trans. by J. M. Edmonds; HERODES, CERCIDAS AND THE GREEK CHOLIAMBIC POETS. Trans. by A. D. Knox.

THEOPHRASTUS: ENQUIRY INTO PLANTS. Trans. by Sir Arthur Hort, Bart. 2 Vols.

THUCYDIDES. Trans. by C. F. Smith. 4 Vols. (Vols. I.-III. 2nd Impression revised.)

TRYPHIODORUS: cf. OPPIAN.

XENOPHON: CYROPAEDIA. Trans. by Walter Miller. 2 Vols. (2nd Impression.)

XENOPHON: HELLENICA, ANABASIS, APOLOGY, AND SYMPOSIUM. Trans. by C. L. Brownson and O. J. Todd. 3 Vols. (2nd Impression.)

XENOPHON: MEMORABILIA AND OECONOMICUS. Trans. by E. C. Marchant.

XENOPHON: SCRIPTA MINORA. Trans. by E. C. Marchant.

THE LOEB CLASSICAL LIBRARY
VOLUMES IN PREPARATION

GREEK AUTHORS

ARISTOTLE: ATHENIAN CONSTITUTION. H. Rackham.
ARISTOTLE: DE ANIMA etc. W. S. Hett.
ARISTOTLE: ON THE MOTION OF ANIMALS, etc. E. S. Forster and A. Peck.
ARISTOTLE: ORGANON. H. P. Cooke and H. Tredennick.
DEMOSTHENES: MEIDIAS, ANDROTION, ARISTO-CRATES, TIMOCRATES. J. H. Vince.
DEMOSTHENES: PRIVATE ORATIONS. G. M. Calhoun.
MINOR ATTIC ORATORS (Antiphon, Andocides, Demades, Deinarchus, Hypereides). K. Maidment.
GREEK MATHEMATICAL WORKS. J. Thomas.
MYTHOGRAPHI GRAECI. D. H. Knappe.

LATIN AUTHORS

AMMIANUS MARCELLINUS. J. C. Rolfe.
CATO AND VARRO: DE RE RUSTICA. H. B. Hooper and R. Ash.
CELSUS. W. G. Spencer.
CICERO: AD HERENNIUM. H. Caplan.
CICERO: AD M. BRUTUM ORATOR. H. M. Hubbell.
CICERO: CATILINE ORATIONS. B. L. Ullman.
CICERO: DE ORATORE. Charles Stuttaford and W. E. Sutton.
CICERO: PRO SESTIO, IN VATINIUM, PRO CAELIO, PRO PROV. CONS., PRO BALBO. J. H. Freese.
COLUMELLA: DE RE RUSTICA. R. Ash.
ENNIUS, LUCILIUS, AND OTHER SPECIMENS OF OLD LATIN. E. H. Warmington.
MINOR LATIN POETS from Publilius Syrus to Rutilius Namatianus, including Grattius, Calpurnius Siculus, Nemesianus, Avianus and others, with "Aetna" and "The Phoenix." J. Wight Duff and Arnold M. Duff.
PLINY: NATURAL HISTORY. W. H. S. Jones.
PRUDENTIUS. J. H. Baxter.
SIDONIUS. E. V. Arnold and W. B. Anderson.
VALERIUS FLACCUS. J. H. Mozley.
VARRO: DE LINGUA LATINA. R. G. Kent.

DESCRIPTIVE PROSPECTUS ON APPLICATION

London . .	WILLIAM HEINEMANN LTD
Cambridge, Mass. .	HARVARD UNIVERSITY PRESS